DISRUPTIVE GRACE

DISRUPTIVE GRACE

Reflections on God, Scripture, and the Church

WALTER BRUEGGEMANN

Edited and Introduced by
CAROLYN J. SHARP

scm press

First published in the USA in 2011 by Fortress Press

This Edition published in 2011 by SCM Press
Editorial office
13–17 Long Lane,
London, EC1A 9PN, UK

SCM Press is an imprint of Hymns Ancient and Modern Ltd
(a registered charity)
13a Hellesdon Park Road, Norwich, Norfolk, NR6 5DR

www.scm-canterburypress.co.uk

British Library Cataloguing in Publication data

A catalogue record for this book is available
from the British Library

978-0-334-04399-7

Printed and bound by
CPI Antony Rowe, Chippenham, Wiltshire

Contents

Part IV. Canon and Imagination

Introduction

Disruptive Grace: The Uncompromising Theology of Walter Brueggemann

Carolyn J. Sharp

WALTER BRUEGGEMANN'S SPEECHES and presentations have captivated and challenged audiences for many years. Long in demand as a speaker at the national level, Brueggemann addresses standing-room-only audiences at annual meetings of the Society of Biblical Literature. His thinking draws unparalleled interest from seasoned scholars and newly minted academics alike, but Brueggemann's appeal is by no means limited to biblical scholars. He is regularly asked to offer his dynamic brand of exegetically grounded theology to church groups and clergy, ecclesial judicatories, and gatherings of preachers and hospital chaplains. This volume collects addresses delivered by Brueggemann from 2002 to 2009. The original audiences included faculty and students at Luther Seminary in St. Paul, Northern Michigan University, Mt. Vernon Nazarene University, the Oblate School of Theology in San Antonio, and his own institution, Columbia Theological Seminary; gatherings of Episcopal bishops in Ontario and at Kanuga Conference Center in North Carolina; church leaders at the Presbyterian Covenant Network in Minneapolis and the Wisconsin Council of Churches; and preachers at Festival of Homiletics gatherings held in Minneapolis and Nashville.

The pieces here are organized in four sections, corresponding to each piece's primary focus: Torah, Prophets, Writings, and the biblical canon and interpretive imagination. In each address, Brueggemann's passion for the Word of God and his eloquence as a writer are well in evidence. Brueggemann offers vibrant and detailed expositions of texts, these always undergirded by a nuanced

1

hermeneutical framework and in service of a trenchant ecclesiology. Brueggemann roots his theology deeply in Scripture. His readings are rhetorically sophisticated in the ways in which they address contemporary concerns, and he challenges the church—repeatedly and without compromise—to take the Word of God seriously. Because the diversity of materials here does not lend itself to systematic description, it may be helpful to situate these addresses within the larger landscape of characteristic features of Brueggemann's interpretive work conceived more broadly.

BRUEGGEMANN ON GOD: BIBLICAL THEOLOGY

The God whom Brueggemann encounters in the pages of Scripture is a powerful God who refuses all human efforts to commodify or manipulate the divine. This God is fully present in covenant relationship yet is never bound to the expectations of believers who find their identity in that relationship. God is the unique other who calls believers in relational and redemptive love, but God's existence remains an irreducible problematic for every human system, including systematic theology. Brueggemann is interested in probing the dialogical relationship between believers and their Creator. Citing thinkers from Martin Buber to Emmanuel Levinas, he insists that "restless, unsettleable relation is the irreducible core of what it means to be human."[1] Dialogical relationship is at the core of faith: we stand in inescapable relation to the one who made heaven and earth, who knows every human heart, and for whom nothing is impossible.

The God of the Hebrew Scriptures cannot be controlled or contained. In Brueggemann's theology, this becomes a crucial point for contemporary believers, given our context of globalization, in which corporations and culture-brokers work tirelessly toward the efficient commodification of everything from natural resources and manufactured goods to political power and social identity. Brueggemann finds that "the God of the Bible is endlessly *irascible*—capable of coming and going, judging and forgiving, speaking and remaining silent—in ways that make the next time endlessly uncertain."[2] God is continually active for transformation, healing, and reconciliation. Much as the church might like to package this holy purpose for evangelism, it inevitably resists commodification and challenges our flawed and exploitative institutions. As Brueggemann puts it, the God of Scripture is "known to be a resilient and relentless advocate of and agent for justice, which entails the complete reordering of power arrangements in the earth,"[3] including ecclesial power relations. Thus Brueggemann finds that the God whom we meet in Scripture can be profoundly destabilizing, not just for secular values but also for the theological platitudes and uneasy compromises that weaken Christian tradition.

His daring interpretations aim to invite us into the drama of the biblical character of God, even though that divine character does not necessarily assent to the goals and values that motivate contemporary readers and faith communities. During his teaching career, Brueggemann was famous in the classroom for his dramatic renderings of biblical texts. He has been quite intentional about this dramatic approach when he teaches and preaches, and we glimpse his flair for the dramatic in his written work as well. He explains,

> The move toward a dramatic sense of the text permits the reading community to stay with the terms of the text, even with its contradictions, incongruities, and unwelcome lines. Thus the text is "unreadable" . . . because the subject and character [God] who dominates the plot does not conform to our flattened reading propensity, theological or critical.[4]

Focusing on the vocabulary and syntax of biblical rhetoric, Brueggemann has explored biblical portrayals of God as merciful, gracious, slow to anger, abounding in faithfulness, righteous, omnipotent, and holy. But he also insists that we attend to Scriptural portrayals of God as hidden, wrathful, inscrutable, conflicted, unreliable, violent, and irrational. The drama of God's character in the Hebrew Scriptures requires that we alternately submit and argue back, yield and wrestle with this Holy One who will not be domesticated by our theologies.

BRUEGGEMANN ON SCRIPTURE: HERMENEUTICS

For Brueggemann, Scripture constitutes a multivoiced chorus of witnesses that continually affirm and contest each other as they seek to make visible the God who has called Israel and who calls each one of us. Brueggemann is committed to elucidating the multivocal nature of Scripture. We see this both in his larger interpretive framework and in the way in which he consistently reflects on many Bible passages in a single address. Brueggemann's hermeneutical commitment to honoring the multivocality of Scripture requires that he name and resist two dominant tendencies in biblical interpretation: confessionalism and reductionism. He has little patience for dogmatic theological claims that attempt to tame or constrain the biblical witness, insisting, "It is the work of a serious theological interpreter of the Bible to pay close and careful attention to what is in the text, regardless of how it coheres with the theological habit of the church."[5] Nor does he care for scholarly ways of constraining the meaning of the text. His interpretive temperament has been strongly influenced by rhetorical criticism, and as a result, Brueggemann has been vigorously critical of the dominance of historical criticism in the scholarly guild. In his view, an aggressively historicist approach to the Bible has tended to mean that "much that is 'odd' in the text is explained away, and serious faith claims are relativized or dismissed."[6] What he seeks, instead, is "a fresh honoring of the ambiguity, complexity, and affront of the text without too much worry about making it palatable either to religious orthodoxy or to critical rationality."[7]

While Brueggemann cannot be said to have escaped a historicist framework entirely—for example, he often acknowledges the importance of Judah's experience of exile in the sixth century BCE for the overall shaping of the Hebrew Scriptures—he is sympathetic to certain trends in postmodernist interpretation. Particularly important within postmodern interpretive culture is dissatisfaction with ways in which "metanarratives"—overarching explanatory systems or scripts—seek to define and control specific instances of cultural expression. While Brueggemann is a master at describing broad themes within Scripture in compelling ways, he also sees clearly that the multivocal nature of Scripture requires us to read slowly and locally. His written oeuvre shows a persistent focus on textual "case studies" and exegetical soundings, precisely because his method is conceptually grounded in sustained attention to passages in their literary microcontexts. Indeed, Brueggemann is adamant that this sort of local exegetical attention is the only way to interpret Scripture that will not falsify what these complex and variegated biblical texts are communicating:

> The Old Testament does not (and never intends to) provide a coherent and comprehensive offer of God. . . . For the most part, the Old Testament text gives us only hints, traces, fragments, and vignettes, with no suggestion of how all these elements might fit together, if indeed they do. What does emerge, in any case, is an awareness that *the elusive but dominating Subject of the Old Testament cannot be comprehended in any preconceived categories*. . . . As a result, most of our categories are unhelpful for the elucidation of this Subject, and we shall have to proceed concretely, a text at a time, a detail at a time.[8]

For Brueggemann, we risk far too much when we hurry past individual Scripture texts in our eagerness to create a coherent metanarrative out of all biblical testimony. We are meant to "linger over the troublesome specificity of the biblical text," for "the Bible offers many small dramas, some of which are not easily subordinated to the large 'drama of salvation.'"[9]

There are two chief hermeneutical models Brueggemann uses to describe the dialogical dynamic that he sees underlying the witness of the Hebrew Scriptures. One model, which has come to fullest expression in his work on the Psalms, identifies biblical texts as being about orientation, disorientation, or reorientation. Some texts serve to orient the reader or faith community to God's power, faithfulness, and trustworthiness. In Brueggemann's words, they "reflect the coherence of life" in a "voice of genuine gratitude and piety for [God's] rich blessings," offering a "continued reaffirmation and reconstruction of this good world" that our Creator has given us.[10] Other texts serve to name difficult circumstances, undercut misguided perceptions of God, or subvert idolatrous claims to power. These texts create a disturbing but salutary disorientation that frees us to see the truth more clearly. Brueggemann says they "have the abrasive effect of dismantling the old systems that hide the well-off from the dangerous theological realities of life," something that is indispensable for the believer because "until there is an embrace of honest helplessness, there is no true gospel that can be heard."[11] Yet other biblical texts serve to reorient the believer anew to God as one who is worthy of all praise. These texts of reorientation testify in wonder and amazement to a God who has exceeded all expectations, in circumstances in which "life has disintegrated but has been formed miraculously again," and in which believers rejoice in "a newness now being given."[12] The dialogical witness of the Hebrew Scriptures taken as a whole, then, offers a lively interplay among texts of orientation, disorientation, and reorientation as those are expressed in the life of the faith community.

Brueggemann's second hermeneutical model is articulated at length in his massive *Theology of the Old Testament: Testimony, Dispute, Advocacy* (1997). Here he explores four categories of witness about God in the Hebrew Scriptures: core testimony, countertestimony, unsolicited testimony, and embodied testimony. Israel's core testimony celebrates God as a righteous sovereign who has created something new, acting on behalf of Israel "in decisive and transformative ways" to heal and to deliver.[13] Israel's countertestimony gives voice to ancient believers' laments that God has not yet saved, that God seems to have abandoned the people, that God seems disproportionately punitive, remote, or uncaring. These texts dare to express God's "hiddenness, ambiguity, and negativity"[14] in hopes that speaking the truth of the people's experience of trauma will spur God to redeem them once again. Israel's unsolicited testimony involves the extravagant and hyperbolic extra testimony of Israel, the human person, the nations, and creation as covenant partners who respond to God in grief and protest, in awe and hope. Finally, Israel's embodied testimony celebrates the ways in which Israel has experienced God's presence through traditions of theophany, kingship, prophetic mediation, ritual practice, and the wisdom of sages.

Elucidating these multiple sorts of testimony requires careful discernment on the part of the interpreter. Thus, in the addresses collected here, Brueggemann displays his characteristic attentive listening to the text and his lavish description of the unique witness that each biblical passage offers. We should note also the seriousness with which Brueggemann takes the speech of ancient Israel. Words not only matter, they are essential; for Scripture is an entirely logocentric witness to the mighty Word of God. In the Bible we have only texts—inscribed speech—about who God is and what God has done. Brueggemann has stirred up considerable controversy with his insistence that we can know God in the Old Testament only through Israel's rhetoric. Critics' misreadings notwithstanding, Brueggemann never intended to suggest that God is not also encountered in prayer, in worship, at the eucharistic table, and in the face of the other—that is, outside of the text. But he has insistently asserted the crucial importance of sacred text precisely as text. For any theology that claims to be biblical, the texts themselves must count as the primary, indispensable, and unique locus of the ongoing revelation of God. Brueggemann was thinking along these lines as early as 1993, when he wrote, "Speech is not merely descriptive, but it is in some sense evocative of reality and constitutive of reality."[15] Here is his later, controversial elaboration of the point:

> For Old Testament faith, *the utterance is everything*. The utterance leads to the reality, the reality of God that relies on the reliability of the utterance. Presumably other utterances could have been accepted as true, but these particular utterances are the ones that have been preserved, trusted, treasured, and given to us. The upshot of this process is, first, that Israel's claim of reality is as fragile as an utterance, and we must be exceedingly wary of flights from utterance to some presumed pretextual reality. Second, this process makes it clear that a student of Old Testament theology must pay close attention to the shape, character, and details of the utterance, for it is in, with, and under the utterance that we have the God of Israel, and nowhere else.[16]

This claim about the profound power of the word explains the loving and sustained attention that Brueggemann gives to every biblical story or poem that he expounds.

Brueggemann's exegetically based view of Scripture has far-reaching consequences for Old Testament theology. His Scripture-centered hermeneutics requires continued listening to the ways in which particular biblical texts make demands on those communities that read and cherish them. The dialogical interpretive model that Brueggemann has plied so robustly poses a challenge for those who encounter it: we must allow our most cherished interpretive notions and habits to be contested and reframed by these strange, holy texts. Brueggemann has said about the potential impact of Old Testament theology that it "invites the academic community away from self-preoccupied triviality that is such a waste, the ecclesial communities away from excessive certitude that is idolatry, and the civic community away from brutality rooted in autonomy long enough to engage this summoning Mystery."[17] These words may be applied not only to Old Testament theology but also to Brueggemann's hermeneutical style as well. In his writing and speaking, Brueggemann alternately rebukes and invites, fumes and implores, confronts and coaxes his audience into heeding the wild words of God no matter how unsettling they may be.

Without being dogmatic about it, Brueggemann models for us the truth that Christian readers necessarily interpret Scripture in light of our redemption in Jesus Christ. He does not tend to introduce sacramental theology overtly into his exposition of biblical texts, but we glimpse this underlying faith conviction whenever we see him attending to scriptural voices of brokenness and despair, voices that struggle to make sense of God in difficult circumstances, voices that dare to speak words of hope despite communal traumas of exile and loss.

Brueggemann may bring his sacramental sensibility to expression relatively infrequently, but it is central to his hermeneutics and visible in nuanced ways throughout much of what he has written. Consider this illuminating articulation of his position:

> Practically, our interpretation is to be done gathered around the Eucharistic table that is an anticipation of our gathering around the throne of mercy. . . . We never come [to the Communion table] without our interpretations. As we watch the bread broken and given to all, we are able to see that faithful interpretation does not speak the truth unless it is broken truth. As we watch the wine poured out, we know that where our lives are not poured out, our interpretation is a lie.[18]

For Brueggemann the witnesses within the Hebrew Scriptures contest every idolatrous gesture that we make toward a spiritually bankrupt autonomy, toward the illusion that we do not need God. These countercultural sacred texts invite us into "a new world of majesty, sovereignty, power, dominion, and splendor where an awful, undisciplined submitting is appropriate and gladly practiced."[19] At its heart, "the biblical tradition is not about control but about vulnerability, not about self-sufficiency but about risky reception of life as gift."[20] For Brueggemann we read Scripture most authentically at the foot of the cross.

BRUEGGEMANN ON THE CHURCH: ECCLESIOLOGY

In Brueggemann's ecclesiology obedience is the fundamental ground on which the identity of the church must be based. Brueggemann is patently uninterested in matters of church dogmatics and the fine points of most ecclesial disputes. His interpretive vision goes broader and deeper even than the clarion call to social justice that is so important to many biblical texts. Brueggemann hears Scripture as calling the church to a radical obedience that goes well beyond Christian platitudes or our comfortable weekly worship services. Heeding the Word of God is not a matter of choice or affinity; it is a matter of divine command. "The God who gives is the God who commands," Brueggemann insists; "Israel's traditioning process continues to exposit and interpret the singular command of Sinai in order to bring every phase of life, personal and public, under obedience to YHWH and to determine what particular form obedience may take amid the vagaries of life where matters of obedience are not clear."[21]

According to Brueggemann, covenantal obedience forcefully contests the obsessive and narcissistic consumerism of mainstream North American culture. Obedience places a non-negotiable claim on the Christian to live in the mode of countercultural witness. Brueggemann writes, "I understand covenant in our time and place to be a radical alternative to consumer autonomy, which is the governing ideology of our society and which invades the life of the church in debilitating ways."[22] He is uncompromising in his indictment: "we live, all of us, in a promiscuous, self-indulgent society that prizes autonomy."[23] Because God declines to be complicit in our addictions and delusions, the grace the Holy One shows to us can be disruptive indeed. This holy disruption challenges ecclesiologies across the denominational spectrum, for those on the left and those on the right alike can fail to hear Scripture in ways that are fruitful for proclamation of the gospel. Brueggemann aims to engage all—even at the risk of offending some—when he writes, "The liberal Christian temptation is to accommodate dominant culture until faith despairs. The conservative Christian temptation is to fashion an absoluteness that stands disconnected from the dominant culture. Neither of these strategies, however, is likely to sustain the church in its mission."[24]

Rarely missing an opportunity to be provocative, Brueggemann seeks to catalyze renewed engagement with a lively and untamable Word that refuses all attempts to "manage" it for any particular ideological program. In our violent and aggressively acquisitive world, the church is called to live otherwise. Brueggemann urges us to embrace our identity as exiles in contemporary culture, to open our hearts and hands freely to those who are dispossessed, to remember our own redemption ("exodus") with a gratitude that issues in generosity toward others, and to practice a prayerful peace ("sabbath" or "shalom") that honors the purposes of God.[25] Looking to the foundation of the Hebrew Scriptures as a sign for the church, Brueggemann avers that "the theological constancy of *miracle* and *gratitude* is implicit everywhere in the Torah . . . and is to be accented in church reading, teaching, and preaching."[26]

Because he is passionate about proclaiming God's newness not only in the classroom but also in the pulpit, Brueggemann has thought long and hard about the ministry of preaching. For him it is a radical act. "We preachers," he writes, "are summoned to get up and utter a *sub-version* of reality, an alternative vision of reality that says another way of life in the world is not only possible but is peculiarly mandated and peculiarly valid. . . . [This sub-version intends] to empower a community of *sub-versives* who are determined to practice their lives according to a different way of imagining."[27] This need not mean that we will all agree. Church should be a place of committed discussion and lively disagreement about ways in which the witnesses of various Scripture texts may be privileged as the Holy Spirit moves in the life of the community. Brueggemann wisely observes, "Because different interpretations in different contexts—driven by different hopes, fears, and hurts—ask different questions from the ground up, it is clear that there will be no widely accepted 'canon within the canon,' which is itself a function of hegemonic interpretation. . . . The ecclesial-academic enterprise of interpretation, like the testimonial process of Israel itself, is a pluralistic one of dispute and accommodation."[28]

Interpretation in community is risky. The church must be both humble and intrepid in its biblical interpretation. It must be humble in acknowledging that even its favorite theological answers cannot suffice to describe our saving God. And it must be intrepid in venturing repeatedly into narrative and poetic texts that insistently deconstruct everything that does not serve the gospel. The risks of biblical theology are quite real, for the world and for the church. Providentially we have in Walter Brueggemann a seasoned and honest guide for the journey.

* * *

In these addresses Brueggemann moves with fluidity across biblical books, so the pragmatic arrangement of essays in this volume—Torah, Prophets, Writings, Canon and Imagination—is meant to signal primary emphases rather than singular focus. This structure is intended to guide readers who are reflecting on one or another kind of text within the Old Testament. But readers may also find it instructive to read through all of the addresses here in order, roughly approximating the way in which the Hebrew Scriptures themselves unfold, since Brueggemann's mode of engagement touches gracefully on many biblical passages and kinds of Scriptural witness.

In these addresses Brueggemann urges us to be candid and courageous. The sacred stories and poems of Scripture demand that we face our terrible flaws— that we tell the whole truth about ourselves, our communities, and our histories. For Brueggemann, to be unsettled and disrupted by the grace of God's Word is a wonderful thing. Indeed, it is urgently necessary to catalyze repentance. Only then can we learn to live in wholehearted obedience to God, yielding lives transformed by praise of our Redeemer.

PART I

TORAH

Demand and Deliverance: Brueggemann on the Torah

Carolyn J. Sharp

As ancient Israel was summoned into covenant, so contemporary believers are summoned to respond to the demands of a holy God who reveals divine love and purpose in covenantal relationship. Faithful memory and faithful practice have always been joined in the life of the faithful. Narrative and covenant are inextricably intertwined for us today, just as the story of Israel's exodus from Egypt and the statutes of the law are woven together in biblical literature. Law can never be understood apart from God's wondrous giving of grace in the life of the people of God. Brueggemann writes, "YHWH's mode of governance is through 'wonders' that lie beyond human possibility, to permit the emergence of the utterly new in the processes of nature and history."[1] Conversely, the stories of the Torah show us that the same God who performs redemption in miraculous ways for the faithful community also demands holiness and righteousness of believers. Thus, deliverance and covenantal demand cannot be separated. As Brueggemann puts it,

> The way in which Israel is to become and remain YHWH's "treasured possession" . . . is not simply by divine designation, but by vigorous, intense, intentional adherence to YHWH's commands given in the Torah of Sinai. By situating "chosenness" at Sinai . . . the tradition witnesses to the *unconditional* commitment of YHWH to Israel that is *conditioned* by Torah obedience.[2]

Brueggemann acknowledges, with many scholars, that the relationship of narrative and legal material in the Torah is an important and unsettled issue. Narrative in the Torah may be "roughly characterized as a recital of miracles wrought by YHWH in which unexpected transformative miracles characteristically happen because the defining Character in this tradition is none other than the YHWH to whom the entire corpus attests."[3] Law, then, becomes the living out of our

13

faith—for Jews, in worship and halakhic observance; for Christians, in worship and following of the great commandments to love God wholly and to love neighbor as self. The Torah's literary richness represents a vast diversity of historical contexts and genres, everything from extremely old and mysterious fragments of poetic tradition to sophisticated postexilic editorial shaping. Each sort of diction—storytelling, poetry, genealogy, legal stipulation—places a distinctive kind of claim on the reading community, yet overall, the coherence of the Torah's witness to the purposes of God remains unmistakable. As Brueggemann notes the Torah "reflects ongoing tension between a *variety of materials* that continue to have something of their own say and a *theological intentionality* that seeks to bring coherence to the complexity and variety of the materials, and, where necessary, to override and trump the initial claims of extant materials."[4]

In the Torah, Israel remembers who they have been in the struggle to walk with God. Brueggemann reflects on this process of memory as both the content of what Israel has learned about God and the ongoing way in which we join ourselves to those who walked in faith in ancient times:

> In this imaginative remembering, the notion of "Mosaic authority" is the thick label that signals Israel's conviction concerning YHWH. It is clear that human agents have been at work through the entire traditioning process. They witness to the will, purpose, and presence of YHWH who remains inscrutably hidden in and through the text and yet who discloses YHWH's own holy Self through that same text. "Moses" is the signal of faithful traditioning that attest that these scrolls are a reliable source upon which to ground faith and life.[5]

In his work on the Pentateuch, Brueggemann has focused on dimensions of spiritual formation that are on offer through the Hebrew Scriptures' representations of covenant. Getting our idea of God right, or at least a little closer to right, is important for biblical theology; but more important, it is essential for our growth in faith. Many biblical texts take pains to combat idolatrous or inadequate views of God. That being so, the faithful reader should attend to theological construals of God in Scripture with deep seriousness. Brueggemann recognizes that on this score, a great deal is at stake, not least for how we understand ourselves:

> If our mistaken notion leads us to an impassive, self-sufficient God in heaven, then the model for humanity, for Western culture, for ourselves, is that we should also be self-sufficient, impassive, beyond need, not to be imposed on. Willy-nilly, we will be made in the image of some God. The one for whose image we have settled is a sure, triumphant God who runs no risks, makes no commitments, embraces no pain that is definitional. Against that, the covenanting God of the Bible protests and invites us to protest.[6]

Covenant thus rejects idolatry, shows us our God, and helps us to understand who we are. Covenant creates us anew in the image of God.

In the addresses here Brueggemann ponders the scandal of covenantal vocation that frees us from the enslavements of the secular world. His exposition of the exodus story draws us into the drama of the contest between our Creator God and the world's fraudulent secular "magicians." Brueggemann challenges us not to collude in the anxious commodification of one another that fuels our society's feverish compulsion to produce and to acquire. And he calls us to hearken to the Torah imperative to remember and trust in the holiness of God. His musings make clear that the Torah is a holy means of reconstituting the community of faith in every age. For through story and law, as Brueggemann has said, "God gathers together folk like us, rich and poor, liberal and conservative, willing and reluctant, slave and free, and bids all sign on for odd songs and hard commands. In that way a community is formed like none other in the world."[7] For all who seek God in these times so distant from Moses' encounter on Sinai, that is good news indeed.

CHAPTER I

Summons to a Dialogic Life

THE CHURCH HAS ITS LIFE from the God of the gospel.[1] For that reason, the wonder and character of God matters crucially for every aspect of our life, the matters about which we trust, about which we are vexed, and about which we quarrel. Thus, I will think with you in these moments about the character of that God and the endlessly unfinished business about how to articulate that God faithfully and how to respond appropriately.

I

As the Bible has it, the God of the gospel bursts into the world with an utterance of promise and summons. There are all kinds of evidences and scholarly strategies to indicate that the God of the gospel in the Bible has important religious antecedents in the ancient Near East. That is not how the Bible has it. The Bible—after mapping the wonder of all creation and the peoples in it—presents the God who bursts in utterance. That divine utterance, in all of its surprise, is addressed to Abram, of whom we only know that he is the son of Terah in Ur of the Chaldeans, husband of a barren woman, Sarai. None of that matters, however, as the divine burst of utterance is unencumbered. It is a word of *summons*, the first word: "Now the LORD said to Abram, 'Go from your country and your kindred and your father's house to the land that I will show you'" (Gen 12:1). Abraham and his kin are summoned to depart their comfort zone in obedience to a God they do not know, toward a zone that remains unidentified. The utterance continues as a *promise*: "I will make of you a great nation, and I will bless you, and make your name great, so that you will be a blessing. I will bless those who bless you, and the one who curses you I will curse; and in you all the families of the earth shall be blessed" (Gen 12:2-3). The speech is dominated by first-person pronouns: "I will make . . . I will bless . . . I will make . . . I will bless." Abraham is on the receiving end, passive recipient of divine commitment. And even the last phrase, "in you," gives Abram no agency, simply a vehicle through which the divine resolve for blessing will extend to all the peoples of Genesis 1–11.

Abraham is required to leave the old regime of his life. Abraham is promised by this divine utterer a future, an heir, a land, and a material bodily well-being in the world. This God of promise and summons defines Abraham's life. In Genesis 15, many heirs are promised: "He brought him outside and said, 'Look toward heaven and count the stars, if you are able to count them.' Then he said to him, 'So shall your descendants be'" (Gen 15:5). And much land is promised:

> On that day the LORD made a covenant with Abram, saying, "To your descendants I give this land, from the river of Egypt to the great river, the river Euphrates, the land of the Kenites, the Kenizzites, the Kadmonites, the Hittites, the Perizzites, the Rephaim, the Amorites, the Canaanites, the Girgashites, and the Jebusites." (Gen 15:18-21)

The vision of "Greater Israel," a force in our contemporary politics, is grounded in covenant: "On that day YHWH made a covenant." It is all promise. In chapter 17, circumcision is a sign of that divine commitment. But there is no commandment. Scholars have noted that *covenant* began in the Old Testament with an unconditional divine promise, a commitment of divine power and divine purpose and divine fidelity to Abraham and his family.

The God of the gospel, we are told, bursts into the world most unexpectedly, to the fugitive slave Moses in the burning bush. That moment does not get much airtime in the Bible. But the components of divine speech are crucial:

- There is an initial *double imperative*:

  come no closer,
  remove your shoes.

  This is an *awesome presence* to which attention must be paid.

- There is holy presence. The ground is holy because it is occupied by the Holy One.

- There is *promise*. Oh my, there is promise:

  > Then the LORD said, "I have observed the misery of my people who are in Egypt; I have heard their cry on account of their taskmasters. Indeed, I know their sufferings, and I have come down to deliver

> them from the Egyptians, and to bring them up out of that land to
> a good and broad land, a land flowing with milk and honey, to the
> country of the Canaanites, the Hittites, the Amorites, the Perizzites,
> the Hivites, and the Jebusites." (Exod 3:7-8)

And the ground of that promise is the fidelity of the promise-maker who looks
back to the book of Genesis: "He said further, 'I am the God of your father, the
God of Abraham, the God of Isaac, and the God of Jacob.' And Moses hid his
face, for he was afraid to look at God" (Exod 3:6). The life of Moses is an interrupted life, interrupted by a *mandate* and *imperative,* interrupted by an *abiding
presence,* interrupted by a *revolutionary future.*

But then, after fearful confrontation with pharaonic power, after dancing at
the edge of the water, and after the risks of the wilderness, they come to Sinai.
Will it surprise you that at Sinai, YHWH interrupts the life of Israel by a burst
of utterance? Everything to be said at Sinai is in the epitome of Exodus 19:4-6.

- There is the remembered miracle of the exodus, how the slaves were
  removed from the comfort zone of Pharaoh to an exposed, risky life
  of sojourn:

  > You have seen what I did to the Egyptians, and how I bore you on
  > eagles' wings and brought you to myself. (Exod 19:4)

  > You have seen! You are here because of that interruptive act of fidelity.

- But then there is an *imperative.* It is a bigger imperative than that
  made to Abraham or by the utterer at the burning bush. Now it is a
  defining imperative:

  > Now therefore, if you obey my voice and keep my covenant, you
  > shall be my treasured possession out of all the peoples. Indeed, the
  > whole earth is mine, but you shall be for me a priestly kingdom
  > and a holy nation. These are the words that you shall speak to the
  > Israelites. (Exod 19:5-6)

Everything about the future of this relationship depends on Israel's meeting the
conditions of the divine "if." *If* you listen, *if* you heed, *if* you pay attention . . .
you will be my people. It all depends on you; you get to choose your future, but
the condition is raw and urgent, and the unspoken negative is that if you do not
respond appropriately, you will not be my covenant partner.

This terse epitome is fleshed out in the more familiar utterance of Exodus 20,
where the emancipator has spoken ten times. This defining burst of utterance has
the same components:

- There is a recalling of *divine generosity*:

  > I am the LORD your God, who brought you out of the land of
  > Egypt, out of the house of slavery; you shall have no other gods
  > before me. (Exod 20:2)

- There is a follow-up of *conditions* for the future that are terse and
  nonnegotiable:

  > You shall have no other gods before me.
  >   You shall not make for yourself an idol, whether in the form of
  > anything that is in heaven above, or that is on the earth beneath,
  > or that is in the water under the earth. You shall not bow down to
  > them or worship them; for I the LORD your God am a jealous God,
  > punishing children for the iniquity of parents, to the third and the
  > fourth generation of those who reject me, but showing steadfast
  > love to the thousandth generation of those who love me and keep
  > my commandments.
  >   You shall not make wrongful use of the name of the LORD your
  > God, for the LORD will not acquit anyone who misuses his name
  >   Remember the sabbath day, and keep it holy. Six days you shall
  > labor and do all your work. But the seventh day is a sabbath to
  > the LORD your God; you shall not do any work—you, your son
  > or your daughter, your male or female slave, your livestock, or the
  > alien resident in your towns. For in six days the LORD made heaven
  > and earth, the sea, and all that is in them, but rested the seventh day;
  > therefore the LORD blessed the sabbath day and consecrated it.
  >   Honor your father and your mother, so that your days may be
  > long in the land that the LORD your God is giving you.
  >   You shall not murder.
  >   You shall not commit adultery.
  >   You shall not steal.
  >   You shall not bear false witness against your neighbor.
  >   You shall not covet your neighbor's house; you shall not covet
  > your neighbor's wife, or male or female slave, or ox, or donkey, or
  > anything that belongs to your neighbor. (Exod 20:3-17)

These are not little moralisms. They are an act of divine resolve about how the
world could be alternatively organized in a faithful way—faithful in letting God
be God and letting neighbor be neighbor. And in Exodus 24, Israel accepts the
conditions and enters into this covenant of fidelity, which has starchy requirements to it:

Moses came and told the people all the words of the LORD and all the
ordinances; and all the people answered with one voice, and said, "All
the words that the LORD has spoken we will do." . . . Then he took the
book of the covenant, and read it in the hearing of the people; and they
said, "All that the LORD has spoken we will do, and we will be obedient." (Exod 24:3, 7)

These encounters with Abraham at the burning bush and at Sinai are the
founding memories. When they are completed a *novum* has appeared in human
history, a linkage of fidelity between the Holy One and an identifiable public
people in history, so that God has become known as "the Holy One of Israel" and
Israel has become known as the holy, chosen people of the God of the exodus.

The tradition is so familiar to us that we do not often notice its oddness. It is
odd because it is so abrupt and disruptive. It disrupts the life of *the rich man in
Ur* who had to go. It disrupts the life of *the fugitive slave in Egypt* who was head-
ing out to the wilderness for safety. It disrupts the slave community that does not
know that it has any peculiar identity. It is a narrative of disruption. But it is a *disruption* that has deep and abiding *durability.* More than that, these three bursts
of utterance are odd because the memory is saturated with deep contradictions
that they were never able to work out. The contradiction is so deep that scholars
have concluded that the Abraham tradition and the Moses tradition originally
had nothing to do with each other and are only loosely joined by editorial work
among the traditionists.

But there they are, these two traditions of Abraham and Moses. They are there
together as the beginning point of covenant. Here is God's covenant to Abraham
that is *unconditional and unilateral.* Here is God's covenant with Moses and
Israel that is *bilateral and conditional.* They are there together, and that interface
of contradiction may offer us the most work to do but also the most honest disclosure of the truth of our life. The full tradition asserts that all of our relationships,
including that with the Holy One, are an unsettled mix of *unilateral and bilateral,*
of *conditional and unconditional,* and it is that unsettled truth of covenant on
which I will dwell for these comments.

II

That is what we get with this God who is a covenant-maker. If you inhabit
the Jerusalem tradition, you get a unilateral covenant given by a God whose
commitments are unconditional. If you inhabit *the Sinai tradition,* you get a
bilateral God with a set of quid pro quo requirements and sanctions to match.
As we read the text and ponder these offers, we tend to choose up sides, select
our rootage, notice our vested interests, and make our advocacy. The problem

with that is that this God, in unutterable holiness, occupies and legitimates all of these transactions. In the biblical tradition that carries the good news of the gospel, it is the one God who is both *unilateral in generosity* and *bilateral in requirement*. It is the same God who can be inordinately demanding, crushing, and reprimanding, and who can be graciously accepting, welcoming, and affirming. It is the one God who sees through hard times with patience and who terminates interactions in cold refusals. It is the God who endlessly negotiates being fully *for us* but who will get glory *for God's own self* and who will not be mocked. It is this God who becomes a threat if approached too casually or carelessly and who warns about drawing too close, but who is nearer to us than our breath or our utterance.

We wonder how this could be. If you would like, you can call it a contradiction. Well, of course. But you can also notice that this God has a rich interior life in which this God in freedom and in fidelity is always processing the world before God's own self, always deciding, always adjudicating, always exercising options, always living in freedom, always repositioning and reengaging afresh. That interior life of God is not available to us, except for the poets and the priests and the singers of songs and the tellers of tales. These makers of texts in uncommon artistry and enormous courage enter into God's own holiness and invite us to go there with them. Because they are artistic, they deliver to us open and imaginative and daring probes. But what they offer is not and could not be flat, one-dimensional, or certain. These poets and singers and tellers of tales make clear to us that *artistry* is required to practice the *complex interiority* of God that makes possible a *dialogical exteriority*. Notice the terms:

- *Artistry* is required concerning the God who comes at covenant practices with ease and restless risk. It is a divine artistry that is matched by the *artistry of human imagination*.
- Such artistry yields *a complex interiority* in which God is capable of self-examination, probe, and critical reflection. Such an interiority evidences that God is capable of more than one possibility, which is why the Bible offers us from time to time probes into divine anguish.
- This complex interiority in turn posits *dialogical externality*, a capacity to come at the covenant partner in a variety of ways, sometimes with the crankiness of self-regard, sometimes with the generosity that considers only the partner.
- Such a flow of *artistry, internal complexity,* and *dialogical externality* issues, does it not, in *fidelity* that arises in *freedom.* Indeed, fidelity, wondrously articulated in the Hebrew triad of *hesed, rahum,* and *amunah* is the hallmark of this God in relationship, not a mechanical predictability but a fully personal capacity for being with and being for and being over against, and staying with and calling out.

You will notice, if you take this sequence of markings of God's holiness—artistry, internal complexity, dialogical externality, and, finally, fidelity—that this characterization of the covenant-making God flies in the face of a long-preferred orthodoxy of "omnipotence, omniscience, and omnipresence." That is the God long confessed among us, present in the catechism traditions, in a mistaken attempt to fully characterize God in God's own self as the one with all the power and all the knowledge and everywhere present in sovereign form. That characterization of God exhibits a God who needs no partners, for whom partners are an "extra," that are not indispensable for divine personhood. Such a God (that requires a quite forced reading of Scripture) results in large measures of *certitude* in which everything is settled well ahead of time. That is the stuff of sovereign *authority* and of unchallengeable *control*.

But it will not work. It will not work biblically because since the first divine utterance to Abraham and the first divine self-disclosure at Sinai, the biblical God has been in relationship. This is a God capable of love and anger, of presence and of absence, of forgiveness and retribution, so much so that we have had to explain it all along the way as "anthropomorphism" and "anthropopathism," language that makes God "too human." It will not work in trinitarian terms because it is impossible that the Father of the Three O's would have sent such a compassionate, self-giving Son into the world. Indeed, the famous football slogan of John 3:16 already gives the game away: "God so loved the world that he sent..." It is this God so committed, so dialogical, so covenantal since Genesis 9 with whom we have to do. It will not work biblically. It will not work in terms of trinitarian theology.

But most of all it will not work pastorally, for who among us in our ecstasy, and especially our agony, needs a God of certitude? For it is the ache of our heart and the yearning of our body that we should finally be attended to by one who is full of grace, and before grace, full of truth. The *narrative* of *the God of fidelity* lives in deep conflict with the *syllogism* of *the God of certitude*. The gods of certitude are often in control, control through some moralism, through settled orthodoxy, through the ideology often allied with the rulers of this age. But in the midst of the gods of certitude there is this burst of the God of fidelity,

- the God *artistically rendered*;
- the God rich in *internal complexity*;
- the God free in *dialogical externality*;
- the God saturated with *fidelity and freedom*.

This God will not settle in certitude, for certitude is finally a cognitive category and not one that is thick with relationship. This God will not settle for certitude but is on the way with Abraham and with Moses and with all their fellow travelers.

And because this God steps out with this people and all such peoples in covenant, the covenanted community comes on hard days. They came on hard days in old Samaria, which the Assyrians destroyed in 722 BCE. They came on hard days in Jerusalem, which the Babylonians destroyed in 587 BCE. And there will be more hard days in Jerusalem in 70 CE, when the Romans put an end to things, and in New York City in 2001 on 9/11, and on and on, always hard days. And those hard days are hard as well for the covenanting God, for how shall the artistically rendered, interiorly complex, externally dialogical God of fidelity respond to such hard days?

The troubles of Samaria and Jerusalem, of New York and Belfast and Sarajevo and Baghdad and Johannesburg and Jerusalem again present the God of covenant with vexation. The troubles, so say the poets, evoke the complexity of YHWH's interiority into dialogical externality in two tensive modes. On the one hand, the God rooted in Sinai speaks out of a bilateral conviction that obedience results in life and disobedience results in death. It figures, of course, that suffering and destruction follow covenantal disobedience. The outcome of poetic utterance is, not surprisingly, poetic oracles of indictment and sentence. This strand of divine utterance offers a tight moral calculus. Thus it follows that Samaria was destroyed because Israel had whored after other gods:

> For they sow the wind,
> > and they shall reap the whirlwind.
> The standing grain has no heads,
> > it shall yield no meal;
> if it were to yield,
> > foreigners would devour it.
> Israel is swallowed up;
> > now they are among the nations
> > as a useless vessel.
> For they have gone up to Assyria,
> > a wild ass wandering alone;
> > Ephraim has bargained for lovers.
> Though they bargain with the nations,
> > I will now gather them up.
> They shall soon writhe
> > under the burden of kings and princes. (Hos 8:7-10)

And it follows that Jerusalem is destroyed for its abuse of the poor:

> Your iniquities have turned these away,
> > and your sins have deprived you of good.
> For scoundrels are found among my people;
> > they take over the goods of others.
> Like fowlers they set a trap;
> > they catch human beings.

Like a cage full of birds,
>   their houses are full of treachery;
herefore they have become great and rich,
>   they have grown fat and sleek.
They know no limits in deeds of wickedness;
>   they do not judge with justice
he cause of the orphan, to make it prosper,
>   and they do not defend the rights of the needy.
Shall I not punish them for these things?
>   says the Lord,
>   and shall I not bring retribution
>   on a nation such as this? (Jer 5:25-29)

It follows in reliable covenantal fidelity. It could not be otherwise. It could not be otherwise in New York and in Washington, in Nanjing and Islamabad, and all other places of violence. Our text of covenant shows the way in which the covenant-making God stays faithful, and the world witnesses moral coherence that cannot be violated with impunity.

On the other hand, the God rooted in Jerusalem—all the way back to Abraham—has a bottomless unilateral freedom that gets expressed as generous fidelity. It is for that reason that the very same daring poets, the ones who imagine and who probe the divine interiority, notice around the edges of divine resolve a countertheme of suffering love that produces costly forgiveness at the very core of divine indignation. The covenant-making God is precisely pressed toward pathos, the capacity to care about, suffer with, and suffer for those in solidarity. Such divine pathos is not an aberration. It is an inescapable enactment of covenantal fidelity.

For that reason the very same poets who speak *bilateral indignation* are recruited to utter, right from God's own heart, *unilateral pathos*. It is this same Hosea, the one who noticed while God responded in rejection against recalcitrant Israel:

They shall return to the land of Egypt,
>   and Assyria shall be their king,
>   because they have refused to return to me.
The sword rages in their cities,
>   it consumes their oracle-priests,
>   and devours because of their schemes.
My people are bent on turning away from me.
>   To the Most High they call,
>   but he does not raise them up at all. (Hos 11:5-7)

It is this same God—through this same poet—who stops short in the middle of the poem, engages in critical self-reflection, and then speaks these awesome words of divine generosity:

How can I give you up, Ephraim?
How can I hand you over, O Israel?
How can I make you like Admah?
How can I treat you like Zeboiim?
My heart recoils within me;
my compassion grows warm and tender.
I will not execute my fierce anger;
I will not again destroy Ephraim;
for I am God and no mortal,
the Holy One in your midst,
and I will not come in wrath. (Hos 11:8-9)

Thus, after a rebuke of Samaria, this northern poet is authorized to speak a future grounded in God's own fidelity.

It is not different in the south, in Jerusalem. This same Jeremiah from Anathoth who noticed the abuse of the poor and drew the inescapable conclusion now articulates the God who grieves the loss of the covenant partner, who is sent away in profound rage. Now speaks the poet again in the voice of covenantal fidelity:

Is Ephraim my dear son?
Is he the child I delight in?
As often as I speak against him,
I still remember him.
Therefore I am deeply moved for him;
I will surely have mercy on him,
says the LORD. (Jer 31:20)

The divine speaker, the same one as in Hosea 11:8, engages in self-criticism. In Hosea 11:8 the self-criticism comes as two questions:

How can I give you up, Ephraim?
How can I hand you over, O Israel?
How can I make you like Admah?
How can I treat you like Zeboiim?
My heart recoils within me;
my compassion grows warm and tender. (Hos 11:8)

Now in Jeremiah 31:20 it is the question again:

Is Ephraim my dear son?
Is he the child I delight in?
As often as I speak against him,
I still remember him.
Therefore I am deeply moved for him;

> I will surely have mercy on him,
> > says the LORD. (Jer 31:20)

And then, as in Hosea 11:8-9, there is a divine response of fresh resolve. I will get my mind off the affront. Indeed, my covenantal attachment to Israel is so intense that I am required to utilize two infinitive absolutes, says the God who has mastered Hebrew grammar:

> I am deeply moved.
> I will surely have mercy.

My intensity of attachment pushes me beyond retaliation to care. I find myself propelled beyond my resolve by a deeper impulse, a love that "will not let me go."

In both Samaria and in Jerusalem, the dialogic God struggles and says both things: *death*—and *new life*. Surely it is so everywhere with this God of complex interiority. It is so in New York and Washington, in New Orleans and Tulsa, and in every village and town where the truth of covenant is observed. It is so wherever there is a poetic pause to cut beneath the flat certitude of control to see that *holiness is a tensive, struggling passion for truth and grace*, for retribution and compassion, for a God whose innards touch lived reality and press toward new possibility. It is so where there is such artistry. And where there is no such artistry, there can only be *denial and despair, resentment, self-indulgence*, and finally, *violence*. The truth of the poetry is that this covenant-making God is never finished and settled; rather, the Holy One is impinged upon and moved to compassion in the same way that the well-beloved Son is moved to compassion when he sees the hungry crowds (Mark 6:34; 8:2). As you know, "compassion" means the cringing stirring of innards moved to new response. Such a moment in the life of God is signaled by Hosea, "My heart recoils within me." And in Jeremiah, "I am deeply moved." This is no unmoved mover, no settled certitude, but a partner evoked and moved to fresh engagement, stringent and caring, passionate and indignant, who variously engages in moral seriousness and generous care.

III

Given that dialogical God who comes toward the world with fidelity and freedom that together constitute covenant, it is the Jewish proposal that human persons are constituted precisely for *dialogical existence* in relationship to this God of fidelity and freedom. The peculiar Jewishness of this offer is made evident in the modern world most especially by Sigmund Freud who, for all his personal struggles against Jewishness, did indeed bequeath to the world a Jewish notion of the human self.[2] For whatever scientific notions of healing that may have occupied Freud's work, at bottom his great insight is that the self can emerge in health only in a candid dialogic transaction with one who listens well and receives honestly. That dialogic self arises only in an exchange with the other who acts freely and faithfully. Freud discerned, moreover, that the thickness ("depth") of the self with layers and layers of meaning is not unlike the thickness of texts that the rabbis could read endlessly for more and more meanings. Thus, the self is essentially a venue for interpretation, an enterprise that requires a trustful exchange. We may notice in addition that, in more recent time, work on a dialogical sense of self in covenant has moved in a more bilateral direction, as the listening partner now is seen to be not simply a passive receiver but also an active participant in a two-way exchange.[3]

After Freud, it is most obviously Martin Buber who has grasped the dialogical quality of the self in his well known "I-thou" formulation and his aphorism that "life is meeting."[4] Buber's work is intended to be a direct and intentional refutation of the modern Cartesian self, a self posited as an isolated, self-sufficient autonomy without regard to any others.[5] The Cartesian self in the modern world has become a narrative of Promethean dimension, and a performance of domination and control that can freely violate any of the others in the pursuit of self.

Buber's more or less mystical sense of I-thou has been given a more formidable articulation in the work of Emmanuel Levinas, notably in his programmatic book, *Totality and Infinity*.[6] By "totality" Levinas means a fully contained and self-sufficient system of power that runs in the direction of totalitarianism, and conversely, "infinity" means an openness to possibility that is not known ahead of time. The defining characteristic of infinity, for Levinas, is the face-to-faceness of human engagement. The supreme act of being human is to look into the face of the other, and in characteristically Jewish fashion, Levinas finds in the face of the other an immediate and elemental ethical demand; having seen the face of the other, one is bound to that other in caring, neighborly ways. It seems clear enough that Buber and Levinas, as alternative to Descartes, could not have written as they have except for the Jewish dialogic tradition of covenant in which they stand.

But clearly, long before Freud, Buber, or Levinas, it is the book of Psalms, which bespeaks the dialogic covenantal self whose vocation is to glorify and enjoy God forever. The book of Psalms, while complex, can in simplistic fashion be understood as a collection of doxologies and complaints-laments. In the doxologies of praise, thanks, and trust, all the energy and attention of the human person (and the human community) are devoted to the enhancement of God. Indeed, praise is the full, glad, exuberant *ceding* of the self over to God. As counterpoint, the complaints and laments of the Psalter are the full, resolved assertion of the *claiming* of the self in the presence of God or even over against God. It strikes one as odd and remarkable that the self in the complaints can address imperatives to God, even if we choose to label those imperatives as petitions. There is no doubt that God is the "thou" who responds to the complaints of Israel in order that the suppliant can be an "I." (At the very edge of this transaction, we may entertain the thought that the human self becomes the "thou" whereby the "I" of God is constituted and signified in the covenantal transaction, which is the self.) Thus the Psalter, before any of the modern thinkers I have cited, provided the script for the performance of *the dialogical covenantal self.* Given the force of the Cartesian self in the modern world, the self necessary to a modern technological society and the self propped up by consumer propaganda, the nurture and performance of the dialogical self is an urgent, subversive activity. That alternative self is one defined precisely by fidelity wherein even lapses into infidelity can be taken as significations of what generates the self. That self, moreover, is constituted in freedom, the freedom to engage, to praise and obey, to command and rejoice, most of all to trust self in a relationship that valorizes the self.

IV

The dialogic self in its interaction with the dialogic God is called to a demanding, energizing way of living in the world. Given that dialogical life is a demanding way in the world, there is an endless temptation to avoid the recurring jeopardy of covenantal existence by embrace by one of two alternatives.

On the one hand, there is the possible flight to *absolutism.* Absolutism is an attractive, seductive alternative because it moves toward the nullification of the risks of dialogue into a flat, settled state of being. Such absolutism can easily become a category into which God is recharacterized and redescribed. Indeed, one can judge that the classical tradition of Western theology, overly informed by Hellenistic categories, has settled for a God who is an absolute sovereign. The familiar characterization of God as "omnipotent, omniscient, and omnipresent" bears witness to a God who is settled and fully self-sufficient, not in any need or in any vulnerability. It is astonishing that Christian theology has sought to accommodate this way of God to the suffering love of the Son, an accommodation that has made trinitarian theology exceedingly problematic. This is a God who cannot be impinged upon and, as Jürgen Moltmann has shown, is a God who cannot suffer in compassionate availability.[7]

Apropos this way of rendering God, the spinoff will predictably be a community of moral conformity that is severe in its demands and unbending toward those who violate the absoluteness of morality that is said to derive from the absoluteness of the deity. It is impossible to measure or provide an inventory of the wounds inflicted by such a self-convinced community of moral certitude that has been experienced as oppressive and unforgiving.

When God is reduced to a settled formula, the notion of God in dialogue seems weak and inadequate. But from the perspective of the covenantal traditions, the lust for absolutism eventuates in *idolatry,* a flat, settled God without dialogic agency who cannot care or answer or engage or respond. The poetry of Israel is capable of contrasting such *absoluteness* with *covenantalism:*

> Their idols are like scarecrows in a cucumber field,
>   and they cannot speak;

they have to be carried,
for they cannot walk.
Do not be afraid of them,
for they cannot do evil,
nor is it in them to do good.
. . . .
But the LORD is the true God;
he is the living God and the everlasting King.
At his wrath the earth quakes,
and the nations cannot endure his indignation.
. . . .
It is he who made the earth by his power,
who established the world by his wisdom,
and by his understanding stretched out the heavens.
When he utters his voice, there is a tumult of waters in the heavens,
and he makes the mist rise from the ends of the earth.
He makes lightnings for the rain,
and he brings out the wind from his storehouses. (Jer 10:5, 10, 12-13)

And so the poetic tradition can dare to mock such absolute gods who can perform none of the functions of "thou-ness" that are so crucial to the health of the world:

Their idols are silver and gold,
the work of human hands.
They have mouths, but do not speak;
eyes, but do not see.
They have ears, but do not hear;
noses, but do not smell.
They have hands, but do not feel;
feet, but do not walk;
they make no sound in their throats. (Ps 115:4-7)

And the Psalm knowingly adds, concerning those who trust such idols:

Those who make them are like them;
so are all who trust in them. (Ps 115:8)

On the other hand and in reaction against such absolutism, there is a flight to *autonomy*. Those who find absolutism too hard to bear flee from it and imagine an unencumbered self. That autonomy is now romantically expressed in the familiar mantra, "I am spiritual but no longer religious," that is, no longer attached to the institutions of holiness that are too demanding and authoritarian. Such a flight merely enacts the Cartesian premise.

Autonomy, the notion that one need to rely on or answer to no other, is the ground for a society that is endlessly acquisitive of the resources of other people and does so with unrestrained violence. That autonomy is also an invitation of the self to live without rootage or tradition, and without the resources or requirements of a community of discipline and expectation. The Bible does not spend as much time on autonomy as on absolutism, because autonomy is a much more modern option. There is, however, enough in the Bible to see the temptation even there. Thus, the prophet Isaiah can imagine the systemic autonomy of the great superpower Babylon:

> You said, "I shall be mistress forever,"
>> so that you did not lay these things to heart
>> or remember their end.
> Now therefore hear this, you lover of pleasures,
>> who sit securely,
> who say in your heart,
>> "I am, and there is no one besides me;
> I shall not sit as a widow
>> or know the loss of children"—
> . . . .
> You felt secure in your wickedness;
>> you said, "No one sees me."
> Your wisdom and your knowledge
>> led you astray,
> and you said in your heart,
>> "I am, and there is no one besides me." (Isa 47:7-8, 10)

The prophetic rebuke is the assertion that the superpower has forgotten that it is permitted no such autonomy. The sapiential tradition can see such autonomy in the action of the arrogant, who know no restraints:

> In the pride of their countenance
>> the wicked say, "God will not seek it out";
>> all their thoughts are, "There is no God."
> . . . .
> They think in their heart, "We shall not be moved;
>> throughout all generations we shall not meet adversity."
> . . . .
>> in hiding places they murder the innocent.
> Their eyes stealthily watch for the helpless;
>> they lurk in secret like a lion in its covert;
> they lurk that they may seize the poor;
>> they seize the poor and drag them off in their net.

They stoop, they crouch,
    and the helpless fall by their might.
They think in their heart, "God has forgotten,
    he has hidden his face, he will never see it." (Ps 10:4, 6, 8b-11)

The upshot of such assured autonomy, inescapably, is the violation of the neighborhood. In Psalm 14, such autonomy is deemed "foolishness," the very foolishness that Gerhard von Rad has termed "practical atheism":

Fools say in their hearts, "There is no God."
    They are corrupt, they do abominable deeds;
    there is no one who does good. (Ps 14:1)

This is, perforce, the same fool who, in the parable of Luke 12:20, engaged in
endless acquisitiveness and who had his life required of him in the night.

   From a covenantal perspective, *absolutism* (which is *idolatry*) and *autonomy*
(which is *atheism*) are two violations of a world ordered for covenant, twin violations that in the end make life unlivable. It is clear, of course, that the twin
practices of *conformist absolutism* and *unfettered autonomy* can be practiced
at the same time and produce a world wherein covenantal dialogue is impossible
to sustain. The outcome of such a practice, even when legitimated by misguided
theology, is a common life that is filled with anxiety that is always again at the
edge of violence and brutality.

V

Given the seductions of absolutism and autonomy, it is the steady alternative of
biblical faith to bear witness to a covenantal existence that is dialogical from the
ground up. The summons of the gospel is always to covenantal existence with all
of its possibilities and risks and inescapable hazards. Covenantal existence eventuates in the pathos of God, the great holy God reaching in vulnerability to be with
neighbors in need. It is for that reason that the most compelling articulation of
God in the Bible is as a *covenanting father* or as a *nursing mother* or as a *suffering
spouse*, or as an *attentive shepherd* or as an *intrusive king and judge*. This is not
to deny that the Bible in its patriarchal presuppositions can flirt with the seductions of absoluteness. But as can be regularly seen, the poetic force of alternative
intrudes on that conventional theology, disrupts it, and says otherwise. Thus,
after God, in the guise of a husband, can file divorce papers against wife Israel,
the poem has God reverse field and make new vows to the practice of covenant
with Israel: "And I will take you for my wife forever; I will take you for my wife
in righteousness and in justice, in steadfast love, and in mercy. I will take you for

my wife in faithfulness; and you shall know the Lord" (Hos 2:19-20). The new vow of fidelity is filled with all of the great words of covenantal loyalty. As we have seen, after God can be a wistful, irate parent ready to abandon the wayward child, the poetry has God flinch from such an orgy of self-satisfaction, reverse field, and make new resolve for fidelity (Hos 11:8-9; Jer 31:20). The intensity of parental connectedness requires a great leap on God's part. Most spectacularly, in Jeremiah 3 there is such a yearning on God's part for the covenant partner Israel that God is prepared explicitly to reject the torah requirements of Deuteronomy 24. That God should violate God's own torah for the sake of the relationship becomes the new arena for hope and possibility in Israel. And surely a new arena for anguish and joy in God's own life.

It is required, then, that we pay attention to the breakout of new image and new metaphor that are necessary for God's great leaps into new depths of fidelity. Of course, one could not build a great superpower on these awkward images of engagement and fidelity. But so it is with this God who, from the first utterance of Abraham, has been on the way to pathos. We say, we Christians, that we have been on the way to the cross from the very outset; and Jews dare say that they have, from the outset, been on their weeping way to the ovens, broken in love for a lost people. God goes to the cross, and to the ovens. And we with God.

Thus covenantal existence, in Christian articulation, eventuates in the Son who suffers. It is this Son who shockingly asked, "Who touched me?" (Mark 5:31) He perceived that power had gone forth from him. He is touchable and reachable and, in that bodily touch, contact is made, power is transmitted, and he is, in that instant, diminished. It is this strange rabbi who came upon a hungry crowd in the wilderness and was moved to do his manna performance. He did so because he was "moved to compassion." The move to compassion that evoked food for the hungry is, of course, an echo of the father who was deeply moved over the suffering of the son in Hosea and Jeremiah. It is not that Jesus had to wait until Friday to suffer. Rather, he is, from the outset, a carrier of covenantal possibility; and so he prefers a covenantal existence, being always impinged upon by those around him.

Covenantal existence eventuates in a community of uncommon generosity and mercy, a community of fidelity and freedom, a community that is not seduced by absolutism and that is not left unrestrained by autonomy. It is a congregation of conservative covenanters and liberal covenanters, all of whom are covenanters before they receive other labels. So imagine a community of covenant, set down in a society of usurpatious absolutism and self-indulgent autonomy come to give self away, ready and able to receive more life from those who are unlike us, ready for fidelity that takes the form of freedom that is disciplined, ready for signs and acts and gestures of forgiveness and hospitality and generosity, more ready to support than to judge. There are, to be sure, in such a community, sanctions, but the sanctions are provisional and penultimate, because the relationships count for more than the rules.

VI

Covenantal life is a life broken and poured out.

God's own life is broken and poured out for the sake of the partner. It is this God of whom Israel can sing:

> . . . who forgives all your iniquity,
>   who heals all your diseases,
> who redeems your life from the Pit,
>   who crowns you with steadfast love and mercy,
> who satisfies you with good as long as you live
>   so that your youth is renewed like the eagle's.
> The LORD works vindication
>   and justice for all who are oppressed. (Ps 103:3-6)

Each of these acts—forgiving, healing, redeeming, crowning, satisfying, vindicating—is an act of self-giving. That self-giving is the order of the day because:

> The LORD is merciful and gracious,
>   slow to anger and abounding in steadfast love.
> He will not always accuse,
>   nor will he keep his anger forever.
> He does not deal with us according to our sins,
>   nor repay us according to our iniquities. (Ps 103:8-10)

The God of life is a father in compassion. This God knows how we are made, contentious, unreliable, and prone to self-destructiveness. And the divine response is forgiveness.

Four times in Psalm 103, Israel utters the quintessential covenantal term *hesed*:

> . . . who redeems your life from the Pit,
>   who crowns you with *steadfast love* and mercy.
> . . . .
> The LORD is merciful and gracious,
>   slow to anger and abounding in *steadfast love*.
> . . . .
> For as the heavens are high above the earth,
>   so great is his *steadfast love* toward those who fear him.
> . . . .
> But the *steadfast love* of the LORD is from everlasting to everlasting
>   on those who fear him,
>   and his righteousness to children's children. (Ps 103:4, 8, 11, 17)

Nothing here of a disengaged absolutism; nothing here of a self-preoccupied autonomy.

The community of faith, knowing about the covenant-keeping God, has long pondered how to be a community apropos of this God, a suitable partner in the ongoing transaction of mutual impingement. In ancient Israel, the poet Jeremiah arrives at the awesome conclusion:

> He judged the cause of the poor and needy;
> > then it was well.
> Is not this to know me?
> > says the LORD. (Jer 22:16)

The case cited is King Josiah. He intervened on behalf of the poor and needy. This is the way to "know God." This is to encounter the covenanting God by loving neighbor. It is neighborliness that is the heart of Sinai. Of course, it is not different in the community gathered around Jesus. The way to love the Son of Man is by commitment to the least:

> Then the king will say to those at his right hand, "Come, you that are blessed by my Father, inherit the kingdom prepared for you from the foundation of the world; for I was hungry and you gave me food, I was thirsty and you gave me something to drink, I was a stranger and you welcomed me, I was naked and you gave me clothing, I was sick and you took care of me, I was in prison and you visited me." (Matt 25:34-36)

The absolutists can be so elevated in their certitude that they do not see the facts on the ground, the facts among "the least." Those in autonomy can be so narcissistic that they also do not notice. But the covenanters have watched their divine partner stop and care, and so they stop and care, and the world is made new.

Truth to tell, it is all about being *broken and poured out*. Jesus specified that, in a desert place, when he came upon the hungry crowd and uttered four great verbs of covenant: "*Taking* the five loaves and the two fish, he looked up to heaven, and *blessed* and *broke* the loaves, and *gave* them to his disciples to set before the people; and he divided the two fish among them all" (Mark 6:41). There is something of the new that wells up in being broken and poured out, five thousand fed and twelve baskets left over. And then he replicated the act in Mark 8 because he intended it to be unmistakably clear: "Then he ordered the crowd to sit down on the ground; and he *took* the seven loaves, and after *giving thanks* he *broke* them and *gave* them to his disciples to distribute; and they distributed them to the crowd. They had also a few small fish; and after blessing them, he ordered that these too should be distributed" (Mark 8:6-7). And the outcome is four thousand fed with seven basketsful left over because covenantal existence is abundant.

The replication continues. So Paul could write:

> For I received from the Lord what I also handed on to you, that the Lord
> Jesus on the night when he was betrayed took a loaf of bread, and when
> he had given thanks, he broke it and said, "This is my body that is for
> you. Do this in remembrance of me." In the same way he took the cup
> also, after supper, saying, "This cup is the new covenant in my blood.
> Do this, as often as you drink it, in remembrance of me." For as often as
> you eat this bread and drink the cup, you proclaim the Lord's death until
> he comes. (1 Cor 11:23-26)

This food is not a weapon; it is a gift for sharing God's own holy self. And the
sharing continues among those who are bound to God and to neighbor. The act is
countercultural subversive activity, but it has been subversive since the first utterance to Abraham.

Jesus is a brilliant, knowing hermeneutist. He works the entire covenantal
tradition:

- He criticizes those who prefer *absolutism*:

  > Woe to you, scribes and Pharisees, hypocrites! For you tithe mint,
  > dill, and cummin, and have neglected the weightier matters of the
  > law: justice and mercy and faith. It is these you ought to have prac-
  > ticed without neglecting the others. You blind guides! You strain
  > out a gnat but swallow a camel! (Matt 23:23-24)

- He criticizes those who opt for *autonomy*:

  > But God said to him, "You fool! This very night your life is being
  > demanded of you. And the things you have prepared, whose will
  > they be?" So it is with those who store up treasures for themselves
  > but are not rich toward God. (Luke 12:20-21).

- And in his parable concerning the rich man and Lazarus, he works
  the covenantal tradition. To *the rich man*, he delivers the *conditional*
  covenant of Sinai:

  > There was a rich man who was dressed in purple and fine linen and
  > who feasted sumptuously every day. . . . He said to him, "If they
  > do not listen to Moses and the prophets, neither will they be con-
  > vinced even if someone rises from the dead." (Luke 16:19, 31)

- To *the poor man*, he welcomes him to the *unconditional promise* of Abraham:

  > The poor man died and was carried away by the angels to be with Abraham. The rich man also died and was buried. (Luke 16:22)

Both receive covenantal payouts, one as *stringent requirement*, one as *abiding abundance*. Our anticovenantal society wants us to be one-dimensional. But we refuse because covenanting is a different way in the world, always requiring, always waiting, always letting us stand alongside neighbors, full of wonder, love, and praise.

CHAPTER 2

Exodus: Limit and Possibility

THE CORE OF THE EXODUS narrative is the contest between the slave community of Moses and the exploitative economy of Pharaoh, between YHWH, who hears the cries of the exploited and the gods of Egypt, who sanctioned such a system (Exod 12:12). In the telling of the story, the contest is between Moses and Aaron on the one hand and the "magicians" of Egypt on the other hand. The term rendered "magicians" comes from the noun "stylus," the ones who engrave, the ones who write, the ones who know the mystery of elite communication, the ones who can manipulate the symbols of power and knowledge in society.

Moses and Aaron, we are told, are there in the contest simply because YHWH has dispatched them. But we may pause over the role of "the magicians." The term occurs in only two other places in Scripture. In Genesis 41:8, 24, they are referenced as the advisors to Pharaoh who are unable to interpret the dream of Pharaoh, the dream that finally Joseph the Hebrew must interpret. The other mention is in the narrative of Daniel, where the magicians of Nebuchadnezzar are named in two stories. In Daniel 1, they are mentioned in passing in order to report that Daniel, who lived on a Jewish diet of water and vegetables, was "ten times better than all the magicians and enchanters in his whole kingdom." In Daniel 2, the narrative closely parallels the Joseph story of Genesis 41. As in the Egyptian account, Nebuchadnezzar has a dream. Here the king summons his magicians not only to interpret the dream (as in Gen 41) but also to tell the dream before they interpret it. Of course, they cannot do it.

> The Chaldeans answered the king, "There is no one on earth who
> can reveal what the king demands! In fact no king, however great and
> powerful, has ever asked such a thing of any magician or enchanter or

Chaldean. The thing that the king is asking is too difficult, and no one
can reveal it to the king except the gods, whose dwelling is not with
mortals." (Dan 2:10-11)

In his demanding rage, the king purports to execute all the wise men in Babylon
who have failed him. They are saved only by the intervention of Daniel, the wise
Jew, who can tell the king his dream and who proceeds to interpret it. And when
Daniel had done his wondrous work for the arrogant king, he goes to Arioch, the
one Nebuchadnezzar had assigned to execute the wise men, and says: "Do not
destroy the wise men of Babylon; bring me in before the king, and I will give the
king the interpretation" (Dan 2:24). And then Daniel says to the king:

> Daniel answered the king, "No wise men, enchanters, magicians, or
> diviners can show to the king the mystery that the king is asking, but
> there is a God in heaven who reveals mysteries, and he has disclosed to
> King Nebuchadnezzar what will happen at the end of days. Your dream
> and the visions of your head as you lay in bed were these: To you, O
> king, as you lay in bed, came thoughts of what would be hereafter, and
> the revealer of mysteries disclosed to you what is to be. But as for me,
> this mystery has not been revealed to me because of any wisdom that
> I have more than any other living being, but in order that the inter-
> pretation may be known to the king and that you may understand the
> thoughts of your mind. You were looking, O king, and lo! There was a
> great statute. This statue was huge, its brilliance extraordinary; it was
> standing before you, and its appearance was frightening." (Dan 2:27-31)

This is a remarkable assertion. It allows, first, that nobody can be expected to
know "the mystery" that the king had dreamed. But then, second, Daniel—good
Jew that he is—acknowledges that it is "God in heaven" who "reveals mysteries."
It is this revealer of mysteries who has disclosed what is to be, and Daniel is his
agent in interpretation. The speech of Daniel thus poignantly contrasts the futility
of imperial wisdom and the disclosure of God offered to the wise, discerning Jew.
    I take this long with the narratives of Genesis 41 and Daniel 1 and 2 (the
only other uses of our term) in order to observe that the magicians are cited in
the narrative only to exhibit their inadequacy and incompetence to do what the
king (Pharaoh or Nebuchadnezzar) requires of them. Now in the "contest" of
the exodus narrative, these same imperial magicians appear for the third time
in Scripture. We will not understand what transpires in the narrative unless we
understand who they are. They are the representative contestants for imperial
power in the contest for the future that is staged by YHWH, the God who hears
the cries of the exploited. They are the "intelligence community" of legitimated
imperial power who know the deep mysteries of how things work. When I read of

them, I could not help but recall the book *The Wise Men* by Walter Isaacson and
Evan Thomas, who consider the six men who dominated U.S. foreign policy for
two generations through the Cold War: Dean Atchison, Averill Harriman, George
Kennan, Charles Bohlen, Robert Lovett, and John McClay.[1] And when I ponder
the futility of those ancient magicians in Egypt, I cannot help but recall that sad
scene traced by Isaacson and Thomas as the "wise men" gathered for the last
time around Lyndon Johnson. They had come, at long last, to the White House
to ponder the souring of the Vietnam War. They, like Lyndon Johnson, held their
heads in their hands in bewilderment and despair, as they could discern no com-
petent way in foreign policy into the future. They could not see, and nothing had
been revealed to them.

It is this cast of characters that appears on behalf of Pharaoh and the Egyptian
gods in the contest that constitutes the narrative of the plagues. That contest is
situated midway in the exodus narrative. Just before the plague narrative begins
in chapter 7, there is the credentialing of YHWH and Moses and Aaron in chapter
6, and a full, adversarial portrayal of Pharaoh's system in chapter 5. The contest
is fully anticipated in Exodus 5:1-2:

> Verse 1: YHWH speaks:
>   Let my people go so that they may celebrate a festival to me in the
>   wilderness.

> Verse 2: Pharaoh speaks:
>   Who is YHWH that I should heed him and let Israel go? I do not
>   know YHWH, and I will not let Israel go.

Thus the issue is joined, arm wrestling between the resolve of YHWH and the
resistance of Pharaoh. The plague narratives detail the struggle. That detail of
struggle makes clear that it is futile to try to understand or "explain" the events as
"natural" occurrences or as "historical" happenings in any modern sense of the
term. Rather, what we have is the articulation of a *theological paradigm*, a screen
through which Israel will read all of its historical experience. Erich Voegelin uses
the terms "paradigm, paradigmatic" in his portrayal of Israel's memory, a memory
that deliberately begs all modernist questions of history.[2] Peter Ochs and David
Halivni, moreover, use the term "pragmatic" for such textual tradition, "because
it serves the needs of a community of practice."[3] The contest undertaken in Exodus
5:1-2 and conducted through chapter 15 is indeed a resource for practice, a tracing
of the world and its history in terms of dispute, conflict, and contest between the
power of coercion and the alternative power of emancipation for new obedience.

The framing of the plague narrative in chapters 5 and 6 is matched by the glorious doxologies of chapter 15, after the contest has been concluded. The initial
doxology is on the lips of Miriam, who sang the victory of YHWH over Pharaoh,
the triumph of the God of ordered justice over the powers of chaos:

And Miriam sang to them:
> "Sing to the LORD, for he has triumphed gloriously;
> horse and rider he has thrown into the sea." (Exod 15:21)

Miriam sang as her sisters danced with their tambourines. It is no small matter to watch as ex-slaves, newly emancipated, sing. Their *song* replaced their *cry*. "Weeping has lingered for many nights, / but now joy has come in the morning" (Ps 30:5). And then Moses appropriates the singing of dancing women. As the authoritative leader, he goes on at much greater length (vv. 1-18), but his song is the same as that of the women. The song is about the failure of Pharaoh and the wondrous transformative victory of YHWH. The contest of chapter 5 is completed in chapter 15. Chapter 5 is a long inventory of Pharaoh's coercive requirements of slave labor, and chapter 15 is about "free at last, free at last, thank God almighty we are free at last." The plague narrative is the detailed tracing of the contest from outset to culmination, a detailed tracing that this remembering, hoping, crying, singing community regularly reenacts in a liturgical performance. Such liturgical performance provides the material for the grandparental instruction of Exodus 10:1-2, in which the children and grandchildren will "know that I am YHWH," this same YHWH of whom Pharaoh said at the outset, "I do not know YHWH."

II

At the outset of the plague narrative, in Exodus 7:5, YHWH asserts and anticipates: "The Egyptians shall know that I am the LORD, when I stretch out my hand against Egypt and bring the Israelites out from among them" (Exod 7:5). And then begins the contest. In 7:14-25, the first encounter begins with the reiterated demand of YHWH given to Pharaoh, only with a test case of water to blood:

> Thus says the LORD, "By this you shall know that I am the LORD." See, with the staff that is in my hand I will strike the water that is in the Nile, and it shall be turned to blood. The fish in the river shall die, the river itself shall stink, and the Egyptians shall be unable to drink water from the Nile. The LORD said to Moses, "Say to Aaron, 'Take your staff and stretch out your hand over the waters of Egypt—over its rivers, its canals, and its ponds, and all its pools of water—so that they may become blood; and there shall be blood throughout the whole land of Egypt, even in vessels of wood and in vessels of stone.'" (Exod 7:17-19)

Sure enough, it happened:

> Moses and Aaron did just as the LORD *commanded*. In the sight of Pharaoh and of his officials he lifted up the staff and struck the water in the

river, and all the water in the river was turned into blood, and the fish
in the river died. The river stank so that the Egyptians could not drink
its water, and there was blood throughout the whole land of Egypt.
(Exod 7:20-21)

That should have been enough. This is the Creator God whom the "powers of
nature" obey. But the narrative continues:

But the magicians of Egypt did the same by their secret arts; so Pharaoh's heart remained hardened, and he would not listen to them; as the
LORD had said. Pharaoh turned and went into his house, and he did not
take even this to heart. And all the Egyptians had to dig along the Nile
for water to drink, for they could not drink the water of the river. (Exod
7:22-24)

Unlike the magicians in Genesis 41 and in the Daniel narratives, here they can
do their work. They are not dysfunctional; they exercise their "secret arts."
Both YHWH and Pharaoh are willing to engage in environmental exploitation
to establish their power just like any great contemporary superpower.[4] The first
encounter is a draw, though it takes the Egyptian wizards seven days to match
YHWH's initial act.

The second plague encounter is more complex in its narrative articulation. In
Exodus 8:1-7, the encounter is in close parallel to that of the water-blood episode. Again, YHWH is on program and intends to release the Hebrews to worship YHWH and so renounce Pharaoh and all his works: "Then the LORD said
to Moses, 'Go to Pharaoh and say to him, "thus says the LORD: Let my people
go, so that they may worship me"'" (Exod 8:1). Only this time, the intending
plague is not simply a show of divine power, as it was in the first case. Now it is
punishment or leverage against a king who should have known to obey the real
king:

If you refuse to let them go, I will plague your whole country with frogs.
The river shall swarm with frogs; they shall come up into your palace,
into your bedchamber and your bed, and into the house of your officials
and of your people, and into your ovens and your kneading bowls. The
frogs shall come up on you and on your people and on all your officials.
(Exod 8:2-4)

The threat is that YHWH can penetrate the security system of the kingdom of
Pharaoh, can reach into the palace, into the private quarters of the king, into
"your bed" and the beds of all the tenants, "your people and all your officials."
The kingdom of Pharaoh, so says YHWH, has no security system to resist this
act of divine terror.

Verse 6 adds tersely, Aaron did it! The frogs came and devoured the land of Egypt. But verse 6 is followed quickly by verse 7: "But the magicians did the same by their secret arts, and brought frogs up on the land of Egypt" (Exod 8:7). More secret arts! Another draw! Thus far, the second encounter is like the first. Except that in the next paragraph things begin to tilt toward YHWH and unravel for Pharaoh. In verse 8 Pharaoh bids Moses and Aaron to lift the frogs from the land: "Then Pharaoh called Moses and Aaron, and said, 'Pray to the LORD to take away the frogs from me and my people, and I will let the people go to sacrifice to the LORD'" (Exod 8:8).

The adversaries then have an exchange that perhaps is for added Israelite enhancement. Moses asks, surely in a mocking voice, "Kindly tell me, when am I to pray to YHWH for you?" Pharaoh answers quickly, "Tomorrow." The exchange shows Moses in complete confidence. He can do this "whenever." The exchange also exhibits Pharaoh in his urgency, "as soon as possible." Both parties seem to agree that YHWH can indeed lift the frogs. Already at this early stage in the longer narrative, Moses can intervene for Pharaoh; for Moses, unlike Pharaoh, has access to the divine agent whose will matters decisively. And Pharaoh, so early in the narrative, seems to concede the decisive point. Moses responds to the royal "tomorrow": "Moses said, 'As you say! So that you may know that there is no one like the LORD our God, the frogs shall leave you and your houses and your officials and your people; they shall be left only in the Nile'" (Exod 8:10-11). Moses will do it, and YHWH will do it "in order that" you may know that there is no one like YHWH in power or attentiveness, no one like YHWH in Egypt, and no one like YHWH in the life of the arrogant superpower. Moses does not deny other gods; but the other gods, the ones who have legitimated Pharaoh, have no power to unleash frogs and recall them, to dispatch death or to bring life.

This time Pharaoh does not answer. Perhaps he is embarrassed. Perhaps he is dazzled by Moses' capacity. Perhaps he is beginning to rethink his theological conviction. In any case, YHWH responded to the petition of Moses and lifted the threat of the frogs. Astonishingly, the narrator adds: "But when Pharaoh saw that there was a respite, he hardened his heart, and would not listen to them, just as the LORD had said" (Exod 8:15). That should have been enough. But it is like every war effort for a great superpower. If there is a challenge, one must mobilize. If there is a pause, one wants to continue. Pharaoh thinks, even yet, that he can have his way. He has seen the power of YHWH, the holy God of departure, but he learns slowly—if at all.

The third encounter concerns gnats (Exod 8:16-19). By now the narrative has established the cadence of contest and need not elaborate on it. YHWH commands Moses to command Aaron to turn dust to gnats throughout the whole land, yet another environmental disaster (v. 16). Verse 17 reports that the command worked: "Aaron stretched out his hand with his staff and struck the dust of the earth, and gnats came on humans and animals alike; all the dust of the earth turned into gnats throughout the whole land of Egypt" (Exod 8:17). The whole land of Pharaoh is under assault from YHWH, and all could see it. Well, you know, after confrontations one and two, what comes next. The Egyptian magicians did the same! Except that the narrative now has a surprise on which the entire contest turns: "The magicians tried to produce gnats by their secret arts, but *they could not*. There were gnats on both humans and animals" (Exod 8:18). They could not! They were not able! They had exhausted the capacity of their "secret arts," which they had spent a lifetime learning. They were not unlike Anthony Eden, the British prime minister who prepared his whole lifetime to be prime minister but then blew it in one week on the crisis of the Suez Canal; the magicians' entire careers had, in an instant, culminated in failure.

The writer does not pause. There were gnats everywhere, all of them caused by YHWH (v. 18). Even the magicians recognize the moment, as they said: "This is the finger of God" (Exod 8:19). Even the learned in the empire now know but not Pharaoh. He would not listen even to his best advisors, who now recognized what he could not acknowledge. Everyone except Pharaoh knew it was a lost cause. But he had to keep on. He had to keep on because his arrogant self-confidence, supported by his ideology of absolute authority, judged that no one else could know anything except him. He had all the data, and he refused to face reality.

The narrator does not linger over verse 18: "They could not!" But we will linger, because this single terse sentence gives away the whole game. The narrator has now reached the extreme limit of royal ideology, of imperial self-deception. The best and the brightest could do no more. The magicians of establishment, coercion, and exploitative power could not perform even one more miracle. The kingdom could not compete with divine resolve. The kingdom and its secret arts could not make safe against holy stirring. The kingdom and its deep learning could not make impact against holy resolve. The kingdom and its learning—"for thine is the kingdom and the power"—has reached the edge of its futile capacity, and there is no more.

Imagine the stir of possibility as this terse verdict moved beyond the arena of contest to the unfortunate and disempowered. Unnamed sources close to the throne reported the moment. Rumors spread that the wise ones were without capacity. The news of royal limit reached very quickly into the slave camp. The workers at the brickyard kept on, for the day, with their slow, resistant pace of work. The old nodded knowingly, and the grandmothers began to gather the children. The children in the slave camp could smell that something enormous was happening, even if they could not yet name it.

The slave community—the workers, the old ladies, the gray mothers, the kids—knew that the "could not" of verse 18 was momentous. You did not need to know "secret arts" to see that this was a seismic shift in world power. No more need to trust Pharaoh, no more need to expect from him, to accept his disciplines of brutality. No more requirement of loyalty to him. Of course it would take a while to trickle down to practicality, but the truth was out. And in that slave community the "they could not" became a mantra like "never again" or "remember the Alamo"; only here it was a mantra of buoyant hope, new futures beyond imagining. The "could not" exposed the fraudulence of royal expectations about more bricks. No more!

III

From here, the narrative is all downhill for Pharaoh. He will not listen, and his heart is hard. He keeps on after everyone else has recognized the futility of it all. The royal consciousness that resists the holy power of newness either could or will not learn soon enough:

- In Exodus 8:25, Pharaoh concedes now, in the face of flies, that Israel can go sacrifice to its God. But it must be within the land of Egypt, under control and under surveillance. Pharaoh wants to compromise only enough but not enough to matter. Moses refuses the offer in the same way that Nelson Mandela refused release from Robben Island until all the others were released as well.
- In Exodus 8:28, Pharaoh permits going into the wilderness, but "not very far away," with the condition that Moses should "pray for me." There is, on Pharaoh's part, a grudging acknowledgment, but not a full recognition of new reality.
- In Exodus 9:11, there are divine boils, and the Egyptian magicians could not stand the affliction. The narrative does not comment, except to call attention to the fact that the royal cast of characters keeps appearing in their accustomed roles but to no effect.

In the seventh plague Moses announces a severe hail storm from YHWH that will, yet again, exalt YHWH, "so that you may know there is no one like me in all the earth" (Exod 9:14). The Egyptians take the threat seriously and respond with a new security alert gone from orange to red! "Those officials of Pharaoh who feared the word of the LORD hurried their slaves and livestock off to a secure place. Those who did not regard the word of the LORD left their slaves and livestock in the open field" (Exod 9:20-21). They tried for a "secure place." But of course the security system failed:

> There was hail with fire flashing continually in the midst of it, such heavy hail as had never fallen in all the land of Egypt since it became a nation. The hail struck down everything that was in the open field throughout all the land of Egypt, both human and animal; the hail also struck down all the plants of the field, and shattered every tree in the field. (Exod 9:24-25)

Pharaoh is helpless, his advisors are without effect, and his people are exposed. The threat comes against the exploitation that runs against holy intention. In Exodus 9:27, Pharaoh has a moment of theological clarity: "Then Pharaoh summoned Moses and Aaron, and said to them, 'This time I have sinned; the LORD is in the right, and I and my people are in the wrong. Pray to the LORD! Enough of God's thunder and hail! I will let you go; you need stay no longer' " (Exod 9:27-28).

Moses responds by another show of authority. But he is under no illusion. He knows that absolute power learns nothing quickly: "Moses said to him, 'As soon as I have gone out of the city, I will stretch out my hands to the LORD; the thunder will cease, and there will be no more hail, so that you may know that the earth is the LORD's. But as for you and your officials, I know that you do not yet fear the LORD God' " (Exod 9:29-30). Moses judges that Pharaoh still does not fear YHWH. Indeed, by verse 34, Pharaoh "sinned once more" and thought he could, via his recalcitrant ideology, make one more stand and prevail in the old power arrangements.

In Exodus 10:7, the advisors to Pharaoh voice their exasperation over the intransigence of their chief: "Pharaoh's officials said to him, 'How long shall this fellow be a snare to us? Let the people go, so that they may worship the LORD their God; do you not yet understand that Egypt is ruined?' " (Exod 10:7). Their words sound like the advisors to Lyndon Johnson who knew that the war in Vietnam was lost. Indeed, they sound like every advisor to absolute power who faces the facts on the ground that do not penetrate the ideology of the leader. The advisors know that continued resistance to YHWH is a path to greater ruin. Everyone now knows except Pharaoh! The advisors have taken into full account the "could not" of Exodus 8:18.

In Exodus 10:8, Pharaoh appears to be at the edge of acknowledgment. He will let some of the slaves go worship: "So Moses and Aaron were brought back to Pharaoh, and he said to them, 'Go, worship the LORD your God! But which ones are to go?' " (Exod 10:8). Some, not all, which ones—still an attempt at control. But Moses knows that he is winning: "We will all go!" And Pharaoh, in a fit of self-deception, once more resists: "He said to them, 'The LORD indeed will be with you, if ever I let your little ones go with you! Plainly, you have some evil purpose in mind' " (Exod 10:10). No, never! If you all go, I will know YHWH is with you. That is not going to happen. The mighty empire has never been defeated, and we will not be defeated now. We will do whatever it takes. The divine response to such uninformed resistance is locusts:

> The locusts came upon all the land of Egypt and settled on the whole
> country of Egypt, such a dense swarm of locusts as had never been
> before, nor ever shall be again. They covered the surface of the whole
> land, so that the land was black; and they ate all the plants in the land
> and all the fruit of the trees that the hail had left; nothing green was left,
> no tree, no plant in the field, in all the land of Egypt. (Exod 10:14-15)

Yet again, Pharaoh relents: "Pharaoh hurriedly summoned Moses and Aaron and said, 'I have sinned against the LORD your God, and against you'" (Exod 10:16). This time he not only confesses his sin against "YHWH your God"; but he also asks forgiveness, "just this once" requesting prayer from Moses to YHWH. YHWH responds and lifts the locusts, but Pharaoh again refuses to let them go.

In Exodus 10:24, Pharaoh gives some ground: "Then Pharaoh summoned Moses, and said, 'Go, worship the LORD. Only your flocks and your herds shall remain behind. Even your children may go with you'" (Exod 10:24). Now he will allow even the children to go—but not the flocks and herds. He insists on keeping a grip on something of value. First children, now livestock. Not surprisingly, Moses will agree to no compromise. Now it is all or nothing:

> But Moses said, "You must also let us have sacrifices and burnt offerings to sacrifice to the LORD our God. Our livestock also must go with us; not a hoof shall be left behind, for we must choose some of them for the worship of the LORD our God, and we will not know what to use to worship the LORD until we arrive there." (Exod 10:25-26)

Moses utilizes a big subterfuge: "We need the animals for sacrifice." Well, yes, but not really. We take them because all of it belongs to YHWH, none to you. All to God, nothing rendered to Caesar. When we go, we all go, because we all know YHWH and the graciousness of YHWH's future for us. We will not stop, and you cannot stop us any more than your magicians were able to compete.

Helpless Pharaoh issues one last cry of indignation: "Then Pharaoh said to him, 'Get away from me! Take care that you do not see my face again, for on the day you see my face you shall die'" (Exod 10:28). No more negotiations. I think Pharaoh could not think of anything else to say, and so he saves face with a dismissal of Moses and his company of slaves. Except that Pharaoh is in no position to dismiss anyone, for he himself—he must know—has been dismissed from power by the greater, uncompromising power of YHWH.

Pharaoh does not appear in chapter 11. The short chapter is a defiant speech by Moses to Pharaoh:

- He anticipates a great cry in Egypt in a night to come;
- He anticipates that the smiting will cause even Egypt to know that YHWH "makes a distinction" between Egypt and Israel;
- He anticipates that the bureaucracy around Pharaoh will bow down to Moses and beg Israel to leave Egypt.

The chapter ends with YHWH's declaration to Moses that YHWH will multiply wonders (miracles, plagues; v. 9). That is, the kingdom that Pharaoh thought he managed is a venue in which YHWH acts well beyond pharaonic management. Egypt is a site for the exhibit and exaltation of YHWH.

And sure enough, in chapter 12, it happens as Moses had foreseen in chapter 11. There was—at midnight—a smiting by YHWH. The terror of YHWH strikes the firstborn prince of Egypt, the firstborn prisoner, the firstborn of the livestock, the best of every species. And there was a loud cry as death invaded empire. Remarkably, Pharaoh summoned Moses and Aaron, and spoke as Moses had predicted: "Rise up, go away from my people, both you and the Israelites! Go, worship the LORD, as you said. Take your flocks and your herds, as you said, and be gone. And bring a blessing on me too!" (Exod 12:31-32). What Pharaoh had so long tried to prevent now he urges: "Depart." Go, and take your herds and flocks with you. Go, and take the holy power of YHWH away from here; just be gone! And then Pharaoh adds, pitifully: "Bless me; bring a blessing on me too" (v. 32). Pharaoh had, finally, after all the others, arrived at the inescapable conclusion that the power for life (blessing) had been entrusted to the slave camp. The narrative process of deconstructing Pharaoh is long and slow paced.[5] The narrative is in no hurry, because it takes time to break absolute power. The narrative is in no hurry because the grandchildren who still remember are entranced by the performance whereby arrogant, coercive, exploitative power is terminated by the inscrutable miracles of the Holy One, wrought through human agents but beyond human agency. The turn was in 8:18; they could not! And now, so says the narrator, YHWH can! YHWH acted, YHWH has prevailed. No wonder that the contest is over; now there is only an embrace of the newness.

IV

This narrative that saturates the imagination of Israel plots public history as a contest, a contest always to be performed again but a contest that each time comes to dancing and departing. The work of interpretation is to take that paradigmatic narrative of "could not" and see how it may be performed among us with compelling authority. In order to show the paradigmatic narrative as paradigmatic, I appeal to the work of Emmanuel Levinas in his programmatic book, *Totality and Infinity*.[6] In that difficult, freighted book, Levinas recasts great philosophic issues, in Jewish fashion, in the direction of the ethical. As his title indicates, Levinas casts his interpretive grid as a great conflict between two contesting articulations of lived reality.

On the one hand, there is "totality," the attempt to contain all imaginable reality within an ideological frame of reference that can lay claim to absoluteness. Thus, totality is a total explanation of reality that allows nothing outside of it and so is tilted toward totalitarianism. It occurs to me, in light of our paradigmatic narrative, that Pharaoh—and Nebuchadnezzar after him—constitutes in Israelite imagination a totalizing system in which all energy is mobilized toward Pharaoh's brick-making and in which all authority is claimed for the "secret arts" of the magicians who serve Pharaoh. It is inescapable that a totalizing system such as that of Pharaoh will become coercive and exploitative, for human persons are viewed not as ends but as tools and means for the enhancement of the system.

It is clear in biblical tradition that the Israelite interpreters never kept Pharaoh back in ancient history. They always treated Pharaoh, in the narrative, as a present threat and reality that may take a variety of forms. It is clear, for example, that Nebuchadnezzar in the narrative is a reperformance of Pharaoh. In Christian tradition, moreover, it is clear that Herod is a replay of Pharaoh (Matt 2:16-18). This narrative taken as paradigm permits us to consider every totalizing system as an idolatrous enterprise that brings suffering and death. Thus we may, in contemporary setting, view heavy-handed moralism as a totalizing system that has no patience with or allowance for the inescapable vagaries of human life. Or more broadly and more importantly, readers of this paradigmatic narrative may refer it to the reality of economic-military globalism in which the United States, with its enormous wealth and power, seeks to leverage other states and other cultures so that the world economy is under mandate for U.S. insatiability. And of course that reach of insatiable legitimacy by the U.S. ideology of freedom and entitlement fosters an ethic of individualism that becomes an excuse for powerfully imposed conformity to the dictates of the corporate economy. As Slavoj Žižek ponders, it is exceedingly difficult to imagine a form of social life that can live beyond the reach of the ideology of insatiability; rather, all efforts and possibilities are contained within that ideology.[7]

But the exodus narrative with its ringing "could not" is shrewd enough to consider that such totalizing systems—after the fashion of Pharaoh—cannot deliver on their promises. Pharaoh turned out to be not as strong or as able or as capable as we had been led to imagine. This narrative taken as paradigm invites us to recognize that the totalizing ideology of our society can make us neither safe nor happy, just as Pharaoh could not. It is clear that the unbridled development of the national security state has made us less safe, and the indices of social pathology suggest that, for all our lavish consumerism, the totalizing system cannot make us happy amid our relatively protected consumerism. We are like young children lavished with too many gifts who prefer to play with the empty boxes. Lavished with consumer goods, we prefer, in knowing candor, the intimate dimensions of human transaction—generosity and hospitality and forgiveness—which ideological consumerism can never offer because such acts are out beyond. Thus, the characteristically human violates the totality. The theological word for such totalizing systems, as Levinas knew so well, is *idolatry*, systems of icons that are powerless to deliver human possibility (see Ps 115:4-8).

Levinas's counteroffer to totality is *infinity*, by which he means open possibility for futures that are not contained and administered. "Infinity" is limitless openness that is constantly generative, making newness possible in dialogical transactions in which neither party sets limits, imposes restrictions, or acts in coercive ways. I note two features of Levinas's "infinity." First, he accents seeing the "face" of the other, so that we understand life as face-to-face engagement and relationship. Levinas contrasts the intense personal and interpersonal quality of dialogic reality with reality understood as statistic or as rule or as proposition. As an heir to Martin Buber's "I-Thou," Levinas understands that it is the willingness to receive the face of the other without coercion, restraint, or control that makes newness possible. Second, Levinas insists that such face-to-face interaction has a defining ethical quality to it, so that open dialogical transaction is generative of compassion and mercy and justice.

It is evident that these two programmatic themes, *totality* and *infinity*, pose a radical either/or for control or generativity that is at the core of Levinas's thinking and at the core of biblical faith. In light of my exposition of the contest of the exodus narrative, I suggest that Pharaoh and YHWH are to be understood, respectively, as agents and embodiments of totality and infinity, *Pharaoh as totality*, *YHWH as infinity*. This transposition of the narrative into the interpretive categories of Levinas provides a way in which a specific historical memory is to be understood as paradigmatic and pragmatic. Levinas surely intends to insist, and is no doubt correct to insist, that the interface of Pharaoh and YHWH in the exodus narrative is a model for the recurring contradiction of totality and infinity that occurs everywhere in social transactions. Thus, the exodus narrative is a primal account and sustaining model of totality and infinity that pervades the world described by the Bible. This description—or redescription—of reality is crucial (1) because those enthralled by totality tend not to notice its coerciveness and (2) because those inured to totality tend not to be alert to the open possibility of infinity. The exodus narrative is about the restless, insistent, purposeful incursion of YHWH's infinity into Pharaoh's totality, thus creating possibilities for Israel not otherwise on offer.

V

I have delineated in some detail the totalizing intentionality of Pharaoh. It remains to consider in a sustained way the infinity authorized by YHWH.

YHWH, evoked by the cry of Israel (Exod 2:23-25; 3:7-9), erupts in the midst of Pharaoh's Egypt with a single command to Pharaoh: "Let my people go that they may serve me" (Exod 5:1), a formula many times reiterated in the narrative. This command contradicts Pharaoh's restrictive coercion. It is the resolve of YHWH to break open the totalitarianism of Pharaoh in order that Israel may have a life and a future beyond the sphere of Pharaoh's exploitation. The command itself is a voice of infinity. Since the second part of the command is, "that they may worship me," it remains to be seen whether the possibility beyond Pharaoh is an infinity or simply a Yahwistic totalism. While we can point to the pressures in the ongoing tradition of Israel to close Yahwism into a new exclusionary totalism, it is also clear that the resilience of YHWH characteristically refuses such totalism.[8] YHWH's capacity to enact "wonders" in the exodus narrative is a demonstration that YHWH is "able" to "prevail" in the generation of newnesses (see Exod 7:3; 11:9-10; 15:11). YHWH's power and capacity to open Israel's future beyond Pharaoh's enslavement is central to the narrative and is never doubted. This claim offers a stunning contrast to the "could not" of the exodus Egyptian magicians and by implication the "could not" of Pharaoh and the Egyptian gods. The powers of totalism are incapable of generating a new possibility but instead use their energy in coercive ways to maintain old order and old control.

This "could" of YHWH's capacity for generative newness, moreover, is on exhibit in the narratives of the sojourn after the departure from Egypt. Thus, YHWH does the "impossible" of bread in the wilderness when no food supplies are available (Exod 16:14-15). YHWH does the impossible in drawing water from rock when there is no water on offer (Exod 17:1-7). These enacted impossibilities become the material of Israel's dialogical memory, as the remembered impossibilities become ground for identity and for hope:

> He split rocks open in the wilderness,
>   and gave them drink abundantly as from the deep.
> He made streams come out of the rock,
>   and caused waters to flow down like rivers. (Ps 78:15-16)

> They asked, and he brought quails,
>   and gave them food from heaven in abundance.
> He opened the rock, and water gushed out;
>   it flowed through the desert like a river. (Ps 105:40-41)

And of course the great doxologies of Israel—along with songs of thanksgiving—regularly detail the wonders of YHWH, who makes a way out of no way. YHWH is on exhibit as a complete contrast to the failed enterprise of Pharaoh, who "could not."

As the contest of Exodus 7–12 exhibits *ten victories* for YHWH that are the grist of grandparental testimony, so the arrival at Sinai yields from divine self-assertion *ten commands*. Now of course the Ten Commandments are open to the coerciveness of totalism and have often been treated so in ongoing tradition. The commandments of Exodus 20:2-17 may be understood as alternative to the commands of Pharaoh, whose command of closure and coercion serve to continue the world of royal productivity. The commands of Pharaoh are vigorously recited in Exodus 5 as a reiterated brick quota: "Make more bricks." That flat, one-dimensional command offers nothing of interaction, nothing of sustained community, nothing of the notice or validation of the workers. But so it always is with totalism. The commands of YHWH, by contrast, are precisely "rules of engagement" for life with the covenanting God and life with the covenanting neighbor in a sustained world of fidelity and responsibility. It is unfortunate indeed that in the popular usage of the Decalogue in American society the commandments have been torn out of the narrative context of covenant-making at Sinai. While the commands are apodictic and nonnegotiable, their intent is to create and sustain a community of human viability that, in the extrapolation of the book of Deuteronomy, will issue in a renovated political economy of neighborliness. It is for that reason that the Decalogue initiates in Israel a wide and open stream of interpretation. Unlike the commands of Pharaoh, these covenantal commands are not one-dimensional directives but are in fact lines of accountability that must always be rearticulated in new circumstances for the sake of the community. The first two commandments (Exod 20:2-4) lay down the theological marker about YHWH and other gods, YHWH and idols. YHWH is exhibited as an engaged, dialogic agent. Idols, by contrast, belong with totalism; they sponsor and legitimate a closed system. As the idols cannot hear or smell or move, so the closed systems they legitimate reflect a fixity in social reality that is commensurate with the theological fixity of the frozen gods. There can be no doubt that, understood in this way, the commands of Sinai extend and continue and the initial command of YHWH in Exodus 5:1. The new community is to "go and to worship YHWH," the guarantor of new social possibility.

Levinas's accent on face is worth recalling as I comment on these texts in the narrative about face:

1. In the penultimate exchange between Pharaoh and Moses, Pharaoh—with hardened heart—contemptuously dismisses Moses from his "presence": "Then Pharaoh said to him, 'Get away from me! Take care that you do not see my *face* again, for on the day you see my *face* you shall die.' Moses said, 'Just as you say! I will never see your *face* again'" (Exod 10:28-29). This indignant statement shows that Pharaoh has not yet understood that his totalizing system is already terminated and that access to his face signifies very little. Beyond that, his formula of dismissal comes close to making a claim of divinity, for to see the face of God is to die. Moses' response to the pharaonic dismissal is one of concurrence. But it is also an ironic response, for Moses knows that he need not again bother with Pharaoh, who is soon to be eliminated from the narrative. While Moses knows the wave of YHWH's future, Pharaoh—in the way of every totalizing agent—completely misconstrues his true situation. Pharaoh is indeed a *force without a face*, incapable of generative interaction, a one-dimensional coercion that traffics in quotas and statistics without acknowledgment of human dimensions of reality.

2. In the YHWH-Moses transaction of Exodus 33, the play on *face* is complex and reflects a complex tradition. On the one hand, YHWH speaks to Moses "face to face" (33:11). The tent is a venue for intimate dialogic transaction, the kind nowhere available in Egypt. On the other hand, YHWH's face is not easily on offer: "'But,' he said, 'you cannot see my face; for no one shall see me and live. . . . Then I will take away my hand, you shall see my back; but my face shall not be seen'" (Exod 33:20, 23).[9] The formula is not unlike that of Pharaoh in 10:28,

except here the hiding of the face is in the context of the graciousness and mercy of YHWH, who acknowledges the partner even as the divine face is protected. While the two formulations for Pharaoh and YHWH are parallel, the narrative context yields a very different transaction—one of dismissal, the other of gracious engagement.

3. The difficult characterization of Moses in Exodus 34:33-35 should be mentioned in this context. To be sure, Moses is never confused with YHWH in the tradition. But it is clear in this text that Moses' face is as it is because it reflects a meeting with YHWH: "Moses came down from Mount Sinai. As he came down from the mountain with the two tablets of the covenant in his hand, Moses did not know that the skin of his face shone because he had been talking with God" (Exod 34:29). Thus the face of presence continues to be generative in the new engagement out beyond pharaonic totalism. Since the face in this little text is likely a cultic reference, it is not too far a reach to mention the familiar benediction of Aaron that concludes:

> The LORD make his face to shine upon you, and be gracious to you;
> The LORD lift up his countenance upon you, and give you peace.
>   (Num 6:25-26)

The outcome of this shone face, albeit in a cultic context, is the divine gift of *shalom*. *Shalom* is perhaps the quintessential mark of infinity, a continuing state of communal well being that is wide and deep and sustainable. The *face* yields *shalom*. The contrast with Pharaoh is complete. In Egypt, there is no face and no *shalom*, only coercive requirement.

It is no wonder that Israel welcomed the initiative of YHWH at Sinai as an alternative to Pharaoh. The God of "eagles' wings" has transported his people from the insatiable totality of Pharaoh to the infinite possibility of YHWH at Sinai.

Sinai, with the Decalogue and the responsive oath of allegiance (Exod 24:3, 7), is not a completed action. It is, rather, the initiation of an alternative process. It is for that reason that the Decalogue becomes the source of a vigorous, contested interpretive tradition of torah. The process of torah interpretation can never be completed, for the good purposes of YHWH extend always into new circumstance, for new forms of obedience are required. The remarkable imagination of Israel, imagination fed by the God of infinity, was able to transpose the meaning of Egyptian emancipation into an ongoing practice of a neighborly ethic. Israel could remember that the break from totalism began in a public cry of pain that totalism finally could not silence. It is the cry of pain that opened the world out beyond pharaonic coercion. It is that same cry of pain given public voice that in recent time has frontally delegitimated coercive regimes. It is that cry of pain uttered privately to pastoral therapists that has often broken the grip of interpersonal totalism.

But the remarkable point is that the cry against totalism has been taken up in ancient Israel for the neighborly "rules of engagement" In Exodus 22:21-22,

Moses, the great voice of infinity, has in purview the needy circumstance of immigrants, widows, and orphans—Israel's characteristic triad of vulnerable people. But Moses can imagine that even these powerless may exercise their voice of engagement, a voice that will be heard by the Lord of the covenant:

> You shall not wrong or oppress a resident alien, for you were aliens in the land of Egypt. You shall not abuse any widow or orphan. If you do abuse them, when they cry out to me, I will surely heed their *cry*; my wrath will burn, and I will kill you with the sword, and your wives shall become widows and your children orphans. (Exod 22:21-24)

In a second commandment, the cry may be on the lips of the poor:

> If you lend money to my people, to the poor among you, you shall not deal with them as a creditor; you shall not exact interest from them. If you take your neighbor's cloak in pawn, you shall restore it before the sun goes down; for it may be your neighbor's only clothing to use as cover; in what else shall that person sleep? And if your neighbor *cries* out to me, I will listen, for I am compassionate. (Exod 22:25-27)

YHWH will hear! YHWH will hear the cry of the powerless outsider—immigrant, widow, orphan, poor. It is impossible to imagine Pharaoh hearing any such cry, for the totalizing system had silenced all such voices. The narrative shows, however, that the totalizing system of silence cannot be sustained. The dialogic practice of "cry-hear" that engages the suffering and the divine yields something new. It only requires, in narrative performance, always again, to depart totalism for the infinity of YHWH's *shalom*. The paradigm continues to be verified by breaks of pain toward *shalom*, even in our contemporary world.[10] How shameful that the church, in its characteristic interpretive practice, has managed to siphon off the risk and the wisdom of this narrative. There are still pharaonic quotas. There are still cries of pain. There are still divine commands to "let go." The narrative always waits, yet again, for another daring performance of contest and of alternative.

CHAPTER 3

Sabbath as Antidote to Anxiety

THERE IS NO DOUBT that anxiety is a constant of the human condition.[1] It may well be, with Rollo May, that we live in "an age of anxiety," a condition that has healthy and/or pathological dimensions to which we may respond in psychological, pastoral, and therapeutic ways. Given that generic acknowledgment, it occurs to me that anxiety of an acute kind is particularly pathological and peculiarly poignant in our society just now and that it constitutes the central social reality to which we seek to make pastoral response. Without denying or minimizing the broader claim about "the human condition," I want here to pursue a quite specific connection between our current social reality of anxiety and the biblical text. In the end, it may well be that faith in our time and place is precisely "Courage to Be," courage to be practitioners of generosity, hospitality, and forgiveness that are decisively upstream against the security, revenge, and grudge that dominate our society.[2]

I

I begin with the Exodus text, where biblical study most properly begins. I begin with this premise that Pharaoh's *system of production and consumption* had, as its major output, systemic anxiety that pervaded every level of society. That system is one of economic consumption, for it is reported in Genesis 47 that Pharaoh achieved a monopoly on the food supply and used food as a weapon, determining who would eat and who would do without (Gen 47:13-26). It is reported, moreover, that the peasants—forced into slavery—signed on for Pharaoh's system. Perhaps they accepted it because they could think of no alternative or because they were too weak to resist or perhaps because they lacked the courage to imagine outside of Pharaoh's system. For whatever reason, they signed on and, in gratitude to Pharaoh, affirmed: "They said, 'You have saved our lives; may it please my lord, we will be slaves to Pharaoh'" (Gen 47:25). And the narrator adds: "So Joseph made it a statute concerning the land of Egypt, and it stands to this day, that Pharaoh should have the fifth. The land of the priests alone did not become Pharaoh's" (Gen 47:26).

That statement now becomes the paradigmatic story of "masters and slaves," all caught up in anxiety that is intrinsic to the system.[3] Pharaoh is anxious because the slaves might quit or resist or depart. Pharaoh is anxious because the production schedule might not keep pace with the requirements of his ambitious state building program. And in his anxiety he becomes more aggressive and more demanding, devising a complete surveillance system to manage his restless slave population, upon which his system depended.

But the slaves are also infected with anxiety about the system. The slaves are anxious that they might not produce enough, that they will be pushed beyond their capacity to produce, that more will be required of them, that their children are in jeopardy before the insatiable requirements of the system.

Consequently, masters and slaves in this production system collude in the generation of and participation in anxiety that leaves none satisfied. The outcome of collusion and anxiety is expressed in the sharp exchanges of Exodus 5, a narrative account of an anxiety system. Pharaoh issues a frantic command: "But the king of Egypt said to them, 'Moses and Aaron, why are you taking the people away from their work? Get to your labors!' Pharaoh continued, 'Now they are more numerous than the people of the land and yet you want them to stop working!'" (Exod 5:4-5). Pharaoh gives instruction to this supervisors:

> You shall no longer give the people straw to make bricks, as before; let
> them go and gather straw for themselves. But you shall require of them
> the same quantity of bricks as they have made previously; do not dimin-
> ish it, for they are lazy; that is why they cry, "Let us go and offer sacri-
> fice to our God." Let heavier work be laid on them; then they will labor
> at it and pay no attention to deceptive words. (Exod 5:7-9)

The taskmasters and supervisors of the bureaucratic system pass the word along: "So the taskmasters and the supervisors of the people went out and said to the people, 'Thus says Pharaoh, "I will not give you straw. Go and get straw yourselves, wherever you can find it; but your work will not be lessened in the least"'" (Exod 5:10-11). The narrative reports the frantic pace of the slave producers: "So the people scattered throughout the land of Egypt, to gather stubble for straw" (Exod 5:12). And the supervisors reinforce the demand system of production: "The taskmasters were urgent, saying, 'Complete your work, the same daily assignment as when you were given straw'" (Exod 5:13). And then they rebuke the slaves who find the quotas impossible: "Why did you not finish the required quantity of bricks yesterday and today, as you did before?" (Exod 5:14). The supervisors, who apparently are kinsmen of the slaves, protest against the system of demand: "Then the Israelite supervisors came to Pharaoh and cried, 'Why do you treat your servants like this? No straw is given to your servants, yet they say to us, "Make bricks!" Look how your servants are beaten! You are unjust to your own people"'" (Exod 5:15-16). But Pharaoh will have none of their rebuke: "He said, 'You are lazy, lazy; that is why you say, "Let us go and sacrifice to the Lord." Go now, and work; for no straw shall be given you, but you shall still deliver the same number of bricks'" (Exod 5:17-18). And the supervisors reinforce the demands: "The Israelite supervisors saw that they were in trouble when they were told, 'You shall not lessen your daily number of bricks'" (Exod 5:19). The system devours all parties in the rigorous requirements, all parties that include Pharaoh, supervisors, taskmasters, and slaves—all caught up in the system. It is an abuse system in which nobody ever arrives at success. The word for the system is "mistreatment."[4] First, Moses accuses YHWH: "Then Moses turned again to the Lord and said, 'O Lord, why have you *mistreated* this people? Why did you ever send me?'" (Exod 5:22). But then he uses the same phrase for Pharaoh: "Since I first came to Pharaoh to speak in your name, he has *mistreated* this people" (Exod 5:23a). But then he circles back and rebukes YHWH: "And you have done nothing at all to deliver your people" (Exod 5:23b). Moses is the speaker who knows firsthand the destructive force of the devouring, insatiable system; he castigates the system by using the same term of indictment for both YHWH and Pharaoh, "mistreat." The chapter offers a picture perfect narrative of a system of anxiety in which all parties are left restless.

Now of course this system is ancient and remote from us. Except that Michael Walzer has powerfully observed:

> So pharaonic oppression, deliverance, Sinai, and Canaan are still with us, powerful memories shaping our perceptions of the political world. The "door of hope" is still open; things are not what they might be— even when what they might be isn't totally different from what they are. This is a central theme in Western thought, always present though elaborated in many different ways. We still believe, or many of us do, what the Exodus first taught, or what it has commonly been taken to teach, about the meaning and possibility of politics and about its proper form:
> —first, that wherever you live, it is probably Egypt;
> —second, that there is a better place, a world more attractive, a promised land;
> —and third, that "the way to the land is through the wilderness."
> There is no way to get from here to there except by joining together and marching.[5]

Our beginning point is the wonderment of how much *our own anxiety system* is parallel to *that ancient system of anxiety*. Of course I believe that there is a close parallel, because I believe that anxiety about production and consumption is at the heart of our social pathology. I mention three points that would suggest the parallel in quite practical ways:

1. My son Jim, an ace of a sales representative and sales manager, tells me that in the business of sales one never does enough. If one makes the sales quota, one is not thanked or given a bonus or allowed time off. One only gets an increased quota for more bricks!

2. Coach Ara Parseghian of Notre Dame is reported to have said that the "point spread" makes it impossible to be a successful coach. If one can win big and beat the point spread, then the consequence is that the next week one gets a bigger point spread and must win by a bigger margin or it turns out all to be a failure.

3. And along with my son Jim and Coach Parseghian, there is Michael Chertoff, Secretary of Homeland Security, who lives in "a zone of orange" and who invites us to live perpetually in the zone of orange anxiety, the purpose of which seems to be the maintenance of high-level public anxiety, out of which come bizarre policies and equally bizarre behavior. I propose that the production of anxiety in the ancient circumstance of Egypt and our own production of anxiety are carefully analogous. It is not that Pharaoh per se is "bad" but that Pharaoh is a player in the anxiety system, in which there can never be relief. The narrative concerning Pharaoh, moreover, exhibits the truth that the anxiety system eventually commits abuse, brutality, oppression, and violence, as though more destructive policies and practice somehow will bring success. All parties are recruited to the system of anxiety and must act accordingly. The narrative is one of acute social exploitation, and everyone now knows that ours is a society of hostility toward all those unlike us in the pursuit of consumer goods that are taken to make us more successful, younger, richer, more secure . . . more in control. But very soon the pursuit of control produces circumstances in which the entire system is out of control, having taken on a life of its own that is remote from the most elemental human realities.

II

In Pharaoh's kingdom of *anxiety*, there was no *Sabbath*, not for Pharaoh, not for the supervisors, not for the taskmasters, not for the brick-producing slaves. Everyone had to reach for *more* in a system of insatiable demand. It is for that reason that Sabbath looms so large in the memory and in the practice of Israel. Sabbath is a refusal to participate in the anxiety system of Pharaoh. It is the dramatic insistence that there is life outside the production-consumption system. And if Exodus be properly understood as "departure," a going out, then it is the departure from the anxiety system of insatiable demand, and a readiness to have life in alternative categories. It is the core claim of my argument here that sustained, public, intentional practice of Sabbath is an act of alternative imagination—outside the imperatives of Pharaoh. It is the practice of an alternative life, alternative to production and consumption. It is a shutdown, work stoppage, of all of the demands that keep life on orange alert, and a readiness to receive and embrace life in alternative categories. In what follows I will outline the principal Old Testament texts on Sabbath and weave them into something of a coherent narrative.

Genesis 2:1-3 and Exodus 31:17

As is well known, the primal authorization of Sabbath is articulated at the end of the creation liturgy in Genesis 1, the conclusion being offered in Genesis 2:1-3:

> Thus the heavens and the earth were finished, and all their multitude.
> And on the seventh day God finished the work that he had done, and he
> rested on the seventh day from all the work that he had done. So God
> blessed the seventh day and hallowed it, because on it God rested from
> all the work that he had done in creation. (Gen 2:1-3)

In this recital of beginnings, YHWH had been meticulously at work on an "intelligent design" for six demanding days. During that time, the creator God commanded the other creatures to "be fruitful," that is, to create more of their own kind: "God blessed them, saying, 'Be fruitful and multiply and fill the waters in the seas, and let birds multiply on the earth'" (Gen 1:22). Terence Fretheim judges that imperative addressed to the creatures to be an invitation to join in the work of creation.[6] And then, as is well known, God created the human couple for governance and management (Gen 1:28). And the concluding verdict, after six days, is "very good" (Gen 1:31). God has variously "said" or "made" or "created," all active verbs.

Nonetheless, the turn to the Sabbath at the end of the liturgy is still something of a surprise. It is usual to say that the goal of the generative work of creation is restfulness. It is usual to say that restful Sabbath is ordained into the fabric of creation. What is not so often said is that God was tired, perhaps exhausted— for generativity is hard work—and had come to the end of God's own energy. That conclusion, moreover, is reinforced by the odd note in Exodus 31:17. In that seldom-read text, God has commanded Moses and Israel for six chapters about the detailed design of the tabernacle, the model for an ordered community. The first six speeches of YHWH in that text concern fabric, design, and workmanship. But the seventh speech, beginning in Exodus 31:12, turns from the design of *space* to purpose for *time*.[7] The seventh speech, not unlike the seventh day of creation, is a command on Sabbath:

> The Lord said to Moses: You yourself are to speak to the Israelites: "You shall keep my sabbaths, for this is a sign between me and you throughout your generations, given in order that you may know that I, the Lord, sanctify you. You shall keep the sabbath, because it is holy for you." (Exod 31:12-14)

It is a God-given rule for the human community. The surprise of the text, however, is the final verse of the entire section, in which it is asserted: "It is a sign forever between me and the people of Israel that in six days the Lord made heaven and earth, and on the seventh day he rested, and *was refreshed*" (Exod 31:17). God rested and "was refreshed." The verb "refreshed," used only three times in the Old Testament, is from the noun *nephesh*, "self." The verb is in the Niphal, a passive or reflexive verb to be translated either "was refreshed" or "refreshed himself." If we pay attention to the frequently used noun that lies behind the verb, then the verb is best rendered "was re-*nepheshed*" or "re-*nepheshed* himself." Either way, the text suggests that God's *nephesh* had been wearied and diminished by generative work, was depleted, and needed time, space, and freedom from responsibility for the recovery of God's own self. It is the same God in world-making and in tabernacle-making, exhausted and diminished after six days of world-making and six speeches of tabernacle design.

This remarkable liturgical assertion, moreover, is that God desisted from the quintessential work of creation and rested. God exhibits no anxiety about creation, no foreboding about tabernacle design, no sense that the world will not work in God's absence. God has complete confidence in the staying power of creation (or of the tabernacle design) and is not committed to more work, more productivity, more accomplishment. God has no anxiety about the world God has made and knows limits to generative investment.

The text, moreover, has a claim that the human couple in Genesis—and Moses in the book of Exodus—is to replicate God's own life in God's own image. Human persons are to be free of anxiety that propels achievement, productivity, or accomplishment. Human persons, along with the Creator, can trust that the world will work without constant attentiveness. I do not need to point out, do I, that YHWH's life-giving system is a sharp and complete contrast to Pharaoh's brick-making system, in which everyone is propelled by production anxiety? It is a radical either/or. When Moses says to Pharaoh, "Let my people go that they may worship me," the intent is to choose *the rest system of YHWH* over the *anxiety system of Pharaoh*, but Pharaoh cannot relinquish his companions in anxiety.

Now I have discerned that Episcopal priests are not an anxious lot, or so it appears to me, largely unflappable and, I suspect, not workaholics. So I do not need to make that point. The point I do make, however, is that Episcopal priests do minister with many people well-placed on the scale of production-consumption anxiety whose creed is "more," who do not know about the unanxious God in whose image we are made. Genesis 1–2 is not a story about beginnings. It is a story about an alternative model of reality that has *restfulness* at its center, of refusal to go beyond appropriate generativity in world-making or in creating a "presence" of worth and money.

Exodus 20:8-11 and Hosea 4:1-3

From Genesis 1 and Exodus 31, it is not a far reach to a second text, one you also know well. In Exodus 20:8-11, Israel has arrived at Sinai. Israel has come out from Pharaoh's anxiety system and is fresh from the risk of wilderness, through many "toils and snares." When they arrived at Sinai in Exodus 19, they assented to the commands of YHWH, even before they had heard the commands in chapter 20: "The people all answered as one: 'Everything that the Lord has spoken we will do.' Moses reported the words of the people to the Lord" (Exod 19:8). They consented eagerly, I suppose, because they understood that the commands of the God of liberation and sustenance, whatever those commands might be, would be preferable to the commands of Pharaoh. That is what is happening at Sinai. Israel is changing its life-defining commands, nothing less than "regime change." At Sinai, they got ten; and in the center of the ten is the command on Sabbath:

> Remember the sabbath day, and keep it holy. Six days you shall labor
> and do all your work. But the seventh day is a sabbath to the Lord your
> God; you shall not do any work—you, your son or your daughter, your
> male or female slave, your livestock, or the alien resident in your towns.
> (Exod 20:8-10)

The text clearly is a reiteration of the Sabbath command in the creation story—or conversely—the creation command is a retrospect on the Sinai command. Either way, Sabbath rest is work stoppage for the entire community—son, daughter, male and female slaves, cattle, and immigrants in your village. The "rest" is comprehensive and systemic. It is, moreover, grounded in creation: "For in six days the Lord made heaven and earth, the sea, and all that is in them, but rested the seventh day; therefore the Lord blessed the Sabbath day and consecrated it" (Exod 20:11). It is "holy," which means it belongs to YHWH and not to Israel. Israel, now having renounced the production-consumption mirage of Pharaoh, is to order its life according to the ordering of creation that is alternative to the craving of anxiety for well-being, more security, more happiness.

These are the "rules for engagement" with the truth of creation that is not negotiable. In this context I call your attention to the remarkable prophetic poem of Hosea 4:1-3 that might, in my judgment, be central to our voicing of "inconvenient truth." In that poem, the prophet offers an "indictment" against Israel. The charge against Israel is:

> For the Lord has an indictment
>   against the inhabitants of the land.
> There is no faithfulness or loyalty,
>   and no knowledge of God in the land.
> Swearing, lying, and murder,
>   and stealing and adultery break out;
>   bloodshed follows bloodshed. (Hos 4:1-2)

This catalog of offenses is surely reminiscent of the Decalogue, even though the Sabbath is not explicitly mentioned. Israel here has violated all the commands of Sinai; that puts it at odds with the nonnegotiable ordering of creation.

And then, in a characteristically daring prophetic move, Hosea says "therefore." That term, in prophetic discourse, regularly connects indictment and sentence, choice and consequence:

> *Therefore* the land mourns,
>   and all who live in it languish;
> together with the wild animals
>   and the birds of the air,
>   even the fish of the sea are perishing. (Hos 4:3)

The phrase "land mourns" in Old Testament poetry means "drought." The drought is so severe that creatureliness across the board is under threat. This statement is a direct allusion to the creation story and anticipates the dismantling and failure of the fabric of creation. *The violation of the Sinai commands has put Israel out of sync with the character of creation so that Israel's misconduct places creation in jeopardy.* Now, I understand that we can reduce this prophetic connection to simplistic moralism or to primitive supernaturalism. But we need do neither. We may take the poetic artistry as a discernment that a society ordered against the fabric of creation (and the will of the Creator) will lose its world. And the center of the fabric of creation is Sabbath rest, an alternative to the anxiety of production and consumption. Serious Sabbath is not just for a good weekend; it is a nonnegotiable condition for viable life in the world. When societies encroach on the day of rest, creation begins to unravel, personally, socially, and cosmically.

Deuteronomy

When Israel arrived at the Jordan River ready to enter the land of promise, Moses stopped at the river and, in the book of Deuteronomy, for thirty chapters he teaches and instructs Israel about their life in the new land. The burden of Moses' instruction in the book of Deuteronomy has, I suggest, two convictions, one negative and one positive. The negative conviction is that, if Israel is not alert about its identity and its vocation as the people of the covenant, it will be seduced by Canaanite practices and forfeit its life in the world. It is for that reason that Moses reiterates the imperative, "Take heed, watch out," or you will lose your way. The warning, cast in religious cadences, is against the gods of Canaan. But the religious claim is inescapably a warning against Canaanite socioeconomic practices of greed and acquisitiveness that were sustained by the Canaanite religion. What used to be called "Canaanite fertility religion" is an effort at can-do, self-help notions that by actions of acquisitiveness inhabitants of the land can secure their own future. This notion is a direct threat to Israel, for Moses reminds Israel that all is a gift and not an achievement:

> When the LORD your God has brought you into the land that he swore to your ancestors, to Abraham, to Isaac, and to Jacob, to give you—a land with fine, large cities that you did not build, houses filled with all sorts of goods that you did not fill, hewn cisterns that you did not hew, vineyards and olive groves that you did not plant—and when you have eaten your fill, take care that you do not forget the LORD, who brought you out of the land of Egypt, out of the house of slavery. The LORD your God you shall fear; him you shall serve, and by his name alone you shall swear. Do not follow other gods, any of the gods of the peoples who are all around you, because the LORD your God, who is present with you, is a jealous God. The anger of the LORD your God would be kindled against you and he would destroy you from the face of the earth. (Deut 6:10-15)

> For the LORD your God is bringing you into a good land, a land with flowing streams, with springs and underground waters welling up in valleys and hills, a land of wheat and honey, a land where you may eat bread without scarcity, where you will lack nothing, a land whose stones are iron and from whose hills you may mine copper. You shall eat your fill and bless the LORD your God for the good land that he has given you.
>
> Take care that you do not forget the LORD your God, by failing to keep his commandments, his ordinances, and his statutes, which I am commanding you today. When you have eaten your fill and have built fine houses and live in them, and when your herds and flocks have multiplied, and your silver and gold is multiplied, and all that you have is multiplied, then do not exalt yourself, forgetting the LORD your God, who brought you out of the land of Egypt, out of the house of slavery, who led you through the great and terrible wilderness, an arid wasteland with poisonous snakes and scorpions. He made water flow for you from flint rock, and fed you in the wilderness with manna that your ancestors did not know, to humble you and to test you, and in the end to do you good. Do not say to yourself, "My power and the might of my own hand have gotten me this wealth." (Deut 8:7-17)

The positive counterpoint to the warning against seduction is the conviction that the land of Canaan is transformable, so that its political economy can be altered and turned into a covenantal neighborhood. That conviction would seem to be the point of the preached torah in the book of Deuteronomy. Israel's insistent obedience to covenantal torah will fundamentally alter the social relationships of the community. It is for that reason that current scholarship refers to Deuteronomy as a "constitution" for an alternative polity in the land of Canaan.[8]

The *warning about seduction* and the *possibility of transformation* are exposited in the book of Deuteronomy by interpretation of the torah of Sinai. I will mention two aspects of that exposition in terms of our subject of Sabbath. First, in Deuteronomy 5:6-21, Moses reiterates the Ten Commandments of Exodus 20. As is well known, this is, except for slight editorial variation, a full and faithful reiteration of the words of Sinai. But as is equally well known, the one substantive variation is in the Sabbath command of Deuteronomy 5:12-15. Again, the commandment is a provision for work stoppage in all parts of the community:

> Observe the sabbath day and keep it holy, as the LORD your God com-
> manded you. Six days you shall labor and do all your work. But the
> seventh day is a sabbath to the LORD your God; you shall not do any
> work—you, or your son or your daughter, or your male or female slave,
> or your ox or your donkey, or any of your livestock, or the resident alien
> in your towns, so that your male and female slave may rest as well as
> you. (Deut 5:12-14)

The most interesting point here is that Moses adds a phrase that does not occur in the Exodus version, "like you" ("as well as you" in the NRSV's translation above). In this rendition Sabbath is the moment of radical social equality in which master and slave, father and son and daughter, livestock and oxen are all equal because none is performing, none is proving anything. Everyone knows that in the rough-and-tumble world of production not all are equal because some are more able, more competitive, more skillful, more motivated; and so they produce more and are awarded accordingly. Everyone knows that in the competitive world of consumption, some have more than others. They are reckoned to be more entitled than others and exercise greater leverage and advantage in the accumulation of goods. But Sabbath is a sabbatical from the rough-and-tumble world of production, from the competitive leverage of consumption, because all, the nonproductive and the nonentitled, are to rest and be treated as a neighbor, just as you are. Such a claim may be inferred at Sinai; here in Deuteronomy it is explicit.

What may interest us more, however, is the motivation offered at the Jordan by Moses for the Sabbath command: "Remember that you were a slave in the land of Egypt, and the Lord your God brought you out from there with a mighty hand and an outstretched arm; therefore the Lord your God commanded you to keep the sabbath day" (Exod 5:15). Here there is no mention of creation and six days of creation. Here there is no reference to the fabric of creation or the unanxious presence of the Creator. In Deuteronomy the matter is more acute and more concrete. It is about Pharaoh and Egypt and exodus deliverance, emancipation from the brutal production-consumption apparatus of Pharaoh, who is reckoned in Israel as the icon of antilife. Sabbath is alternative to Pharaoh. Work stoppage is an alternative to unreachable brick quotas. Rest is a counter to the complexity that is endemic to the pharaonic system. Israel is to rest as a public statement that life does not consist in the compulsions of production or consumption. It may be seen, then, that the Sabbath commandment is the middle term and the connection between the first commandment, on *false gods*, and the tenth commandment, on *compulsive acquisitiveness*, that Moses takes to be rooted in the attractive power of the gods of Egypt and Canaan. At the center of the Deuteronomic Decalogue is the insistence that if Israel is to *resist seduction* and if Israel is to *enact a transformative alternative*, then the key and starting point is the refusal of the commoditization of life in order to make room for social relationships that are not so ordered in coercion.

Second, it is the view of some scholars that the Torah corpus in Deuteronomy 12–25 is in fact an ordered exposition of the Decalogue, so that the Torah commandments that appear to be miscellaneous and ad hoc in fact are sequenced according to the Ten Commandments.[9] I do not know if that case is compelling, but it has heuristic value in any case. If we entertain that option and look to see where the Sabbath commandment is exposited in the more extended corpus, we will conclude that it shows up in the commandment on the "year of release" in Deuteronomy 15:1-18. The "year of release" is the Sabbath writ large and made concrete in the political imagination of Israel.

This statute, extended by a great deal of didactic material, provides that debt held by creditors in the community must not be extended beyond six years. This commandment, plus its exposition, is likely the fount of all thinking about *forgiveness* in the Bible. Forgiveness has to do with the overcoming of indebtedness, whereby the economy is subordinated to neighborly relationships and is pressed into the service of healthy social relationships.[10] The commandment itself is terse in verses 1-3 and only provides and asserts that the requirement pertains only to neighbors in the community of covenant and not to outsiders. What is particularly interesting is the extended exposition that pertains to the poor or, as the NRSV prefers, "the needy." I will mention five aspects of the exposition of Sabbath, but we are already into fresh territory by connecting Sabbath to the economy of the poor whereby rest is understood as a neighborly curb on social practices of acquisitiveness.

1. The Sabbath is linked to the needy. In verse 11, a text quoted by Jesus (Matt 26:11; Mark 14:7), Moses affirms that there will always be poor people, and so the commandment must be kept: "Since there will never cease to be some in need on the earth, I therefore command you, 'Open your hand to the poor

and needy neighbor in your land'" (Deut 15:11). Clearly the statement is a motivation for obedience and is not to be taken cynically, as now often happens, to imagine that nothing can be done. On the other hand, in verse 4, the cruciality and effectiveness of the command are asserted: "There will, however, be no one in need among you, because the LORD is sure to bless you in the land that the Lord your God is giving you as a possession to occupy" (Deut 15:4). The year of release makes it possible that there need be no poor in the community, certainly not an underclass. Thus Moses imagines a radical covenantal act of sabbathing that transforms social relationships.

2. It is clear that the teaching of Moses met with resistance from those who saw no reason to curb acquisitiveness, that is, who wished to replicate Pharaoh in terms of production and control. Moses acknowledges a propensity toward pharaonic practice that had been alive in Israel from the beginning:

> If there is among you anyone in need, a member of your community in
> any of your towns within the land that the LORD your God is giving you,
> do not be hard-hearted or tight-fisted toward your needy neighbor. . . .
> Be careful that you do not entertain a mean thought, thinking, "The seventh year, the year of remission, is near," and therefore view your needy
> neighbor with hostility and give nothing; your neighbor might cry to the
> LORD against you, and you would incur guilt. (Deut 15:7, 9)

Moses takes this resistance and refusal to be a dangerous practice for the community because it will evoke "a cry," the same cry that the slaves voiced to YHWH in Egypt.

3. Moses mobilizes his most urgent rhetoric of imperative concerning this commandment, more than any other in the corpus of Deuteronomy. Five times Moses employs *the absolute infinitive*, a peculiar grammatical construction in Hebrew that intensifies a verb by its reiteration. This usage is not visible in English translation, but we can, even in the English translation, notice the urgency of the rhetoric:

- diligently observing (v. 5);
- opening your hand (v. 8);
- willingly lending (v. 8);
- giving liberally (v. 10);
- providing liberally (v. 14).

The imperatives are the most elemental urging toward covenant, for it is in the treatment of the needy that Israel is most Israel. And it is in Sabbath disengagement from production and consumption that Israel most evidences its peculiar covenantal character.

4. The motivation for this elemental requirement is the same as that given in Deuteronomy 5 for the Sabbath: "Remember that you were a slave in the land of Egypt, and the LORD your God redeemed you; for this reason I lay this command upon you today" (Deut 15:15). It is clear that Sabbath and the derivative practice of debt cancellation are militantly anti-Pharaoh. And, of course, the same conviction is insisted on for the even more extravagant imagination of the jubilee year in Leviticus 25:

> I am the LORD your God, who brought you out of the land of Egypt, to give you the land of Canaan, to be your God. . . . For they are my servants, whom I brought out of the land of Egypt; they shall not be sold as slaves are sold. . . . For to me the people of Israel are servants; they are my servants whom I brought out from the land of Egypt: I am the LORD your God. (Lev 25:38, 42, 55)

5. Moses adds a final rhetorical flourish, asserting that the practice of the year of release also has practical implications: "Do not consider it a hardship when you send them out from you free persons, because for six years they have given you services worth the wages of hired laborers; and the Lord your God will bless you in all that you do" (Deut 15:18). The promise of a "blessing" draws the exposition of Moses back into the sphere of creation, for "blessing" refers to the good, productive world of creation and the bearing of much economic fruit. This statement represents a modest departure from the exodus theme in order to insist that such an economic practice that is exodus-shaped brings the community into sync with creation. Such an economy that is not exploitative or acquisitive will work better because the earth yields its gifts to a neighborly society.[11]

It is worth noting that, in the ordering of Deuteronomy, this extended instruction is followed in Deuteronomy 15:19-22 and 16:1-17 by provisions for sacrificial offerings and celebration of festivals, each act a glad performance of gratitude for the goodness of life granted by the God of the exodus.

Exodus 16

If the Sabbath commandment constitutes resistance and alternative to Pharaoh, and if we work backward from the commandment of Sinai (and Deuteronomy) to Pharaoh, we will again come to Exodus 16 as an important way station, whether we read forward from Pharaoh to Sinai or backward from Sinai to Pharaoh. Either way, we have noticed the narrative of bread from heaven that was freely given in abundance, with only one imperative attached: "And Moses said to them, 'Let no one leave any of it over until morning'" (Exod 16:19). That is all. Bread cannot be stored. It cannot be accumulated. It cannot be carried over until the next day. That provision perforce limits the amount of bread to be gathered to be sure that your eyes are not bigger than your stomach and that your grasping hands do not overreach. Sufficient for the day is the bread thereof! For that reason we are profoundly taken by surprise when Moses adds the next statement:

> He said to them, "This is what the Lord has commanded: 'Tomorrow is a day of solemn rest, a holy sabbath to the Lord; bake what you want to bake and boil what you want to boil, and all that is left over put aside to be kept until morning.'" So they put it aside until morning, as Moses commanded them; and it did not become foul, and there were no worms in it. (Exod 16:23-24)

In this statement Moses violates his own rule just uttered about bread for the day. Moses makes an exception for Sabbath, because Sabbath is an exceptional day in Israel. The test case is that they tried it. The bread acted differently on the seventh day. It did not become foul; there were no worms in it. And Moses issues his concluding command: "Moses said, 'Eat it today, for today is a sabbath to the Lord; today you will not find it in the field. Six days you shall gather it; but on the seventh day, which is a sabbath, there will be none'" (Exod 16:25-26). Bread will not be given on the seventh day—because the Creator is at rest. There will be none! Earth rests because heaven does not grant the commodities that would evoke work.

Likely too much should not be made of this little paragraph, terse as it is. But what an utterance, what a prohibition, what an assurance! Even in the wilderness, the place without viable life support, Sabbath will be kept. Israel will enact its antipharaonic identity, and Israel will see that even in this place bereft of life support, sustenance is given. Israel did not need to violate its identity, even in a place of deepest deficiency.

Amos 8:4-6

It is remarkable that, after this accent on Sabbath in Sinai Torah provisions, the prophetic corpus of the Old Testament makes few references to it. Perhaps it makes few references because it was so ingrained in Israel that it did not need to be reiterated or because it was overrun by bigger issues or because on historical-critical grounds Sabbath was not yet established in Israel. In any case, I cite one of the few Sabbath texts in the prophetic corpus, one that seems to me to be peculiarly pertinent in its urgency, Amos 8:4-6. The poem begins with a rather generic indictment:

> Hear this, you that trample on the needy,
> and bring to ruin the poor of the land. (Amos 8:4)

The indictment concerns economic exploitation of the poor, a standard theme of Amos. The economic exploitation is, in Old Testament horizon, an imitation of

Pharaoh and an embrace of Canaanite practice. In verse 5, Amos gets specific; he does so by putting in the mouth of his adversaries all of the material of verses 5-6 with a "you say":

- You say:

> When will the new moon be over
> so that we may sell grain? (Amos 8:5a)

You wonder how long the festival service will last. You look at your watch, you fidget, and you wonder how long you have to stay in the meeting, the "new moon" that comes once a month, the Sabbath that occurs every week. You endure the discipline of it all, but you already are making notes for what comes next.

- You say:

> . . . so that we may offer wheat for sale? (Amos 8:5b)

When can we get back to the market? When can we reengage the economy from which we have taken a break, an enforced break? When can we get back to the normal processes of dishonest measures and rigged scales?

- You say:

> . . . buying the poor for silver
> and the needy for a pair of sandals,
> and selling the sweepings of the wheat. (Amos 8:6)

When can we get back to exploitation of the poor, through high interest rates, exploitative prices, poor goods, because they do not know their value and do not care?

Amos posits a profound contradiction between pious practice and compulsive intention,[12] sketching out double-mindedness in which the pursuit of commodity has crowded in on the quintessence of Israelite reality, so that even in the moment of Israelite rest, energy is given to pharaonic commoditization. (I know about making notes in church for the next thing that comes along, though I have not yet had my own cell phone ring during a worship service.)

It strikes me that what Amos describes is multitasking, the contemporary agile capacity to do more than one thing at a time, to rest or to worship, but to maximize the time by doing more, doing more in order to get ahead, having an advantage, improving one's life. I submit that *multitasking* may be the visible enactment of *anti-Sabbath*; I could imagine Pharaoh in Egyptian liturgy engaging in text messaging to see how the production of bricks goes—no Sabbath rest! And then I thought of the ultimate teaching of Jesus on multitasking: "No one can serve two masters; for a slave will either hate the one and love the other, or be devoted to the one and despise the other. You cannot serve God and wealth" (Matt 6:24). However the last word is rendered—mammon, wealth, capital—it is a telling counterpoint to God, to the God of the exodus. It is no wonder that at its very beginning in Deuteronomy Moses had summoned Israel: "Hear, O Israel: The LORD is our God, the LORD alone. You shall love the LORD your God with all your heart, and with all your soul, and with all your might" (Deut 6:4-5). Moses urges an undivided God and an undivided Israel in alliance with God—one heart, one mind, one will, one relationship, one act of loyalty, one practice of imagination. Could it be that multitasking with juggled loyalties bespeaks our primal restlessness and militates against exodus emancipation and the assurances of creation? If one thinks about multitasking and single-mindedness, it is of interest to me that on CNN and such news channels one gets scrolling updates at the bottom of the screen with the news so that we may multitask—but none during the ads! The advertisers invite single-mindedness and do not want divided attention or a contradiction to the demands of Pharaoh and all other anxious, self-securing systems.

III

All of this thus far might be obvious and well known to you. I have taken so long with it for two reasons. First, I believe that Sabbath-defying anxiety is at the heart of our social pathology and that this Sabbath-defying anxiety is the primal datum in the horizon of an early Christian trajectory of faith. I have made the surface exploration through an old book by Philip Carrington who, in the book, is identified only as "Bishop of Quebec."[13] His study concerns these sets of either/or counsel, which he situates in the practice of baptism, whereby the candidate for baptism embraced a very different life in the world.

Carrington suggests that the evidence of the New Testament epistles reflects a fourfold formulation familiar to us in the cadences of the baptismal liturgy and that must have been, according to Carrington, a recurring liturgical usage:

1. Put off all evil:

> Rid yourselves, therefore, of all malice, and all guile, insincerity, envy, and all slander. (1 Pet 2:1)

> Therefore rid yourselves of all sordidness and rank growth of wickedness, and welcome with meekness the implanted word that has the power to save your souls. (Jas 1:21)

2. Be in subjection (a code of subordination):

> For the Lord's sake accept the authority of every human institution, whether of the emperor as supreme, or of governors, as sent by him to punish those who do wrong and to praise those who do right. (1 Pet 2:13-14)

> Submit yourselves therefore to God. Resist the devil, and he will flee from you. (Jas 4:7)

3. Be vigilant:

> The end of all things is near; therefore be serious and discipline yourselves for the sake of your prayers. (1 Pet 4:7)

> Devote yourselves to prayer, keeping alert in it with thanksgiving. (Col 4:2)

4. Be in resistance:

> Discipline yourselves, keep alert. Like a roaring lion your adversary the devil prowls around, looking for someone to devour. (1 Pet 5:8-9)

> Submit yourselves therefore to God. Resist the devil, and he will flee from you. (Jas 4:7)

The sum of these imperatives is to urge active intentionality, as everything is at stake in being disciplined and single-minded. The urgency is not because of a small, calculating moralism but because the world is under threat from the power of evil that would override faith and undo humanness.

The fourfold formulation of Carrington amounts to an either/or decision of resistance and affirmation that Paul lines out in terms of "flesh and spirit." I am aware that it is easiest to read Paul's radical either/or in terms of ontological realities. But when read in Old Testament perspective, a perspective that is characteristically dramatic, political, and socioeconomic, the bid for resistance and affirmation sounds exactly like that of Moses in Deuteronomy concerning rejection of Canaanite modes of life and embrace of neighborly covenant.

Given this family resemblance, I read the Pauline either/or of "flesh and spirit" as the antithesis of *pharaonic, Sabbathless society* and a *neighborly, Sabbath-grounded alternative.*

I do so by asking about what a restless acquisitiveness may do, and I suggest that such acquisitiveness may produce people who are anxious, fearful, aggressive, mean-spirited, self-indulgent, and selfish. My thought is that such modes of participation in society are not accidental or incidentally chosen. They are, rather, the predictable results of a systemic ordering of social relationships around insatiable production and equally insatiable consumption. Thus, I read the "fruits" of Sabbathless society:

> Now *the works of the flesh* are obvious: fornication, impurity, licentiousness, idolatry, sorcery, enmities, strife, jealousy, anger, quarrels, dissensions, factions, envy, drunkenness, carousing, and things like these. I am warning you, as I warned you before: those who do such things will not inherit the kingdom of God. (Gal 5:19-21)

> They are darkened in their understanding, alienated from the life of God because of their ignorance and hardness of heart. They have lost all sensitivity and have abandoned themselves to licentiousness, greedy to practice every kind of impurity. . . . Put away from you all bitterness and wrath and anger and wrangling and slander, together with all malice. (Eph 4:18-19, 31)

> Put to death, therefore, whatever in you is earthly: fornication, impurity, passion, evil desire, and greed (which is idolatry). On account of these the wrath of God is coming on those who are disobedient. These are the ways you also once followed, when you were living that life. But now you must get rid of all such things—anger, wrath, malice, slander, and abusive language from your mouth. Do not lie to one another, seeing that you have stripped off the old self with its practices. (Col 3:5-9)

The sum of these lists constitutes the horizon and the practice of destructive human conduct that makes human community impossible.

By contrast, Paul commands the fruit of the spirit:

> By contrast, *the fruit of the Spirit* is love, joy, peace, patience, kindness, generosity, faithfulness, gentleness, and self-control. There is no law against such things. And those who belong to Christ Jesus have crucified the flesh with its passions and desires. If we live by the Spirit, let us also be guided by the Spirit. Let us not become conceited, competing against one another, envying one another. (Gal 5:22-26)

> Let no evil talk come out of your mouths, but only what is useful for building up, as there is need, so that your words may give grace to those who hear. . . . And be kind to one another, tenderhearted, forgiving one another, as God in Christ has forgiven you. Therefore be imitators of God, as beloved children. (Eph 4:29, 32; 5:1)

> . . . and [you] have clothed yourselves with the new self, which is being renewed in knowledge according to the image of its creator. In that

renewal there is no longer Greek and Jew, circumcised and uncircumcised, barbarian, Scythian, slave and free; but Christ is all and in all!

As God's chosen ones, holy and beloved, clothe yourselves with compassion, kindness, humility, meekness, and patience. Bear with one another and, if anyone has a complaint against another, forgive each other; just as the Lord has forgiven you, so you also must forgive. Above all, clothe yourselves with love, which binds everything together in perfect harmony. And let the peace of Christ rule in your hearts, to which indeed you were called in the one body. And be thankful. (Col 3:10-15)

Here is offered a portrayal of a community in which its members are predisposed to the habits of neighborliness.

In the early church, the drama of baptism was a life or death matter that required resistance and fresh embrace. If we read back from Paul (by way of Carrington), we dare imagine that the drama of exodus-Sinai is likewise a repeated liturgical performance of departure and arrival. In that ancient drama, it is a move,

- from a Sabbathless society of anxiety,
- to a wish for bread with enough given for Sabbath in the wilderness,
- to a set of commands that connect idolatry to covetousness and refuses both.

IV

I conclude this exercise with the conviction that such *systemic anxiety* no doubt feeds the war effort, feeds the crisis of gays and lesbians, feeds the loudness about immigration. The body politic is restless and, because Sabbathless, is devoured by the urgency of control that is willing to violate neighbor and to violate the Constitution.

In that matrix that seethes with fear and resentment, the community of covenant bespeaks an urgent alternative. That unanxious alternative concerns genuine social relationships that can be neighborly. That unanxious alternative, I believe, depends on a centered restfulness that does not perceive others as threats or as competitors but as brothers, sisters, and neighbors. I believe, and have found it true for myself, however, that such neighborly possibility depends on some intentional disengagement from the pursuit of money, control, and power. I have, moreover, the conviction that the best strategy for slowing down the motor of anxiety is precisely the willful performance of Sabbath.

I understand that Episcopalians have never entertained the thought of becoming Mennonites, and neither have Calvinists! But the Mennonite discipline of disengagement is likely urgent for our time and place—not in order to remain withdrawn, as Mennonites do not—but to reengage with a buoyant, unintimidated spirit. The church, in its practice of baptism—performance, remembrance, and "improving"—is the practice of disengagement from Sabbathless existence that leaves us fractured and exhausted and short of our best selves. In parallel fashion, Israel's departure from Egypt through wilderness to Torah is not a one-time memory but a frequently reenacted decision.

Paul has the right language:

> For freedom Christ has set us free. Stand firm, therefore, and do not submit again to a yoke of slavery. (Gal 5:1)

> So then, putting away falsehood, let all of us speak the truth to our neighbors, for we are members of one another. (Eph 4:25)

> . . . and have clothed yourselves with the new self, which is being renewed in knowledge according to the image of its creator. In that renewal there is no longer Greek and Jew, circumcised and uncircumcised, barbarian, Scythian, slave and free; but Christ is all and in all! (Col 3:10-11)

We have been at this forever. It is my thought that Moses might be a larger pattern in this enterprise, even as he placed the Sabbath command at the center of the Decalogue, a barrier against the commoditization of neighbor and of self.

CHAPTER 4

The Countercommands of Sinai

THE NEWS WE CONFESS together is that God has loved the world, us as creatures in the world, and all of our neighbors, human creatures and all other creatures.[1] The reason this is news is that there is deeply rooted in creation a contradiction of that love that makes the news a scandal. And yet we cling to that news against the evidence of contradiction. As we cling to the news, we are left with all the ethical questions of attitude, behavior, and policy that are demanding, elusive, and complex. Of course, none of that is new, as we have been at this issue of response to the gospel for the sake of the world at least since the Second Isaiah and his self-conscious use of the term "gospel." And even that poet had his antecedents in gospel response. But the question is fresh for us, as it always is, because our faith is always as new and urgent as the most recent shape of the world and our existence within it. To pose the question as the planning committee has done invites us to venture afresh as we ask about "response to the gospel for the sake of the world."

I

I am willing to take a try at that fresh venture that is bound to be vexatious and contentious. But as I do so, I am aware of three impediments that I face:

The first impediment in this company is that I am not good at "Lutheran." I have old Lutheran genes in my body and no less than Kathleen Norris has labeled me as a Lutheran. I am a child of *Kirchenverein des Westes*, the Evangelical Church Fellowship of the West that was a transport from the Prussian Union of 1817. In that moment of German history, the king of Prussia forced Lutherans and Calvinists into the same church, weary as he was of their eucharistic quarrels. In my seminary education at Eden Seminary, down the street from Concordia Seminary, the center of the curriculum was the Epistle to the Romans, read, as we now call it, in a Lutheran way concerning "grace alone." My toughest, most demanding theological teacher was Lutheran in perspective, though not of the C. F. W. Walther variety.

Since seminary I have mostly breathed Calvinist air. This is true of my membership in the United Church of Christ, which is Calvinist if it can claim any theological tradition. During my years on the Eden Seminary faculty, I was increasingly tilted toward Calvin, as it was not easy to be our kind of Lutheran in St. Louis. And that Calvinism was reinforced at Columbia Theological Seminary, where I have been for the last twenty years—Calvinism largely through the prism of Karl Barth. Given that tilt, I must think in terms of "the third use of the law," the law as guide for new life. I understand that our theme of response to the gospel comes down to "gospel and law," though only a good Lutheran could find enough to say on gospel and law to make it last fifty minutes.

My second impediment is that my conversation partner is Professor Terence Fretheim. Terry has been the master of the text for me and has been my teacher right along, as I regard Terry as the premier reader of texts in my generation of Old Testament readers. As a consequence, after each paragraph of this, as I wrote it, I had to ask, "What would Terry say about that?" I am going to stay in this presentation with the exodus narrative, and I regard Terry's most important contribution to our common work to be his remarkable study of the exodus narrative in terms of creation and Pharaoh as the great disturber of the environment. I am aware that he has done much more than that on creation, but that interpretive twist seems to me the most stunning of his many insights. Terry has more than a few times chided me for moving outside the range of viable Christian reading, and I could perhaps find warrant for doing so by observing that YHWH, as well as Pharaoh, did not blink from disturbing the creaturely environment. In any case I am delighted at the opportunity to be with Terry in this venue.

But after speaking only broken Lutheran and after intimidation by Professor Fretheim, the third and most important impediment for me is that there is no easy or obvious or direct move from Scripture study to our theme of response to the gospel for the sake of the world. The theme invites a reference to the typology of H. Richard Niebuhr in *Christ and Culture*, except that in all quarters it is now considered that Niebuhr's influential typology is much too simplistic and static, that neither "Christ" nor "culture" will accommodate such monodimensional articulation. Thus our response, as it is informed and propelled by the gospel and as it makes the connection to "the world," runs toward a moving target that will not stand still or wait for us.

As a result, our mode of "response" requires an enormous act of imagination, the kind of act of imagination that the church is always committing, whether knowingly or not. Such imagination is never innocent, moreover, because it is always permeated with our interests and hurts and hopes. Such an imaginative response is, consequently, inescapably disputatious. For when the gospel is heard and embraced by others with different interests, hurts, and hopes, the outcome is very different; and there is no answer in the back of the book.

Any response to the gospel that is imaginative and endlessly disputatious is inevitably provisional, never full, complete, or settled. That is because all elements of the engagement—the voice of the gospel, the reality of the world, the imagination of the church—all are part of a fluid interaction. That means not only that we must be prepared to try it again in the next instant, it also means that our response in any given circumstance cannot honestly claim much absoluteness because our articulation of what is absolute depends to some great extent on who is in the room. And whenever there is an entrance or exit, the formulation requires freshness. So I acknowledge this impediment and proceed boldly.

II

The question with which I begin is this: Can we get a *rule* out of a *story*? The grandparents of Exodus 10:1-2 are instructed and expected to retell the exodus narrative. And they, like all effective grandparents, tell stories because we find them not only entertaining but also instructive. We imagine in our retelling them repeatedly (as in the liturgy) that the grandchildren will receive through the telling an identity and a vocation and an angle of vision and a passion and an obligation. So we would answer, yes, rules come from stories. But not clearly, not exactly, not necessarily, but only by an act of traditioning imagination as each new generation watches to see how the grandparents make that move in their time and place.

The pivot point of the tradition of exodus-sojourn-Sinai, I propose, is in that familiar, awesome divine utterance by YHWH at Sinai: "I am YHWH your God. . . . You shall have no other gods before me" (Exod 20:2-3). Before we ask about the rule—the first and decisive commandment—we have to ask who speaks. And when we ask that, it is clear that the one who speaks is the one "who brought you out of the land of Egypt, out of the house of bondage" (Exod 20:1). The one who speaks is the one who is embedded in the earlier narrative of emancipation. It does not matter at all that there is a strong critical judgment that the exodus tradition of the Sinai materials had no connection to each other. It will not do to say that the canonical tradition connected the two distinct units of text. What counts is that the dominating character of YHWH—the deliverer, the commander— stretches across the transition from one unit of tradition to the other. The one who is to speak ten times in the commandments is the one who acted decisively and triumphantly ten times in the plague narratives. The authority of the one who commands at Sinai is given in the exodus narrative, which is not hindered in its compelling power by all of the critical energy that we can muster. The narrative is retold because it is remembered. It is remembered and retold, not proven. It is not proven the way we thought it was when Terry and I began our graduate study. It is not proven but treasured, sustained on the lips of the grandparents.

It turns out that the exodus narrative is on the mind of all parties who come to Sinai. It is on the mind of the *grandparents* who tell the story. The grandparents never tire of telling the story in its many refractions, trusting the story to make its own delivery of rule. It is on the mind of *YHWH*: "You have seen what I did to the Egyptians, and how I bore you on eagles' wings and brought you to myself" (Exod 19:4). "You remember what I did in Egypt," YHWH is saying. "I carried you and brought you not to Sinai but 'to me.'" And the grandparents tell it so that one can see that YHWH made fools of the Egyptians. You cannot come to Sinai unless you know that YHWH made fools of the Egyptians. But the exodus narrative is also on the mind of the *Israelites* at the foot of that dangerous mountain. Already in Exodus 19:8 we read, "The people all answered as one: 'Everything that the LORD has spoken we will do.' Moses reported the words of the people to the LORD" (Exod 19:8). They say this in Exodus 19:8 even though the commands of YHWH are not enunciated until Exodus 20. The pledge of obedience to YHWH by Israel precedes the announcement of the commandments. The Israelites are eager for the new obedience. Why are they eager? Because they have seen enough of YHWH to know that whatever YHWH commands will be better than the commands of Pharaoh. They will try the alternative because the commands of Pharaoh have quickly become unbearable. The new commandments will still bear echoes of YHWH's first utterance. YHWH first said:

> Let my people go, so that they may celebrate a festival to me in the
>   wilderness (Exod 5:1);
> Let my people go, so that they may worship me in the wilderness
>   (Exod 7:16);
> Let my people go, so that they may worship me (Exod 8:1);
> Let my people go, so that they may worship me (Exod 8:20);
> Let my people go, so that they may worship me (Exod 9:1);
> Let my people go, so that they may worship me (Exod 9:13);
> Let my people go, so that they may worship me (Exod 10:3).

Seven times. Let them be free and conduct a liturgy to me, free to imagine a world before me, free to perform an alternative, free to commit an act of subversion. Let my people have time, space, and energy in order to commit an act of imagination that is not framed and controlled by Pharaoh. You have seen what I did. I made it possible for you to perform the world beyond the reach of Pharaoh, even if you had to do it in the wilderness.

So imagine the community at Sinai—grandparents, YHWH, and Israel—knit together to see whether the exodus memory can be consolidated into an institutional practice, a form of public life that shapes political economy into a durable form of neighborly solidarity. That much arises from the narrative memory, for up to this point all I have cited is, first, the mandate to the parents in Exodus 10:1-2: "Then the LORD said to Moses, 'Go to Pharaoh; for I have hardened his heart and the heart of his officials, in order that I may show these signs of mine among them, and that you may tell your children and grandchildren how I have made fools of the Egyptians and what signs I have done among them—so that you may know that I am the LORD.'" Second, I have cited the memory of YHWH in Exodus 19:4: "You have seen what I did to the Egyptians, and how I bore you on eagles' wings and brought you to myself." And third, I have cited the eagerness of Israel in Exodus 19:8: "The people all answered as one: 'Everything that the LORD has spoken we will do.' Moses reported the words of the people to the LORD" (Exod 19:8). All of these acts of narration, remembering, and eagerness move together toward the summary enunciation of YHWH in Exodus 20:2: "I am the LORD your God, who brought you out of the land of Egypt, out of the house of slavery."

<h2 style="text-align:center">III</h2>

But we must linger over *the commands of Pharaoh* from the initial narrative if we are to have full appreciation for *the commands of YHWH*. In Exodus 5, the narrator has Pharaoh speak his harsh, relentless commands concerning insatiable productivity:

> Get to your labors. . . . You shall no longer give the people straw to
> make bricks, as before; let them go and gather straw for themselves. But
> you shall require of them the same quantity of bricks as they have made
> previously; do not diminish it, for they are lazy; that is why they cry,
> "Let us go and offer sacrifice to our God." Let heavier work be laid on
> them; then they will labor at it and pay no attention to deceptive words.
> (Exod 5:4, 7-9)

Then speak the taskmasters and supervisor on behalf of Pharaoh: "So the taskmasters and the supervisors of the people went out and said to the people, 'Thus says Pharaoh, "I will not give you straw. Go and get straw yourselves, wherever you can find it; but your work will not be lessened in the least"'" (Exod 5:10-11). And then again the taskmasters: "The taskmasters were urgent, saying, 'Complete your work, the same daily assignment as when you were given straw'" (Exod 5:13). And then the taskmasters toward the supervisors: "And the supervisors of the Israelites, whom Pharaoh's taskmasters had set over them, were beaten, and were asked, 'Why did you not finish the required quantity of bricks yesterday and today, as you did before?'" (Exod 5:14). The supervisors, apparently trusted Israelites who are held accountable for low-level management chores, answered back in protest to Pharaoh for his severe demands: "Then the Israelite supervisors came to Pharaoh and cried, 'Why do you treat your servants like this? No straw is given to your servants, yet they say to us, "Make bricks!" Look how your servants are beaten! You are unjust to your own people'" (Exod 5:15-16). But Pharaoh responds to them without conceding anything: "He said, 'You are lazy, lazy; that is why you say, "Let us go and sacrifice to the LORD"'" (Exod 5:17). Finally, in exasperation, the supervisors—seeing that they are helpless in their ineffective appeal to Pharaoh—turn on Moses and Aaron and accuse them of causing the problem: "They said to them, 'The LORD look upon you and judge! You have brought us into bad odor with Pharaoh and his officials, and have put a sword in their hand to kill us'" (Exod 5:21). Moses in turn directs his accusation against YHWH: "Since I first came to Pharaoh to speak in your name, he has mistreated this people, and you have done nothing at all to deliver your people" (Exod 5:23). Both the protest of the supervisors and that of Moses let Pharaoh off the hook and turn the blame against their own. It is likely that this redirection of anger in protest represents the triumph of Pharaoh's ideology, which turns out, in the narrative, to be above blame.

While that ending to the narrative gives a curious turn to the narrative account of Egyptian exploitation, it is clear that it is the relentless, uncompromising demand of Pharaoh that is the root cause of the problem and the trigger for the narrative of departure that is to follow. We may draw together the terse demands without their narrative elaboration:

> Get to your labors (v. 4);
> You shall require of them the same quality of work as they have made previously (v. 8);
> Let heavier work be laid on them (v. 9);
> Go and get straw yourselves (v. 11);
> Complete your work, the same daily assignment (v. 13);
> Make bricks (v. 16);
> Go now and work (v. 18);
> You shall not lessen your daily number of bricks (v. 19).

Or, if you like, all of these severe injunctions can be reduced to a single pharaonic command, "Make more bricks"; you can imagine his institutional statement of purpose that expressed the same singular goal in finer language.

It is all about productivity. It is all about productivity to enhance the political-economic apparatus of Pharaoh. It is all about productivity at enormous human expense, without regard to human well being. Indeed, the "slaves" (the narrator would have us tremble at the word) are not perceived as human beings but only as "hands"—tools, instruments, and vehicles that produce wealth for those who command the project. This single command of productivity has dehumanized the labor force so that they are nameless contributors to an inscrutable, insatiable requirement.

The capacity to dehumanize the labor force is already evident in the Joseph narrative, another account of power in Egypt. There it is written that Joseph was served food to eat by himself when he had already established himself as a person of prominence in Egypt: "Then he washed his face and came out; and controlling himself he said, 'Serve the meal.' They served him by himself, and them by themselves, and the Egyptians who ate with him by themselves, because the Egyptians could not eat with the Hebrews, for that is an abomination to the Egyptians" (Gen 43:31-32). He is in a commanding position in the kingdom. But even so, he does not share table with the Egyptians, for his presence at the table would be an abomination, that is, an elemental act of contamination of the Egyptians. It is not, I submit, a far step from ritual degradation to economic exploitation, for the "unclean" are subhuman creatures without claim or sensitivity. Their only "value" lies in production.

That much Pharaoh knows. What Pharaoh does not know (but the narrator understands) is that even helpless, nameless, dehumanized people are capable of the most elemental human act of pain. The pain in the slave camp must have been acute. But only belatedly does it find voice: "After a long time the king of Egypt died. The Israelites groaned under their slavery, and cried out. Out of the slavery their cry for help rose up to God" (Exod 2:23). The cry of pain from abusive, dehumanizing labor practices at the command of Pharaoh is placed early in the text, in chapter 2. It is placed early because it is that cry of pain that becomes the primal engine for what follows in the narrative of departure. I was taught in seminary about "divine initiative"; it was good theology. But in narrative performance it is not divine initiative that began the process of exodus. The initiative is found in human pain that the commands of Pharaoh cannot silence. This cry in Exodus 2 is not the cry of Jews, it is not the cry of Israelites. It is the raw, elemental human reality of pain that will not be silent. The cry is precluded by the uncompromising command of Pharaoh; but the cry is also the refusal of the domination of Pharaoh, the refusal to be eliminated as an abomination. The slaves refused to be reduced to productivity, to be submerged invisibly in the self-indulgent requirements of Pharaoh.[2]

And, says the narrator, more than that, the cry is heard by the God of the book of Genesis, who has not yet appeared in the book of Exodus. Now, finally, there is a triangle in the narrative:

Pharaoh, whose commandment produces the cry;
The slaves, who cry against the demand for more bricks;
YHWH, who hears the cry.

It is not any wonder, then, that when the erstwhile slaves arrive with YHWH at the mountain, YHWH recalls the exodus miracle. YHWH identifies himself as the exodus God: "I am YHWH who brought you up out of the land of Egypt." And Israel, with vivid memories and scars to exhibit—but without any of the specificity of torah—welcomed the commands about to be produced by YHWH. The steady beat of "make more bricks" pounds in their ears and on their sore bodies. They are, not unlike Rosa Parks, just too tired to move. They assemble now to be addressed by new commands, and they are ready.

IV

I propose then to take the Ten Commandments—and the entire Torah corpus that derives from them—as countercommandments, counter to the severe commandments of Pharaoh. I intend to avoid a positivistic approach to the commandments; nor do I want to treat them in a vacuum as absolutes. The opener by YHWH, "I am the LORD who brought you out," insists that the Decalogue be taken in narrative setting as a performance of contrast to the commands of Pharaoh. I do not propose to correlate in any way the Ten Commandments with the commands of Pharaoh. Indeed, as we have seen, Pharaoh has only one commandment. But then, YHWH also has only one commandment, "I am YHWH . . . no other gods." All the rest is exegesis. YHWH offers himself as alternative sovereign to the slaves just emancipated. YHWH is a counter-God who enacts a countergospel and invites a counterresponse for the sake of the world.

The first three commandments (counting as a Calvinist) exposit the ways in which YHWH is unlike Pharaoh:

YHWH who brought you out, who caused emancipation, who willed living space and time and circumstance outside the world of severe production, is the singular God who can transform.

There will be no other gods, no competitors or rivals, no consort, no associates, no divine hierarchy, no drama among the gods that can distract from YHWH's drama with human history. There were other gods. They are often implied in the narrative but mentioned only once in Exodus 12:12, as YHWH institutes the practice of Passover, YHWH asserts: "For I will pass through the land of Egypt that night, and I will strike down every firstborn in the land of Egypt, both human beings and animals; on all the gods of Egypt I will execute judgments: I am the LORD" (Exod 12:12). YHWH, the violent emancipator, will enact judgment on the gods of Egypt. These gods are the sponsors and legitimators of the dehumanizing process of insatiable production. Thus, the first commandment is not a theological construct about monotheism. It is a performative dismissal of the very gods who have made the brick system into a viable social arrangement. YHWH intends to dismiss, discount, and defeat the divine power that makes it possible to regard dehumanization as a legitimate arrangement of social power.

No graven images. It is not necessary to cite the usual references about imagery to get the point. I have read that when Karl Marx wrote about "commodity fetishism," he did so in an intellectual world in which anthropologists were discovering and investigating "primitive peoples" with their religious "fetishes." Marx makes the cleverly mocking, ironic move to say that late Western capitalism practiced commodity fetishism, in parallel to primitive peoples, investing commodities with religious significance. Isn't it the case now that, while we have gotten over such primitive anthropological ideas, we have kept religious passion in relationship to commodities? It is clear that our society is propelled by the pursuit of more commodities that claim to have the transcendent power to make us whole and safe and happy, and keep us young and beautiful.

So it was with Pharaoh. Bricks, the immediate production, could be traded or assembled into emblems of beauty and power and control. "More bricks" bespeaks a society in which the dream of more culminates in pyramids, pyramids of power and wealth, a convergence of human energy and inscrutable divine blessing. That is the self-indulgent goal of Pharaoh. It is no wonder that Israel at Sinai is prepared to try for an imageless world, for images bespeak production, exploitation, and commoditization. Pharaoh is the image-maker par excellence, and they embrace the alternatives.

Do not take the name in vain; do not seek to attach the divine power to vested agenda or interest. The Egyptian gods were intimate allies of the pharaonic system of exploitation. Obviously there is the endless temptation in ancient Israel to attach YHWH to human programs—to monarchy, to temple, to holiness programs. There is a steady resistance in ancient Israel to such domestication of YHWH, who needs or wants nothing from Israel and who signs on for none of Israel's religious posturing. So in the oracle of Nathan to David: I do not want a house from you. . . . I will make a house for you (2 Sam 7:4-7). And in psalmic protest, YHWH refuses any thought that he is dependent on or needful of or expectant of any religious gesture of Israel:

> Hear, O my people, and I will speak,
> O Israel, I will testify against you.
> I am God, your God.
> Not for your sacrifices do I rebuke you;
> your burnt offerings are continually before me.
> I will not accept a bull from your house,
> or goats from your folds.
> For every wild animal of the forest is mine,
> the cattle on a thousand hills.
> I know all the birds of the air,
> and all that moves in the field is mine.
> If I were hungry, I would not tell you,
> for the world and all that is in it is mine.
> Do I eat the flesh of bulls,
> or drink the blood of goats?
> Offer to God a sacrifice of thanksgiving,
> and pay your vows to the Most High.
> Call on me in the day of trouble;
> I will deliver you, and you shall glorify me. (Ps 50:7-15)

The commandment concerns the connection between faith and the practice of power in the world. The commandment refuses the reduction of YHWH to the program of priest or king or prophet, or right or left:

> only YHWH, none of the gods of productivity;
> no fetishes that domesticate YHWH into anything graspable by human production;
> no alliance with the powers of production.

The contrast to Pharaoh is complete:

> Pharaoh's hierarchy of gods, all of them busy legitimating Pharaoh's enterprise, and totally contained therein;
> Pharaoh's gods committed to the multiplication of commodities since the enhancement of power, wealth, and control is the proper business of religion.
> Pharaoh's gods signed on into a system in which they are no more than a legitimating agent for interests other than their own.

In the plague narrative, the opponents of Moses and Aaron are, in popular translation, "the magicians." They are the scientists, technicians, and "intelligence community" of Pharaoh's regime. They know the mystery of how things work. They are, according to the narrator, able to match the miracles of Moses and Aaron. But then, in the third plague, they cannot perform. They cannot make gnats (Exod 8:16-19). They marvel that Moses and Aaron—and YHWH—can do what they cannot, and they exclaim: "This is the finger of God." To be sure, they do not refer here to the gods of Pharaoh. They mean the real God, the God above all gods, the one who has freedom outside the sphere of pharaonic power. This is as close as the Egyptian intelligence community will come to making a Yahwistic confession. But it is enough. No wonder Israel signed on with the first three commandments of YHWH against the command of Pharaoh: No other gods, no commodity fetishism, and no domestication for a program. They marvel, as do we.

The tenth commandment in Calvin's enumeration is "Thou shalt not covet." The command is a prohibition against acquisitive economics, the mad pursuit of commodities at the expense of the neighbor. Without any exposition, the command puts YHWH in contradiction to Pharaoh. Pharaoh is the quintessential coveter. He is concerned with "more bricks." More! And behind the command of Exodus 5 is the narrative of Genesis 47, in which Joseph buys up all the land and monopolizes all the food for Pharaoh, all because Pharaoh had had nightmares of scarcity. This entire enterprise is designed to accomplish a monopoly. And YHWH, at the mountain, in this tenth utterance, says, do not crave like Pharaoh!

The pivotal final commandment is picked up in the Pauline instruction to the baptized in a most compelling way: "Put to death, therefore, whatever in you is earthly: fornication, impurity, passion, evil desire, and greed (which is idolatry)" (Col 3:5).[3] What an amazing juxtaposition, "coveting, which is idolatry." This remarkable sentence draws the tenth commandment back to the first commandment and recognizes that the practice of *acquisitiveness* is a manifestation of *idolatry*, so that the first and tenth commandments provide an envelope for the whole. It is a linkage that Karl Marx would have understood well.

The series of commandments five through nine (in the count of Calvin)—parents, killing, idolatry, stealing, false witness—bespeak covenantal community in which folks are neighbors to each other who have regard for the life, the property, and the well being of neighbors, both the powerful and the marginalized. All are neighbors! Norman Gottwald has proposed that such an imagined society is "egalitarian." Because of critique of his radical imagining, Gottwald has more recently pulled back from "egalitarian" to "communitarian," but the claim is the same. In that covenantal society ordered at Sinai, there are no "slaves" among the Israelites, with special provision made for those who fall into poverty. And there are no "masters," as is evident in the grudging allowance for kingship in Deuteronomy 17:14-20. This community has no masters and no slaves—only neighbors.

The intent of the ordering of Pharaoh's Egypt is clear enough—a system of masters and slaves without any human interaction at all. We have no immediate evidence for the kind of violent abusiveness in Egypt that is prohibited by the commandments of Sinai. It is, however, not unreasonable to extrapolate. We know enough to know that absolute power breeds exploitative violence. We know, moreover, that a system of aggressive acquisitiveness that values only production is impatient with and dismissive of any who are not productive—in sum, widows, orphans, aliens, and the poor. Thus we may imagine that commandments five through nine seek to draw a line against the practices of a predatory system that is devoid of neighborliness and that treats the powerless as replaceable parts.

We may go one step further in imagining the brutalizing society detailed in Exodus 5 and mourned in Exodus 2. Once I heard a rabbi say that at Auschwitz, all Ten Commandments were systematically violated. And then he added, "When you violate the Ten Commandments, you will get Auschwitz every time." It is not reasonable or fair to transpose pharaonic Egypt into contemporaneity. Of course not. It is, however, reasonable and fair to imagine an economy of abusive exploitation that becomes unreasonably violent in its predatory insistences, that becomes increasingly violent in incremental steps so that what was once abusive becomes accepted as normative, like a frog slowly submitted to very hot water.

So at Sinai we have:

> Honor father and mother (the authorization of family values);
> Do not kill;
> Do not commit adultery;
> Do not steal;
> Do not bear false witness.

When you violate these norms, you create a competitive society in which there are no neighbors and no neighborhoods, but only practices of use and abuse.

At the core of the tenfold divine utterance at Sinai is the Sabbath command. As you know, Sabbath is not about worship. It is about rest—work stoppage that is grounded in the rhythms of creation. The work stoppage includes all members of the neighborhood, sons, daughters, slaves, livestock, and immigrants. And in Deuteronomy 5:14, Moses will go further to say that on the day of work stoppage, all these others in the neighborhood will be "as you." Sabbath rest, unlike productivity, is an equal-opportunity practice that overrides all distinctions of social valuation. Sabbath discipline is the visible public insistence that work, productivity, consumption, and commoditization do not define one's life, because we are not fundamentally workers. We are fundamentally neighbors.

It follows, obviously, that there was no Sabbath in Egypt. Clearly there was no Sabbath for the brick-makers, for the quotas were relentless. But surely there was no rest for Pharaoh, restless and demanding, endlessly checking the production schedules, the price of straw, and the value of bricks. Pharaonic restlessness is evoked in the strictures of Amos with his condemnation of those who cannot wait for Sabbath to end in order to get back to the fascination of the economy:

> Hear this, you that trample on the needy,
>   and bring to ruin the poor of the land,
> saying, "When will the new moon be over
>   so that we may sell grain;
> and the sabbath,
>   so that we may offer wheat for sale?
> We will make the ephah small and the shekel great,
>   and practice deceit with false balances,
> buying the poor for silver
>   and the needy for a pair of sandals,
>   and selling the sweepings of the wheat." (Amos 8:4-6)

Sinai is an act of alternative imagination that affirms that the neighborhood need not be a seething, restless turmoil of busyness wherein social relationships become a contest between rats in a rat race.

Now I am aware that Professor Fretheim has shown the exodus narrative to be about creation and the desolation of creation. I would wish that the alternative to environmental destructiveness had been more explicit in the Decalogue. But there is enough there to satisfy me, and surely to satisfy Terry. In the second commandment idols are prohibited in the form of anything that "is in the heavens above or that is in the earth beneath, or that is in the waters under the earth" (Exod 20:4). This act of alternative imagination clearly has the coherence of an ordered creation in purview. In the Sabbath command, as noted, the grounding for disciplined rest is the rest of the Creator, who has no anxiety about the viable coherence of creation. The unanxious practice of Sabbath is testimony to the trustworthy coherence of the creation; and workaholism, even on a good day, bespeaks a mistrust of creation. Only once—but once!—the Decalogue speaks directly of the land: "Honor your father and your mother, so that your days may be long in the land that the LORD your God is giving you" (Exod 20:12). The rhetoric sounds like the insistence of covenant in Deuteronomy. The phrasing is attestation to respect for parents and occurs in the very center of the ten words. I suspect that the phrasing could have been attached to any of the commandments, though it cannot be incidental that it occurs here. From familial fidelity out into every zone of existence, "honor" is the condition of a workable environment. This is a society in which mother and father are taken seriously, and in the previous command on Sabbath, slaves, sons, daughters, and livestock are honored. And in the terse commands six through nine, all neighbors are honored. Such neighborly honoring will enhance the earth, because the earth is diminished precisely because of anxious, aggressive productivity. Wendell Berry has shown in his writings how diminished neighborliness inevitably dismisses the land as well. The juxtaposition of honor in commandment five and the Sabbath in commandment four may suggest also an honoring of time (Sabbath) and an honoring of space (creation), all made possible because of unanxious fidelity. As a consequence, I entertain the thought that the violation of environment in overproduction and overdevelopment may arise from an elemental anxiety about creation, that it will not hold. Israel is entrusted with a parcel of creation—land/earth—and may order it alternatively. The backdrop of these commands is the seething anxiety of Pharaoh that has diminished all parties.

V

Thus, I propose that Sinai, echoed by Deuteronomy and the prophets and eventually Jesus, sets before God's people a radical either/or—either the covenantal neighborliness of common destiny or a restless predatory contest of abusive violence. The urgency of Sinai is that Moses and his company knew full well that intentionality about covenantal neighborliness is necessary in order to prevent a return to pharaonic Egypt. That return may be because the powers of Pharaoh are coercive. More likely, it is because the offer of Egypt is seductive:

> The rabble among them had a strong craving; and the Israelites also wept again, and said, "If only we had meat to eat! We remember the fish we used to eat in Egypt for nothing, the cucumbers, the melons, the leeks, the onions, and the garlic; but now our strength is dried up, and there is nothing at all but this manna to look at." (Num 11:4-6)

> And all the Israelites complained against Moses and Aaron; the whole
> congregation said to them, "Would that we had died in the land of
> Egypt! Or would that we had died in this wilderness! Why is the LORD
> bringing us into this land to fall by the sword? Our wives and our little
> ones will become booty; would it not be better for us to go back to
> Egypt?" So they said to one another, "Let us choose a captain, and go
> back to Egypt." (Num 14:2-4)

It is an either/or that takes many different forms in many different circumstances, but it is always the same. The imaginative act of Sinai is a demanding reminder to Israel that it was summoned by YHWH and borne on eagles' wings for an alternative existence in the world.

I have taken this long with the exposition of these texts because I believe that the exodus-Sinai narrative lays out the key issue that the church in our society faces. From a Calvinist perspective it is not a gospel/law choice (though I do not much mind a Lutheran cast); it is the either/or of *covenant* or *predatory violence* that precludes neighborliness. In what remains I want to turn that either/or of the ancient narrative toward our contemporary circumstance. I understand that such "dynamic analogues" are precarious and open to question. But I suggest that such a transposition is not a mechanical "now/then" transposition; it is, rather, an inescapable transport of an ancient text into the matrix of our fears and hopes and hurts and anger.

The predatory economy of Pharaoh, sanctioned by impotent gods and practiced by "magicians" who know the "secrets" but who cannot produce, shows up in our narrative imagination as the *global market economy* supported by an *undisciplined militarism* in the service of a *limitless consumer entitlement*. There are three components to that thick characterization:

- the *global market economy* centers on securing more commodities;
- *undisciplined militarism* diminishes our societal resources by a bloated military budget, which is legitimated by a durable "orange alert";
- this is done in the service of *entitlement* for consumer goods.

None of us would say it so in church. But truth to tell, we are overstressed and overburdened by our endless preoccupation with email and cell phones and iPods and multitasking, with no time left for critical reflection or the nurture of an intentional life of freedom and imagination. The outcome of such seething anxiety is that neighborliness and random acts of kindness are rare. Our society is driven by market greed, in which the middle class—the glue of a durable society—is dissolved into rich haves and dismissed have-nots, in which homelessness lives alongside gated communities, and in which the indices of violence are everywhere on the rise. And beyond all of that, oil prices!

Into that matrix erupts the cry of those who are not so numbed that they cannot voice pain. They are the ones who refuse to accept the rat race of anxiety as normal. The narrative erupts with the imperative of the holy God, "Let them go. . . . Let them serve me." Let them change gods, let them commit acts of alternative imagination. Let them move from pain and beyond the system in which pain is the normal price of survival. Let them depart.

The exodus narrative is all about departure from the pharaonic system, in which we are kept enthralled. It is a departure to the wilderness of scarce water and flaky bread. It is a departure to an ominous mountain where the holy God who bested Pharaoh speaks ten times. In that utterance too ominous for Israel to bear, the holy God who has defeated the Egyptian gods declares an alternative existence, and Israel signs on without reservation.

- It is an alternative to defining life as production, an alternative to seething anxiety that jeopardizes the neighborhood and reduces the neighborhood to a threat;
- It is an alternative to Egyptian gods who cannot make safe and cannot make happy;
- It is an alternative to predatory coveting that will never provide enough;
- It is an alternative to antineighborliness in which neighbors are expendable others whom we may dismiss by killing, adultery, stealing, or false witness;
- It is an alternative to anxiety as a way of life that refuses Sabbath rest;
- It is an alternative of honor that specializes in fidelity to family and to land.

It is the news, from Sinai and always again, that the pharaonic enterprise among us is not legitimate and need not be the story of our life. So how to respond to the gospel news of *otherwise*? The response is to *talk the talk* of an alternative that exposes the pharaonic system among us as not legitimate but as a cruel aberration from which we may and can depart. The response is to *walk the walk* of neighborly fidelity and thereby to witness against the predatory values of our society, predatory toward children and old people and immigrants and gay people and all the others who are not well-connected "suits" on the make. So consider:

- Response to the gospel is to be a *truth-teller*, to name the ways in which our world is organized according to the gospel of greed—which is idolatry.
- Response to the gospel is to be a *hope-teller*, that the political economy can be organized differently, not man for the Sabbath but Sabbath for man, not man for the economy but the economy for men and women.

- Response to the gospel is the daily practice of *generosity, hospitality*, and *forgiveness*, the generosity that is a disruption in the chain of anxiety that creates a wee Sabbath whereby the land is enhanced. Generosity: Paul in Romans 12:8: "those who give in generosity"; hospitality: Paul in Romans 12:13: "contribute to the needs of the saints"; "practice hospitality to the stranger"; forgiveness: Paul in Romans 12:19-21: "Beloved, never avenge yourselves, but leave room for the wrath of God; for it is written, 'Vengeance is mine, I will repay, says the Lord.' No, 'if your enemies are hungry, feed them; if they are thirsty, give them something to drink; for by doing this you will heap burning coals on their heads.' Do not be overcome by evil, but overcome evil with good."

We may not underestimate such acts, as they are harbingers of alternative, as Wendell Berry says:

> I have no large solution to offer. There is, as maybe we all have noticed, a conspicuous shortage of large-scale corrections for problems that have large-scale causes. Our damages to watersheds and ecosystems will have to be corrected one farm, one forest, one acre at a time. The aftermath of a bombing has to be dealt with one corpse, one wound at a time. And so the first temptation to avoid is the call for some sort of revolution. To imagine that destructive power might be made harmless by gathering enough power to destroy it is of course perfectly futile. William Butler Yeats said as much in his poem "The Great Day":
>
> > Hurrah for revolution and more cannon shot!
> > A beggar upon horseback lashes a beggar on foot.
> > Hurrah for revolution and cannon come again!
> > The beggars have changed places, but the lash goes on.
>
> Arrogance cannot be cured by greater arrogance, or ignorance by greater ignorance. To counter the ignorant use of knowledge and power we have, I am afraid, only a proper humility, and this is laughable. But it is only partly laughable. In his political pastoral "Build Soil," as if responding to Yeats, Robert Frost has one of his rustics say,
>
> > I bid you to a one-man revolution—
> > The only revolution that is coming.[4]

Response to the gospel includes not only an immediate practice of alternative. It includes, surely, in Mosaic-prophetic horizon and surely in Calvinist tradition, a mandate to impinge upon public life in order that the social enterprise of political-economic power can be mobilized for an effective neighborhood. The mandate is given, for example, in familiar cadences:

> Is not this the fast that I choose:
>   to loose the bonds of injustice,
>   to undo the thongs of the yoke,
> to let the oppressed go free,
>   and to break every yoke?
> Is it not to share your bread with the hungry,
>   and bring the homeless poor into your house;
> when you see the naked, to cover them,
>   and not to hide yourself from your own kin? (Isa 58:6-7)

But of course in a complex urban society, face-to-face neighborliness must also take the form of policy commitments that mobilize the resources of the community for the common good. So far as we may imagine, Pharaoh had no plans for the common good. But clearly the Sinai alternative reaches beyond one-on-one practices to systemic concerns for which there is no clearer example than the "year of release" in Deuteronomy 15:1-18, a command that provides for debt cancellation for poor people. That command is rooted in exodus memory: "Remember that you were a slave in the land of Egypt, and the Lord your God redeemed you; for this reason I lay this command upon you today" (Deut 15:15). Fretheim, moreover, would be prompt to point out that this command is extrapolated even further to the Jubilee, whereby the land is rested. That provision, as well, is grounded in exodus memory:

> If any who are dependent on you become so impoverished that they sell
> themselves to you, you shall not make them serve as slaves. They shall
> remain with you as hired or bound laborers. They shall serve with you
> until the year of the jubilee. Then they and their children with them shall
> be free from your authority; they shall go back to their own family and
> return to their ancestral property. For they are my servants, whom I
> brought out of the land of Egypt; they shall not be sold as slaves are sold.
> You shall not rule over them with harshness, but shall fear your God. . . .
> For to me the people of Israel are servants; they are my servants whom I
> brought out from the land of Egypt: I am the LORD your God.
> (Lev 25:39-43, 55)

It is the exodus ethic that seeks to relieve land and people—especially the poor—from the passions of "survival" economics.

It is an obvious move to say that that response to the gospel includes policy formation concerning housing, healthcare, education, and all the contested spheres of the neighborhood. These are not "add-ons" from liberals but are the core mandates of the Sinai alternative. I understand that this is a tall order of truthful talk, of hopeful walk, of daring practice, and of policy initiatives. All of that is beyond the imagination of most congregations. Well, it is a tall order because Sinai is a tall order in a society where Pharaoh decides what is normative. Moreover, it is beyond our imagination because we have a quite shriveled imagination, having shrunk our theological hungers away from the thickness of the narrative. Thus, the primal work of ministry in response to the gospel, I submit, is to evoke the evangelical imagination of the baptized community out beyond the shriveled imagination suppressed by Pharaoh. For when our imagination catches up to the awesome holiness of Sinai, there come energy and courage for an alternative life in the world.

It occurs to me, as I conclude this reflection, that the Sinai summons is a summons to vigorous, active, constructive engagement. That kind of engagement is not usual in a settled, established church in which the "orders" of life are all given and tacitly received. Pharaoh wants passionately to have passive people who are wooed to shopping and commoditization because they are easy to administer and ready for conformity. But those who "depart" the settled conformity of Pharaoh are dangerous. It is true that when we depart the weary symmetry of Pharaoh, we do have energy. If we depart the liturgies of television, we have more time. If we truth-tell against the powers of death, we are enlivened. The work of Israel is always a departure to covenant, a journey made repeatedly. And Jesus did not say to his early disciples, "Sit." He said, "Follow." Follow into the alternative kingdom, the one we pray for, that it might be on earth as it is in heaven. Such prayers are acts of revolutionary hope, the kinds not prayed by those who have not departed.

PART II

PROPHETS

Refusal and Redescription:
Brueggemann on the Prophets

Carolyn J. Sharp

Among the dozens of books that Brueggemann has written, *The Prophetic Imagination* may be the most beloved and best known in the church. His reflections in that volume have stirred the hearts of Christian leaders and social activists for over three decades since its original publication in 1978. One suspects that it may be here, in these early musings on prophetic witness, that Brueggemann first came fully to authentic voice. Of the prophets, he has said,

> They are primarily poets who bring the world to voice outside of settled convention. While the future is implied in their discernment of the reality of God and while justice is intrinsic to their characteristic utterance, the most important aspect of their speech is their reperception of the world as the arena of God's faithful governance.[1]

We might say that this definition of the prophets could be applied to his own work in Old Testament theology, for Brueggemann himself happily operates outside of settled convention. Alert to the tensive interplay between judgment and salvation that characterizes the biblical prophetic corpus, Brueggemann does not content himself with simply reiterating the famous prophetic calls for social justice (Amos 5:24; Micah 6:8) that are so beloved in Christian tradition. Instead, taking account of all of what the prophets tell us, he articulates forcefully their refusals of idolatry, arrogance, and misguided self-reliance—sins that are no less relevant today than they were in the centuries before Christ. Brueggemann moves on to illumine for his audiences the daring ways in which the prophets redescribe reality for their people as they reach for new ways of living faithfully in a tumultuous and uncertain world.

Prophetic witness is particular and even idiosyncratic, for it must be responsive to the needs, failures, and hopes of communities struggling through specific historical moments with their God. Thus, Brueggemann's hermeneutical method of locally attentive reading is especially well suited for exposition of prophetic oracles. He insists,

> The sovereign word of YHWH is not an absolute, everywhere and always the same. It is a particular, concrete word spoken to particular persons in particular contexts, to impact persons, to impinge upon perception and awareness, to intrude upon public policy, and if possible to evoke faithful and transformed behavior. The prophetic word is not a proposition or the announcement of set truths. It is often the playful exploration and processing of insight that is not known until it is brought to precisely the right shape of expression.[2]

The prophetic word always unfolds dynamically in service of a specific cause: "No prophet ever sees things under the aspect of eternity. It is always partisan theology, always for the moment, always for the concrete community, satisfied to see only a piece of it all and to speak out of that."[3] So too Brueggemann himself is unabashedly partisan in his hermeneutics and in his theology. Brueggemann's exegesis unfolds in each instance with loving care for the particulars of his text and the needs of his audience as he understands them.

Brueggemann characteristically positions prophetic witness over against empire. "Empire" in his oeuvre is a broad metaphor signifying such things as spiritual smugness, political and social heartlessness, economic addiction to profit, and the fetishizing of technology and efficiency over human life. He sees the prophets as working to dismantle the dehumanizing and exploitative logic of imperial power, which he names in ancient Israel's context as "pharaonic" or "royal consciousness" and in contemporary terms as the "national security state." The advocacy of the prophets emboldens the oppressed to own their vulnerability. Further, it spurs believers to dare to expect an answer—from secular authorities in power and from God. The prophets' redescription of reality shows us that we may dare to hope for liberation and transformation despite the trauma that we may have known and the hopelessness that may surround us. The prophets invite us into the pathos of God. They alternately rage and grieve, thundering indictments and suffering agonies on behalf of their communities. Jeremiah, the prophet on whose book Brueggemann has spent the most interpretive attention throughout his career, suffers deeply with his people. In Isaiah, too, the prophetic figure known as the Suffering Servant embodies the anguish of his people. For Brueggemann, the pathos and dissent of the prophets may be read christologically, in the shadow of the cross:

> The cross is the ultimate metaphor of prophetic criticism because it means the end of the old consciousness that brings death on everyone. The crucifixion articulates God's odd freedom, his strange justice, and his peculiar power. . . . Without the cross, prophetic imagination will

likely be as strident and as destructive as that which it criticizes. The cross is the assurance that effective prophetic criticism is done not by an outsider but always by one who must embrace the grief, enter into the death, and know the pain of the criticized one.[4]

The prophetic imagination is for Brueggemann a means of evangelical proclamation that does not overlook the terror and grief of the marginalized, the exploited, and the forgotten, but rather stands in solidarity.

In the addresses here, Brueggemann explores layers of biblical prophetic tradition from different angles. He invites us to see the prophets as mediators standing in the liminal cultural space between ancient truth and present risk. He names the reality of exile for today's displaced persons (the poor, gays and lesbians, and others who are vulnerable) and advises that it is in practices of generosity, Sabbath rest, and prayer that we constitute the alternative community of God. He celebrates the courage of truth-tellers who walk with their people into the abyss in order to proclaim the surprise of grace. And he reminds us of a fundamental prophetic truth: notwithstanding the scheming of those who wield economic power and military aggression for their own gain, the earth and its fullness belong to God.

CHAPTER 5

Every City a Holy City:
The Holy City in Jeopardy

THERE IS IN THE BIBLE, of course, only one Holy City.[1] It is Jerusalem. The Bible, taken in one way, is a meditation on the Holy City of Jerusalem all the way from Father Abraham's offering there (Gen 14:18-20) and his near killing of his Isaac on Mount Moriah (Gen 22:2), through David's purchase and legal entitlement to the City (2 Sam 24:18-25) to the death of Jesus there, and finally the vision of a new Jerusalem in Revelation 21:1-4, where there will be no more tears. Jerusalem is the Holy City. It is holy because it is set apart by God and for God, especially loved and protected and inhabited by God. It is holy as well, however, because there reside the *priests* to make it holy, and there operate the *media experts* to say it is holy, and there are lodged all the forces of *technology, finance,* and *power* to generate the juices of life on which the countryside depends. It is clear in the ancient world that the agricultural community supported the economy of the city, but it was the city—God's natural habitat—that had a sustaining, symbiotic relationship with all the mountains to the north and all the cotton fields to the south.

I

In the Bible there is only one holy city, and it is Jerusalem. There are, however, many holy cities, and every city imagines that it is holy. Every city, every "world-class city," has its share of *priests* to make it holy. Every world-class city has its *media experts* to say it is holy. Every world-class city, not unlike Jerusalem, possesses *technology* like CNN and *finance* like the Nations Bank and *power* like Delta and Coca Cola and Home Depot to generate the juices of life—hospitals that do research, universities that serve business, and on and on. Every city puts up the bright lights, and the young come there for jobs and excitement and freedom. It is holy, the place where dwell the secrets of control and security and well-being. We speak here of Jerusalem as holy city, or at least the Old Testament does. But such talk as we conduct here is never about only Jerusalem. It is about this holy city and every holy city, each of which in its distinctive way relives the story of Jerusalem as holy city, usually learning only late, if at all, the hard lessons of Jerusalem. So I speak of *one holy city*—but you, as you read, may dream of *other holy cities.*

If we consider the failure of the Holy City of Jerusalem in the Old Testament, we quickly notice that the whole story of Jerusalem pivots around 587 BCE, about the wrenching catastrophe of that grim moment when the Babylonians came and destroyed the city where God was said to dwell. The Old Testament is mesmerized by that strange, nearly inexplicable disaster, for who would have thought that this blessed, beloved, impregnable city would be attacked and taken, leveled and reduced to silent tears? Everything in the Old Testament is about the city *going into 587* or *coming out of 587*. It is this *going into 587* and *coming out of 587* that give me my topic.

In this general topic, I take up the first, not very happy theme of *Jerusalem into 587*. Or, as I put it succinctly, "The Holy City in Jeopardy." The phrase is odd because the subject "Holy City" does not go with "jeopardy"; it should be a first property of "Holy City" to be immune to "jeopardy," a property claimed in "The Songs of Zion" (see Pss 46 and 84). Of course, that is what they thought in ancient Jerusalem and what they wanted so badly to believe. David had funded the Israelite version of the Holy City, "City of David"! It is under David's son Solomon that the city blossomed visibly with a whole new building program, supported by immense wealth made possible by international trade (1 Kgs 10:23-25). The blossoming of the city was heightened by a liturgical-ideological blossoming as well. Suddenly, all at once, this sleepy little mountain town displayed a new skyline of magnificence, and such pride as the new city took on made use of high powered adjectives: "*Holy* city, *Eternal* Jerusalem, Zion, city of our God" (see Ps 87:1-3). Growth, exuberance, wealth, happiness, extravagance, and liturgy, all without lament:

> God is in the midst of the city; it shall not be moved;
> God will help it when the morning dawns. (Ps 46:5)

> Glorious things are spoken of you,
> O city of God. (Ps 87:3)

But not jeopardy! Not risk, because the liturgies of the Holy City were saturated with the adverb "forever" (see 2 Sam 7:16; Ps 89:36-37; 1 Kgs 8:12-13). It was not even imaginable that this magnificence could ever wane or fail, or end in silent tears.

II

But of course it is my obligation—with such a theme—to report that there were those in the ancient city who looked underneath at the urban "facts on the ground" and who were not impressed by the self-congratulatory slogans and liturgies of throne and temple. We call these underneath people "prophets," and that makes them sound so fabulous. But we must think of them in the first instance, I believe, as odd voices of discernment, mostly poets and unwelcome dissenters who had a sinking feeling in their gut. Here and there they found words that unnerved the city; because they offered a shrill reminder that even slick logos do not change or nullify the facts on the ground in the city.

There were other poets who dissented. Here I will focus here on the best known, the three major prophets, Isaiah, Jeremiah, and Ezekiel. They were all based in Jerusalem, and they all looked to the destiny of the city. They all were unpersuaded by the press releases of the Jerusalem Chamber of Commerce, presided over by the king and the priests. My simple work in this discussion is to consider the *jeopardy to the Holy City* in the presentation of these three truth-tellers.

I have come to the judgment that the reason we have "three major prophets" in the Old Testament is that they are the three spokespersons for the three dominant theological traditions of the Old Testament, these traditions that correlate with the three major strands of the Pentateuch commonly called J, D, and P.[2] If this correlation between Pentateuchal tradition and prophet is correct, then what we consider is how these heavyweight traditions viewed the loud theological-ideological claims of Jerusalem and how they identified the reality of jeopardy in an urban environment that was thought to be risk free. Their work from conviction to articulation was upstream because they testified against the self-satisfied claims of the urban establishment that was supported both by the monopolistic power of the throne and by the dominant liturgical force of the temple. Against that claim made by the royal priestly establishment that they regarded as an illusion, these three voices of jeopardy had only words, images, and symbols; they were carriers of *old truth* that connected to *present risk*. I take them in turn and invite you to ponder how it is that a holy city had come under the spell of a self-congratulatory illusion, and how it is that *old truth* that connects to *present risk* can be uttered in ways that count as truth to which attention must be paid.

III

I begin with Isaiah, first, best known, and best loved of the major prophets. He is a well-connected urban presence who lived easily amid power and who believed that temple and monarchy were divine gifts that must be relished. He is not easily a dissenter, and one can imagine that he was welcomed and at ease at the tables of the rich and powerful. He is one termed by Robert Wilson as a "central prophet," meaning that he is located inside the power structure.[3]

Isaiah has drunk deeply at the wells of tradition. He is schooled in and accepts Davidic claims of power and legitimacy. If, moreover, we assume that the David traditions in the Old Testament are correlated to the Abraham traditions, as seemed likely, then we may conclude that Isaiah was especially attuned to the unconditional promises that God had made to Abraham and to David, that God's faithful sustenance of the Jerusalem establishment would be reliable.[4] (This leads me to the judgment that Isaiah is attuned to what we term the *J tradition* of the Pentateuch, which understood that Jerusalem is a decisive fixture in the shape of the world as God intends it.)

The ongoing tradition of Isaiah after his death, moreover, continued to unfold with hope and promise for the Holy City, for it is the Isaiah tradition that announces:

> Comfort, O comfort my people,
>> says your God.
> Speak tenderly to Jerusalem,
>> and cry to her
> that she has served her term,
>> that her penalty is paid,
> that she has received from the LORD's hand
>> double for all her sins. (Isa 40:1-2)[5]

It is the same tradition, eventually, that offers lyrical hope:

> But be glad and rejoice forever
>> in what I am creating;
> for I am about to create Jerusalem as a joy,
>> and its people as a delight.
> I will rejoice in Jerusalem,
>> and delight in my people;
> no more shall the sound of weeping be heard in it,
>> or the cry of distress. (Isa 65:18-19)

> As a mother comforts her child,
>> so I will comfort you;
>> you shall be comforted in Jerusalem. (Isa 66:13)

So here is this poet in the midst of urban illusion, stretched between *old promises* that are very sure and *new hopes* that are very powerful.

We catch him in between old promises and new hopes, in a moment of terrible anguish, a sharp moment of recognition when the prophet senses that for all the old promises and for all the new hopes, this is a moment that requires a different utterance. It is an utterance that he does not want to speak, but he is sure of it even if it is a minority report in the midst of urban self-congratulations, so sure is he that he takes it as God's word upon the Holy City.

Isaiah takes a deep breath. The first word he utters, in Isaiah 5:8, is "woe." (It is too bad the NRSV translates "ah," because it is not "ah"; it is "woe.") "Woe" is a word whereby the Bible invites us in imagination to death, to a funeral. "Woe" is deep grief for trouble coming that is in the cards and that cannot be avoided. *Death* in the *Holy City* . . . a profound oxymoron. It was a very difficult word for Isaiah to utter in 5:8 because the very utterance created an aura of jeopardy that was unwelcome in the Holy City and that he himself surely did not relish. It was a difficult syllable to utter, but once he said "woe" in 5:8, he repeated it six times: in 5:11; 5:18; 5:20; 5:21; and 5:22. And for good measure, in 10:1. All together *seven* times "woe," a number of completeness for the demise of Jerusalem, the stench of death, the trace of loss in this city where the proponents are still singing:

> God is in the midst of the city; it shall not be moved;
> God will help it when the morning dawns. (Ps 46:5)

No doubt Isaiah would rather have joined that chorus. But he knows better. He breathed hard and swallowed deep to arrive at "woe," that the Holy City is under threat of death.

Once he had said "woe" in 5:8, then he had to finish the section of poetry and complete the seven. What is it that would bring wholesale jeopardy on a city so well loved and guaranteed by God? Well, this:

> Woe to you who join house to house,
>   who add field to field,
> until there is room for no one but you,
>   and you are left to live alone
>   in the midst of the land! (Isa 5:8)

Woe to those who join house to house. Woe to those who add field to field. Woe to those who chase more property and more wealth and more real estate. Woe to those who keep buying up large tracts of land and getting bigger houses, so that there is no room for the neighbors and so no neighborhood and so to live alone, isolated, privatized, "safe and secure from all alarms." The prophet comments on the wild pursuit of private economic gain at the expense of the community, wherein some have so much that they can drive out the small, vulnerable people. And that, says Isaiah "will bring death to the city." In verse 8, he doesn't even mention YHWH. The trouble will not be by divine intervention but by the inescapable processes of urban self-destruction.

To be sure, he reinforces the woe of verse 8 in verse 9 by mention of the divine name:

> The LORD of hosts has sworn in my hearing:
> Surely many houses shall be desolate,
>> large and beautiful houses, without inhabitant. (Isa 5:9)

Something bad will happen to the many houses, to the big houses, to the beautiful houses, to the many beautiful houses that will be deserted, left empty, abandoned—no longer sustainable. Because, in the purview of the poet, big houses, big buildings, big landgrabs at the expense of the others are unsustainable and will bring down the whole business.

And then in verse 10, as an addendum:

> For ten acres of vineyard shall yield but one bath,
>> and a homer of seed shall yield a mere ephah. (Isa 5:10)

It will take ten acres of vineyard to produce a modest supply of wine. The land simply will not produce, and we will not, as we say on the farm, "get our seed back." The connection between the destruction in verse 9 and the agricultural crisis in verse 10 is not obvious. Apparently the poet means that, when people live in urban life, no longer related to or aware of the slow requirements of food production, when they imagine that extravagant food is simply brought out of the kitchen without thought to the wonder of growth, then the land will surely be neglected and turned over to bureaucratic agribusiness. The land will, says Isaiah, simply conduct a sit-down strike and refuse to produce under those circumstances.

Isaiah saw the big ones eating the little ones; he knew that the city, from Solomon on, was creating an unbearable economic inequity that could only end in failure and alienation. Let us imagine from Isaiah that the jeopardy of the city is caused by *commoditization*, the reduction of daily life to things, to buying and selling and getting and having and owning and eating, with the emerging impression that everything is purchasable, everything is for sale, everyone is a "thing"—no more people, because you are alone in the land. (This is the same misperception in 1 Kgs 21, concerning Naboth's vineyard, wherein a treasured inheritance is reduced to a commodity.) And if all is commodity, then *acquisitiveness* is the order of the day; monopoly is not just a game but also a strategy and an urban ideology celebrating the ambitious ones who can get the most. Jeopardy for the city is rooted in the misperception that the city is a place to play at monopoly, because what emerges in such a practice is "woe." And verse 13 adds, moreover, an ominous "therefore":

> Therefore my people go into exile without knowledge;
> their nobles are dying of hunger,
>> and their multitude is parched with thirst. (Isa 5:13)

Alas!

IV

The second major prophet I cite is Jeremiah, a voice very different from that of Isaiah. Jeremiah lived a century after Isaiah, thus very close to the crisis of 587. For many reasons, his bubble-piercing word is more poignant than that of Isaiah. He is rooted differently from Isaiah, from the village and not the city. He is identified as "from the priests of Anathoth" (1:1), Anathoth being a village north of Jerusalem, across the boundary of Judah in the tribe of Benjamin.[6] Thus, he is something of an outsider to the ethos of Jerusalem. There is, however, another factor that makes Jeremiah even more of an outsider to Jerusalem. His connection to the "priests of Anathoth" links him to Abiathar, a priest of David who disapproved of Solomon and who was, perforce, banished by Solomon to his village of Anathoth (1 Kgs 2:26-27; see 1 Sam 2:33). Jeremiah's rootage is in a community that had, for the last four hundred years, disapproved of Solomon and the entire royal program of global economy and self-aggrandizement in Jerusalem.

More than that, there is reason to think that Jeremiah and his family of priests had been studying the book of Deuteronomy for a very long time. There is no doubt that Jeremiah is deeply linked to the subcommunity that fostered and prized the book of Deuteronomy and its ongoing tradition.[7] And if we know the book of Deuteronomy, then we know that, of all of the literature of the Old Testament, it is Deuteronomy that stays closest to Moses, to Sinai, and to the torah; this tradition believes not in unconditional promises but in covenant blessings that are given to covenant-keepers. Jeremiah is unlike Isaiah and remote from the promises of the J tradition, and conversely deep into the commandments of the D tradition, the Deuteronomic tradition.[8] It is looking for four hundred years at the city of Jerusalem from the village of Anathoth through the lens of the Deuteronomic torah that produces the tradition of Jeremiah. And that tradition has known—forever—that a city that imagines itself, as did Jerusalem, to be autonomous and self-referential and self-serving is headed for a fall.

The book of Jeremiah stays with the city into 587 and out beyond 587. In the end, the book of Jeremiah is lyrical about the restoration of Jerusalem but not ever as buoyant as the voice of Isaiah. In Jeremiah the coming future is more modest. Jeremiah thinks of the future as a remnant of scroll-people who study, thus a vision of what became Judaism. Jeremiah goes so far, in fact, to be a part of that company that meditate on the torah "day and night," because for all of the imagined autonomy of the city, says he, it is not autonomous. The torah is in, with, and under the city, and there can be no viable city apart from a torah. Jeremiah champions the tradition of *Moses* while Isaiah is celebrating *David* and, perhaps, *Abraham*.

But think what it means for this village guy in the city to study torah day and night.

If you spend four hundred years leafing through the book of Deuteronomy, it will inevitably fall open to *chapter 15*, with the Bible's most radical teaching, that of the year of release. This is a command from Moses that says, in an economy where the poor must work their debts off, no poor person, no matter how much indebted, will need to work off the debt for more than six years. The provision insists that the economy must be made to serve the community, and the foremost thought on Moses' mind is to prevent the formation of a permanent underclass in Israel, the kind of underclass that had been forced, in Egypt, into slavery (see Gen 47:13-26).

If you spend four hundred years leafing through the book of Deuteronomy, you will come eventually to 17:14-20, the only commandment of Moses pertaining to kingship. There it is provided that kings—read "urban managers of the economy"—must not collect horses and chariots or silver and gold or wives. Power of a public dimension is not for self-aggrandizement! This commandment proposes as an alternative to acquisitiveness the practice of the study of the torah day and night and thereby to be reminded of solidarity with others in the community.

And just past that, we come to a series of little commands from Moses:

> When you reap your harvest in your field and forget a sheaf in the field,
> you shall not go back to get it; it shall be left for the alien, the orphan,
> and the widow, so that the LORD your God may bless you in all your
> undertakings. When you beat your olive trees, do not strip what is left; it
> shall be for the alien, the orphan, and the widow. When you gather the
> grapes of your vineyard, do not glean what is left; it shall be for the alien,
> the orphan, and the widow. Remember that you were a slave in the land
> of Egypt; therefore I am commanding you to do this. (Deut 24:19-22)

The force of the exodus memory looms large for this villager, just when the city was into the pathology of amnesia. Jeremiah, and every careful reader of Deuteronomy, has noticed the mantra "widow, orphan, alien" . . . "widow, orphan, illegal immigrant," a recurring slogan to refer to the most vulnerable and exposed members in a patriarchal economy (see Deut 14:29; 16:14). This commandment, designed for a modest agrarian economy, is as Frank Crüsemann says, an early "social safety net" whereby the community must attend to all of the neighbors, the ones often invisible, the ones without social power, the ones without social utility who will contribute nothing of their own to the community's well being.[9]

All these teachings are very old in Israel. It was clear to Jeremiah that the city had forgotten the most elemental, nonnegotiable aspects of covenant. And so Jeremiah had to go public. He did so, we are told, as he occupied the public square in Jerusalem with his famous "sermon" in chapter 7:

> For if you truly amend your ways and your doings, if you truly act justly
> one with another, if you do not oppress *the alien*, the *orphan*, and *the
> widow*, or shed innocent blood in this place, and if you do not go after

other gods to your own hurt, then I will dwell with you in this place, in
the land that I gave of old to your ancestors forever and ever. (Jer 7:5-7)

This remarkable, quite representative, speech of Jeremiah places a weighty conditional "if" over the Holy City. In fact, four *ifs* (three in Hebrew) yield a *then*:
"then I will dwell with you." The condition of YHWH's presence, the condition
of the viability of the city, is to act justly in terms of "widow, orphan, and alien."
What an incredible interruption in the illusion of the city sponsored by Solomon,
a city that was in the habit of thinking that you could leave some behind and
ignore some and have a quota of discarded, useless people and yet have a good
city.

And then comes this starchy voice of torah from an ancient village that says,
"No. No, you cannot discard some and have a viable city." The starchy "if" of
prose is matched in lively poetry in Jeremiah:

> For scoundrels are found among my people;
> > they take over the goods of others.
> Like fowlers they set a trap;
> > they catch human beings.
> Like a cage full of birds,
> > their houses are full of treachery;
> therefore they have become great and rich,
> > they have grown fat and sleek.
> They know no limits in deeds of wickedness;
> > they do not judge with justice
> the cause of the *orphan*, to make it prosper,
> > and they do not defend the rights of the *needy*. (Jer 5:26-28)

The "scoundrels" are people the city judges to be honorable. They are scoundrels
because they exclude and conduct antineighborly policy that makes neighborhood
impossible. The prophet understands very well that "deeds of wickedness" are not
just little ugly acts; they are, rather, great policy commitments about taxes and
mortgages and rents and loans and interests and collateral—all legal, all commonly accepted, all ways of becoming "great and rich and fat and sleek." It is the
dominant narrative of most holy cities that such practices leave some behind. In
such an environment, the *grossly entitled* do not remember the neighbor who is
leanly entitled. And the entitlements of schools and housing and jobs and police
protection and healthcare of the vulnerable, all in the gift of the city, are siphoned
off in greed that destroys the weak neighbor.

And then God says in verse 29:

> Shall I not punish them for these things?
> > says the LORD,

and shall I not bring retribution
on a nation such as this? (Jer 5:29)

The utterance of God is only a question, not a verdict. It is a question designed
to haunt. Shall I not punish? What would you think if you were God? Well, if
you were the high God of urban capitalism you might say, as Secretary O'Neill
said recently when Enron collapsed: "That's the beauty of the system. Companies come and companies go."[10] Blessed be the name of the company! But if you
are *the curmudgeonly God of Deuteronomy* you might answer differently. You
might say, "Yes, I must punish, because these are my people, and they are not
available for such antineighborly acts." And so the haunting question of Jeremiah lingered over the Holy City in its antineighborliness until 587; and then the
answer came. How astonishing, to attribute the loss of the city to maltreatment
of widows and orphans! More than that, the text persists and the question keeps
sounding: shall I not punish? And we answer tentatively to acknowledge that the
city is in jeopardy.

VI

The third of the major prophets, the one least known and least read among us, is
Ezekiel. He is least known because Reformed people of the affluent sort do not
talk much about holiness, and certainly liberals do not talk much about holiness.
Ezekiel is said to be a priest (1:3). Of that identity we may say two things. First,
Ezekiel clearly belongs with and is a participant in the emerging group of Aaro-
nide priests, said to be rooted in Zadok, who emerged as the dominant holy interpreters of Jerusalem after there was no king.[11] These are the "big steeple priests"
of Judaism in the sixth century, who left as their legacy the capacity to classify
and protect sacerdotal things because they believed that a rightly ordered liturgy
created a zone of coherence in a world that is otherwise incoherent and chaotic.
And, indeed, that is the proper, generative function of ordered worship, so that
the reality of good worship is a contrast and alternative to the shabbily disordered
world that is out of control and beyond recall. As you may know, this priestly
group gave us the book of Leviticus, with its endless distinctions about things holy
and profane, clean and unclean (see Ezek 22:26). And while we may lose patience
with the punctiliousness of Leviticus, intentional holiness is not to be mocked. We
will understand *Ezekiel* in his links to *Leviticus* only if we contrast it to *Jeremiah*
with his links to *Deuteronomy*. In the Pentateuch, Leviticus and Deuteronomy
represent two dominant options for Judaism; whereas Deuteronomy is fundamentally concerned with civic communal justice, Leviticus concerns rightly ordered
religious matters with only slight attention to economic issues. It is the argument
of this tradition that the community (and the city) will be secure only if there is a
zone of holiness at its center.

On that basis I comment on Ezekiel 8 as a case study in holiness. Ezekiel reports that God addressed him and that God took him on a tour of the Jerusalem temple, likely in 593, the sixth year of Jehoiachin's exile (8:1). In his dismay, Ezekiel reports what he saw in the Jerusalem temple:

> He said to me, "Go in, and see the vile abominations that they are committing here." So I went in and looked; there, portrayed on the wall all around, were all kinds of creeping things, and loathsome animals, and all the idols of the house of Israel. (Ezek 8:9-10)

> Then he brought me to the entrance of the north gate of the house of the LORD; women were sitting there weeping for Tammuz. Then he said to me, "Have you seen this, O mortal? You will see still greater abominations than these." (Ezek 8:14-15)

Ezekiel uses the term "abomination." The term is the stringent language of the Old Testament for ritually defiling practices that render a place unworthy of God. In priestly horizon, YHWH cannot stay in an impure place. And now the holy temple became uninhabitable by the holy God. God's proper place in the Jerusalem temple is absent of God's own self. The affront to God that Ezekiel saw in the temple was of "creeping things and loathsome animals" (those long since ruled out by Levitical law); and in the liturgies addressed to Tammuz, he saw liturgies of weeping addressed to a foreign God. The temple has become a place from which God must flee, or God's own holiness will be diminished. In the next two chapters, Ezekiel narrates the way in which the "glory of YHWH" flies away from the Holy City to exile in Babylon (see Ezek 10:9-22). Ezekiel of course knows that when the glory departs, the city can no longer imagine itself as "world class" and can no longer perform according to its reputation. It is left empty of what matters.

Ezekiel's devastating characterization concerns a city that has forfeited holiness because of a mindless embrace of shameless *pornography*. I understand that the use of the term "pornography" is problematic because it conjures up sex shops and all of that smut, the critique of which gives aid and comfort to good people like us. But of course that is what I mean—sex shops and loaded magazine racks and unbelievable internet exposés and young women pressed into prostitution, and so on. There is enough affront in the rawness of it, but we must not stop there. We must go on to notice that pornography bespeaks an entire culture that has lost its sense of shame and that can settle for mindless exploitation, abuse, and violence that turns into big bucks. The term signifies a profound loss of human dignity, a pursuit of cash from the use of human persons and the attempt to dispel what is most hidden and mysterious and precious in human personhood and in human interaction.

Pornography, as Ezekiel condemns it, is not just distortion in sexuality; it is a matching distortion in economics in which it is imagined that the whole world is manipulatable for use, as though unutterable respect for and unimaginable awe before God's giftedness in creation has evaporated, as though urban culture has "exchanged the glory of the immortal God for images resembling a mortal human being or birds or four-footed animals or reptiles" (Rom 1:23). A society cannot be sustained in such shamelessness because the infrastructure of dignity and respect will be overcome by a diminishing kind of violence. I think, moreover, that we must reflect seriously on how it is that *pornography* is deeply connected to *unbridled militarism*, with its byproduct of torture and *uncontrolled market economics*, all of which serve together in cheapening trivialization and exploitation. Eventually a culture of pornography becomes craven; it finds expression in limitless market, equally limitless sports, and an endless voyeurism of a thousand extremeties. The city is in jeopardy when the body politic has lost its will and capacity for self-criticism and self-transcendence. Ezekiel could think of no more effective way to chronicle the demise of the city than the narrative of God's departure when pornography has overwhelmed generative imagination:

> Then the glory of the LORD went out from the threshold of the house and stopped above the cherubim. The cherubim lifted up their wings and rose up from the earth in my sight as they went out with the wheels beside them. They stopped at the entrance of the east gate of the house of the LORD; and the glory of the God of Israel was above them. (Ezek 10:18-19)

VII

These several traditions that I have traced in very different idioms bespeak a visible jeopardy that has a deep theological dimension.

The great traditions of the Pentateuch can be distinguished in their expectations and articulations:

- J is designed to celebrate the *great promises* to Abraham and David;
- D is designed to insist on *torah imperatives*;
- P is designed to sort out the close distinctions of *holiness and purity*.

The great traditions of the major prophets extrapolate from pentateuchal traditions to diagnose the jeopardy of the Holy City:

- Isaiah in his denunciation of *acquisitive commoditization* as he probes the great urban promises and eventually must say "woe":

> Ah, you who join house to house,
> who add field to field,

> until there is room for no one but you,
>> and you are left to live alone
>> in the midst of the land! (Isa 5:8)

- Jeremiah in his meditation on Deuteronomic torah and his acute awareness of *exclusionary antineighborliness*:

> They have grown fat and sleek.
> They know no limits in deeds of wickedness;
>> they do not judge with justice
> the cause of the orphan, to make it prosper,
>> and they do not defend the rights of the needy. (Jer 5:28)

- Ezekiel in his pondering of priestly holiness from Leviticus, and his abhorrence at *life-emptying pornography*:

> So I went in and looked; there, portrayed on the wall all around, were all kinds of creeping things, and loathsome animals, and all the idols of the house of Israel. (Ezek 8:10)

This is quite a triad: *acquisitive commoditization, exclusionary antineighborliness, life-emptying pornography*!

No wonder, in prophetic purview, that the city failed. There came the "woe" to visibility, much weeping, and then, awed, bewildered, painful silence.

The texts persist. The prophetic tradition continues:

- with Isaiah: there can be a human economics instead of acquisitive commoditization;
- with Jeremiah: there can be a neighborly engagement instead of exclusion with some left behind;
- with Ezekiel: There can be holiness about the mystery of life with no wish for pornography.

The options persist. The jeopardy persists as well. And we are left to answer concerning our own holy city.

CHAPTER 6

Every City a Holy City:
The City of Possibility

I

THE DIRE OPTION concerning Jerusalem announced by the great prophets—Isaiah, Jeremiah, and Ezekiel—came to fruition.[1] The city did fail. The visible reason for failure was the irresistible force of Babylon. Some said, of course, that the failure was because of weak leadership on the throne. Some said, remarkably enough, that the imperial sack of Jerusalem was at the behest of YHWH. Among the ones who said that of YHWH, some said YHWH was angry. Others said it was due to YHWH's neglect and negligence. But they all made a connection between *the truth of YHWH* and *the failure of the city*. Such a connection is an act of prophetic imagination that one can never demonstrate.

Whatever else one may say by way of theological imagination or insight, the fact on the ground is that the city had failed. Whatever the interpretation, it was unmistakable that the city fell and had failed. The facts on the ground are incontrovertible. The city of preeminence and promise, the one founded by David, enhanced by Solomon, and saved by Isaiah, was finished. The city celebrated in song and liturgy was terminated. They said it could not happen here, and then it did! The word writ large in the feverish dismay of Israel is the verdict given to Ezekiel, "The city has fallen" (Ezek 33:21). It happens to cities—Gary, East St. Louis, Sarajevo, Youngstown—but surely not here, not in Israel, not in David's city. Yet it happened! It happens to holy cities!

And then a pause! A loss of breath, a rush of reality. An emptiness, a wistfulness, a yearning, a blink of dislocation, a shudder of dismay. The grip of anxiety, and then long-term grief. And then empty silence, silent emptiness:

> How lonely sits the city
> that once was full of people!
> How like a widow she has become,
> she that was great among the nations!
> She that was a princess among the provinces
> has become a vassal.
>
> . . . .
>
> Zion stretches out her hands,
> but there is no one to comfort her;
> the LORD has commanded against Jacob
> that his neighbors should become his foes;
> Jerusalem has become
> a filthy thing among them. (Lam 1:1, 17)

It happened in Jerusalem. What an oxymoron! "Israel silent, silent Israel." Because Israel will not keep silent. Israel had learned, long before contemporary feminists, that silence kills:

> I was silent and still.
> I held my peace to no avail;
> my distress grew worse,
> my heart became hot within me. (Ps 39:2-3)

In response to the stillness of failure, the voices of Israel rallied. They had to speak. Dislocation required speech. God granted speech. It was like 9/11: In the time after 587, everyone who could had to speak. Every poet, every pastor, every prophet, every public figure was summoned in dread to voice something.

The aftermath of 587 features a profound cacophony of voices in ancient Israel. The crisis required comment.[2] And among the commentators came our three great prophets, Isaiah, Jeremiah, and Ezekiel. The book of Isaiah had tailed off with the words of Hezekiah in the end of chapter 39 in anticipation of exile: "Then Hezekiah said to Isaiah, 'The word of the LORD that you have spoken is good.' For he thought, 'There will be peace and security in my days'" (Isa 39:8).

The book of Jeremiah had gone silent after the letters to the exile, anticipating a long exile without prospect of homecoming:

> Thus says the LORD of hosts, the God of Israel, to all the exiles whom
> I have sent into exile from Jerusalem to Babylon: Build houses and live
> in them; plant gardens and eat what they produce. Take wives and have
> sons and daughters; take wives for your sons, and give your daughters in
> marriage, that they may bear sons and daughters; multiply there, and do
> not decrease. (Jer 29:4-6)

And Ezekiel had ended in a divine silencing, no longer permitted to speak: "I will make your tongue cling to the roof of your mouth, so that you shall be speechless and unable to reprove them; for they are a rebellious house" (Ezek 3:25-26). Only at 24:27 is that silencing at last reversed. But until then, silence. All three prophets employed silence to match failure.

And then, all three, in different voices, must move on to speak the future of the failed city. Their capacity to speak and so extend the literary corpus in each case is a sign and permit that *there is more* for the city. The city will not end in the deep dysfunction of 587. There is more, because the God who leveled the city is the God who makes promises. It is those promises, outrageously against circumstance, that are my concern here. It is no small matter to trust a promise, for a promise is simply a word uttered. If trustworthy, the promise has durability because the one who speaks is "as good as his word" (see Isa 40:8; 55:10-11). But notice that a promise over a city is an odd mix of categories, because promise bespeaks intimate speaking and listening, a deep relational matter that depends on fidelity. In contrast, a city is bricks and mortar and traffic, banks and media, police protection and garbage pickup, all marked by competence or incompetence, by money and power and effectiveness. In such a mix of intense busyness, a promise is an odd ingredient.

If, however, we are to speak faithwise of the city, the promise becomes a defining ingredient, even if an odd ingredient. And that, of course, is exactly what is claimed for Jerusalem, the Holy City gone shabby and incompetent. The divine promise is uttered over the city by the one who is "as good as his word," and therefore the city failed is a city still with possibilities. It was a daring act of imagination for these poets to interface *promise* and *city*. And now, on the basis of their daring, we commit a second daring act, an act of extrapolation, to say that like Jerusalem, *every city as a holy city is under promise*. The city cannot be understood with a future, moreover, unless we entertain the conviction that precisely in such a *place* as a city the Creator of heaven and earth has promises to enact that are being guaranteed by the vigilant fidelity of the promise-keeper. That is why faith dares to speak of "a new Jerusalem," and by daring extension a new Atlanta, a new Prague, a new Johannesburg.

II

The book of Isaiah, in its final form, is about the Holy City of Jerusalem being re-uttered and reimagined under promise. The book of Isaiah traces the demise of the city—as we have suggested on the basis of *acquisitive commoditization*—until chapter 39. In that chapter the prophet Isaiah declared to the good King Hezekiah that the city would fall into the hands of Babylon:

Hear the word of the LORD of hosts: Days are coming when all that is in your house, and that which your ancestors have stored up until this day,

shall be carried to Babylon; nothing shall be left, says the Lord. Some
of your own sons who are born to you shall be taken away; they shall be
eunuchs in the palace of the king of Babylon (Isa 39:5-7).

And it did indeed fall into Babylonian hands.

It did, and the book of Isaiah waited two hundred years for the next word
to sound, until finally by the stirring of heaven in new resolve the good word of
comfort would be delivered to the city for which there was "none to comfort"
(Lam 1:2):

> Comfort, O comfort my people,
>   says your God.
> Speak tenderly to Jerusalem,
>   and cry to her
> that she has served her term,
>   that her penalty is paid,
> that she has received from the Lord's hand
>   double for all her sins. (Isa 40:1-2)

The poetry following chapter 40 anticipates that the Jewish exiles, long absent
from the city, would come home in triumph. YHWH, long exiled from the city,
would come back in splendor, and "all flesh" would see the wondrous return of
people and God. The city would prosper; the walls would dance with delight. The
desert would bloom. Creation would flourish, and the city, as crown of creation,
would flourish above all.

Of course, in fact it was not so easy or so grand. The economy could not
match the poetry. The politics became disputatious, and even the returned God
received only a small and modest temple. Rebuilding cities is slow, hard, contentious work that requires imagination and vision in order to know where to put
the streets and how to renovate the temple in order to secure divine presence yet
again. Or said another way, rebuilding cities requires promises that are made by
a trustworthy promise-maker. And that in turn depends on a *compelling poet*
who knows what comes next and why.

That poet, in this Holy City, showed up in Isaiah 65. He summoned Jerusalem away from petty dispute to large vision; he called away from despair that
issued in private dreams to a large public hope, as large as the words he could
imagine:

> For I am about to create new heavens
>   and a new earth;
> the former things shall not be remembered
>   or come to mind.
> But be glad and rejoice forever

> in what I am creating;
> for I am about to create Jerusalem as a joy,
>   and its people as a delight.
> I will rejoice in Jerusalem,
>   and delight in my people. (Isa 65:17-19)

Utterly new! Not a rearrangement of what is old, not a replication of what was with the same old patterns of dysfunction. If the old city had failed because of endemic *acquisitiveness* and *the rash pursuit of commodity*, then the new city must not be about acquisitiveness and commodity. It must, rather, be an infrastructure that focuses on the protection of the unprotected and valuing of the unvalued.

Among the sounds of the city are always cries of distress and the weeping of the exposed and forgotten. And now this poet promises:

> No more shall the sound of weeping be heard in it,
>   or the cry of distress. (Isa 65:19)

Imagine a city where the unprotected and devalued no longer lived daily in distress and vulnerability.

So who are the unprotected and unvalued? For starters, the very young who are not noticed and the very old who are forgotten. We take them as representative of the nonproductive, about whom the poet says:

> No more shall there be in it
>   an infant that lives but a few days,
>   or an old person who does not live out a lifetime;
> for one who dies at a hundred years will be considered a youth,
>   and one who falls short of a hundred will be considered accursed.
>   (Isa 65:20)

Think of that! No more infant mortality, because there will be good family services and good medical care. A caring policy of public money, public institutions, and public attentiveness. As for babies, so for the aged, who will not die of neglect. They will be well cared for, to live out a long life of dignity and well being, so that even the undeserving will live to be a hundred, and that in a culture of short lifetimes.

Quite clearly the poet envisions an infrastructure that values those who contribute nothing to the economy; the economic future of the vulnerable will be secure.

> They shall build houses and inhabit them;
>   they shall plant vineyards and eat their fruit.
> They shall not build and another inhabit;
>   they shall not plant and another eat;

> for like the days of a tree shall the days of my people be,
>> and my chosen shall long enjoy the work of their hands. (Isa 65:21-22)

There will be adequate housing, guaranteed by adequate housing policy. The vulnerable will not lose their houses by urban development or the right of eminent domain; they will not be taxed out of them or scammed out of them; security and well being will last long after one's productiveness has ceased.

In verse 23 the poet returns from the old to the young, here to the unborn. Since the curse of Genesis 3, Israel has known that birthing babies is hazardous and the whole process of pregnancy and labor is dangerous. That beginning point of life is a sign of how skewed life in the world has become. And now, in one poetic verse, the curse of Genesis 3 is lifted. The city and all of its inhabitants can now expect that from birth on life will be wondrously under blessing from God, blessing of well being willed by God, given through good administration:

> They shall not labor in vain,
>> or bear children for calamity;
> for they shall be offspring blessed by the LORD—
>> and their descendants as well. (Isa 65:23)

The last two verses of the poem offer an astonishing vista. In verse 24 it is promised that God will be present in the renovated city, God's power for life and well being fully invested, and this after God had had to flee the unbearable place the city had become. God will not only be present but also remarkably attentive, like a mother who can anticipate every need of the child:

> Before they call I will answer,
>> while they are yet speaking I will hear. (Isa 65:24)

The city will be a place of common well-being because it has become an acceptable habitation for the holy God.

Finally, the poet takes up the environmental crisis and imagines a creation sustained in a new harmony:

> The wolf and the lamb shall feed together,
>> the lion shall eat straw like the ox;
>> but the serpent—its food shall be dust!
> They shall not hurt or destroy
>> on all my holy mountain,
>>> says the LORD. (Isa 65:25)

No hurting, no exploitation, no acquisitiveness, no destruction, no violence, because the city is reordered to make such negations unnecessary.

Of course, this is only poetry with a little concluding marker, "says the LORD" (v. 25). But think what the city will become without summoning poetry! And think where generative poetry could have resonance. And think who it is that can imagine the city new and humane. The city may now bet its future on the book of Isaiah, a book that in the end is a long poem about Jerusalem. Near its conclusion, the book of Isaiah anticipates of the city:

> For thus says the LORD:
> I will extend prosperity to her like a river,
>   and the wealth of the nations like an overflowing stream;
> and you shall nurse and be carried on her arm,
>   and dandled on her knees.
> As a mother comforts her child,
>   so I will comfort you;
>   you shall be comforted in Jerusalem. (Isa 66:12-13)

A mothered city! Wrought by a poet! The poem only awaits concrete enactment, a deed that is utterly doable.

III

The long book of Isaiah envelops the reality of the Babylonian threat. The long book of Jeremiah sits in the midst of that very same threat, watching in detail while the holy city is dismantled. Jeremiah, sent by YHWH, stood desperately against the ideology of the Holy City that imagined it could do whatever it wanted. Against that illusion, the prophet had exposed the city as a fraud:

> For from the least to the greatest of them,
>   everyone is greedy for unjust gain;
> and from prophet to priest,
>   everyone deals falsely.
> They have treated the wound of my people carelessly,
>   saying, "Peace, peace," when there is no peace.
> They acted shamefully, they committed abomination;
>   yet they were not ashamed,
>   they did not know how to blush.
> Therefore they shall fall among those who fall;
>   at the time that I punish them, they shall be overthrown,
>   says the LORD. (Jer 6:13-15)

The prophet characterizes a city so busy with itself that it is no longer capable of critical reflection on its cynical, rapacious operation. The poet anticipates big trouble, and then in a prose voice details the loss of the city:

> In the fifth month, on the tenth day of the month—which was the nine-
> teenth year of King Nebuchadrezzar, king of Babylon—Nebuzaradan,
> the captain of the bodyguard who served the king of Babylon, entered
> Jerusalem. He burned the house of the LORD, the king's house, and all
> the houses of Jerusalem; every great house he burned down. All the army
> of the Chaldeans, who were with the captain of the guard, broke down
> all the walls around Jerusalem. . . .
>
> The pillars of bronze that were in the house of the LORD, and the
> stands and the bronze sea that were in the house of the LORD, the Chal-
> deans broke in pieces, and carried all the bronze to Babylon. They took
> away the pots, the shovels, the snuffers, the basins, the ladles, and all
> the vessels of bronze used in the temple service. The captain of the guard
> took away the small bowls also, the firepans, the basins, the pots, the
> lampstands, the ladles, and the bowls for libation, both those of gold and
> those of silver. (Jer 52:12-14, 17-19)

Everything lost, confiscated, usurped by alien powers. Such a silence! Such an
unbearable silence, designed to match the unspeakable demise of the Holy City.
They said it could not happen here . . . and then!

This prophetic tradition broods, and brooding will not give in to the inescapable fact of the failed city. Through a long silence, YHWH, the destroyer of the
failed Holy City, speaks yet again:

> For surely I know the plans I have for you, says the LORD, plans for your
> welfare and not for harm, to give you a future with hope. Then when
> you call upon me and come and pray to me, I will hear you. When you
> search for me, you will find me; if you seek me with all your heart, I
> will let you find me, says the LORD, and I will restore your fortunes and
> gather you from all the nations and all the places where I have driven
> you, says the LORD, and I will bring you back to the place from which I
> sent you into exile. (Jer 29:11-14)

YHWH still has resolve. And out of that resolve for newness and restoration
rooted in YHWH's own heart, Jeremiah manages two exquisite chapters of new
possibility (chapters 30–31). The city had been lost, we have seen in chapter 5,
because of the absence of neighborliness.

And now the poet speaks of a city beyond failure. Of all of these rich texts,
I have selected one of the most familiar, that of the new covenant in Jeremiah
31:31-34. At the outset we must clear up a deep misunderstanding. You know
how the text begins: "The days are surely coming, says the LORD, when I will

make a new covenant with the house of Israel and the house of Judah" (Jer 31:31). The phrase "new covenant" got translated into *novum testamentum* in the Latin, and so Christians readily heard it as referring to the New Testament of Jesus and the early church. This odd misreading, moreover, was taken up in Hebrews 8:8-12, where the whole of the passage of Jeremiah is quoted, after which the writer says dismissively: "In speaking of 'a new covenant,' he has made the first one obsolete. And what is obsolete and growing old will soon disappear" (Heb 8:13).

At the outset we Christians must be clear that the remarkable passage in Jeremiah 31:31-34 is not about Jesus or the Christian faith or the supersession of Jewishness. Rather, it is a newness promised by YHWH precisely to the house of Israel and to the house of Judah. That is, uttered in the sixth century, the text asserts YHWH's resolve to begin again with this failed people, this time to make it new and to make it right. Thus the text is about the end of exile, the homecoming of YHWH's people, and the restoration of a blessed life in the land and in the city.

I will here comment on only two aspects of this wondrous promise. First, the anticipated restored city will be a city of torah:

> But this is the covenant that I will make with the house of Israel after those days, says the LORD: I will put my law within them, and I will write it on their hearts; and I will be their God, and they shall be my people. No longer shall they teach one another, or say to each other, "Know the LORD," for they shall all know me, from the least of them to the greatest, says the LORD. (Jer 31:33-34)

Everyone in the new regime will "know me," will know who YHWH is and what YHWH wills. And the reason they will know is that all will have inhaled the torah, which is the gift of YHWH's pleasure. The new city will be torah-based, with a consensus about the public good. Of this anticipated torah community, it is clear that this text in Jeremiah and this tradition is rooted in Deuteronomy, either directly by Deuteronomists or by Jeremiah, who had studied Deuteronomy. Either way, the torah envisioned here is the tradition of Deuteronomy, which, unlike other elements of the torah, is fixed on civic justice. Thus the promise is that all will study, ponder, and work at neighborly justice. If we draw close to Deuteronomy, moreover, then it is clear that this torah envisions a well-being and dignity for widowed, orphaned, and alien, a triad that shows up everywhere in Deuteronomy:

> When you reap your harvest in your field and forget a sheaf in the field, you shall not go back to get it; it shall be left for the *alien, the orphan, and the widow*, so that the LORD your God may bless you in all your undertakings. When you beat your olive trees, do not strip what is left; it shall be for the *alien, the orphan, and the widow*.

> When you gather the grapes of your vineyard, do not glean what is
> left; it shall be for the *alien, the orphan, and the widow.* Remember that
> you were a slave in the land of Egypt; therefore I am commanding you to
> do this. (Deut 24:19-22)

These three social categories typify all those who lack social power and social
clout and who fail to be socially productive. The new community of torah will
attend precisely to the neglected and disadvantaged, who are the test of viable
urban life in that Holy City or in any holy city.

The tradition of Deuteronomy, moreover, poses a "year of release" whereby
poor people have their debts canceled after six years (Deut 15:1-18). The provision is in order that there should be no permanent underclass in Israel. One might
think this is socialism, but in fact it is torah teaching that the economy must be
made to serve the infrastructure of the neighborhood. Thus, the new covenant is
not just a spiritual idea; it is a set of practices that reorder the economy to make a
neighborhood possible. That is what the torah of Deuteronomy cares about. The
new community will not be a collection of "free market" profiteers; rather, it will
be ordered by people who understand, via torah, that the public task is the construction and maintenance of a covenantal infrastructure that leaves behind no
orphan, no widow, no needy, no illegal immigrant. The torah knows that such an
ordering is economically doable. All that is lacking is public will, and that comes
by poetry.

I understand, of course, that this torah-based ethic is difficult in a pluralistic
city such as ours, more difficult than Jeremiah could have imagined. It is clear,
however, that in addition to the commands of Sinai that constitute a specifically
Israelite torah, that prophetic faith also assumed a wider, more generalized notion
of command that was larger than Sinai—as large as creation—to which all people
in every city, of any persuasion, are subject. Thus, to care for the human infrastructure as an alternative to acquisitive commoditization is not a tradition on
which Israel has a monopoly. Thus, we may imagine that many peoples can locate
something of the requirement of "new covenant" and "new commandment" in
their own cultural and historical horizon (see John 13:34).

The other dimension of new covenant I comment on is that it concludes with
a ringing affirmation of YHWH's readiness to *forgive and forget.* The prophet
anticipates a genuine social newness that cannot be grounded in old affronts.
What an incredible word in the Holy City. All holy cities, especially holy cities,
remember too much too long, so that the substructure of political-economic layers
have old wounds never dealt with and never resolved. Jeremiah's twofold work
of *exposé* and *transformation* is like a Truth and Reconciliation Commission, in
which *truth-telling* makes *wound-relinquishment* possible. In that ancient city,
the accent on forgiveness is urgent, because Jerusalem is enthralled in its past to
the third and fourth generation, a point acknowledged in Jeremiah 31:29-30, just
before the new covenant passage.[3]

It is not (is it?) different in our holy city. The political-economic advances have behind them old wounds of slavery, and the city waits for truth-telling and wound-relinquishment. Or said in different horizon, the city continues to ponder General Sherman and Tara, the general who has so much for which to answer, and the city cannot move on until there is *truth-telling* and *wound-relinquishment*. And then says the poet:

> Again I will build you, and you shall be built,
>   O virgin Israel!
> Again you shall take your tambourines,
>   and go forth in the dance of the merrymakers.
> Again you shall plant vineyards
>   on the mountains of Samaria;
> the planters shall plant,
>   and shall enjoy the fruit.
> For there shall be a day when sentinels will call
>   in the hill country of Ephraim:
> "Come, let us go up to Zion,
>   to the LORD our God." (Jer 31:4-6)

The rebuilding requires a turn from antineighborliness to neighborly covenant. The newness requires a turn to torah that attends to the widow, the orphan, the poor, and the sojourner. There is something profoundly conditional about this urban newness, the conditionality of the God who presides over every holy city:

> For *if* you truly amend your ways and your doings, *if* you truly act justly
> one with another, *if* you do not oppress the alien, the orphan, and the
> widow, or shed innocent blood in this place, and *if* you do not go after
> other gods to your own hurt, then I will dwell with you in this place, in
> the land that I gave of old to your ancestors forever and ever. (Jer 7:5-7)

IV

In the priestly tradition of Ezekiel we have seen how YHWH's holiness is driven out by pornography, pornography taken broadly and comprehensively to refer to the cheapening of life and the trivializing of God into pettiness and entertainment. God's awesome holiness deported the Holy City that thereby ceased to be holy, ceased to have "the force" that permitted it to function. The glory of God had evacuated the city.

And then came shabbiness and despair, and finally silence. The prophet is reduced to muteness in the absence. The city is reduced to shabbiness and brutality in the absence, for no city can long survive the absence. Then the destruction, and with that urban descent into hell, newness began.

It was a newness whereby God's own self accepts the vocation of shepherd in the new age when all other shepherds have failed:

> I myself will be the shepherd of my sheep, and I will make them lie
> down, says the LORD God. I will seek the lost, and I will bring back the
> strayed, and I will bind up the injured, and I will strengthen the weak,
> but the fat and the strong I will destroy. I will feed them with justice.
> (Ezek 34:15-16)

It was a newness whereby God would vindicate God's holy name in the only way possible, by imposing well being on this pornographic people:

> I will sprinkle clean water upon you, and you shall be clean from all
> your uncleannesses, and from all your idols I will cleanse you. A new
> heart I will give you, and a new spirit I will put within you; and I will
> remove from your body the heart of stone and give you a heart of flesh.
> I will put my spirit within you, and make you follow my statues and be
> careful to observe my ordinances. Then you shall live in the land that I
> gave to your ancestors; and you shall be my people, and I will be your
> God. (Ezek 36:25-28)

It was a newness whereby God's spirit would blow in the valley of dry bones and Easter the diaspora back to the land, out of the grave of the exile:

> And you shall know that I am the LORD, when I open your graves, and
> bring you up from your graves, O my people. I will put my spirit within
> you, and you shall live, and I will place you on your own soil; then you
> shall know that I, the LORD, have spoken and will act, says the LORD.
> (Ezek 37:13-14)

It was a newness whereby the prophet commits a great ecumenical act of reunion by joining symbolically the community of the north and the community of the south into one new community:

> I will make them one nation in the land, on the mountains of Israel;
> and one king shall be king over them all. Never again shall they be two
> nations, and never again shall they be divided into two kingdoms. They
> shall never again defile themselves with their idols and their detestable
> things, or with any of their transgressions. I will save them from all the
> apostasies into which they have fallen, and will cleanse them. Then they
> shall be my people, and I will be their God. (Ezek 37:22-23)

Such a newness is wrought by God's own holiness. All of that, however, is pre-
liminary. For the priestly tradition knows that the city has no future unless holiness is somehow housed visibly in its center—holiness that set firm limits against
every pornographic reduction. A voice said: "The man said to me, 'Mortal, look
closely and listen attentively, and set your mind upon all that I shall show you, for
you were brought here in order that I might show it to you; declare all that you see
to the house of Israel'" (Ezek 40:4). What follows is a careful, precise, punctilious,
detailed plan for the new temple. The detail of the temple plan stretches through
three chapters (Ezek 40–42). And when all is ready, the holiness of God flies back
from exile to take up residence again in the city:

> And there, the glory of the God of Israel was coming from the east; the
> sound was like the sound of mighty waters; and the earth shone with its
> glory. The vision I saw was like the vision that I had seen when he came
> to destroy the city, and like the vision that I had seen by the river Chebar;
> and I fell upon my face. As the glory of the LORD entered the temple by
> the gate facing east, the spirit lifted me up, and brought me into the inner
> court; and the glory of the LORD filled the temple. (Ezek 43:2-5)

The city can begin again, because the holiness of God will be visibly present,
appropriately housed in its center. Holiness is the singular Godness of God never
to be confused with things urban, a presence that emits life but life on terms of
the resident God, never life in terms of acquisitive commoditization, never life in
terms of antineighborliness, never life cheapened to pornography. Holiness evokes
a public sense of reality that what happens here matters in the courts of heaven.
And now it begins again in Jerusalem, with due provision for priestly responsi-
bilities, proper offerings, and festivals, all of which give sacramental force to the
urban community, sacramental force without which the city cannot live or prosper.

And then in chapter 47, the prophetic vision leaps to what must surely be its
most spectacular claim. The priests around Ezekiel of course could remember the
old Yahwist tradition of Genesis 2:10-14 and the claim that life flows from the
garden of paradise:

> A river flows out of Eden to water the garden, and from there it divides
> and becomes four branches. The name of the first is Pishon; it is the one
> that flows around the whole land of Havilah, where there is gold; and the
> gold of that land is good; bdellium and onyx stone are there. The name
> of the second river is Gihon; it is the one that flows around the whole
> land of Cush. The name of the third river is Tigris, which flows east of
> Assyria. And the fourth river is the Euphrates. (Gen 2:10-14)

Four rivers fed life in the four directions of the creation! The Tigris was known
along with the Euphrates in Mesopotamia, that is, "the land between the rivers."

About Pishon, we know nothing at all. But it is the fourth river we might notice, the Gihon. Whatever else, the Gihon is the stream that flowed through Jerusalem and made the city safe, even under siege. The Gihon had sacramental significance, for it is the place Solomon went for induction into kingship:

> So the priest Zadok, the prophet Nathan, and Benaiah son of Jehoiada,
> and the Cherethites and the Pelethites, went down and had Solomon ride
> on King David's mule, and led him *to Gihon*. There the priest Zadok
> took the horn of oil from the tent and anointed Solomon. Then they
> blew the trumpet, and all the people said, "Long live King Solomon!"
> (1 Kgs 1:38-39)

It is, moreover, likely the river about which the psalmist gives lyrical articulation:

> There is a river whose streams make glad the city of God,
>   the holy habitation of the Most High.
> God is in the midst of the city; it shall not be moved;
>   God will help it when the morning dawns. (Ps 46:4-5)

They knew about the cruciality of rivers, and they talk in poetic fashion about the rivers that sustained the entire earth as God's creation. Ezekiel, among the priests, however, had a different take and a daring interpretive maneuver. Now Ezekiel dares to imagine that the rivers of life flow not from some poetic Eden; rather, the rivers of life flow from below the threshold of the new temple:

> Then he brought me back to the entrance of the temple; there, water
> was flowing from below the threshold of the temple toward the east
> (for the temple faced east); and the water was flowing down from below
> the south end of the threshold of the temple, south of the altar. Then
> he brought me out by way of the north gate, and led me around on the
> outside to the outer gate that faces toward the east; and the water was
> coming out on the south side. (Ezek 47:1-2)

What a river! It is the river of life! And it flows in all directions from the temple. It derives from the seat of YHWH's own holiness. The river is a sacramental gift whereby the urban world of finance and technology and weapons can live.

The river is a sign of YHWH's utter abundance in a city that disputes too much about resources—taxes, medical supplies, school bonds. Now there will be abundance, luxury, extravagance, "abundantly far more than we can ask or imagine" (Eph 3:20). Do you know how much water is given in this river? "Going on eastward with a cord in his hand, the man measured one thousand cubits, and then led me through the water; and it was ankle-deep" (Ezek 47:3). The water is *ankle deep*!

"Again he measured one thousand, and led me through the water; and it was knee-deep" (Ezek 47:4a). The water is *knee deep*!

"Again he measured one thousand, and led me through the water; and it was *up to the waist*" (Ezek 47:4b). The water is up to the waist!

"Again he measured one thousand, and it was a river that I could not cross, for the water had risen; it was deep enough to swim in, a river that could not be crossed" (Ezek 47:5).

And then the voice asked, "Mortal, have you seen this?" (Ezek 47:6). Have you seen the abundance of life that flows crystal clear from the residence of the holy God to give life to the city? The gift of water is a sacramental phenomenon; the priests in Jerusalem have known long before the disputants in the tri-state Chattahoochee Commission that a city must have water to live. The water, moreover, must be loaded with sacramental force in order to keep the mundane realities of life from the pornographies of wealth and selfishness and brutality and alienation. Have you seen this, mortal?

More than that, this water is as transformative as the waters of baptism, for it will turn death to life: "He said to me, 'This water flows toward the eastern region and goes down into the Arabah; and when it enters the sea, the sea of stagnant waters, the water will become fresh'" (Ezek 47:8). The Dead Sea comes to life! The Dead City made fresh! All creation, after the absence that causes acute environmental failure, now alive as the creator wills, all because of sacramental waters:

- Many fish:

  Wherever the river goes, every living creature that swarms will live, and there will be very many fish, once these waters reach there. It will become fresh; and everything will live where the river goes. (Ezek 47:9-10)

- Many kinds of trees for food:

  On the banks, on both sides of the river, there will grow all kinds of trees for food. Their leaves will not wither nor their fruit fail, but they will bear fresh fruit every month, because the water for them flows from the sanctuary. (Ezek 47:12a)

- Much food and much healing:

  Their fruit will be food, and their leaves for healing (Ezek 47:12b).

Nothing cheap, nothing tawdry, nothing scarce, nothing failed. Life from holiness! The words attest the full luxuriant resumption of creation!

V

What an extraordinary act of imagination are these three great poets, Isaiah, Jeremiah, and Ezekiel. They tell the truth, and they do not flinch from the jeopardy in which stands their holy city—and every holy city. They share that dread judgment of jeopardy before which every holy city is at risk, for every holy city stands under the aegis of the holy God. With their common truth-telling, however, they go further to tell hope for the Holy City and for every holy city.

Isaiah, rooted in great royal promises as old as the *J tradition*, knows that the city will be made new by the power of the Creator God. Isaiah knows that *acquisitive commoditization* will cease, and there will come a new Jerusalem.

Jeremiah, rooted in the *Deuteronomic tradition of torah*, knows that a city cynical about widows, orphans, and aliens—the star performers of the Deuteronomic torah—will fail. Beyond that, he knows that *antineighborliness* will sooner or later, "in the days to come," yield to a new covenant of neighborly torah rooted in YHWH's good forgiveness.

Ezekiel, rooted in the *priestly traditions of holiness*, knows that *pornography* taken most broadly will drive out YHWH's holiness and the city will die. He also knows, however, of the deep readiness of this holy God to return to and reside in the holy city. The Creator God will bring sacramental waters along in return, so that the temple will be the instrument through which the holy God will infuse all creation with new life.

The three prophetic traditions together constitute a remarkable *urban theology*. We may imagine, of course, that while the three dominate the canonical literature, they did not dominate the city. The city is always dominated by bankers and planners, by people in media technology, research and development, people who engage practical issues. Yes, and thank God! But the movers and shakers at their best know that no city has a viable future if in, with, and under the men and women of practical matters there were not carriers of vision, oracle, and promise. The city must refer beyond itself to the Creator God, who makes covenant and who gives water, or the city will turn in on itself in indulgence and eventually in cynical indifference and brutality.

I imagine these poetic traditions did not count for much in old Jerusalem. I imagine, likewise, that vision, oracle, and promise, prayer and hymn and sermon, do not count for much in this city or in a thousand like it. Who notices or who cares? Except the old truth is still true! No city has a viable future if in, with, and under the men and women of practical matters there are not carriers of vision, oracle, and promise. And so this church and many more like it in God's great ecumenical enterprise keep at the task.

The good news entrusted to us is not simply personal and spiritual. Rather, it goes to the core of *commoditization* and *new possibility of homecoming*, of *antineighborliness* and *new covenant*, of *pornography* and *rivers of holiness*.

I refer one more time to the lyric of Walt Whitman, that great poet of urban America:

> After the seas are all cross'd, (as they seem already cross'd)
> After the great captains and engineers have accomplish'd their work,
> After the noble inventors, after the scientists, the chemist, the geologist,
>   ethnologist,
> Finally shall come the poet worthy of that name,
> The true Son of God shall come singing his songs.[4]

Finally comes the poet! Isaiah, Jeremiah, and Ezekiel were not practical men, but men of poetry. Ministry in the end is not "practical." It is about *oracle*, *vision*, and *promise*, about *truth-telling* and about *hope-telling*. This is no time to stop such testimony, for urban life lives from a poetic imagination that seeps into bricks and mortar, into tax policy and media coverage. We have much weeping to do over old holy cities that have failed. And after weeping long and slowly, by God's gift we have many new visions and oracles to speak—imagine visions and oracles, poems and promises—ankle deep, knee deep, waist deep, too deep to cross, making old dead places fresh . . . fresh from the Word.

CHAPTER 7

Prophetic Ministry
in the National Security State

CELEBRITY PROPHECY is important among us.[1] Celebrity prophets continue to push the edges of thought and imagination to create space for the rest of us in which to maneuver. Celebrity prophets among us say things that sound to some folk to be utterly outrageous, but then the rest of us sound less outrageous. You can name celebrity prophets and give thanks for them—Desmond Tutu, William Stringfellow, William Sloane Coffin, Jim Wallace, Barbara Brown Taylor, Tony Campolo, Michael Lerner, Brian McLaren, and sometimes me. Other names could be added. But after all of them, there is still the day-to-day parish task of the prophetic, not so daring, not so space-creating, not so crazy-sounding. That prophetic ministry is much more difficult, because of pastoral entwinements, because of face-to-faceness that makes everything complex, because budgets must be raised and institutions must be nurtured, tasks not so obvious for the celebrities among us.

My thought in these remarks is to reflect with you on prophetic ministry that is much closer to home, more complex, and more risky—but nevertheless urgent. The outcome of my comments, I hope, will be an invitation for you to marvel at what has been entrusted to us, for you to ponder how urgent is the prophetic task, and for you to think for a moment that which is *entrusted to us* and that which is *urgent in context*. I will develop my thought in five themes in a way that I hope will be useful.

I

The core of preaching is what Jürgen Moltmann has somewhere termed, "the dialectic of reconciliation," the crucifixion and resurrection of Jesus. There is

129

no doubt that the concrete, history-transforming, world-redefining happenings of Friday and Sunday constitute the core of our faith and of our preaching. Paul has familiarly summarized for us, "of first importance what I too had received," namely the core proclamation of the church (1 Cor 15:3), all of this "in accordance with the scriptures." The church, in its mumbling, unthinking fashion, regularly recites the creedal formulation, and even after that it "proclaims the mystery of faith," that "Christ has died, Christ is risen, Christ will come again."

We are entrusted to *preach Christ crucified*. That Friday turn of the world was the exposure of the vulnerability of God to the violence of the empire. Jesus' trial before Pilate—which turned out to be a trial of the empire before Jesus—and his subsequent conviction and execution is the best show of power and authority that the world can muster.[2] In that exhibit of power and authority, the world is exposed as fraudulent in its claim of ultimacy, a papier-mâché practitioner of violence and good intention. That effort by the world to eliminate him did not work. However one outlines the claim that we are "saved by the cross"—without the niceties of a theory of atonement—something decisive happened there in which God's vulnerability is exhibited as ultimate truth. It is for good reason that Moltmann terms the cross not only the "foundation" of Christian theology but also the "criticism" of Christian theology.[3] The cross, in its raw, abrupt, quotidian fleshliness, testifies against our smoother theological truth that gives false assurances and that makes easy alliances in the world. Luther's famous phrase "the crucified God" calls us always back to the raw claim that the utter self giving of God in weakness is the true exhibit of holiness that eludes the control of the world. That has been entrusted to us.

We are empowered to *preach Christ risen*. From the beginning, the church has struggled and mumbled about this miracle. No doubt we have four Gospel narratives because the church could not agree on how to say it. And in our own time, "modernist" preachers have been too long engaged in explanation whereby they try to subsume Easter in generic categories, while this has been countered by insistence on the "literal" and the "physical" in a way that dissolves the claim of truthful power.[4]

What has been entrusted to us is the news that the death systems of the world lack staying power and authority and do not merit our loyalty. They do not merit our loyalty because they disappear after two days, driven from the field by the overflowing power of new life invested in the body of the risen Christ. While the church has mumbled about the particular way of Easter, it has been forthright in God's gift of energy and freedom and joy that comes when our lives depart the death systems and move in a myriad of ways into the uncharted territory of well-being given as the gift of the Spirit.

The church and its preachers are instructed to attest to the saving *vulnerability of Friday*, even while we are citizens of a society that wants no vulnerability at all. The church is invited to witness to the intense *surprise of Easter*, even though we live in a society that by technological anxiety wants to reduce and overcome all surprise, to make it a world in which no gifts are given and no compassion enacted that makes all things new. The church is invited to *the great violent festival of vulnerability* and to *the great exuberance of surprise*. Of this the church knows two things.

First, the church knows that the connect between Friday and Sunday, the move from *vulnerability* to *surprise* is by way of dread *absent Saturday*, which is more than Sabbath and more than "weekend," a brooding silence wherein the life-giving urges of God come to fruition, and so we linger in the dread.[5]

Second, the church knows that the dramatic movement from *Friday vulnerability* through *Saturday dread* to *Sunday surprise* is only made by narrative particularly, not by scientific proof, not by universal truth, not by logical discourse. It is done, rather, by narrative acknowledgment that subverts *a world of power* by vulnerability, that exposes *a world of dread* through brooding absence, that rejects *a world of control* through surprise. All of that is entrusted to the preacher, to be lined out each time we meet, a little imagination, a little cleverness, a few gimmicks, but mostly a stark alternative to a world that has failed in its extravagant claims that lack any life-giving power.

II

That core claim of Friday–Sunday, crucifixion and resurrection, vulnerability and surprise is firmly linked to the particularity of the life of Jesus. But that particularity did not arise in the first century de novo. It is rooted deeply in Israel's lived experience that constitutes the shaping memory and abiding reality for Jews and Christians. That shaping experience has been stylized by liturgy and tradition; such stylization, however, only mediates and makes available the raw bodily reality, the scars of which continue to be carried in the community of faith. It is the truth of our narrative that life *led to an abyss* that foreshadows the Friday crucifixion. That abyss had anticipations in the history of Israel; but whatever anticipations there were, the crisis is singularly the dislocation of the Holy City of Jerusalem, the loss of a temple, monarchy, and political identity, and the deportation of leading citizens at the behest of the empire. Empires are always dislocating people and producing refugees as a sure outcome of imperial policy; so it was in the sixth century at the hands of the Babylonians. Whatever may be the historical details of destruction and deportation, that abyss is seared into the imagination of God's people, an abyss before which faith is powerless and silent. The raw reality is the crude imposition of force that culminates in the capture of "the last king" in Jerusalem. It is reported that Zedekiah watched his sons, the princes, being executed, and then his eyes were put out (2 Kgs 25:6). Many suffered, but Zedekiah's suffering is Jerusalem's epitome of helplessness, vulnerability, and humiliation; he is representative of his people that had lost its way in the process of geopolitics. His blinding and execution signify the roughshod termination of the lead figure in the Davidic line, a humiliation for the God who had made promises. The Old Testament does not flinch from the geopolitical reality of imperial power, the sort of imperial power enacted by Rome on a later Friday. Empires produce abysses, and faith cannot resist or counter that reality.

It is the truth of our narrative, moreover, that life in displacement eventuated in a *restoration*, albeit a modest, even feeble restoration. The leading Jews of Babylon did indeed return to Jerusalem and recover some semblance of Jewish identity and social reality.

There apparently was a modest return of Jews to Jerusalem just after 537 BCE, just after Cyrus the Persian had come to imperial authority. The evidence is sparse, but apparently Cyrus made Sheshbazzar a prince of the Davidic house, the leader of a returning contingent (Ezra 1:5-11). It was a most modest enterprise, and John Bright suggests, "Only a few of the boldest and most dedicated spirits were willing to accompany Shesh-Bazzar."[6]

After that feeble effort, there was a more visible effort in the years 520–516 BCE, noted by Haggai and Zechariah, at the modest accomplishment of the "Second Temple."

These returnees, however, were not very significant, for we learn, with reference to Nehemiah, the continuing sorry state of the city: "They replied, 'The survivors there in the province who escaped captivity are in great trouble and shame; the wall of Jerusalem is broken down, and its gates have been destroyed by fire'" (Neh 1:3). Out of that report, with deep and troublesome sadness and with cunning negotiations with the Persians, Nehemiah leads a more effective effort at restoration in Jerusalem. In the wake of Nehemiah came the torah enterprise of Ezra that is commonly regarded as the reconstitution of Judaism.

This experience of being *led into abyss* and *eventuation in restoration* proved to be the defining marks of Jewishness and surely the large truth of the Old Testament. This twofold movement with genuine discontinuity between them can hardly be doubted, even if the historical scale of the movement is modest compared to the theological maximization of it in the tradition. The reality is a geopolitical one; Israel found itself as exposed and vulnerable to the vagaries of the empire, as was the body of Jesus in the Christian narrative.

The reason I take this much time with historical detail (which will not preach well in most of our congregations) is that there surely is an interpretive connection between the *core tradition of the church* and the *core memory of Israel*.

Behind *Friday vulnerability* lies the stamp of the *Jewish abyss*.

Behind the *Sunday surprise* lies the *wonder of restoration* of Jerusalem, even on a small scale.

Behind the *dread silence of Saturday* lie the *long years of displacement* wherein we were coerced into "Songs of Zion" in a strange land, in order that we should be mocked for our faith and scorned for its failure (see Ps 137:1-3).

It belonged to the church to make the trek from *Friday vulnerability* through *Saturday dread absence* to *Sunday surprise*. Before that trek made by the community around Jesus, it belongs to Jews—and continues to belong to Jews—to make the journey into the *abyss of displacement* through the mocking of *humiliation in historical absence* to the *miracle of restoration*. It belongs to the truth of history and to the truth of faith. At the center of faith, for Christians as for Jews, is the gap of discontinuity, where we are led into the dismantling power of the world; this gap of discontinuity arises in a way and in a depth that is beyond our construction or imagination. The truth of lived faith is engagement with that lived experience that is given liturgical articulation. It is, however, a lived experience that defies stylized articulation, about which every pastor knows. Every pastor walks the walk with folk into that journey of *vulnerability, dread, and surprise.* And every pastor is compelled to talk the talk of *vulnerability, dread, and surprise*, a task that we rightly call "prophetic."

III

It belongs to Jews and Christians to walk the walk of discontinuity, to move from *vulnerability* through *dread absence* on to *surprise*. Characteristically, we do not want to go. Jews did not want to go, in that ancient world. And Christians with whom we minister do not want to go; nor do we ourselves much want to go. We do not want to walk the walk.

There is huge *resistance to being led into the abyss*. It is called *denial*. I believe that denial is now a major pathology in our society, as it was in that ancient Jewish society. It is, rather, a "don't ask, don't tell" policy in which, if one does not know and is not told, one need not have to go.

In that ancient world of Jerusalem as they walked closer and closer to the abyss that had the fingerprints of empire all over it, the Jews pretended that it was not happening and that they could manage their future without walking that dread journey. I will cite three texts that exhibit the vigorous *denial* of the coming abyss.

In Jeremiah 6:13-15, Jeremiah issues one of his many poems of sad truthfulness. He begins with a standard indictment:

> For from the least to the greatest of them,
>   everyone is greedy for unjust gain;
> and from prophet to priest,
>   everyone deals falsely. (Jer 6:13)

He describes an acquisitive society in which everyone is on the make with the kind of deception that makes neighborliness impossible. That acquisitiveness, moreover, is rooted in a sense that acquisitiveness is possible and legitimate because "everything is coming up roses":

> They have treated the wound of my people carelessly,
>   saying, "Peace, peace,"
> when there is no peace. (Jer 6:14)

There was a wound in Jerusalem society. That was the wound of external threat and internal alienation. It was, so Jeremiah concludes, a lethal wound; but his contemporaries had managed by easy words to "heal" the wound, to cover it over, to make it invisible, to remove it from the screen by smooth talk. The word is *shalom*, "all shall be well, and all manner of thing shall be well." It was the cant of the temple liturgy sustained by political ideology:

> God is our refuge and strength,
>   a very present help in trouble. (Ps 46:1)

Jeremiah follows his assault on deceptive words with the most acute indictment, "They do not know how to blush." They have no more shame. They are incapable of being embarrassed at their true situation. Abraham Heschel remarks that the loss of embarrassment is the quintessential loss of human capability.[7] And so Jeremiah issues a massive "therefore," a consequence of such denial:

> *Therefore* they shall fall among those who fall;
>   at the time that I punish them, they shall be overthrown,
>   says the LORD. (Jer 6:15b)

And just in case the oracle was not noticed, the tradition of Jeremiah permits the prophet to say it yet again in chapter 8:

> Therefore I will give their wives to others
>   and their fields to conquerors,
> because from the least to the greatest
>   everyone is greedy for unjust gain;
> from prophet to priest
>   everyone deals falsely.
> They have treated the wound of my people carelessly,
>   saying, "Peace, peace,"
>   when there is no peace.
> They acted shamefully, they committed abomination;
>   yet they were not at all ashamed,
>   they did not know how to blush.
> Therefore they shall fall among those who fall;
>   at the time when I punish them, they shall be overthrown,
>   says the LORD. (Jer 8:10-12)

Here the poem reverses matters and begins with anticipation that wives and fields will be taken over by conquerors (Babylon). The juxtaposition of wives and fields surely echoes the tenth commandment, "Thou shall not covet your neighbor's wife or your neighbor's field." The empire covets and will have its way, so says the prophet, because of Jerusalem's denial.

The second exemplar of denial is the narrative transaction between Hananiah and Jeremiah in chapter 28. The latter prophet's name means "YHWH is gracious," and Hananiah expected YHWH to be gracious enough to save the city in its current crisis. Indeed, Hananiah had meditated on the rescue of Jerusalem a century earlier from the hand of the Assyrians at the time of Hezekiah and Isaiah, and he reckoned that the same rescue would happen again. Jeremiah has just announced the coming onslaught of Babylon against Jerusalem, and Hananiah refutes his words:

> Thus says the LORD of hosts, the God of Israel: I have broken the yoke of
> the king of Babylon. Within two years I will bring back to this place all
> the vessels of the LORD's house, which King Nebuchadnezzar of Babylon
> took away from this place and carried to Babylon. I will also bring back
> to this place King Jeconiah son of Jehoiakim of Judah, and all the exiles
> from Judah who went to Babylon, says the LORD, for I will break the
> yoke of the king of Babylon. (Jer 28:2-4)

Hananiah anticipates, according to YHWH's promises, that the little deportation of 597 BCE will be ended; everyone will come home, including the boy-king Jehoiachin. The yoke of the empire will be broken, and there will be return to normalcy, within two years. The two prophets argue the point, and Jeremiah is put on trial for his life. In the end, the narrative dismisses Hananiah tersely as a false prophet whom YHWH has not sent: "In that same year, in the seventh month, the prophet Hananiah died" (Jer 28:17).

Though Hananiah dies, his message is an important one because *denial* of the coming abyss is a major establishment enterprise. We may imagine that Hananiah, unlike Jeremiah, enjoyed good access to the establishment and his patter of cheap grace was welcomed as free grace: God is good all the time, and all shall be well. Just pretend.

A third pertinent text is Ezekiel 13, in which the prophets who oppose Ezekiel are accused of falsehood: "Because, in truth, because they have misled my people, saying, 'Peace,' when there is no peace; and because, when the people build a wall, these prophets smear whitewash on it" (Ezek 13:10). The political leaders may have been at fault; but the religious leaders are the ones who put a good face on their fault and enact a cover-up. The outcome, of course, is that members of the community do not need to face reality. It is as though it were not happening! And therefore one need only pretend.

Just pretend:

- that the economy has bottomed out;
- that the war has turned and we are making great progress;
- that the addiction can be controlled with discipline;
- that the index of teenage suicides is societally insignificant;
- that date rape is just boys who will be boys;

- that generous gun laws will make us safer;
- that if people work harder they will prosper like us.

There is also a huge resistance to life *eventuating in restoration*; it is called *despair*. It is the mood of those who have looked clearly into the abyss, who have gone reluctantly but necessarily into it, and who have come to regard the abyss as bottomless and perpetual, a world without end. Despair is the conclusion that we reach in the pit of our stomachs that we are trapped here forever, and we had best make the most of it. In the end, there will be no well-being, so get what you can now. Eat and drink and own all that you can because there are no new gifts to be given. There are no dreams, no visions, no possibilities, only this—the worst kind of eschatology, sadly "realized." Here are some texts on despair in ancient Israel in the midst of the abyss.

The book of Lamentations, sad poems of grief, concludes with a stunning realization:

> Why have you forgotten us completely?
>   Why have you forsaken us these many days? (Lam 5:20)

The verse assumes that God has forgotten and God has forsaken. The poem does not debate that claim but accepts and asks "Why?" To be sure, the verse is followed in the penultimate verse of the book by a petition, indicating that hope is not completely voided. But the final verse, Lam 5:22, leaves us with a notion of rejection and divine anger:

> unless you have utterly rejected us,
>   and are angry with us beyond measure. (Lam 5:22)

The poem cannot make a move toward restoration because the abyss is all-defining. The use of the word "forsake" of course anticipates the Friday lament of Jesus in his forsakenness, in which he replicates the pain of Jerusalem in his own body (Matt 27:46; Mark 15:34). In the abyss, there is only rejection.

In Isaiah 40:27, the lyrical poet of hope begins by quoting Israel's utterance of despair, perhaps a liturgical formulation of despair:

> Why do you say, O Jacob,
>   and speak, O Israel,
> "My way is hidden from the LORD,
>   and my right is disregarded by my God"? (Isa 40:27)

In its abyss, Israel could only conclude that YHWH did not know and did not care.

Isaiah 49:14, in what appears to be a quote from the liturgical formulation of Lamentations 5:20 that I have already cited, again uses the double terminology of "forsake":

> But Zion said, "The LORD has forsaken me,
>   my LORD has forgotten me." (Isa 49:14)

That is what Zion said. That is what they said in shabby, shattered Jerusalem. That is what they said in Babylon, where they had been taken against their will. The big defining terms again are "forsake" and "forget."

In Isaiah 50:2, YHWH asks in indignation:

> Is my hand shortened, that it cannot redeem?
>   Or have I no power to deliver?
> By my rebuke I dry up the sea,
>   I make the rivers a desert;
> their fish stink for lack of water,
>   and die of thirst. (Isa 50:2)

YHWH is indignant because when YHWH comes to rescue, God finds no takers. When God called there were no respondents. And why did Israel not respond? Because they had drawn the conclusion that YHWH's hand was short. They remembered when YHWH had delivered them from Egypt with "a strong hand and an outstretched arm." But now, by contrast, there was no evidence of a strong divine hand, no show of a divine outstretched arm. All the evidence suggested that YHWH's arm, a vehicle of divine power, had shriveled to uselessness. It is as though YHWH had become disabled. All around, the Israelites could see the geopolitical outcomes of an empire no longer kept in check by divine restraint. They had drawn the only conclusion that the evidence permitted. There was no reason to answer YHWH, no motivation to receive or welcome the coming of YHWH, no ground for any hope at all. They were, they judged, alone in the world, without an advocate or a strong intervener.

We can see, from Isaiah 59:1, that this way of voicing despair must have been prevalent in displaced Israel. An affirmative voice answers the doubt of 50:2:

> See, the LORD's hand is not too short to save,
>   nor his ear too dull to hear. (Isa 59:1)

The Israelites concluded that YHWH did not save because YHWH could not save. The world is beyond YHWH's recovery, and the news is not good.

Jeremiah had dealt with *denial* among those who could not see the disaster coming. The tradition of Isaiah, somewhat later, deals with *despair* among those who are caught in the abyss. The denial is among those who refuse to see and so imagine that Israel will not be destroyed, that the Messiah will not die. The despair is among those who know but cannot imagine a future, cannot discern a way out of no way; they could not believe that Messiah will be raised from the dead to new life. *Denial resists abyss—and so crucifixion.*

Denial fends off vulnerability. *Despair resists homecoming—and so resurrection*. Despair fends off surprise. Faith is to walk that walk, but *denial and despair* refuse the walk.

IV

Prophetic ministry is among those who refuse the walk. The wonder of faith is that the *talk* sometimes authorizes, empowers, and emboldens the *walk*. Prophetic ministry *talks the talk* that the community may *walk the walk* of faith into the abyss and walk the walk of faith out of the abyss into restoration. Thus, it is my thesis that prophetic ministry is neither *prediction*, as some conservatives would have it, or *social action*, as some liberals would have it. Prophetic ministry is to talk in ways that *move past denial* and that *move past despair* into the walk of vulnerability and surprise, there to find the gift of God and the possibility of genuine humanness. Because the deniers and the despairers do not want to go, prophetic talk is characteristically upstream against great resistance. I shall insist in what follows that in the reality of abyss and restoration, in the practice of vulnerability and surprise, in the face of denial and despair, the prophetic task has a twofold accent about the shape of reality in a world where the living God is on exhibit.

The walk into the abyss is fended off by *denial*. The prophetic antidote to denial is *truth-telling*. It is the task of truth-telling that belongs to prophetic ministry, an act that is sure to provoke resistance and hostility among those in denial, because it requires seeing and knowing and engaging with that which we have refused to see, know, or engage. The truth that is to be told is that the world is out of sync, that we live against the grain of God's holiness, and that such living has immense negative consequences because the sync and the grain are God-given and cannot be outflanked. Such talk of "out of sync" and "against the grain," put theologically, is the truth that the world is under divine judgment. That is the primal burden of truth-telling among these ancient prophets in the face of the abyss enacted—at the behest of YHWH—by Babylon. The rhetorical tradition of the prophets suggests that there are two modes of such truth-telling as divine judgment, a "hot mode" that imagines the intrusive agency of YHWH as punisher, and the "cool mode" that makes connections between cause and effect and so traces the consequences of actions, consequences that belong intrinsically with the choices and the policies.

The truth-telling is an insistence that we live, by the goodness of the Creator God, in a morally coherent creation. For that reason, matters are connected in terms of present choices and future outcomes. It is to be noticed that prophetic truth-telling—whether hot or cold—is characteristically poetic. It is not excessively confrontive, unless of course there is objection to subversive poetry that is not especially issue-oriented. Such poetry aims, characteristically, below social specificities to the brooding anguish and dismay of the God who will not be mocked. It is always the propensity of the powerful to imagine that with enough technology or shrewdness, the holy intransigence of creation can be outflanked. The poets arise to bear witness to the deep conviction that God is not mocked and that the moral coherence of the creation will hold.

I have selected seven obvious occasions of truth-telling in the prophetic tradition, though one might choose others. As I pondered them, it struck me that these ancient utterances require almost no interpretive imagination, so contemporary are they. And therefore, as belated prophetic voices, we ourselves can appeal to the ones who uttered before us and trade on their imagination and courage.

Isaiah 5:20

The verse is among a series of "woes." "Woe" means big trouble coming that cannot now be averted:

> *Ah*, you who call evil good
>   and good evil,
> who put darkness for light
>   and light for darkness,
> who put bitter for sweet
>   and sweet for bitter! (Isa 5:20)

In the NRSV "woe" is translated as "ah." The verse asserts that big trouble that cannot be averted will come to those who engage in euphemism, who call things by their wrong names, and so disguise the truth of social reality. Prophetic ministry consists of calling things by their right names and so summoning folk to face the social reality of being out of sync. Consider, for example, "friendly fire," "collateral damage," "welfare reform," "outsourcing," "downsizing," to name a few; and perhaps the most shameless usage, to term a lethal missile "peacekeeper." Ancient Jerusalem, in its liturgies of complacency, disguised reality, as do we. The church is the place for naming things faithfully, because euphemism is a tool for denial.

Amos 6:4-7

Amos offers another "woe," though the term is not in the Hebrew and must be borrowed from verse 1. Amos describes the indulgent entitlement of his contemporaries in Samaria with their exotic ivories, their at-ease lounging, and their killing of young animals for veal—which only the affluent can do—their idle entertainment, and their self-indulgent society out of control:

> *Alas* for those who lie on beds of ivory,
>   and lounge on their couches,
> and eat lambs from the flock,

> and calves from the stall;
> who sing idle songs to the sound of the harp,
>   and like David improvise on instruments of music;
> who drink wine from bowls,
>   and anoint themselves with the finest oils. (Amos 6:4-6a)

The poem moves inescapably to the "but" of verse 6b: "*but* are not grieved over the ruin of Joseph!" (Amos 6:6b). Not grieved! Not upset! Not in touch with reality! This is consumerism run amok, without notice. And there comes the big prophetic "therefore" of verse 7:

> *Therefore* they shall now be the first to go into exile,
>   and the revelry of the loungers shall pass away. (Amos 6:7)

They had not noticed at all and were not worried; they surely could not have extrapolated the deportation into exile, for "exile" was nowhere on the screen of the folks at the club, as it was not on the screen with the shah or with the czar or with any who are narcoticized in power. When they heard the poem of Amos they must have wondered. Perhaps "exile" does not follow from self-indulgent entitlement; that is a connection only in the rash thrust of the poem, and besides, it is only a poem.

Now I know that such poetry, if made contemporary, cannot comfortably be uttered in most of our venues of ministry. But here it is, a text inviting other texts, a poem inviting other poems, an act of imagination authorizing other acts of imagination that seek to do truth-telling.

Hosea 4:1-3

YHWH has an "indictment" against Israel. The poem announces YHWH to be a litigator who sues God's people. The bill of particulars is the Decalogue, which has been violated:

> There is no faithfulness or loyalty,
>   and no knowledge of God in the land.
> Swearing, lying, and murder,
>   and stealing and adultery break out;
>   bloodshed follows bloodshed. (Hos 4:1-2)

This is a clever poetic utilization of the Ten Commandments, for who would have thought to turn the Sinai charter into subversive poetry? There is an edginess to the rhetoric when command becomes poetry.

And then the big "therefore" of verse 3:

Therefore the land mourns,
   and all who live in it languish;
together with the wild animals
   and the birds of the air,
   even the fish of the sea are perishing. (Hos 4:3)

"Land mourns" means there is a drought. Violation of commandment, in poetic construal, causes drought. Violation of Sinai impinges on the ordered fruitfulness of creation. Talk about environmental crisis! Such talk makes no sense unless it is *creation* behind which sits *the Creator*, who is not to be mocked. Hosea can use the triad, "wild animals, birds, fish," because he has studied Genesis 1. He takes old liturgy and makes poetry. Prophetic talk is not explanation and rational argument. It is, rather, poetic declaration that is outrageous in its performance. And when once performed in utterance, the poetry lingers with its own force and cannot be recalled. Technical achievements in our contemporary world require us to imagine our autonomy; but Hosea, long before Al Gore, knew that such autonomy is a joke. The divine commands are ways in which we answer for creation to the Creator.

Micah 2:1-4

Yet another "woe," this one portraying a luxurious land speculator staying in his bathrobe until noon, walking around the house with a cup of coffee on a cell phone, talking to his broker:

Alas for those who devise wickedness
   and evil deeds on their beds!
When the morning dawns, they perform it,
   because it is in their power. (Mic 2:1)

What is he doing? He is coveting. He is not doing this on the side; it is his business. That is what he does. He buys up cheap property, he finds vulnerable people, he seizes his oil fields, he imagines that everything is available and purchasable and usable, on the prowl for underpriced possibilities, naive widows, and vulnerable orphans:

They covet fields, and seize them;
   houses, and take them away,
they oppress householder and house,
   people and their inheritance. (Mic 2:2)

Well, now we know what comes next:

Therefore thus says the LORD:
Now, I am devising against this family an evil
    from which you cannot remove your necks;
and you shall not walk haughtily,
    for it will be an evil time.
On that day they shall take up a taunt song against you,
    and wail with bitter lamentation,
and say, "We are utterly ruined;
    the LORD alters the inheritance of my people;
how he removes it from me!
    Among our captors he parcels out our fields." (Mic 2:3-4)

Another "therefore," an imagined vision of land loss, because the Assyrians are coming. The coming crisis concerns "the inheritance of my people," a phrase that reaches all the way back to Father Abraham and the earliest land arrangements.

And now, in poetic anticipation, "We are utterly ruined." Ruined because of coveting. Ruined for speculating. Ruined for seizing what is not ours. Ruined for thinking we are entitled to whatever we can usurp. You might be interested to know that in the next verse, verse 6, it is written as a counter-opinion of resistance:

One should not preach such things.
Disgrace will not overtake us. (Mic 2:6)

Jeremiah 5:23-29

Closer to the abyss, Jeremiah offers a poem:

But this people has a stubborn and rebellious heart;
    they have turned aside and gone away.
They do not say in their hearts,
    "Let us fear the LORD our God,
who gives the rain in its season,
    the autumn rain and the spring rain,
and keeps for us
    the weeks appointed for the harvest." (Jer 5:23-24)

They live as though they were not dependent. They are incapable of gratitude, let alone obedience. They do not remember to be compassionate about the neighborhood:

For scoundrels are found among my people;
    they take over the goods of others.
Like fowlers they set a trap;
    they catch human beings.

> Like a cage full of birds,
>> their houses are full of treachery. (Jer 5:26-27)

The big ones eat the little ones. And the outcome is incredible prosperity:

> Like a cage full of birds,
>> their houses are full of treachery;
> therefore they have become great and rich,
>> they have grown fat and sleek.
> They know no limits in deeds of wickedness;
>> they do not judge with justice
> the cause of the orphan, to make it prosper,
>> and they do not defend the rights of the needy. (Jer 5:27-28)

The outcome of such assumed autonomy is to create an economic crisis in which the vulnerable—the orphan, the needy—have no public defender. And YHWH ends the poem in probing indignation:

> Shall I not punish them for these things?
>> says the LORD,
> and shall I not bring retribution
> on a nation such as this? (Jer 5:29)

Shall I not? YHWH is trying to persuade listening Israel—would you not draw the conclusion I draw? What conclusion would you draw? The poem links *the rainmaker God* and *the most vulnerable*, the linkage that self-indulgent, narcoticized society most wants to deny.

Jeremiah 9:17-19

Now a different style from Jeremiah. YHWH gives an instruction to the village elders:

> Thus says the LORD of hosts:
> Consider, and call for the mourning women to come;
>> send for the skilled women to come;
> let them quickly raise a dirge over us,
>> so that our eyes may run down with tears,
>> and our eyelids flow with water. (Jer 9:17-18)

Call the professional mourners. Every church and every rural village I know has women—always women with casseroles—who know how to manage grief. At a death they need to be notified and mobilized. In their intuitive ways they legitimate grief, bring it to visibility, give public expression to pain, and let the community participate in the loss. Only here the loss is not simply a loved one. It is a city. It is a culture. It is a community rooted in tradition. Death has come, and we have not noticed:

> raise a dirge;
> eyes run down with tears;
> eyelids flow with water.

Because:

> For a sound of wailing is heard from Zion:
>   "How we are ruined!
>   We are utterly shamed,
> because we have left the land,
>   because they have cast down our dwellings." (Jer 9:19)

Ruined, shamed, gone, cast down! The poet looks ahead and sees what the numbed cannot see and do not want to see. The mechanism of death has been put in motion. In verses 21-22, the poet imagines death entering palaces to "cut off" young men—the body count mounts! The corpses accumulate, and there is none to gather them up, perhaps because we have refused to acknowledge the reality. The poet seeks to penetrate the practice of an economy that rewards those at the top and does not notice the determined power of negation that robs those who sustain the enterprise. The killing and the dying constitute a process that will touch, says the poet, even the privileged.

Jeremiah 18:14-17

Yet another mode of utterance, beginning with two rhetorical questions:

> Does the snow of Lebanon leave the crags of Sirion?
> Do the mountain waters run dry,
>   the cold flowing streams? (Jer 18:14)

Yes, snow melts and runs down the great mountains. No, mountain streams, when snow melts, are not dry. The two questions and the two implied answers witness to what is natural and reliable. You can count on the ordered performance of creation. Snow will melt, and mountain streams will have water.

By contrast,

> But my people have forgotten me,
>   they burn offerings to a delusion;

> they have stumbled in their ways,
>   in the ancient roads,
> and have gone into bypaths,
>   not the highway,
> making their land a horror,
>   a thing to be hissed at forever.
> All who pass by it are horrified
>   and shake their heads. (Jer 18:15-16)

My people have committed an unnatural act, as unnatural as snow not melting and not causing flowing streams. So unnatural is it to forget the God of Sinai and the paths of torah obedience. So unnatural to do the routines of worship like burnt offerings that are delusional, that are pretend and denial, while not walking the walk. So unnatural as to be repulsive.

There is a result to such failure:

> Like the wind from the east,
>   I will scatter them before the enemy.
> I will show them my back, not my face,
>   in the day of their calamity. (Jer 18:17)

A wind from the East, from Iran, for God's sake? A scattering before the enemies, and all Israel will get is God's back and not God's face, God's shunning, God's abandonment, left to calamity.

I know this is too hard. But it is now as urgent as it is hard. Because the truth must be told, told in image and figure and poem. Told sideways, told by one who lives alongside the others who are narcoticized. The text will tell more than we can utter, because without the text we are left in denial, imagining that it is not so. Except that many folk who show up for the poetry hunch the truth and wait to have it given voice. Many who hunch deeply are most resistant, for we do not want to know what the Spirit is saying to the church. No wonder texts like these do not make the lectionary.

V

The walk out of the abyss into newness is fended off by despair. The prophetic antidote to despair is *hope-telling*. It is the task of *hope-telling* that belongs to prophetic ministry, an act that is sure to evoke doubt and resistance among those in despair, because hope-telling requires risk and venture that we characteristically do not want to undertake. When an alternative is possible, it requires us to leave present circumstance, even if that present circumstance is debilitating, and to move out to new gifts that we thought would not be given. The hope to be told is that the abyss will not defeat God or deter God from bringing creation to full *shalom*. The news of prophetic utterance is that the world is under promise. That is the primal burden of hope-telling among these ancient prophets who spoke in the midst of the abyss. That hope takes a modest political form in regard to the recovery of Jewish society in Jerusalem. But it also takes a larger, lyrical form in grand doxological exuberance that does not doubt that the world is on its way to well-being. That doxological exuberance invites us to be the vanguard of newness that will arise among the bold, exactly in the abyss. One of the great wonders is that the exile is precisely the venue for hope, a venue out of which comes the promises of God, upon which we continue to count.

I have selected seven occasions of hope-telling in the prophets, though one might have chosen others. As I pondered these promissory texts, it struck me that they are now very difficult to enunciate in a world that knows too much and that is largely emptied of the mystery of God. But then it struck me as well that they must have been very difficult in ancient time, for they are in defiance of facts on the ground. But then, in this tradition of faith, the future will be given by God to those who act in defiance of the apparent facts on the ground.

I imagine all of these seven texts (and many others) are summarized by the words on God's lips, "I have a dream." It is a dream that rushes beyond present circumstance, a dream in which God, like Martin Luther King, has no strategy for getting from here to there. But the dream, and the utterance of the dream, keep the abyss from being absolutized. The news is that there is more and there is other. It is on offer to those who refuse to abide in despair, the despair of defeat or the despair of entitled affluence. It is on offer to those who move out according to the God who has one more trek to make across the wilderness.

Amos 5:14-15

Amos is not much of a hoper, fixed as he is on the coming abyss in Samaria. Nonetheless in chapter 5, there is a series of imperatives that culminate in this way:

> Seek good and not evil,
>> that you may live;
> and so the LORD, the God of hosts, will be with you,
>> just as you have said.
> Hate evil and love good,
>> and establish justice in the gate;
> it may be that the LORD, the God of hosts,
>> will be gracious to the remnant of Joseph. (Amos 5:14-15)

Such imperatives are acts of hope. They assert that things may still be turned but that such a renewing turn will require radically altered conduct. The new conduct is "good" (not evil), hate of evil and love of good, good finally equated with social justice, that is, economic reform. It is an act of hope to perform in this way, because "it may be"—the prophetic "perhaps"—it may be that YHWH will be gracious. Hope is active, transformative conduct.

Hosea 2:18-23

The crisis is deeper in Hosea. In Hosea 2:2-13, the prophet has announced divorce and termination of the covenantal relationship. At the end of verse 13 comes the abyss. The remarkable fact is that the poem does not end at verse 13.[8] There is a very long pause after verse 13, long enough to inhale the reality of abyss, of being God-abandoned. But then God says more. In verses 14-23, YHWH speaks Israel out of abyss and into renewed covenant. It is a covenant that renews creation and that rescues the environment from a meltdown: "I will make for you a covenant on that day with the wild animals, the birds of the air, and the creeping things of the ground; and I will abolish the bow, the sword, and war from the land; and I will make you lie down in safety" (Hos 2:18). It is a covenant that reaches to God's forsaken people. The people divorced will be reembraced, reloved, and remarried: "And I will take you for my wife forever; I will take you for my wife in righteousness and in justice, in steadfast love, and in mercy. I will take you for my wife in faithfulness; and you shall know the LORD" (Hos 2:19-20). All the great words of Israel's covenantal faith are mobilized to bespeak YHWH's renewal of faithfulness. Beyond abyss lies passionate, divine fidelity. Along with the *restitution of covenant* comes full, glad *restoration of fruitful creation*, the very creation that had been plunged into the abyss:

> On that day I will answer, says the LORD,
>   I will answer the heavens
>   and they shall answer the earth;
> and the earth shall answer the grain, the wine, and the oil,
>   and they shall answer Jezreel;
>   and I will sow him for myself in the land.
> And I will have pity on Lo-ruhamah,
>   and I will say to Lo-ammi, "You are my people";
>   and he shall say, "You are my God." (Hos 2:21-23)

The earth will answer in fruitfulness: Israel will luxuriate in its new status: "You are my people." It is never so in the abyss. The poet, however, refuses despair and asks his poem-listeners to move beyond abyss into glad expectation.

Micah 4:1-5

There will be days to come! The abyss is not the last day. The description of exile (and Friday) does not disrupt YHWH's rule. The poet imagines, as does every prophet, a world out beyond despair. In this case, it is the scenario of all nations and peoples on the road together:

> In the days to come
>> the mountain of the LORD's house
> shall be established as the highest of the mountains,
>> and shall be raised up above the hills.
> Peoples shall stream to it,
>> and many nations shall come and say:
> "Come, let us go up to the mountain of the LORD,
>> to the house of the God of Jacob." (Mic 4:1-2a)

The nations will refuse to sink in mutual deterrence and destruction. They will gather together peaceably to make a trip into YHWH's future. The reason they will go to the house of the God of Jacob—going joyously and peaceably—is in order to learn what they do not yet know:

> that he may teach us his ways
>> and that we may walk in his paths.
> For out of Zion shall go forth instruction,
>> and the word of the LORD from Jerusalem.
> He shall judge between many peoples,
>> and shall arbitrate between strong nations far away. (Mic 4:2b-3a)

From Zion comes "instruction," that is, torah. From the temple come commandments for all, commandments of discernment and disarmament and peace. There are days coming when wars will end. The weapons will be overcome; they will be transposed by torah. Nations will eventually decide that obedience beats oppression:

> They shall beat their swords into plowshares,
>> and their spears into pruning hooks;
> nation shall not lift up sword against nation,
>> neither shall they learn war any more;
> but they shall all sit under their own vines and under their own fig trees,
>> and no one shall make them afraid;
>> for the mouth of the LORD of hosts has spoken. (Mic 4:3b-4)

It is only a poem, a vision, a hunch, a hope. But that is all you get in the abyss. Such a hunch, however, on the lips of a bold poet is enough. It asserts, without explanation or apology, that it will be otherwise.[9] Listeners are to be ready for otherwise, because God's world will not remain in the abyss, not more than three days' worth.

Jeremiah 31:31-34

This utterance of hope is the best known. It is a full admission that the covenant has been broken, fidelity shattered, old traditions of relating null and void. But—listen to this!—the days are surely coming! They are coming because the God of the abyss is the God of utter newness. This God so vexed by disobedience is the God who will make new covenant, beyond the breakage, freely, generously, compassionately. There will be a new wave of divine fidelity. It will be torah-based, but the torah will now be inhaled. And beyond torah, the basis of the future is divine forgiveness:

> The days are surely coming, says the LORD, when I will make a new covenant with the house of Israel and the house of Judah. It will not be like the covenant that I made with their ancestors when I took them by the hand to bring them out of the land of Egypt—a covenant that they broke, though I was their husband, says the LORD. But this is the covenant that I will make with the house of Israel after those days, says the LORD: I will put my law within them, and I will write it on their hearts; and I will be their God, and they shall be my people. No longer shall they teach one another, or say to each other, "Know the LORD," for they shall all know me, from the least of them to the greatest, says the LORD; for I will forgive their iniquity, and remember their sin no more. (Jer 31:31-34)

The ground for torah receptivity and torah obedience is full pardon. No more grudge, no more alienation, no more resentment, no more calculation. Now face-to-face generous companionship, all the disobedience forgiven, all the recalcitrant welcomed back, all the alienated restored. It will happen and is sure, as sure as prophetic imagination, as certain as prophetic utterance, because God's future rests on the lips of the hope-tellers.

Jeremiah 33:10-11

I cite this little text because it is lesser known. Do you remember that after 9/11 there was a debate about when to resume major league baseball and the NFL? The theaters were closed, the world shut down. To resume too soon, it was generally understood, would dishonor the dead. Well, it was like that in the ancient abyss. The world ceased. There were no poems, no songs, no parties, no new babies, no weddings—because there was no future.

And then this:

> There shall once more be heard the voice of mirth and the voice of gladness, the voice of the bridegroom and the voice of the bride, the voices of

those who sing, as they bring thank offerings to the house of the LORD:
>   "Give thanks to the LORD of hosts,
>   for the LORD is good,
>   for his steadfast love endures forever!"
> For I will restore the fortunes of the land as at first, says the LORD.
> (Jer 33:10-11)

Weddings will happen—again! People will fall in love. They will woo each other and meet new in-laws. There will be singing and dancing and food . . . and then babies. And pledges of fidelity and joy and forgiveness and all the things that make for a marriage. Life in its fullness will begin again, without sadness or reticence. Who would have believed Sunday would come so soon and so abruptly? We say it in the creed but we do not notice:

> He was crucified under Pontius Pilate
>   was dead and buried.
> He descended into the abyss.

And then without missing a beat:

> On the third day he was raised from the dead.

But the newness is not spiritual and private. It is public and concerns everyone in the village, including the vulnerable. If you hear the dancing and the singing of a wedding, you will know that futures have been restored, that the old despair has been overcome. No wonder the wicks should be trimmed, for the bridegroom is on his way and everybody is beyond despair (Matt 25:10-12).

Isaiah 43:1-5

The ultimate defeat of despair is delivered by this remarkable poem that contains the quintessential overthrow of despair. It begins and ends the same way.
    At the beginning in verse 1:

> But now thus says the LORD,
> he who created you, O Jacob,
>   he who formed you, O Israel:
> *Do not fear*, for I have redeemed you;
>   I have called you by name, you are mine. (Isa 43:1)

It ends in verse 5:

Do not fear, for I am with you;
I will bring your offspring from the east,
and from the west I will gather you. (Isa 43:5)

The beginning and the end are the same: *Do not fear!* It is an assurance in the form of a command. It is an imperative requiring moving out of the abyss, out of a world defined by imperial cynicism, out of a world of abuse that discounts the displaced.

The ground for such assurance-as-imperative is twofold. First, "I am with you." You thought I had abandoned you; the reason you thought that is that you accepted imperial definitions of reality that are not true (see Isa 54:7-8). Second, "You are mine." You had forgotten that because you accepted the definitions of the empire that identified you as subject of the empire. Thus, the assurance is a vigorous contestation of the reality accepted too easily in the abyss. I am with you, not absent, not negligent, not indifferent. You are mine, not theirs! This *assurance-as-imperative* is the rock-bottom assurance of hope, that the world—and our particular context—is inhabited by the Holy One, who will prevail in the same way that the same Holy One has prevailed over the powers of death when he descended into Saturday hell.

Do not fear:

- It is the word of the angels to the shepherds in Bethlehem (Luke 2:10);
- It is the word to the visitors of the tomb on Easter morning, because "Do not fear," is the substance of Easter power (Matt 28:5, 10);
- It is the word every parent speaks to every child in the midst of a nighttime nightmare, "Do not fear; I am right here." That utterance ends the child's nightmare; and in the abyss of Israel, that divine utterance ended the long nightmare of displacement and transformed exile into home;
- It was the primal utterance of John Paul II when he first came back to Poland as pope, a word uttered to Solidarity leaders who had much to fear.

The empire in all of its manifestations—and its various shapes of red/orange/yellow alert—is, "Be very afraid."

- Be very afraid of not conforming to social authority and social expectation;
- Be very afraid of peer pressure;
- Be very afraid for your life, your food, your home, your future.

And then, "Do not fear." The world waits for hope-filled truth. But the word must not be spoken too soon or the word of hope will only reinforce denial. It is a word among those who despair, not among those who deny.

Isaiah 65:17-25

The ultimate hope-telling at the edge of the Isaiah tradition speaks the ultimate hope of new possibility—new heaven, new earth, new Jerusalem:

> For I am about to create new heavens
>   and a new earth;
> the former things shall not be remembered
>   or come to mind.
> But be glad and rejoice forever
>   in what I am creating;
> for I am about to create Jerusalem as a joy,
>   and its people as a delight.
> I will rejoice in Jerusalem,
>   and delight in my people;
> no more shall the sound of weeping be heard in it,
>   or the cry of distress. (Isa 65:17-19)

It is Israel's mode for the great affirmation:

> Christ has died.
> Christ is risen.
> Christ will come again.

Christ will come again, and so we pray for God's kingdom on earth, as it is in heaven, that creation will be a venue where God's will will be done as it is done in heaven.

The poem in Isaiah dares to assert that creation will be renovated.

There will be good health care:

> No more shall there be in it
>   an infant that lives but a few days,
>   or an old person who does not live out a lifetime;
> for one who dies at a hundred years will be considered a youth,
>   and one who falls short of a hundred will be
>   considered accursed. (Isa 65:20)

There will be safe neighborhoods:

> They shall build houses and inhabit them;
>   they shall plant vineyards and eat their fruit.
> They shall not build and another inhabit;
>   they shall not plant and another eat;
> for like the days of a tree shall the days of my people be,
>   and my chosen shall long enjoy the work of their hands. (Isa 65:21-22)

There will be a healed earth:

> The wolf and the lamb shall feed together,
>> the lion shall eat straw like the ox;
>> but the serpent—its food shall be dust! (Isa 65:25a)

There will be peace on earth:

> They shall not hurt or destroy
>> on all my holy mountain. (Isa 65:25b)

While we dwell in the abyss, newness does not seem possible. To those Jews in Babylon, the newness did not seem possible. To those disciples that Saturday, it did not seem possible. It never seems possible to those who accept the abyss as a perpetual fate. But hope breaks fate. Hope for newness cracks open what seemed to be true in perpetuity. The world waits for the hope-tellers among us, for it will be from people like us that "finally comes the poet"![10]

I know this is too hard. It is too hard because we would rather tinker and solve problems that promote programs and give advice. But this hope is as urgent as it is hard because where despair rules, the life-destroying furors of the empire of death will prevail.[11] Hope must be told, in image, in figure, in poem, in vision. It must be told sideways, told as one who dwells with the others in the abyss. The text will tell more than we are able to utter, because without the text we are left in despair, imagining that the abyss is our final home. Except, many folks show up for the utterance of hope and wait for it to be given voice. Many who hunch about an alternative hold their breath in fear, dreading that it may not be uttered, that it may not ring true. No wonder we have grown timid and calculating and explanatory! But this Isaiah at the brink of homecoming was not timid. He spoke of the God who makes all things new. And the women on the third day were not explanatory. They said: "Christ is risen!" In their saying, the world opened beyond abyss.

VI

So I offer you a simple structure for pondering the poetry that you have yet to utter:

- crucifixion . . . resurrection;
- exile . . . homecoming;
- abyss . . . newness;
- denial . . . despair;
- truth-telling . . . hope-telling.

We Christian utterers have only to *speak of Friday* and the exhibit of the death of all that we have treasured. We have only to *speak of Sunday* and the exhibit of newness that we thought not possible.

My last task is to reflect specifically on the context in which we are to be truth-tellers against denial and hope-tellers against despair.

We are situated, as prophets most often are, in a national security state that imagines itself to be autonomous and ultimate, an act of distorted imagination that puts us on a path to death. The reach of the national security state touches our life in all its aspects and influences all sorts of people who have never heard the phrase *the national security state*.

- The national security state *makes promises* it cannot keep, promises of well being and safety;
- The national security state invites systemic and *pervasive anxiety* from which it offers no respite;
- The national security state breeds efforts at a *religion of certitude* that is sure to be idolatrous.

Prophetic ministry is to expose such a state of mind and such an ideology of public life, to name the false *promises*, the pervasive *anxiety*, and the ill-gotten *certitude*. Prophetic ministry, in the face of such lethal practice, offers a world of fidelity that is alternative to the ersatz world of security and certitude. Against such formidable claims, prophetic ministry proceeds one text at a time—one oracle, one poem, one narrative, one metaphor—that leads to *vulnerability* and *surprise*. The news of the prophetic tradition is that this practice of vulnerability and surprise is the gift of Jewishness, given by God, waiting to be performed. Prophets have always understood that such high-risk practice is urgent. I cannot imagine a time when it was more urgent than our present time. Such practice is not carping; it is not scolding; it is not confrontation. It is, rather, *a truth* that makes free, *a hope* that heals. There is a desperate waiting among us for such a performance. Amos, in justifying his venturesome vocation, did so with two statements and two rhetorical questions (Amos 3:8):

Statement: The lion has roared;
Question: Who will not fear?
Statement: The Lord God has spoken;
Question: Who can but prophesy?

From Amos to us, the question lingers and haunts, Who indeed?

CHAPTER 8

The Land Mourns

THE BIBLE, and the Old Testament in particular, is the story of a people with God.[1] It is, at the same time, the story of God and the land, God and the earth, God as Creator, and land as creation. When religious communities are excessively preoccupied with issues of personal salvation and redemption, the big issues of Creator-creation suffer disregard. Our present work in biblical interpretation and in communities of faith is to recover the large horizon of Creator-creation and so to reconstrue the natural environment as God's gift that invites our full joy and our responsible management. In what follows I will outline how the crisis of creation appeared in ancient Israel and consider textual resources in the Old Testament for our own thinking and practice of responsible creatureliness in the world.

I

In the Old Testament, King Solomon radically shifted the presuppositions of public life and public practice in ancient Israel.[2] He did so, moreover, in imitation of the powerful regimes around him, most especially Pharaoh's regime in Egypt. In the older practice and memory of Israel, public life and public policy were shaped essentially by the covenant of Sinai, which had summoned Israel to a responsible public ethic in the world. That hard-nosed and uncompromising covenantal tradition sought to bring every aspect of life under the aegis of YHWH, the Creator of heaven and earth who had saved Israel from slavery in Egypt. The big accent of the Sinai covenant mediated through the book of Deuteronomy was to organize the political economy of Israel as a *neighborhood*, in which each member of the community was summoned to invest in the well being of all of the neighbors. It was a kind of communitarianism that moved toward egalitarianism, though it never arrived there.

But Solomon, as he is remembered in the Old Testament, did not share the passions of Sinai. Rather, he embraced the *appetites of acquisitiveness* that contradicted the *neighborly insistences* of Sinai. While Solomon is popularly regarded in the church as a model for wisdom, in fact the biblical report on him tells otherwise and traces out his foolishness. It tells us that he created a great apparatus of control and wealth and self-indulgence that operated on the backs of his vulnerable neighbors.

Solomon's wealth

Solomon was a great practitioner of *wealth*. In fact, he turned out to be a money machine. His political-military strength caused the money to flow into Jerusalem, money as taxes, tributes, and customs fees:

> Solomon was sovereign over all the kingdoms from the Euphrates to the land of the Philistines, even to the border of Egypt; they brought tribute and served Solomon all the days of his life. (1 Kgs 4:21)

> The weight of gold that came to Solomon in one year was six hundred sixty-six talents of gold, besides that which came from the traders and from the business of the merchants, and from all the kings of Arabia and the governors of the land. King Solomon made two hundred large shields of beaten gold; six hundred shekels of gold went into each large shield. He made three hundred shields of beaten gold; three minas of gold went into each shield; and the king put them in the House of the Forest of Lebanon. The king also made a great ivory throne, and overlaid it with the finest gold. The throne had six steps. The top of the throne was rounded in the back, and on each side of the seat were arm rests and two lions standing beside the arm rests, while twelve lions were standing, one on each end of a step on the six steps. Nothing like it was ever made in any kingdom. All King Solomon's drinking vessels were of gold, and all the vessels of the House of the Forest of Lebanon were of pure gold; none were of silver—it was not considered as anything in the days of Solomon. For the king had a fleet of ships of Tarshish at sea with the fleet of Hiram. Once every three years the fleet of ships at Tarshish used to come bringing gold, silver, ivory, apes, and peacocks. . . . Every one of them brought a present, objects of silver and gold, garments, weaponry, spices, horses, and mules, so much year by year. (1 Kgs 10:14-22, 25)

That enormous amount of wealth permitted a high standard of living that contrasted with the life of the peasants who supported him:

Solomon's provision for one day was thirty cors of choice flour, and
sixty cors of meal, ten fat oxen, and twenty pasture-fed cattle, one
hundred sheep, besides deer, gazelles, roebucks, and fatted fowl. For he
had dominion over all the region west of the Euphrates from Tiphsah to
Gaza, over all the kings west of the Euphrates; and he had peace on all
sides. (1 Kgs 4:22-24)

Solomon as commercial genius

Solomon was a *commercial genius* who controlled the trade routes and the flow
of resources north and south. His geographical location made him the middleman
in international trade:

King Solomon built a fleet of ships at Eziongeber, which is near Eloth on
the shore of the Red Sea, in the land of Edom. Hiram sent his servants
with the fleet, sailors who were familiar with the sea, together with the
servants of Solomon. They went to Ophir, and imported from there four
hundred twenty talents of gold, which they delivered to King Solomon.
(1 Kgs 9:26-28)

Solomon's import of horses was from Egypt and Kue, and the king's
traders received them from Kue at a price. A chariot could be imported
from Egypt for six hundred shekels of silver, and a horse for one hundred
fifty; so through the king's traders they were exported to all the kings of
the Hittites and the kings of Aram. (1 Kgs 10:28-29)

Solomon's supply of cheap labor

Solomon's enormous military, political, and economic success depended on the
supply of cheap labor. It is reported that he pressed into service in state labor the
subjects of other countries that he controlled and perhaps also his own subjects.
We can tell that the biblical narrators are nervous about this forced labor, because
it reminded them too much of slavery in Egypt. So they vacillated on the data
they wanted to report. On the one hand, it is reported that the men of Israel were
forced into labor camps:

King Solomon conscripted forced labor out of all Israel; the levy num-
bered thirty thousand men. He sent them to the Lebanon, ten thousand a
month in shifts; they would be a month in the Lebanon and two months
at home; Adoniram was in charge of the forced labor. Solomon also had
seventy thousand laborers and eighty thousand stonecutters in the hill
country, besides Solomon's three thousand three hundred supervisors
who were over the work, having charge of the people who did the work.

> At the king's command, they quarried out great, costly stones in order to lay the foundation of the house with dressed stones. So Solomon's builders and Hiram's builders and the Gebalites did the stonecutting and prepared the timber and the stone to build the house. (1 Kgs 5:13-18)

But on the other hand, a second report qualifies the matter:

> All the people who were left of the Amorites, the Hittites, the Perizzites, the Hivites, and the Jebusites, who were not of the people of Israel—their descendants who were still left in the land, whom the Israelites were unable to destroy completely—these Solomon conscripted for slave labor, and so they are to this day. But of the Israelites Solomon made no slaves; they were the soldiers, they were his officials, his commanders, his captains, and the commanders of his chariotry and cavalry. (1 Kgs 9:20-22)

Whether or not Solomon recruited his own subjects to forced labor to enhance his regime or not, it is clear that there was no neighborly regard but only use made of persons reduced to production performance.

Solomon as temple builder

As is well known, Solomon is *the great temple builder* in the Old Testament. His temple was famous for its ornamentation and its extravagance in which no expense was spared. The report asserts the goal that marked the new construction:

> The interior of the inner sanctuary was twenty cubits long, twenty cubits wide, and twenty cubits high; he overlaid it with pure gold. He also overlaid the altar with cedar. Solomon overlaid the inside of the house with pure gold, then he drew chains of gold across, in front of the inner sanctuary, and overlaid it with gold. Next he overlaid the whole house with gold, in order that the whole house might be perfect; even the whole altar that belonged to the inner sanctuary he overlaid with gold. (1 Kgs 6:20-22)

> So Solomon made all the vessels that were in the house of the LORD: the golden altar, the golden table for the bread of the Presence, the lampstands of pure gold, five on the south side and five on the north, in front of the inner sanctuary; the flowers, the lamps, and the tongs, of gold; the cups, snuffers, basins, dishes for incense, and firepans, of pure gold; the sockets for the doors of the innermost part of the house, the most holy place, and for the doors of the nave of the temple, of gold. (1 Kgs 7:48-50)

The king obviously made an enormous display of his wealth, his power, his capacity to control, and his savvy management. The temple was, of course, to the glory of YHWH; but as it happens with such immense projects, it turned out to be *to the glory of Solomon,* a Solomon who dazzled not only his own people but also leading foreign leaders like the Queen of Sheba. It is reported that "there was no more spirit in her" (1 Kgs 10:5). Better rendered, he "took her breath away" with his opulence and his extravagance.

Solomon in the twenty-first century

Now, if we reflect on Solomon's accomplishment from the perspective of the twenty-first century, we can see what he was about. He organized a whole economic world around his government, so that he was an early practitioner of *globalization.* His globalization depended, as it always does, on controlling matters so that he created a *national security state,* an institution of acquisitiveness that depended on enormous military muscle. It is easy enough for us, as citizens of the United States, to see how this worked for Solomon; for we also live in a national security state that manages *globalization* in the interest of *acquisitiveness* that depends on *military muscle.* We may note, moreover, one other ingredient in Solomon's oppressive achievement. The temple served as a visual articulation of a religious ideology that gave legitimacy to Solomon's entire enterprise. The temple in Jerusalem was a monument that helped everyone to see that YHWH, the God of Israel, was Solomon's patron and that Solomon was YHWH's chosen, special agent in the world.

A great national security state cannot exist without religious legitimization that believes for itself that it is God's messianic agent to do God's will in the world. I do not have to tell you that what invariably happens is that God signs on for the purposes and goals of the national security state, so that YHWH became an appendage to Solomon. It is easy enough to see that this ancient God who guaranteed the national security state is now replicated in the United States as a national security state that claims for itself the rule of God to establish democratic capitalism in the world, a claim that supports militarism and economic aggression everywhere. It is not new among us; Solomon had already done it.

In the Solomon memory, there is no direct mention of abuse of the environment, except this. Everything and everyone has become a commodity. Everything and everyone can be bought and sold and owned and used and traded. Solomon referred nothing beyond himself to a greater good but regarded himself as the point of it all. It follows that reduction of everything to a commodity means that the environment is simply an expendable resource for self-indulgence and self-enhancement. Thus, we may imagine that Solomon is a great abuser of creation, because he did not acknowledge the will and purpose of the Creator. In all of this Solomon replicated the policies and practices of his father-in-law, the Egyptian pharaoh, who abused the environment, including the Nile River, for the great acquisitive ends of the state.[3] It is no wonder that Solomon's government fell apart in a tax revolt, because his subjects in northern Israel were weary of paying taxes to fund his aggressive acquisitiveness (see 1 Kgs 12:1-19). By the time he was finished, Solomon had created a practice and a perspective that was ready to use up all available resources for short-term benefits to the regime without regard for the vulnerability of the environment. He cared no more for the environment than he did for his subjects. He is, in all respects, a drastic contradiction to the ancient covenant of Sinai.

II

The Solomonic enterprise, the attempt in ancient Israel at a national security state, worked its slow, weary way to self-destruction. That of itself is not news, for every national security state works itself to destruction, never learning in time the limits of exploitative acquisitiveness, giving full rein to satiation.

What is news, rather, is that ancient Israel, all through the heady Jerusalem years, witnessed sporadic, ad hoc protests, dissents, and warnings. While these peculiar voices may be seen altogether as a sustained corpus, in fact these voices appear here and there, roughly informed by old memories of Sinai neighborliness. We call these voices "prophets," and we can see that the biblical memory functions through them in an ongoing interaction between the *power of acquisitiveness* and the *poetry of alternative*. Here I will consider five examples of the poetry of alternative before I move to the decisive example for our topic of the environment. The question before is, How shall we understand the earth (*'erets*), which in Hebrew is also land (*'erets*). The *power of acquisitiveness* viewed the earth-land as a *commodity*; the *poetry of alternative* insisted that earth-land is a *trust* to be cherished, respected, and well cared for. The dispute over *commodity* or *trust* is a very old dispute that runs through the Old Testament. And, of course, we dwell on these old text traditions because the same issue of *commodity* or *trust* is an urgent one among us.[4] It is astonishing that when one puts a new question to these classic texts, new worlds of interpretation open up.[5] We are now, in our time, compelled to put new questions to the text, questions that arise from our context of jeopardy. When we do so, we are led to new and occasionally compelling new worlds.

1 Kings 21

The narrative account of Naboth's vineyard in *1 Kings 21* is well known to us. It concerns a member of the covenant community of Israel who had a vineyard, a choice property that the king wanted. The king, Ahab, had no notion of neighborliness and assumed that land was property and could be bought and sold and traded. He is an honorable man, given his focus on commodity, for he offers to buy the vineyard from Naboth or to trade for it. But Naboth will not part with the vineyard. Indeed, he cannot part with it. Because it is his inheritance. He belongs to it. It is a family trust, and it must be held. Thus, the issue sharply divides between two views of land, land as *commodity* or land as *trust*, land as market goods or land as a place in a neighborly society.

The narrative account exhibits the way in which Ahab, and his wife Jezebel, exercise the new ruthless power of the crown, frame Naboth as a traitor, have him executed, and so seize the property by default. In the narrative account, *commodity* defeats *trust*, as perhaps it always will.

But, of course, in Israel's telling, the story does not end there. In fact, it only begins now, in verse 17, when the prophetic character, Elijah, enters the drama. That entry is marked in the narrative by the introduction of "the word of God" that dispatches Elijah to confront the king. By telling the story in this way, the text attests that there is more to social transactions than power and acquisitiveness. The "more," about which the king knows nothing, is the silent but intransigent intentionality of YHWH, the God who presides over land and keeps royal possessors as only penultimate social reality. The appearance of Elijah attests to the old doxology, "The earth is the LORD's and the fullness thereof" (Ps 24:1). The earth does not belong to the national security state, and it cannot be abused or confiscated with impunity. If land could be managed without this "third agent," then the exploiters could do what they want. But according to the text tradition, that third agent is always present. King Ahab recognizes immediately that the prophetic voice of Elijah is a threat to royal authority. He greets him by saying, "Have you found me, O my enemy?" (v. 20). The poet of alternative is always an enemy of unbridled acquisitiveness. The story ends with a prophetic declaration that such commoditization of reality will come to a sorry end.

Amos 6:4-7

A century after Elijah, the prophet Amos appears in his poetic way. I cite only one text, *Amos 6:4-7*. The oracle begins with a "woe," big trouble coming![6] The poem provides an inventory of the practices of self-indulgence that are common for the power class in the ancient city of Amos:

> Alas for those who lie on beds of ivory,
>   and lounge on their couches,
> and eat lambs from the flock,
>   and calves from the stall;
> who sing idle songs to the sound of the harp,
>   and like David improvise on instruments of music;
> who drink wine from bowls,
>   and anoint themselves with the finest oils. (Amos 6:4-6a)

The list of acquisitive practices shows the limitless utilization of consumer goods without reference to those in great need. The economy is skewed so that some live so well. Thus, the power class can eat lamb and veal, while the poor must let their animals grow to maturity for the sake of more meat. The days of the power class are at the club, with frivolous music and other entertainment, wine in large bowls, much body care with extravagant oils—all expensive uses.

That inventory might not be so appalling were it not followed in the poem by the strong adversity "but": "*but* are not grieved over the ruin of Joseph!" (Amos 6:6b). Not vexed! Not troubled about the jeopardy of the community of covenant. The ones Amos critiques have been narcoticized by their self-indulgence so that they are immune to the world out beyond them. They do not notice, and they do not care. Now this poetry does not use the word "land," but the term "Ephraim" means the land and the society of northern Israel. They have not yet noticed that the economy is under acute strain, and they certainly do not connect that economy to the overuse of costly commodity goods at the expense of the community.

In verse 7 the poet introduces a dramatic "therefore" in which the consequences of undisciplined self-indulgent results:

> Therefore they shall now be the first to go into exile,
>   and the revelry of the loungers shall pass away. (Amos 6:7)

Therefore exile! Therefore displacement! Therefore land loss! The poetry, as all such poetry, is elliptical. We are not told how self-indulgence and narcoticization are linked to land loss. The poet does not tell us and perhaps does not know. The poet only knows that the land that is used and exploited is God's creation. There are limits to be honored. There are restraints to be exercised. There are trusts to be cared for. And when self-aggrandizement overrides limits and restraints and trusts, creation has a way of circling back to bring negation and death. Poetry is perhaps the only way to say this, because the power class has confiscated all other modes of discourse. The poet in dissent does not explain but only imagines. And that prophetic imagination discloses what the power class could not foresee.

Isaiah 5

Isaiah, perhaps a contemporary of Amos, saw the same self-indulgence in the south in the land of Judah. In *Isaiah 5*, the prophet offers a series of "woes"—seven times—big trouble coming! In that recital Isaiah mentions strong drink, falsehood, euphemism, and self-sufficiency as the causes of the trouble to come. I will focus on the first of the woes, spoken in verses 8-10. The indictment introduced by "woe" is against agribusiness or perhaps even military aggression that seeks to occupy and control the land:

> Ah, you who join house to house,
>   who add field to field,
> until there is room for no one but you,

> and you are left to live alone
> in the midst of the land! (Isa 5:8)

The poet sees that acquiring and controlling huge tracts of land—for the sake of production and security—will bring trouble. For starters, such accumulation destroys neighborliness. So much land diminishes the habitation that none are left. There are no neighbors, and there can be no neighborhood.

Beyond loss that follows from economic acquisitiveness, the poet intrudes YHWH into the transaction and puts on the lips of God a decree:

> The LORD of hosts has sworn in my hearing:
> Surely many houses shall be desolate,
>   large and beautiful houses, without inhabitant. (Isa 5:9)

The Lord of military force ("hosts") has declared as a coming social reality that big houses and beautiful homes and large estates will be abandoned, without habitation. The lines conjure the ruined Tara Plantation and many such plantations that are left abandoned by war. But here it is not war that causes abandonment. Rather, it is an agricultural, economic crisis. In a remarkable act of imagination about creatureliness, Isaiah imagines that the land, when it is organized into huge private tracts, will simply refuse to produce. The poetry is quite precise. It will take ten acres of grapes to produce a small measure of wine. We do not know exactly what those measures are, but clearly the poet means that it will take a huge piece of land to produce very little. The land will become resistant to fruitfulness. The land will resist the Creator's command to "be fruitful." Such resistance on the part of creaturely land is what we know as an almost certain result of absentee ownership and agribusiness, in which land becomes commodity. In such an arrangement, the land is no longer caressed and honored, as would be done by a small farmer with an intimate connection to the land. The poetry offers no explanation for this outcome, but the poet knows that big-time acquisition of land is inimical to fruitfulness. The land is abandoned because of loss of agricultural income. The land requires ownership that is partnership; without such partnership, the creation loses interest in fruitfulness.

Micah 2:1-5

Micah, a later contemporary of Isaiah, continues the same dire warnings given with a "woe" of big trouble coming. The indictment of the landgrabbers describes an aggressive process of real estate transactions:

> Alas for those who devise wickedness
>   and evil deeds on their beds!
> When the morning dawns, they perform it,

> because it is in their power.
> They covet fields, and seize them;
> houses, and take them away;
> they oppress householder and house,
> people and their inheritance. (Mic 2:1-2)

The power class schemes about real estate even before they get out of bed in the morning. They lie awake at night thinking how to buy up the land. And as soon as the sun comes up, they call their agents. Even before they have breakfast, they have taken legal steps to advance their holdings at the expense of the community, for they know who is vulnerable and what land is available, and they have very smart agents. More than that, the poet pushes behind the acts to the motivation: They "covet." The poet uses the term from the tenth commandment of Sinai, "Thou shall not covet" (Exod 30:17). The ones that the poet critiques are propelled by avarice, wishing for much more than they need. They buy up fields and houses, and in so doing they act aggressively against those who cannot defend their houses or their fields. They violate the neighborhood, and they take advantage of those who are not as sharp. And then the poet uses the word we have already seen in the Elijah narrative. They oppress household and house, people and *inheritance*. They violate old family trusts and old tribal arrangements. They have no interest in such ancient arrangements because now it is all about profit and gain. Now the economy has to do with commodity, nothing about covenant or neighborliness.

Then comes, predictably, another prophetic "therefore." Such attitudes and such rapacious acts have consequences in a world ordered by the Creator. God plans trouble for such coveters. They do not go unnoticed by the divine guarantor:

> *Therefore* thus says the LORD:
> Now, I am devising against this family an evil
> from which you cannot remove your necks;
> and you shall not walk haughtily,
> for it will be an evil time. (Mic 2:3-4)

Coming soon will be an evil time, a time of profound trouble. Notice that the means of misery are not specified. There will come threats that will reduce the big land speculators to weeping mourners. They will lament bitterly, giving grieving voice to their economic ruin. They will say, "We are utterly ruined" just when we thought we would be on top of the heap. The mention of "captors" suggests that the land will be occupied by a foreign army, in this context, the Assyrians. Notice the remarkable symmetry of the poetry. If the power class *seizes* land from vulnerable neighbors, now the enemy will *seize* the land from the power class. This is poetry, not logic. The logic of it is that the Creator will not tolerate the ultimate despoiling of creation. Of course, the connection is outrageous, as outrageous as if a contemporary poet were to say that abuse of land and poor people would pro-voke a terrorist threat—because the world is morally coherent. Abuse of the land and the neighborhood has its costs, a connection that can only be voiced in poetry.

Hosea 4:1-3

Hosea's sense about land and environment is one he shares with his companion prophets. In 4:1-3, Hosea issues a clear speech of condemnation that concerns land. Of special interest is the fact that in his brief oracle of the three verses, the term land (*'erets*) occurs three times:

- the Lord has an indictment against the inhabitants of *the land;* (v. 1)
- there is no knowledge of God in *the land;* (v. 1)
- therefore *the land* mourns. (v. 3)

The case against Israel concerns violation of creation that leads to destruction of the land. The violation concerns the transgression of the Ten Commandments:

Swearing, lying, and murder,
and stealing and adultery break out;
bloodshed follows bloodshed. (v. 2)

This is the clearest appeal to the Ten Commandments in all of prophetic litera-ture. That guilty verdict against Israel is followed by a prophetic "therefore":

Therefore the land mourns.

As a prophet enunciates the consequence of a society out of control, the phrase "land mourns" refers to a drought. If, however, we take the imagery seriously, the land is reduced to weeping sadness. It causes grief to the environment to see the commandments broken, because such transgression bespeaks a society out of control, alienated from God, set against the neighbor, passionate for its own advantage without regard to social or "natural" reality.

In poetic imagination the land responds to such disorder with a drought. Cre-ation simply refuses to function because the keeping of the commandments is the condition of a well-functioning creation. The connection that Hosea makes is an anticipation of Wendell Berry's insight that distorted social relationships will inescapably distort the environment, a distortion caused by greed, acquisitiveness, and self-indulgent entitlement.[7] The commandments articulate the restraints that are necessary to the maintenance of the environment. But when there is excessive greed, the land is overused, the oceans are overfished, and the forests are stripped, until the entire ecosystem is made to be dysfunctional. Hosea did not express the matter scientifically, but the point is unmistakably clear in poetic formulation.

These four texts, from Amos 6:4-6, Isaiah 5:8-10, Micah 2:1-5, and Hosea 4:1-3, are agreed on the threat to the environment that is caused by the crisis of society. All are dated to the eighth century BCE, wherein Israel and Judah were flexing their muscles, and imagining their status as God's "chosen" peoples gave them freedom to live beyond limit. During that time, they were simply living out the dream of Solomon, who had imagined he could have it all immediately. But then came the poets! The word is uttered that exposes the illusion that has become the basis of public policy and public practice. It takes no imagination to transpose this confrontation between such public policy and practice and the poets to our own time and place. Our society lives in an illusion of no restraints in which the global economic-military reach of the United States seizes and controls everything. And now we face, as they did in that ancient society, an inconvenient reminder to the contrary. Al Gore is not the first to educate us. Already in ancient Israel there were those "inconvenient poets" who asserted that creatureliness is curbed in its entitlement and self-indulgence by the Creator. They saw, as we are now recovering, that creatureliness requires, in quite concrete ways, an embrace of nonnegotiable limit; a violation of that nonnegotiable limit leads to the dysfunction of creation, and eventually death to creation.

III

After this cluster of poetic texts from ancient Israel in the 700s, the collision course between God's poets and public policy became more and more acute in the 600s, that is, in the seventh century. That collision course is best voiced and embodied in the prophet Jeremiah, whose poetry occurs just as Jerusalem society comes to a stunning crisis. On his watch the city, the king, the temple, and civil society were all terminated—by the judgment of YHWH, the Creator and Lord of the commandments. Jeremiah is unflinching in his poetry, which speaks the truth of the crisis. I will cite four remarkable texts from Jeremiah.

Jeremiah 9:23-24

In *Jeremiah 9:23-24*, the poet stakes the radical, nonnegotiable either/or of life in the world: "Thus says the LORD: Do not let the wise boast in their wisdom, do not let the mighty boast in their might, do not let the wealthy boast in their wealth" (Jer 9:23). The great triad he critiques—wisdom, might, wealth—is the legacy of Solomon. It was Solomon who acquired the know-how to manage the world, the might to control trade routes, and the wealth to build a capital of gold. He was a celebrated success. But, says Jeremiah, do not brag about that, because it is not the stuff of faithful life in the world.

And then Jeremiah offers a countertheme of three qualities: "But let those who boast boast in this, that they understand and know me, that I am the

LORD; I act with steadfast love, justice, and righteousness in the earth, for in these things I delight, says the LORD" (Jer 9:24). The poet commends steadfast love, justice, and righteousness, which constitute the sum of covenantal, neighborly living. The three terms, steadfast love, justice, and righteousness are at the center of the biblical ethic. They all have to do with the sense of solidarity according to the limits and commands of YHWH. Thus, Jeremiah offers a radical either/or that pertains directly to the social and environmental crisis of his time:

> Either: wisdom, might, wealth;
> Or: steadfast love, justice, righteousness.

In prophetic rhetoric the either/or is total and without compromise. The first three, inherited as the legacy of Solomon, lead to the destruction of Jerusalem. They are the same three that are embodied by the national security state, by global exploitation, and by unfettered economics; and they are, says the poet, the route to death. The good news is that there is an alternative in covenantal faithfulness that curbs appetites for the sake of communal solidarity that conforms to creatureliness. All that remains, according to the poet, is to decide.

Jeremiah 4:23-26

In *Jeremiah 4:23-26*, Jeremiah issues one of his brilliant and most devastating poems:

> I looked on the earth, and lo, it was waste and void;
>   and to the heavens, and they had no light.
> I looked on the mountains, and lo, they were quaking,
>   and all the hills moved to and fro.
> I looked, and lo, there was no one at all,
>   and all the birds of the air had fled.
> I looked, and lo, the fruitful land was a desert,
>   and all its cities were laid in ruins
>   before the LORD, before his fierce anger. (Jer 4:23-26)

The poet says five times, "I looked and behold," an act of imagination in which he looks out beyond the present to conjure the future. And what he sees with his uncommon visionary capacity is

> chaos without light,
> mountains and hills destabilized,
> birds gone, and
> the land a desert.

Interpreters recognize that this fivefold vision is a reference to the creation text in Genesis 1. The poet is describing the dismantling of creation, the loss of creatureliness—fruitful land, birds, mountains, lights, all ending in chaos. The poem attests that *creation can be undone*. Be undone, says the poet, by the fierce anger of God because the Creator God is deeply vexed by the abuse of creation. For us, the poem attests that creation is not unconditionally guaranteed; it depends on responsible care and partnership with God. Human community can either be *partner in creation* or can be *enemy of creation* that eventually negates the life systems willed by God. The poetry is radical and terse, but it voices a truth not to be denied.

Jeremiah 22:29

I cite the brief text of *Jeremiah 22:29*. In this poem Jeremiah is grieving the fact that the last king of Judah, Coniah, will be taken away into exile. In the middle of the poem there is this stunning verse:

> O land, land, land,
> > hear the word of the LORD!

That is all. It is a sad summons to the land (*'erets*) that is now addressed by the Creator God. And what God has to say to the land is that the end has come; that is, as the last king in Jerusalem goes, so goes the creaturely order. The voice in the poem is no longer angry; now it is sad. The poet looks ahead to see a future that derives from practices and policies of greed and autonomy.

Jeremiah 31:4-5; 31:13-14

At the edge of the poetry of Jeremiah, spoken in the depth of loss, anger, and sadness, there is an anticipation that when Jerusalem is sobered in its loss and hurt in its failure, the Creator God will act to restore creation, to cause—in a quite concrete way—a new creation:

> Again I will build you, and you shall be built,
> > O virgin Israel!
> Again you shall take your tambourines,
> > and go forth in the dance of the merrymakers.
> Again you shall plant vineyards
> > on the mountains of Samaria;
> the planters shall plant,
> > and shall enjoy the fruit. (Jer 31:4-5)

> Then shall the young women rejoice in the dance,
> > and the young men and the old shall be merry.

> I will turn their mourning into joy.
>> I will comfort them, and give them gladness for sorrow.
> I will give the priests their fill of fatness,
>> and my people shall be satisfied with my bounty,
>>>> says the LORD. (Jer 31:13-14)

Life will resume! But it is after the death. It is a promise made but only to later generations. The good news is that the Creator God will not quit because God wills a workable, fruitful, joyous creation. The sober news is that it is no time soon when God will re-create. The prophet intends to walk his contemporaries, through his utterance, into the crisis and, belatedly, out of the crisis. It was a hard word when he spoke it, because it contradicted all of their present continuities. It is still a hard work because the truth of dismantling contradicts our pet convictions, namely, that democratic capitalism of our preferred variety is willed by God as a wave of the future. The word of the poet, then as now, is that that conviction is out of control. There is an alternative, but the alternative that is announced is enormously costly.

IV

I have summarized the poetry that opposed official policy in ancient Israel, poetry that comes in many forms but that is coherent in its main claims. The point of the poetry is that the arrogant assumption that we can do whatever we want and fall back on the sustaining life-support system is an illusion. The creation is fragile and can be defeated. But in such defeat for creation the Creator is not defeated. There is long-term assurance about the Creator alongside short-term news about the creation.

The last text I mention is *Hosea 2:2-23*, which I take to be a summation of prophetic imagination about the environment. As many already know, Hosea, out of his personal experience, represents life with God as a marital crisis, God as husband and Israel as wife. There is in such usage an unfortunate patriarchal bias.[8] Given that, however, the poetry still moves with a powerful, compelling claim. The poem is divided into two parts.

The first part is a *scenario of divorce* in which YHWH is a grieved, angry husband who is terminating the marriage covenant with Israel. Like all such serious marital disputes, YHWH makes accusations of infidelity against Israel and then makes sweeping threats, introduced as always by "therefore":

> For their mother has played the whore;
>> she who conceived them has acted shamefully.
> For she said, "I will go after my lovers;
>> they give me my bread and my water,
>> my wood and my flax, my oil and my drink." (Hos 2:5)

> Therefore I will take back my grain in its time,
>   and my wine in its season;
> and I will take away my wool and my flax,
>   which were to cover her nakedness. (Hos 2:9)

YHWH is angry because Israel had received from the generosity of YHWH the Creator the best produce, grain, wine, and oil. But, according to YHWH's rant, Israel did not realize that these were gifts of the Creator and refused (1) to be grateful or (2) to use them in ways appropriate to YHWH. Indeed, Israel mistakenly thought the fruitful gifts came from their own cleverness and their religious technology, not knowing that all they produced was a pure gift from the Creator.

In poetic discourse, the Creator-husband threatens to remove the fruitfulness so that creation will no longer work. Beyond that, there will be an end to public life, the cessation of festivals, and a drought that dries up vines and fig trees. The final word is that YHWH is angry because "they forgot me" (v. 13). They forgot in their autonomy that they were creatures. They forgot in their self-indulgence about the commandments as condition of fruitfulness. They forgot in their sense of entitlement that they lived by a gift. The poem comes to a silence at the end of verse 13. There is a stillness as the poet imagines that God gives up on Israel and on creation.

And then, after a long, devastating silence of absence, YHWH speaks again in the second half of the poem. In verses 14-23, YHWH promises to renew creation. YHWH will take an initiative, woo Israel back to faithful obedience, so that Israel and creation can be reordered. There will be a new covenant with creation: "I will make for you a covenant on that day with the wild animals, the birds of the air, and the creeping things of the ground" (Hos 2:18a). There will be a cessation of war, because war is the great devastator of the land: "and I will abolish the bow, the sword, and war from the land; and I will make you lie down in safety" (Hos 2:18b). There will be a new marriage covenant with Israel, the same Israel that had been unfaithful: "And I will take you for my wife forever; I will take you for my wife in righteousness and in justice, in steadfast love, and in mercy. I will take you for my wife in faithfulness; and you shall know the LORD" (Hos 2:19-20). The new marital vows of YHWH contain all the great terms of faith, words of fidelity and solidarity and care and sustainability and well being. And finally, as the poem ends, there will be the resumption of fruitfulness:

> And the earth shall answer the grain, the wine, and the oil,
>   and they shall answer Jezreel;
> and I will sow him for myself in the land.
> And I will have pity on Lo-ruhamah,
>   and I will say to Lo-ammi, "You are my people";
>   and he shall say, "You are my God." (Hos 2:22-23)

This is a poem of extraordinary sweep. It moves from divorce to remarriage, from alienation to reconciliation, from failed creation to new creation. How we read the poem depends on where we are situated in the poem. Think how the poem reads if we position ourselves in the poem just at the end of verse 13, when God's termination of this covenant is voiced, just before verse 14, when God begins to woo again. In that dread moment of silence, we are placed before a deep failure in which the Creator is, for now, ready to end creation. This is not science. It is poetry. It discloses to us the deep things of God. It requires us to wait and to receive, to hope, and to repent before we hope. It invites us not to quit but to change and to live, yet again, as glad creatures of the Creator. But we cannot get to the second part of the poem unless we ponder for a very long time the truth of the first part of the poem, in which there is a shortage of fidelity and gratitude and excessive practice of control and abuse. Our entire life is lived out in the poem, and it is the life *in the land with God*.

V

There are no easy moves from biblical testimony to our contemporary environmental crisis. I do believe, nonetheless, that it is women and men of faith who are active in public life who can make the urgent move from this basis in faith to the reality of our economic-political world. To that end, I note five conclusions.

1. The environmental crisis requires a rethinking and a reformulation of faith, with particular reference to creation. The church's faith has been so preoccupied with salvation and redemption that we have forgotten how to think theologically about the earth as our true home, a gift from God that comes, like every true home, with demanding chores. Recovery of creation requires us to see that the world is neither an absolute given nor a commodity to possess; it is, rather, a long, caring partnership with the creation.

2. The recovery of creation leads to a candid recognition of limit. It is the reality of the creation that limits the freedom of the creature, a truth already given in a creation story about not eating of the tree of knowledge and good and evil. In the modern world, we have been on a binge of entitlement and self-indulgence with regard to energy and resources. No doubt the recognition of limit will require serious adjustment to our standard of living, but for the sake of our future, we must adhere to limits that summon to serious inconvenience. We cannot overlook the crisis simply because we want to keep the economy at its present level.

3. Addressing these issues requires us to exercise daring imagination that thinks beyond autonomous capitalism. Such imagination, grounded in biblical texts and led by the Spirit of God, may permit us to see and act differently in the world. The truth is that most of our imagination has been co-opted and domesticated by our present circumstance of privilege in the world as citizens of the last

superpower. We imagine unrestrained freedom to do what we want, because there is no serious challenge to such autonomy that legitimates harmful adventurism. Faithful imagination refuses to accept the narrative of unrestrained capitalist ideology and conjures neighborly relationships in a very different way.

4. I have been attentive to the promissory notes of Jeremiah 31 and Hosea 2 because I do not think that faithful people end in defeatism. In these texts God has spoken another word about new possibility, a new creation, a new earth, a restored environment. God has gifts yet to give. It is important that the faithful not end in a kind of dismal fatalism, even if it is very late among us. The Creator has more gifts to give but will give them only to a receptive society.

5. Finally, alternative imagination must impinge on policy. Good intentionality and heroic personal practices are important but they are not adequate. What is necessary now is political will to reverse the politics of self-indulgence and the economics of commoditization that places our world in jeopardy. There are deep technological problems, but the hard issues concern political will. It is precisely the task of religious communities to summon political will so that there can be freedom and courage to do the right thing.

As Hosea says, the land mourns. It weeps for the way it has been exploited and raped. It cries over negligence and misuse. It is sad because it has not been honored or respected. We can imagine that the Creator weeps over the land as Jesus wept over Jerusalem. It is the chance of faithful people to weep with the land and with the Creator who loves the land. We are, in our weeping, summoned to thanks. Thus the psalmist concludes:

> For his anger is but for a moment;
>> his favor is for a lifetime.
> Weeping may linger for the night,
>> but joy comes with the morning. (Ps 30:5)

We are in the night. It is the weeping that makes newness possible—not sure but possible.

Part III

Writings

SKEPTICISM AND DOXOLOGY:
BRUEGGEMANN ON THE WRITINGS

CAROLYN J. SHARP

THE WRITINGS in their final literary form reflect the Judean postexilic period, with its debilitating economic pressures under Persian rule and strong pressure toward cultural assimilation in the Hellenistic period. Mindful of this historical context, Brueggemann notes that "immense courage and interpretive flexibility were required in order to sustain Jewish canonical coherence and identity"[1] in those centuries before the Common Era. The biblical texts that make up the Writings address themselves in a wide and creative variety of ways to the maintenance of Judean cultural and theological identity. To oversimplify, we might say that three main trajectories obtain within these diverse materials. Some texts give themselves to extended and highly sophisticated epistemological discourse (Job and Ecclesiastes). Some weave dramatic tales of believers' heroic negotiations of Diaspora and colonization (Ruth, Esther, Daniel). And finally, some use poetry to express the trust (Proverbs), lament (Lamentations), delight (Song of Songs), and praise (Psalms) of a displaced yet faithful people.

When he interprets Job, Proverbs, and Ecclesiastes, Brueggemann hears the friction of conflicting testimonies and their contestatory epistemologies. The supreme assurance of the courtly maxims of Proverbs is met in the skeptical writings, Job and Ecclesiastes, by a "theological vexation that is beyond the horizon of the founding narratives" of Israel's faith.[2] Positivist wisdom "asserts that the God who decrees and maintains a particular ordering of reality toward life is a sovereign beyond challenge whose will, purpose, and order cannot be defied or circumvented with impunity."[3] But the disillusionment of Ecclesiastes and the anguish of Job speak their own dissenting truths, and their countertestimony must be honored if we are to appreciate Scripture's witness in all its fullness. Brueggemann does not always relish attending to what he characterizes as the strident negativity of Job and Ecclesiastes. There is most certainly risk in these texts, and threat. Hope is muted there, and one may guess that this is difficult for the ebulliently hopeful Brueggemann. But he knows that these biblical books offer believers something vital for mature faith: a thoroughgoing candor about the frustrations and desperations of human life. The profound honesty of these ancient texts gives the larger biblical dialogue an authenticity that otherwise might have seemed too easy. Brueggemann is swift to acknowledge that the ironic countertestimony of skeptical Wisdom literature is integral to Israel's religious expression; as he notes, "Israel's faith is a probing, questioning, insisting, disjunctive faith."[4] Surely we who are grafted into Israel by the grace of God in Christ (Romans 11) must claim this apophatic stream of biblical witness as our rightful heritage as well.

Risk and threat of a different kind suffuse the Diaspora stories of Ruth, Esther, and Daniel. Deprivation and persecution loom for the protagonists, quintessential outsiders who must be true to themselves and their God in order to survive. These narratives create faithful community anew through their vivid stories of their protagonists' perseverance and trust in God's future. Such storytelling, in Brueggemann's words, "is witness to the rule of God who sustains the practitioners of truth in the presence of power" against all odds.[5]

Faithful community is voiced in richest tones in the Psalms. The Psalter has proven to be an extraordinarily fertile ground for Brueggemann's exegetical imagination. These ancient liturgical texts insist on dialogue between the faithful and God, employing a boldly poetic self-assertion that amounts to nothing less than "chutzpah before the throne" of the Sovereign of the cosmos.[6] The psalmist may shout a wrenching cry of despair or sing a jubilant doxology: either way, a claim is pressed and the attention of God is demanded. The turbulent mélange of protests, hymns, laments, and affirmations in the Psalter lends itself beautifully to Brueggemann's exegetical fascination with dialogical relationship and biblical polyphony. The dialogue in the Psalter engages not just the individual believer but also the body politic, not only the congregation but also all the nations of the world. Not surprisingly, given his interest in the subversion of empire, Brueggemann has probed the political dimensions of these poems that are so often received as vehicles of private spiritual devotion. What he writes of Psalms 9 and 10 applies to every instance in which the psalmist cries out for God to act:

> The psalm as a voice of inexplicable hope—surely rooted in an unquench-able sense of Yahweh as a third party in social relations—in its utterance creates a new social possibility that did not exist before or outside this utterance. . . . This text is itself a practice of alternative politics. It is not mere wishful thinking, nor is it a description of what happened elsewhere. The psalm itself, each time it is boldly uttered in its criticism, polemic, celebration, and anticipation, is the place of *redefined power relations.*[7]

For many centuries, such reconfigured relationships have been the catalyst for our movement from dutiful obedience to unbridled, joyous praise of the God who redeems.

In his addresses on the Writings, Brueggemann plumbs many theological dimensions of these unique and sometimes idiosyncratic biblical texts. He rejoices at the prospect of recovering lament in the life of the church, something he sees as crucial for authentic pastoral care and public healing. He urges that we rediscover wisdom as discernment of the mystery and hiddenness of God. He invites us to embrace the startling oddness of the Holy One who saves us. He gestures toward the ethical and missional implications of practicing wisdom as a way of mending the world and reclaiming creation on behalf of God. Finally, he argues that the courageous defiance of Daniel in Diaspora provides us with a model for asserting our baptismal identity in a world that does not honor the gospel. Readers will find Brueggemann's musings on these varied topics to be provocative, exuberant, and wise.

CHAPTER 9

A Necessary Condition of a Good, Loud Lament

THE ENACTMENT OF LAMENT in our world today is *a sign!*[1]

It is a sign that we focus on lament.

It is a sign that we—and our church and society around—have come of age in a new way.

It is a sign that we—our church and society—are ready to recover a practice (and its rootage in a text) too long denied.

It is a sign that we are prepared to break through the façade of easy triumphalism so powerful among us.

It is a sign that needs to be relished and fully appreciated, not trivialized or taken for granted.

It is a sign, perhaps of a new sense of health and fresh faith, of new missional energy without illusion.

It is a sign from God, and so we must begin in thanksgiving to God, who has signed us in this new way.

I want to reflect, first, on the staged way through which we have come to this fresh focus on lament; second, on the preconditions and prerequisites that make the recovery, retrieval, and practice of lament a serious theological possibility among us; and third, on the ways in which this practice of lament rooted in these texts is a serious countercultural activity that bespeaks a fresh chance to be the faithful church.

I

It is a truism that the church in the modern world has been unfamiliar with and uninterested in the laments of the book of Psalms. Of that unfamiliarity and lack of interest, Claus Westermann, in his wave-making article, writes:

> It would be a worthwhile task to ascertain how it happened that in
> Western Christendom the lament has been totally excluded from man's
> relationship with God, with the result that it has completely disappeared
> above all from prayer and worship. We must ask whether this exclusion
> is actually based on the message of the New Testament or whether it is
> in part attributable to the influence of Greek thought, since it is so thor-
> oughly consistent with the ethic of Stoicism.[2]

In the context of Luther's "theology of the cross," the lament Psalms (including Psalm 88) were important theological data. The new self-confidence of the
Enlightenment, rooted in the reasonable capacity of the autonomous self, however, needed no such voice and, indeed, rendered such a voice nonsensical. Consequently, the lament psalms (with the inescapable exception of Psalm 22) dropped
out of the lectionary and the liturgy. The exception of the liturgical churches
cause such psalms to be disguised in lovely music so that no one notices and no
one is bothered. As a general consequence, the modern church made use of and
indeed produced no representations of lament beyond a Good Friday horizon.
My judgment is that the cultural temptation to triumphalism that has beset the
church was powerfully reinforced by the scholastic catechism tradition that took
God as "omnipotent, omniscient, and omnipresent." Thus, *self-sufficient selves*
in communion with an *all-managing God* had no room for lament, and that theological premise is now powerfully replicated in so-called praise hymns, in which
"never is heard a discouraging word."

   Theological certitude plus cultural self-sufficiency together caused a disregard
of one-third of the Psalter. One may, moreover, imagine that through this studied
repression of those psalms, there was eventually a studied repression of one-third
of faith resources and one-third of the theological reality of our common life.
Thus, I think it is worth considering how we have arrived—with a history of theological certitude and cultural triumphalism—at this place of recovery. I will trace
this movement of the recovery of the laments in three stages, though it clearly is
more complex than that.

The scholarly recovery of lament

The course of scholarship in the twentieth century has been a slow tale of the
recovery of the laments. The great founder of modern Psalm study, Hermann
Gunkel, had, in his commentary of 1926 and in his introduction of 1933,

identified the laments as a primal genre of Israel's Psalter.[3] Nothing of theological importance came of that until the work of his equally important successor, Claus Westermann. Westermann, who has written endlessly on Psalms, did his basic work as a Russian prisoner of war during the Second World War, when he worked out his taxonomy of praise and lament. But, of course, publication and circulation took a very long time. In 1954, he published his "Structure and History of the Lament in the Old Testament."[4] In 1961, he published *The Praise of God in the Psalms*, but it was not until 1977, in the fifth edition of his study, that it became *Praise and Lament in the Psalms*.[5] It was Westermann who worked out the dramatic components of the lament Psalms that Gunkel had not pursued and who saw that they moved characteristically *from plea to praise*. It is this sense of dynamism that is the key discovery of Westermann and, I believe, the most important theological insight for us.

There clustered around Westermann other younger scholars who continued to develop his awareness that the lament occupies a powerful place in the faith of Israel and constitutes a primal datum of biblical theology. I will mention two of his students. First, Erhard Gerstenberger. In many ways, Gerstenberger is Westermann's true successor in Psalm study. He issued his astonishing study of the lament Psalms, *Der bittende Mensch* ("the petitioning person"), but it was not published until 1980.[6] Gerstenberger has since published a full essay on the several genres of the Psalms and has recently issued through Eerdmans a two-volume study of the Psalms.[7] It was Gerstenberger's argument that the capacity of Israel to petition God in the lament is a defining dimension of the anthropology of the Old Testament. In 1978, a second student of Westermann, Rainer Albertz, published his study *Personal Piety and Official Religion*, in which he outlined the remarkable tension in the Psalter between the personal and the public.[8] Since that time, there has been a spate of studies of the Psalms in this country as well, culminating in Patrick Miller's magisterial book *They Cried to the Lord* in 1994.[9]

It is clear that Westermann's new impetus came out of the dread reality of war and, in particular, his savage experience as a prisoner of war. That project, however, did not take on a serious life until the literature had expanded, particularly through the work of Gerstenberger and Albertz in the 1970s. It was the merit of the journal *Interpretation* to have published an issue in January of 1974 on the laments that I believe was pivotal in fixing the lament in the center of the discussion in the United States.[10] In that issue, articles by John Bright and Elizabeth Achtemeier concerned exegetical analyses, and I offered my first foray into the study of the laments. But the key article was by Westermann, "The Role of the Lament in the Theology of the Old Testament."[11] It is not and cannot be unimportant that this development happened in the 1970s, when everything began to fall apart in our society, particularly with reference to the civil rights movement, Watergate, and Vietnam. It became inescapable that wide cultural vulnerability would be freshly noticed, that things had become deeply skewed and distorted in our society. When women and men of faith noticed vulnerability and distortion, moreover, that notice had to be brought to speech. It has to be brought to speech in the face of an ideology that had been too sure and too settled, and in such speech, alert people looked for a text out of which to speak and *voila*! There it was, had always been, unnoticed in the Scriptures because ideologies of triumphalism had taught us not to notice.

The relationship between context and scholarship is, of course, complex and opaque, but I have no doubt that the deep cultural fissures of the 1960s and the 1970s, highlighted by the student revolts of Paris in 1968 and the Chicago Democratic National Convention in the same year, hastened the work and set us on a path to a recovery of the laments. Rootage in the scholarship of Westermann and his students is immensely important and has made available fresh categories of interpretation that were deeply enhanced by a cultural context in which the illusion of self-sufficiency could no longer be sustained.

The pastoral recovery of lament

Church usage often lags behind scholarship. When *Interpretation*, led by Westermann, published its issue in January 1974, the work was genuinely new to many of us. It took another two decades or so as the pastoral care movement began to notice that these scripts of lament were congruent with therapeutic practice. For good reason, the earlier form of the pastoral care movement had turned away from authoritarian theology to the freedom and depth of psychology; by the 1980s, however, it was increasingly clear that pastoral care could not be reduced to psychology. There was more than psychology; it involved reference to the holiness of God as the ground of health.

When that awareness dawned, these lament texts came front and center as a way of voicing from below uncensored pain, anger, and need. Thus, by the end of the 1980s, a large number of books began appearing that explored the interface between pastoral theology and the Psalms. There the authors discovered that what the pastoral care movement under Seward Hiltner and Anton Boisen had learned had been long known in ancient Israel, particularly in the demanding liturgical resources and practices of the Psalms. A large number of derivative books appeared that were related to the practice of ministry. Some of the best of these include books by Michael Jinkins, Katherine Billman and Daniel Migliore, and Stephen McCutchan.[12]

We need to recognize, I believe, that much of the early use of the Psalms in pastoral care was understood in a thin, therapeutic mode of catharsis; that is, we felt better if we said "stuff" without taking too seriously the fact that these texts are prayers addressed to God, who is addressable and who responds to petition and protest. Thus, after initial rediscovery, there was still a necessary effort to go beyond *catharsis* (important as that is) to genuine *conversation with God*. On this point, Harold Fisch is helpful:

Can we therefore conclude that the Hebrew term "meditation" suggests something like romantic self-consciousness—a self-consciousness that expresses itself essentially in monologue? The answer is that the Psalms are not monologues but insistently and at all times dialogue-poems, poems of the self but of the self in the mutuality of relationship with the other.

To speak of relationality pure and simple is, however, misleading. The Psalms are not exercises in existential philosophy; we are not speaking of an encounter for the sake of merely discovering the existence of the other and of the self in relation to the other. The "Thou" *answers* the plea of the "I" and that answer signals a change in the opening situation. The Psalms are in this sense dynamic, they involve action, purpose. W. H. Auden said in his elegy on the death of Yeats, "For poetry makes nothing happen." This is not true of the Psalms. In nearly every psalm something does happen. The encounter between the "I" and the "Thou" is the signal for a change not merely in the inner realm of consciousness but in the realm of outer events.

Against the purity of the inner dialogue, or rather in addition to it, we have the emphasis repeated here, as in many other psalms, on the comforts of the Temple worship, where the well-tried and well-established forms of ritual observance bring to the dialogue with God an institutional basis and framework.[13]

This pastoral dimension continued to be refined. It was widely recognized that the laments in ancient Israel already had the form of what became the "Twelve-Step movement" in Alcoholics Anonymous. The interface between ancient awareness and present rediscoveries has received huge practice support by Ann Weems, who has powerfully dramatized the practice of lament in her voice of grief from below that legitimated a demanding approach to God.[14] Most recently, a paper by Brad and Brent Strawn has urged that expressions of lament evoke a bodily, physiological transformation that hastens the move from plea to praise.[15] This latter insight is parallel to the urging of Joachim Begrich and Westermann about the utterance of salvation oracle that facilitates the plea-to-praise dynamic.[16] Thus, Begrich matches the hypothesized utterance of oracle with a suggested physiological transformation. By the turn of the century, consequently, the interface of *lament and pastoral care* is well established and now available in a wide variety of books.

The public recovery of lament

The capacity of the church to reengage with and reappropriate the laments as important theological pastoral data has mostly been confined to a therapeutic, interpersonal horizon. This in itself is not a bad thing, except that it has confined the practice significance of lament to the personal—indeed, the private—realm. I suggest that we may, with September 11, 2001, identify a new phase of reengagement with the laments of ancient Israel whereby the use and practice of the lament has abruptly gone *public*. The devastation of 9/11 has awakened consumer America from its narcotized notion of self-sufficiency. Beyond the violence to property and persons enacted that day, the real issue has been the piercing of the ideology of invulnerability. Suddenly even the affluent, well-defended United States has recognized vulnerability that has characteristically marked elsewhere in the world.

One consequence of this new status of wakefulness has been the ready engagement with the lament, most especially the book of Lamentations, which rings true from the very first lines of the poetry:

> How lonely sits the city
>   that once was full of people!
> How like a widow she has become,
>   she that was great among the nations! (Lam 1:1)

I believe that this new interface of text and crisis is a healthy sign of the recovery of the text and, through it, engagement with creaturely reality that has moved slowly but relentlessly from *scholarly recovery* to *pastoral recovery* and, finally, to *public recovery*. In all three waves of fresh awareness, it is surely clear and unmistakable among us that our life is profoundly penultimate in its vulnerability and need. For women and men of faith, that acknowledgment of penultimate status invites, even requires, reference to the ultimate one, toward whom we turn variously in need, in trust, in indignation, in doubt and rage, in flattery and demand; but we do turn, deeply, utterly, viscerally, doxologically beyond ourselves. Our mothers and fathers in faith have known that forever and so made it central to our normative text. But we, too long beguiled by layers of ideology, are now in a rapid learning curve of recovery. We enact lament as a sign of glad recognition concerning this originary text tradition entrusted to us. As we reengage in that recognition, we are aware that recovery of the text and the practice of lament are no peripheral matters; rather, text and practice together invite rethinking, reimagination, and repractice in every facet of our faith and of our life from the ground up.

The depth and significance of that recovery is nowhere more elegantly voiced than in a new book by my treasured colleague Kathleen O'Connor. She writes:

> Lamentations is about the collapse of a physical, emotional, and spiritual universe of an entire people, not about individual sorrows except in a metaphoric and symbolic manner. Yet the power of its poetry can embrace the sufferings of any whose bodies and spirits are worn down and assaulted, whose boundaries have shrunk, who are trapped, and who face foreclosed futures. And although, or perhaps because, Lamentations holds intense

personal resonance for me, I find in it ethical challenges to my American society, as well as a tool for cultural and social healing. . . .[17]

I am convinced that our profound spiritual hunger undermines not only our own humanity; it also affects our relationships with other peoples and with the earth itself. We feed that hunger in our frenzied self-centeredness and with anesthetizing abundance and violence. This is the "spiritual catastrophe in which the rich live" (Soelle 48), and it continues to endanger the world. I find in Lamentations food for this hunger and a healing balm for hidden wounds. The hunger of the rich is not comparable to the material hungers of the poor, but our inhumanity, or inability to be empathic, and our denial of our own deep hungers directly impinge upon the lives of the poor, who often have much to teach us about humanity.[18]

The recovery of the lament in practice is an embrace of creaturely reality amid bewitching ideologies that benumb us. It is at the same time, however, an enormous gift to the church and an enormous invitation to those who manage the text resources and practices of the church. It is an invitation to a public practice in a society that has no other text that is adequate to our newly embraced loss and vulnerability.

II

We are agreed that the practice of lament is a sine qua non for believing people who embrace need and vulnerability in the presence of God. I want to insist, however, that the serious practice of lament is difficult to the point of impossibility for persons and communities that are deeply and uncritically situated in the ideologies of technological therapeutic military consumerism. Thus, I submit that pastors must do intentional interpretive, instructional work to create an evangelical context in which lament can be serious. This is work that is difficult and demanding because it entails for us a departure from the all-comprehending ideologies that are deeply resistant to lament, a departure that mostly we no more want to undertake than did the reluctant want to depart Egypt or the hesitant want to return from Babylonian exile. Thus, in the main body of this chapter, I consider ten theological preconditions that allow lament to be a serious theological datum and a pertinent theological practice.

1. An addressable "Thou"

First, we need *a Thou* who looms large enough and strong enough and good enough to generate a responding *I*. Lament is not possible if God is only a

shadowy warm fuzzy or a settled scholastic proposition incapable of forceful dialogical engagement. Of course, the laments in the Psalms are situated with the
Thou who is so commonplace we scarcely notice, a Thou celebrated in wonder
and a Thou addressed in imperatives:

> But *you*, O LORD, are a shield around me,
>   my glory, and the one who lifts up my head.
> I cry aloud to the LORD,
>   and he answers me from his holy hill. (Ps 3:3)

> But *you* do see! Indeed you note trouble and grief,
>   that you may take it into your hands;
> the helpless commit themselves to you;
>   you have been the helper of the orphan. (Ps 10:14)

Nowhere is this more evident than in the sixfold repetition in Psalm 86 of the full
second-person pronoun *'attah*:

> *You* are my God
> *You*, O LORD, are good and forgiving
> *You* are great and do wondrous things
> *You* alone are God
> *You*, O LORD, are a God merciful and generous,
>   slow to anger and abounding in steadfast love and faithfulness
> *You*, LORD, have helped me and comforted me. (vv. 2, 5, 10, 10, 15, 17)

The rhetoric is direct, immediate, face-to-face, not theological reflection on an
object but intense engagement with a subject.

2. Fidelity and issues of infidelity

Second, we need a *practice grounded in fidelity about which issues of infidelity
can be boldly raised*. When our theological rhetoric traffics in scholastic certitude, no questions can be raised; the classic traditions of catechism, moreover,
have made it so. But certitude is not fidelity, because fidelity is an interpersonal,
dynamic, ongoing process that is endlessly negotiated, never settled, as scholastic
notions of certitude might be. In addresses of lament trouble is not immediately
turned to guilt, as in classic tradition, but it becomes a part of dispute between
partners. The premise of fidelity is everywhere in the Psalter, well voiced in the
Thou statements of Psalm 86 just cited. The premise of fidelity, however, is premise and not conclusion. It is premise against which the vicissitudes of lived reality
come, and when reality clashes with premise, issues must be raised.

The issue is raised in personal psalms, most acutely in Psalm 88, a series of Thou statements that entertain the breakdown of YHWH's pledged loyalty:

> You have put me in the depths of the Pit,
>> in the regions dark and deep.
> Your wrath lies heavy upon me,
>> and you overwhelm me with all your waves.
> You have caused my companions to shun me;
>> you have made me a thing of horror to them.
> I am shut in so that I cannot escape;
>
> . . . .
> You have caused friend and neighbor to shun me;
>> my companions are in darkness. (Ps 88:6-8b, 18)

This psalm gives no hint, as is present for example in Psalm 39, that the trouble is with the speaker. The psalm is a full-voiced wonderment that the God of fidelity can behave in this death-dealing way.

The personal grief of Psalm 88 is matched in the vigorous public statement of Psalm 44:

> Yet you have rejected us and abased us,
>> and have not gone out with our armies.
> You made us turn back from the foe,
>> and our enemies have gotten spoil.
> You have made us like sheep for slaughter,
>> and have scattered us among the nations.
> You have sold your people for a trifle,
>> demanding no high price for them.
> You have made us the taunt of our neighbors,
>> the derision and scorn of those around us.
> You have made us a byword among the nations,
>> a laughingstock among the peoples. (Ps 44:9-14)

This psalm, moreover, takes the trouble to assert Israel's attentiveness to covenant, eschewing any infidelity on Israel's part, thus making YHWH's infidelity an inescapable judgment:

> All this has come upon us,
>> yet we have not forgotten you,
>> or been false to your covenant.
> Our heart has not turned back,
>> nor have our steps departed from your way,

> yet you have broken us in the haunt of jackals,
>> and covered us with deep darkness. (Ps 44:17-19)

This sort of speaking is only possible because of fidelity. It is precisely fidelity that poses the question in ragged circumstance.

3. Moral coherence of the world

A faithful *Thou* about whom issues of *infidelity* can be raised concerns our third precondition for lament, the Creator's *reliable governance of the creation*—that is, the Thou of the Creator issues in a universe of moral coherence and reliability wherein distributive justice is a credible assumption. The move from *Thou* to the *moral coherence of the world* is a huge move, but Israel makes it readily and constantly. Theological framing of lament is not simply a subjective, interpersonal transaction; it involves God's larger guarantees to the world. The laments are premised on and made possible by the assumption that the world works to the positive benefit of the righteous and obedient even as it punishes those who mock God and diminish torah. Patrick Miller has made the case that the Psalms echo the theology of Deuteronomy, and Deuteronomy is an assurance of life for the obedient and death for the disobedient.[19] This fundamental confidence is the premise of Psalm 1:

> Happy are those
>> who do not follow the advice of the wicked,
> or take the path that sinners tread,
>> or sit in the seat of scoffers;
> but their delight is in the law of the LORD,
>> and on his law they meditate day and night.
> They are like trees
>> planted by streams of water,
> which yield their fruit in its season,
>> and their leaves do not wither.
> In all that they do, they prosper. (Ps 1:1-3)

That premise pervades the Psalter, so that laments pray against the God of Psalm 1:

> God is my shield,
>> who saves the upright in heart.
> God is a righteous judge,
>> and a God who has indignation every day. (Ps 7:10-11)

> Cast your burden on the LORD,
>> and he will sustain you;
> he will never permit

the righteous to be moved.
But you, O God, will cast them down
    into the lowest pit;
the bloodthirsty and treacherous
    shall not live out half their days.
But I will trust in you. (Ps 55: 22-23)

The righteous will rejoice when they see vengeance done;
    they will bathe their feet in the blood of the wicked.
People will say, "Surely there is a reward for the righteous;
    surely there is a God who judges on earth." (Ps 58:10-11)

It is my judgment that this conviction, so central to faith in Israel, is a conviction that has been lost among us. It has been lost either through the conviction of militarism that affirms that "might makes right," or it has been lost through a fuzzy existentialism that regards the world as a series of meaningless fragments. Consequently, we do not count much on the intrinsic, inviolate connection of "deeds and consequences" in the structure of creation. There are many reasons to doubt, and the poem of Job makes clear why the claim is so difficult. Nonetheless, it cannot be given up:

For thus says the LORD,
who created the heavens (he is God!),
who formed the earth and made it
    (he established it;
he did not create it a chaos,
    he formed it to be inhabited!):
I am the LORD, and there is no other,
I did not speak in secret,
    in a land of darkness;
I did not say to the offspring of Jacob,
    "Seek me in chaos."
I the LORD speak the truth,
    I declare what is right. (Isa 45:18-19)

The laments are occasionally on the lips of the wicked who plead for help. But characteristic of a lament is the voice of the righteous who believe they have claims to make according to God's fidelity that has made the world faithful:

The LORD brings the counsel of the nations to nothing;
    he frustrates the plans of the peoples.
The counsel of the LORD stands forever,
    the thoughts of his heart to all generations.

Happy is the nation whose God is the LORD,
   the people whom he has chosen as his heritage.
The LORD looks down from heaven;
   he sees all humankind.
From where he sits enthroned he watches
   all the inhabitants of the earth—
he who fashions the hearts of them all,
   and observes all their deeds.
A king is not saved by his great army;
   a warrior is not delivered by his great strength.
The war horse is a vain hope for victory,
   and by its great might it cannot save.

Truly the eye of the LORD is on those who fear him,
   on those who hope in his steadfast love,
to deliver their soul from death,
   and to keep them alive in famine. (Ps 33:10-19)

4. An emancipated sense of self

Fourth, we need *an emancipated sense of self* fully present to self, who is able to recognize harm, hurt, and dysfunction in one's own bodily existence or in one's own community. This may seem self-evident, but it is not. It is possible to be so enveloped in an act of renunciation for a greater good that one does not attend to one's present circumstance. It is possible to be so colonized into a larger project that one's "role" or "place" in the larger scheme can be justified! As Simone Weil puts it,

> The truth is that, to quote a famous saying, slavery degrades man to the point of making him love it. . . . The conditions of the factory engendered submission and docility not revolt. . . . Marx underestimated the power of force. He failed to recognize the effectiveness and pervasiveness of force and ideological legitimatization—that is, the way in which the sentiments and interests of the masters are internalized and appropriated by the slaves. In other words, the scorn and disregard that the masters show for those who obey is internalized by slaves and directed against themselves.[20]

My sense is that the petitioning, insisting, and demanding prayers of Israel are not willing to defer or justify pain but—fully in touch with bodily existence—tell the truth. Indeed, the laments are notorious for paying concrete attention:

I am poured out like water,
    and all my bones are out of joint;
my heart is like wax;
    it is melted within my breast;
my mouth is dried up like a potsherd,
    and my tongue sticks to my jaws;
    you lay me in the dust of death. (Ps 22:14-15)

But as for me, when they were sick,
    I wore sackcloth;
    I afflicted myself with fasting.
I prayed with head bowed on my bosom,
    as though I grieved for a friend or a brother;
I went about as one who laments for a mother,
    bowed down and in mourning. (Ps 35:13-14)

My heart is in anguish within me,
    the terrors of death have fallen upon me.
Fear and trembling come upon me,
    and horror overwhelms me. (Ps 55:4-5)

I cry aloud to God,
    aloud to God, that he may hear me.
In the day of my trouble I seek the LORD;
    in the night my hand is stretched out without wearying;
    my soul refuses to be comforted.
I think of God, and I moan;
    I meditate, and my spirit faints. (Ps 77:1-3)

These prayers have no interest in generalization and become intensely concrete. They know, muscle by muscle, limb by limb, nerve by nerve, about diminishment. Moreover, they wave such creaturely concreteness in the face of the Creator. If it is true, as the catechism says, that every hair on the head is accounted for, then concreteness about one's bodily situation is crucial.

In parallel fashion the speaker of the lament is knowing enough to understand the power of social exploitation that causes dysfunction:

Their mouths are filled with cursing and deceit and oppression;
    under their tongues are mischief and iniquity.
They sit in ambush in the villages;
    in hiding-places they murder the innocent.

> Their eyes stealthily watch for the helpless;
>> they lurk in secret like a lion in its covert;
> they lurk that they may seize the poor;
>> they seize the poor and drag them off in their net. (Ps 10:7-9)

> Guard me as the apple of the eye;
>> hide me in the shadow of your wings,
> from the wicked who despoil me,
>> my deadly enemies who surround me.
> They close their hearts to pity;
>> with their mouths they speak arrogantly.
> They track me down; now they surround me;
>> they set their eyes to cast me to the ground.
> They are like a lion eager to tear,
>> like a young lion lurking in ambush. (Ps 17:8-12)

> All day long they seek to injure my cause;
>> all their thoughts are against me for evil.
> they stir up strife, they lurk,
>> they watch my steps.
> As they hoped to have my life,
>> so repay them for their crime;
>> in wrath cast down the peoples, O God! (Ps 56:5-7)

This self-knowledge makes no divorce between bodily failure and social imposition because both are enactments of evil that violate well being and thereby violate the *entitlement* of fully functioning health that lies behind the lament.

5. The capacity to remember well-being

Fifth, this sense of diminishment that is stated with bodily particularity and social discernment has as its counterpoint the *quotidian capacity of the body that can remember or that can imagine*—given what was said about Creator and creature—*a fully functioning body at ease* with all systems working in a fully functioning body politic. These prayers can immediately contrast the dread way it is now with the wondrous way it was and is supposed to be. There is no erosion of the knowledge of health that was promised and guaranteed by the Creator and that is known from other times:

> These things I remember,
>> as I pour out my soul:
> how I went with the throng,

and led them in procession to the house of God,
with glad shouts and songs of thanksgiving,
 a multitude keeping festival. (Ps 42:4)

I say to God, my rock,
 "Why have you forgotten me?
Why must I walk about mournfully
 because the enemy oppresses me?" (Ps 42:9)

I consider the days of old,
 and remember the years of long ago.
I commune with my heart in the night;
 I meditate and search my spirit:
"Will the LORD spurn forever,
 and never again be favorable?
Has his steadfast love ceased forever?
 Are his promises at an end for all time?
Has God forgotten to be gracious?
 Has he in anger shut up his compassion?" (Ps 77:5-9)

I remember the days of old,
 I think about all your deeds,
 I meditate on the works of your hands.
I stretch out my hands to you;
 my soul thirsts for you like a parched land. (Ps 143:5-6)

The one who prays such prayer is not alive simply in an isolated moment but has the cadences of other, better times pulsing deeply in the body. Of course, it is the case that deep affliction concentrates the mind and obliterates all other references. But these prayers—so focused on the immediacy of suffering dysfunction—do not lose context. The ground of prayer is the conviction that this present condition is not bearable, is not right, and cannot be permanent. In Psalm 77, the speaker is restlessly awake all night, perhaps with sleep apnea! In such exhaustion, however, the speaker does not concede anything, does not seek the light comfort of any kind, but goes deep into protest that voices the contrast of the unbearable "now" with the remembered "then." The naming of "days of old, years of old," perhaps in this particular life but likely beyond that, goes behind one's short life to the long life of faith in the community. The memory evokes questions about promises of steadfast love that make the present void stark, but that make that stark void penultimate and transient at best. And finally, after the reference to the memory in verse 5, the psalm leaps, in verse 11, back to the large claims of the community:

> I will call to mind the deeds of the LORD;
> > I will remember your wonders of old. (Ps 77:11)

This troubled, sleepless speaker appeals to the exodus memory and behind that memory to the large silencing of the chaotic waters. That is not to say that the present suffering of the speaker is not as deep as all chaos, but in that suffering chaos, Israel can recall the wondrous power of God, who turns the pain, who overrides the oppression, and who vetoes the devastation. The recall made by the speaker moves into the night of churning, into the body of disease, to yield, I imagine, not only comfort and reassurance but, in fact, transformation.

6. A voice of assertion

A body noticed in suffering, a *body of well-being remembered*, sets up *the contrast* out of which lament comes. Such notice of contrast, however, is itself not enough. Sixth, there must be a *voice capable of shrill assertion*, equally capable of yielding gladness. The temptation toward silence is immense. It can seem that silence is a positive virtue of a certain kind:

> But the LORD is in his holy temple;
> > let all the earth keep silence before him! (Hab 2:20)

Silence can be imposed, as was the case back in slavery in Egypt until "after a long time"—a very long time—"the King of Egypt died" (Exod 2:23). Only after the death of the enforcer is there voice. Or silence can be self-willed and self-imposed:

> I said, "I will guard my ways
> > that I may not sin with my tongue;
> I will keep a muzzle on my mouth
> > as long as the wicked are in my presence."
> I was silent and still. (Ps 39:1-2a)

But such silence is so costly:

> I held my peace to no avail;
> my distress grew worse,
> > my heart became hot within me.
> While I mused, the fire burned;
> > then I spoke with my tongue. (Ps 39:2b-3)

Silence is the great vehicle for the match of empire and colony, as William Cavanaugh, Elaine Scarry, Alice Miller, Judith Hermann, and Rebecca Chopp, among others, have noticed.[21] It is white silencing black, men silencing women, Westerner silencing Asian, straight silencing gay, the power of "the established God" silencing all. Indeed, God's own self is sometimes seduced to the passivity and submissiveness of silence:

> For a long time I have held my peace,
>   I have kept still and restrained myself;
> now I will cry out like a woman in labor,
>   I will gasp and pant. (Isa 42:14)

> For Zion's sake I will not keep silent,
>   and for Jerusalem's sake I will not rest. (Isa 62:1)

But finally, silence is not possible in this Jewish community of utterance. Finally, imposed silence is unbearable. Finally, self-willed silence is impossible. It belongs to this community of fidelity to break out of every silence and speak. Such speech is at least inconvenient, and the powers of silencing are like the people who tried to silence the blind Bartimaeus when he cried out for help to Jesus, because such asking exposes dysfunction and begins the process of dismantling what was (Mark 10:48). This capacity to break the silence is a characteristic reply of Israel already in the slave camp of Egypt. Israel's characteristic way is loud, shrill insistence against every mannered control. Israel's speech after silence is profoundly regressive and hyperbolic, flailing out at many enemies, spilling over in rage and lust for vengeance. Unsettling as that is, more unsettling is the daring mouth of Israel that addresses YHWH in huge demanding imperatives. Listen, hear, save, rescue, rise up!

> Rise up, O LORD!
>   Deliver me, O my God!
> For you strike all my enemies on the cheek;
>   you break the teeth of the wicked. (Ps 3:7)

> Rise up, O LORD; O God, lift up your hand;
>   do not forget the oppressed. (Ps 10:12)

> Break the arm of the wicked and evildoers;
>   seek out their wickedness until you find none. (Ps 10:15)

> But you, O LORD, do not be far away!
>   O my help, come quickly to my aid!
> Deliver my soul from the sword,
>   my life from the power of the dog!
>   Save me from the mouth of the lion! (Ps 22:19-21)

> O God, break the teeth in their mouths;
>> tear out the fangs of the young lions, O LORD! (Ps 58:6)

> Deliver me from my enemies, O my God;
>> protect me from those who rise up against me.
> Deliver me from those who work evil;
>> from the bloodthirsty save me. (Ps 59:1-2)

Serious study of the lament leads us to recognize how we have trivialized prayer, not daring much, partly because it is impolite and partly because we will not be embarrassed at not receiving.

But, of course, Jesus authorized petition in that terse triad of imperatives: Ask, knock, seek (Matthew 7:7)! And in that odd parable of Luke 18:1-8, Jesus legitimated importunity, which in a lesser term seems to mean to "nag to death" about life-urgent matters. Only Jews could countenance such chutzpah at the throne. Only Israel could risk the urgency of dialogical transaction. Only covenanters could imagine seizing the initiative before the throne. Only the prophets understood that such crying at the throne bespeaks other voices where truth—quotidian bodily truth—speaks to power in imperatives.

7. An arena for protest

There is this Thou who pledges fidelity and who guarantees a world of moral coherence. There is this speaker who notices the shameless dysfunction and who contrasts that dysfunction with a remembered normalcy and who finds voice for a sharp contrast in order to ask about fidelity and moral coherence. The lament is essentially a transaction between this dangerously voiced one and the listener who has made promises. But the two of them do not live in a vacuum. The one who speaks is an Israelite, or perhaps Israel. The one who hears, "I, the God of Israel, creator of heaven and earth."

All around the transaction of the two *hovers Israel*. The rest of what I have to say about preconditions and prerequisites for lament concern communal context, a context that makes the intimate, abrasive transaction possible and credible. Israel has been a practitioner of this utterance since Exodus 2:23-25, long before any current utterer comes on the scene.

Needed for lament is our seventh precondition, a body politic as an arena for voicing full extremes of life in a free, shameless way, the extremes of lyrical affirmation in vigorous protest. Practitioners of lament must live in a community capable of limit expressions that give lived access to limit experiences. The lament cannot be voiced in a safe, flat, conventional context of techno-speech.

Consider Israel as exactly such an arena where from early on, candidates for lament have been hearing radical cadences that Israel utters full throated, precisely because Israel has never been narcotized to quotidian suffering and quotidian joy. Speaking of contemporary mainline churches, Charles Mathewes allows that they are

> spaces of encounter, both "spiritually" speaking—where the congregation encounters God—and "civically" speaking—where the various members of the congregation in the larger communities of which they are a part encounter each other. Simply by offering physical spaces the churches provide "public spaces.". . . Most significant, the churches serve, however partially and weakly, as almost unique sites of genuine moral conversation, including sustained moral disagreement.[22]

James Plastaras has seen that the exodus narrative, perhaps Israel's most elemental script, begins in lament in Exodus 2:23-25 and ends in doxology in Exodus 15:20-21.[23] Indeed, it is clear that Israel cannot tell its life with YHWH in any other way. Plastaras notices this of course in a critical way, so that this act of rhetoric from lament in 2:23-25 to praise in 15:20-21 is a late, highly stylized utilization of older patterns and texts. No doubt. But now, in "final form," this dramatic movement in the exodus narrative is paradigmatic. Israel is always moving, as did that generation of slaves, from lament to doxology, or with Westermann, from plea to praise. Israel is always beginning yet again in lament, anticipating a culmination in praise, anticipating but not knowing.

As a consequence, every time a girl or boy attended Passover—and many other times—the young were inducted into such speech of extremity. They understood intuitively that any less dangerous speech, any safe speech in the safer rhythm of the world would lead them back into the brickyard, with its endless memos of brick quotas. They understood, at the edge of the water, that extreme speech fends off memos and quotas and slavery. They understood that emancipation required emancipated speech that refused to conform to the censored imperial order of the day. And so they groaned and cried out and later had the chance for singing and dancing. They cried out, to be sure, in guilt. But that went only so far. After that, they groaned and cried out in pain, the pain of ruthlessness, of alienation, of loss.

The Passover children could hear at the very edge of the groan, moreover, the coming cadences of Miriam's feet and the tambourines of her sisters, ready to dance on the grave of Pharaoh, ready but waiting, waiting until morning. They knew that

> Weeping may linger for the night,
>> but joy come comes in the morning. (Psalm 30:5)

They knew about that paradigmatic drama. They knew of its many, each time contemporary reenactments. They knew that the regular performance of the drama kept them free. And while they loved the conclusion in praise, they knew each time they had to begin again in moaning and groaning, keeping their bodies in touch with the travail they preferred to silent submissiveness. As a consequence, it was a matter of course that communal cadences came to their lips for personal matters and for public matters, for war and disease and drought. This is the script of extremity, adequate for life's extremities taken up intimately, personally, urgently but never privately.

8. Vigorous contestation

Eighth, this body politic, this particular exercise of extreme speech that is Israel, is a community that is designed for and committed to *vigorous contestation*. This may be obvious by now; it is, however, no small matter. It is no small matter to be in contestation, because conventional understandings of faith are calm and serene with a God who presides over all evenhandedly. Unlike all of that pious nurture, however, Israel has been a community of contestation from the outset. It is in part propelled by moral passion, as in Amos. It is in part propelled by righteous indignation, as in Job. It is in part driven by vested interest in which bartering has gone on long before Elisabeth Kübler-Ross disclosed bargaining as the third stage of grief.

The practice of contestation, of speaking up in favor or against, runs all the way back from father Abraham to Job. In Genesis 18, as you know, Abraham pressed his God to practice justice. He asks the question that must forever ring in the ears of this God who occasionally slacks on the justice question: "Far be it from you to do such a thing, to slay the righteous with the wicked, so that the righteous fare as the wicked! Far be that from you! Shall not the Judge of all the earth do what is just?" (Gen 18:25). The question must have caught the Almighty up short, as though it were a new idea. And then the two of them must arm wrestle over the price of saving the city. Of course, it is not different at the end of the exchange in the poem of Job. It is a bitter Job who will say:

> Though I am innocent, my own mouth would condemn me;
> > though I am blameless, he would prove me perverse.
> I am blameless; I do not know myself;
> > I loathe my life.
> It is all one; therefore I say, ·
> > he destroys both the blameless and the wicked.
> When disaster brings sudden death,
> > he mocks at the calamity of the innocent.
> The earth is given into the hand of the wicked;
> > he covers the eyes of its judges—
> if it is not he, who then is it? (Job 9:20-24; see also 31:35-37)

This deep habit of contestation, engrained in Israel and characteristic of YHWH, has given the Christian Bible this juridical cast that culminates in the Pauline teaching on justification.

As a consequence, when a single petitioner finds voice for lament, it is not new and it is not in a vacuum. It is an extension of the long contestation that characterizes our people, precisely because God is never as single-minded as anticipated and the world never works as fully as promised.

9. *A community of truth-telling*

So consider, for our ninth precondition, this community of extremity and contestation that is the brooding house for lament. Finally, lament becomes an ecclesial question in which we ask what kind of community is required, over a long span of practice, whereby laments may be possible and credible—it is *a community of truth-telling* that will not fudge on truth-telling in order to protect our mannered sensibilities or to protect the character and reputation of God. Kathleen O'Connor writes,

> Truth-telling is an act of survival, because it affirms the humanity of victims, gives them agency, and places a wedge between their experience of suffering and expression. Lamentations is ancient poetry of truth-telling, an act of survival that testifies to the human requirement to speak the unspeakable, to find speech in traumatized numbness, and . . . to assert boldly the "sheer fact of pain."[24]

Israel's praise is not a practice of "praise hymns" that cover over the reality of life in the world. A habit of truth-telling is a primal resolve in Israel, most extremely in Job, but other voices also wonder about Israel's much promised *hesed*:

> Do you work wonders for the dead?
>   Do the shades rise up to praise you?
> Is your steadfast love declared in the grave,
>   or your faithfulness in Abaddon?
> Are your wonders known in the darkness,
>   or your saving help in the land of forgetfulness?
> But I, O LORD, cry out to you;
>   in the morning my prayer comes before you. (Ps 88:10-13)

> How long, O LORD? Will you hide yourself forever?
>   How long will your wrath burn like fire?
> Remember how short my time is—
>   for what vanity you have created all mortals!

Who can live and never see death?
  Who can escape the power of Sheol?

LORD, where is your steadfast love of old,
  which by your faithfulness you swore to David? (Ps 89:46-49)

Truth-telling asks hard questions that frequently remain unanswered. But the
questions are not withdrawn. Israel waits for an answer, waits till hell freezes
over, and imagines that it can, in its bodily distress, outwait even the Creator of
heaven and earth.

It is a *memory-cherishing community* that can recall other times in contrast to
this time, times overwhelmed by wonder, gift, and miracle, other times in which
doxology was normative, unqualified, and untroubled. There are many such voic-
ings, none more patterned than Psalm 136. That psalm, verse by verse, identifies
a particular act of YHWH, and then in each verse, Israel generalizes YHWH's
definitive *hesed*:

O give thanks to the LORD of lords,
  for his steadfast love endures forever;

who alone does great wonders,
  for his steadfast love endures forever;
who by understanding made the heavens,
  for his steadfast love endures forever;
who spread out the earth on the waters,
  for his steadfast love endures forever;
who made the great lights,
  for his steadfast love endures forever;
the sun to rule over the day,
  for his steadfast love endures forever;
the moon and stars to rule over the night,
  for his steadfast love endures forever;

who struck Egypt through their firstborn,
  for his steadfast love endures forever;
and brought Israel out from among them,
  for his steadfast love endures forever;
with a strong hand and an outstretched arm,
  for his steadfast love endures forever;
who divided the Red Sea in two,
  for his steadfast love endures forever. (Ps 136:3-13)

Even in distress, the cadence of praise sounds to remember better times. These memories serve to exhibit the shabbiness of need in the present; but they also function as ground for petition:

> In you our ancestors trusted;
>> they trusted, and you delivered them.
> To you they cried, and were saved;
>> in you they trusted, and were not put to shame. (Ps 22:4-5)

The petition is that God do yet again only what God has done in past times, not more but that much, not something exceptional but something characteristic for YHWH and glorious for Israel.

It is a *hope-practicing community* that refuses to submit to imposed circumstances. The classic case is the neediness of Israel in exile. In the book of Lamentations, there is not much ground for hope when Israel's hope is gone. But then this:

> But this I call to mind,
>> and therefore I have hope:
> The steadfast love of the LORD never ceases,
>> his mercies never come to an end;
> they are new every morning;
>> great is your faithfulness.
> "The LORD is my portion," says my soul,
>> "therefore I will hope in him." (Lam 3:21-24)

Of these verses and this practice of hope, O'Connor writes,

> Biblical hope does not emerge from proper reasoning or new information.
> It is not optimism or wishful thinking. It is not a simple act of the will,
> a decision under human control, or a willful determination. It emerges
> without clear cause like grace, without explanation, in the midst of despair
> and at the point of least hope. It comes from elsewhere unbidden, elusive,
> uncontrollable, and surprising, given in the pit the place of no hope.[25]

Israel in its depth of abandonment can remember and hope. It does not, in such texts, dream of global power or exotic wealth. It dreams only of the relational gifts of fidelity, steadfast love, mercy, faithfulness; it imagines that even in this circumstance and just beyond it, the fickleness will end and the abandonment will be overcome.

What a context for prayer and faith—*truth-telling, memory-cherishing, hope-practicing*! This is an environment for lament, amid the thickness of community, cadences that support quivering lips in a quite intimate contestation, immediately joined by many voices who do not know the particulars but who never cease the beat of covenantal anticipation.

10. A miracle-prone community

All three parties in this transaction of lament—the *Thou* addressed, the *I* who protests, and the *we* who remember and hope—are *miracle-prone*, our tenth precondition. If we characterize "miracle" as a gift given outside the delivery systems of the dominant establishment, we are able to see that the whole life of Israel with YHWH has as its defining preoccupation of miracles inexplicable transformations rendered in the real life of Israel but outside the systems of control, prediction, and normal expectation. Israel's vocabulary for miracle is rich and multidimensioned, precisely because Israel is in the "miracle business":

> One generation shall laud your works to another,
>   and shall declare your mighty acts.
> On the glorious splendor of your majesty,
>   and on your wondrous works, I will meditate.
> The might of your awesome deeds shall be proclaimed,
>   and I will declare your greatness.
> They shall celebrate the fame of your abundant goodness,
>   and shall sing aloud of your righteousness. (Ps 145:4-7)

Israel is able to sing, remember, hope, and exult in this day, however, only because YHWH is a God who has the will and power to generate inexplicable transformations:

> Bless the LORD, O my soul,
>   and do not forget all his benefits—
> who forgives all your iniquity,
>   who heals all your diseases,
> who redeems your life from the Pit,
>   who crowns you with steadfast love and mercy,
> who satisfies you with good as long as you live
>   so that your youth is renewed like the eagle's. (Ps 103:2-5)

> The LORD is gracious and merciful,
>   slow to anger and abounding in steadfast love.
> The LORD is good to all,
>   and his compassion is over all that he has made. (Ps 145:8-9)

It is this God who opens the life of Israel with a promise to effect precisely such healing, forgiving, ransoming, and satisfying:

> Then the LORD said, "I have observed the misery of my people who are
> in Egypt; I have heard their cry on account of their taskmasters. Indeed,
> I know their sufferings, and I have come down to deliver them up out of
> that land to a good and broad land, a land flowing with milk and honey.
> (Ex 3:7-8)

What Israel was promised at the outset keeps recurring out of God's fidelity.

It is no wonder, then, that a speaker of lament, child of Israel and beloved of Israel's steadfast miracle worker, prays for gifts to be given outside the delivery systems of the dominant establishment. Every time Israel speaks a lament, it issues an urgent, impassioned imperative. It addresses God Almighty with a command from below, commanding the Creator of heaven and earth to do what the world judges impossible: save, heal, give life! The prayer is uttered because the state cannot save, the medical community cannot heal, and the church cannot give life. These are prayers of extremity when lesser petitions to lesser agencies have failed and gone unanswered.

The petitioners pray so passionately because the history of Israel's recital emboldens them to do so. There is, however, a second reason for such daring imperatives. The voice arises out of the body—or the body politic—and the body knows about its creaturely entitlements. It knows that by its very "being there," it has been promised goodness by the verdict of the Creator. And this petition, attentive to such elemental entitlement, moves from body to voice and will settle for nothing less!

In many places such miracle-anticipating imperatives sound strange but not in this miracle-prone community. Such miracle-anticipating imperatives sound embarrassing in a military-industrial community where everything is on program. They sound strange in church communities inured into technological horizons. They sound strange in bourgeois communities of the self-sufficient, where little is hoped and little is expected and, consequently, little is asked. And when asked, that little asking is timid and polite and deferential. But not here. Not in this community. Not with these bodies voiced. Not with pain brought candidly, hopefully to speech. Not in address to this Thou, whose work is in, with, under, and stunningly beyond our little systems that have their day and cease to be.

Those are ten preconditions and one may think of others. I propose that these ten preconditions require nerve in communities of faith that have had a longtime failure of nerve. I propose that the fostering of these conditions is the peculiar work of the text managers in these communities. I propose that this is important work because only these communities have such a text. I anticipate that as these texted communities seize on this dangerous practice, the world will notice because the world is coming to know that the dominant texts are very, very thin; those texts permit no assertion in need, no submission in gladness, and no surprise toward life.

III

The legitimate and credible practice of lament and the fostering of the preconditions and prerequisites for that legitimate, credible practice invite pastors of congregations to ponder what is entrusted to us, what is required of us, and what risk
we are summoned to. I propose that in every dimension, the legitimate, credible
practice of lament and the fostering of the necessary preconditions for lament is
an engagement in countercultural activity. That is, it is to assume, practice, and
evoke a world that stands against the assumed world of the dominant script of our
culture. I propose, briefly, to enumerate the ten prerequisites that I have listed one
more time, and this time to notice how in each case the precondition tells against
a dominant cultural assumption:

1. The reality of an *addressable Thou* is against the model of self-
   invention, self-sufficiency, and self-actualization that is ever among us.
   There are of course gods out there but none generative of an *I*, none
   addressable.
2. The premise of fidelity and the issue of infidelity assumes *dialogical
   engagement*. Such dialogical engagement is impossible in an environment defined by power and control in which engagements of fidelity
   are next to impossible.
3. *The claim of a morally coherent universe* as a premise for lament is
   impossible when the world belongs to the strong, the quick, and the
   well connected for whom there are no norms or restraints or judgments, a world in which the outsider has no court of appeal.
4. *An attentively engaged bodily self* is against a practice of numbed
   economics, narcotized to the value of what we know to be the most
   elemental requirements for personal well being.
5. *The memory of a better time* of health is impossible among those
   narcotized to the past, in which there is no thick practice of tradition
   transmitted from generation to generation.
6. *The practice of voice*, shrill and extreme, is immensely subversive in a
   culture devoted to silence and conformity without courage or cadence
   for criticism or protest.
7. *A body politic* as a matrix for speech of extremity is impossible when
   a sense of the public is dissolved into endless privatism, when real
   public speech is reduced to techno-speech without human depth or
   staying power.
8. *The public practice of contestation* is an act of enormous nerve in a
   society that has no patience for disputatious voice, in which everything must be smoothed over into agreeable consensus that conceals
   the deep fractures that are never silenced.

9. *A community of truth-telling*, memory-cherishing, hope-practicing passion, tells against a culture in thrall to commodity, the pursuit of commodity, and the reduction of all issues to commodity.

10. *The inclination to be miracle-prone* constitutes a capacity to step outside the epistemological world of modernity upon which our culture, in its power and wealth, is based. And who wants to step outside?

It is, of course, possible to nurture church communities that remain gladly inside dominant cultural assumptions. We are learning, belatedly, that such insider contentment breeds denial, despair, amnesia, and all of the deadly pathologies that are all around us. There are, indeed, ways of life and ways of death that are profoundly complex. On the main issues, however, matters are not very complex. They simply require courage, energy, and imagination among those who are not ashamed of the gospel. We know, we liberals and we conservatives, that the gospel is the power of God unto salvation. That conviction, deep and common among us, is the fundamental ground from which to nurture communities of praise, obedience, and mission that live in a world of evangelical reality. Those ashamed of the gospel can never lament. Those who are unashamed are the ones who dance and sing in the morning after a night of voiced grief.

CHAPTER 10

The Fearful Thirst for Dialogue

I TAKE MY CUE from the verdict of the great Jewish critic George Steiner:[1]

> It is the Hebraic intuition that God is capable of all speech acts except
> that of monologue, which has generated our acts of reply, of question-
> ing, and counter-creation. After the Book of Job and Euripides' *Bacchae*,
> there *had* to be, if man was to bear his being, the means of dialogue with
> God, which are spelled out in our poetics, music, art.[2]

Steiner's point, from his book *Real Presences*, is that great art must be dialogic. Behind that point, however, the argument of his book is that great art is
only possible if it is rooted in faith in God. And if art is to be dialogic, it must be
rooted in a sense of a God who is dialogic, a holy agent who is engaged interac-
tively with creaturely subjects in a mutuality that impinges on both parties. I take
that theological conviction as my beginning point and extrapolate from it two
further convictions that the work of the church in its preoccupation with God's
holiness is to bear witness to dialogic holiness and to engage in the practice of
that dialogic holiness. My thesis is that the church is a venue for dialogue in the
midst of a monologic culture that finds such dialogue to be an unbearable threat
that must be mightily resisted. Dialogue, I shall suggest, is not merely a strategy
but it is also a practice that is congruent with our deepest nature, made, as we are,
in the image of a dialogic God.

I

There is no doubt that we, in our society and in our churches, are sorely tempted to monologue. Such a temptation imagines absolute certainty and sovereignty, and uncritically imagines that any one of us can speak with the voice and authority of the monologic God. There can be no doubt that such a shrill voice of certitude, in any arena of life, is an act of idolatry that is characteristically tinged with ideology.

It is evident that in the public arena, the military-economic hegemony of the United States exercises a monologic practice of power that by force imposes its will on others and silences voices to the contrary. The same propensity is evident in government that is now largely co-opted and controlled by wealth interests and amounts to nothing less than an oligarchy, wherein voices of need can scarcely be heard.

It is not, in my judgment, very different in the churches wherein judgments are made and positions taken that make sounds of absolute certainty without any sense either that God's own life in the world is dialogical or that there is inevitable slippage between God's will and our perception of that will.

II

There can be no doubt that such monologic practice seeks to silence, and there can be no doubt that such imposed silence kills. It is, of course, the hope of U.S. imperialism to silence voices to the contrary, most recently even that of "old Europe." The manipulation of the media, moreover, is an effort to still the critical voice of a free press. Such silencing in the long run will kill the spirit of our democracy and create an environment of distrust and resentment that will readily issue in violence, as is already apparent in the shrillness of the Right in its readiness to violate the law in the service of its ideology.

I do not need to tell you that the same effort at silencing is alive and well in the church. And so that you may know that this is not simply a critique of the Right, I report to you that in my own church, the United Church of Christ, the same silencing is done from the Left, so that there is no room remaining in our national church for those who dissent from the dominant voice. Such silencing in the church, as in our society, of course does immense damage to the church, robbing it of its healing capacity and diverting its energy from missional transformation to keeping the lid of control on the body.

A subset of such singular silence that kills occurs when individual persons arrive at absolute certainty and claim to identify their own view with the mind of God; such persons are characteristically engaged in profound denial about the complexity and conundrums that constitute the self. There can be no doubt that such repressed, denied complexity of self issues at least in the source of alienation and at worst in violence toward neighbor or toward self. Most of us, in our season of denial, do not go so far as overt violence, but every congregation and every diocese knows about the absolute, one-dimensional selves of shrill certitude that function as profound impediments to the life and faith of the body.

III

My simple thesis is that the church, summoned, formed, and empowered by the God of all dialogue, has in our anxiety-driven society an opportunity to be deeply dialogical about the most important issues, dialogical in a way that keeps our judgments penultimate before the holy throne of God. It is important, in the practice of *dialogue that moves against absoluteness* to see that the evidence of Scripture itself provides data for such a theological practice. I will name four such examples of dialogue, and then in the next section I will proceed to two texts of dialogue that have preoccupied me.

First, in the remarkable text of *Genesis 18:16-33*, God is engaged in a plan concerning the coming destruction of Sodom. God has resolved to destroy the city, but Abraham confronts God about that decision. Of particular importance, in Genesis 18:22 there is a rabbinic adjustment of the text that matters to our theme. Our translations, following the rabbis, have, "Abraham remained standing before the LORD." But before the rabbis made that theological adjustment, the text said, "YHWH remained standing before Abraham." That is, in the original form of the text, Abraham is the senior partner in the dialogue and calls YHWH to account. In that narrative, Abraham bargains YHWH down to a minimum of ten righteous people, a clear dialogic act of chutzpah.

Second, Moses undertakes a like dialogic challenge to YHWH. In *Exodus 32*, YHWH is prepared to consume Israel because of the production of the golden calf. In the narrative, the act is retarded because of the intervention of Moses.

> But Moses implored the LORD his God, and said, "O LORD, why does your wrath burn hot against your people, whom you brought out of the land of Egypt with great power and with a mighty hand? Why should the Egyptians say, 'It was with evil intent that he brought them out to kill them in the mountains, and to consume them from the face of the earth'? Turn from your fierce wrath; change your mind and do not bring disaster on your people. Remember Abraham, Isaac, and Israel, your servants, how you swore to them by your own self, saying to them, 'I will multiply your descendants like the stars of heaven, and all this land that I have promised I will give to your descendants, and they shall inherit it forever.'" (Exod 32:11-13)

And the narrative reports, in response, "YHWH changed his mind" (v. 14).

Third, Jeremiah notoriously remonstrates with YHWH about his unbearable prophetic vocation. In his extreme prayer at the end of all of his prayers, Jeremiah accuses YHWH of seduction; only after he has made the charge, only after he has broken his silence in accusatory fashion, does his accusation turn to confidence in YHWH:

> O LORD, you have enticed me,
>   and I was enticed;
> you have overpowered me,
>   and you have prevailed.
> I have become a laughingstock all day long;
>   everyone mocks me.
> For whenever I speak, I must cry out,
>   I must shout, "Violence and destruction!"
> For the word of the LORD has become for me
>   a reproach and derision all day long.
> If I say, "I will not mention him,
>   or speak any more in his name,"
> then within me there is something like a burning fire
>   shut up in my bones;
> I am weary with holding it in,
>   and I cannot.
> For I hear many whispering:
>   "Terror is all around!
> Denounce him! Let us denounce him!"
>   All my close friends are watching for me to stumble.
> "Perhaps he can be enticed,
>   and we can prevail against him,
>   and take our revenge on him."
> But the LORD is with me like a dread warrior;
>   therefore my persecutors will stumble,
>   and they will not prevail.
> They will be greatly shamed,
>   for they will not succeed.
> Their eternal dishonor
>   will never be forgotten. (Jer 20:7-11)

And fourth, Job, likely modeled after Jeremiah, engages YHWH in the most extreme exchange in the Old Testament. As you know, the speech of the whirlwind trumps Job and seems to reduce him to silence. Except that in the end, YHWH says of Job, in contrast to the conventional predictable friends, "You have not spoken what is right, as has my servant Job" (Job 42:7-8). The conclusion I draw is that Job's willingness to engage YHWH and challenge both conventional theology and the justice of God is welcomed by the God of daring dialogue.

These four cases are examples, the most striking examples, of the *dialogue of ancient Israel with God*, of an intensely theological undertaking. I take these texts as background because unless with Steiner we know that *God is dialogical*, we will never understand that truth takes dialogical form among members of church and society in a way that precludes ready settlement. Such a theological awareness requires among us a huge unlearning of conventional monological theo-logic in the church, and I think in society as well. It requires the manifestation of a dialogical God who becomes the premise for dialogic human community, the sort of community that precludes both absolute authority and absolute submissiveness. In every case of dialogue I have cited, the human partner to the exchange must have enormous energy and courage to enter the zone of holy power and issue self-announcement.

And of course more generally, this same chutzpah before the throne is evident in many psalms of complaint. It is evident in the Old Testament that the community of faith—and by inference the human community—has an enormous stake in dialogue that subverts the destructive combination of authoritarianism and submissiveness. The breaking of silence that makes newness possible is nicely voiced in Psalm 39:

> I said, "I will guard my ways
>   that I may not sin with my tongue;
> I will keep a muzzle on my mouth
>   as long as the wicked are in my presence."
> I was silent and still;
>   I held my peace to no avail;
> my distress grew worse,
>   my heart became hot within me.
> While I mused, the fire burned;
>   then I spoke with my tongue. (Ps 39:1-3)

Everything in faith depends on such utterance.

IV

I want now to conduct two forays into the Psalms as practices of dialogue, with the general insistence that the *church in dialogue* represents a transformative subversion of *society in monologue* and *church in monologue*. I intend to exhibit two cases in which dialogic practice is at the heart of our faith. Such dialogue on the one hand requires courage and energy; on the other hand, it yields newness that can never be generated through monologue.

My first case is *Psalm 35*. I will show that in this psalm the human person is himself/herself an *ongoing internal conversation*, a conversation conducted before God. My own experience of such conversation is that, during the day when

I am awake and in control, I can give expression to my life in a single voice. At night, however, when I am defenseless, all the other voices sound, and the honoring of them becomes the condition of my humanness. Thus, my first example concerns pastoral care that, in our common understanding, is shaped and informed by Freud's discernment of self. There is no doubt that Freud—in his sense that the human self is thick, layered, and conflicted—is profoundly Jewish in his perception. His sense of self as multivoiced is clearly parallel to a rabbinic awareness that the text is multivoiced—that is, thick, layered, and conflicted.

Psalm 35 is a fairly standard psalm of lament, with the usual accent on *complaint* that tells God how bad and urgent the need is and *petition* that recruits God to be active and effective amid the voiced trouble. What interests me, however, is that this psalm, more than any other I know, includes a candid announcement of the complexity of voices that make a single integrated person impossible. I will identify four voices that constitute something of a sociogram of the life and practice of faith.

In verses 1-3, the psalm begins with a series of six imperative petitions addressed to YHWH. The first five are, contend, fight, take hold, rise up, draw. The imagery mixes the judicial and the military, asking God be both judge and warrior. But it is the sixth imperative that interests me: "Say to my soul, your salvation am I." After the vigorous and violent petitions, this sixth imperative asks YHWH to speak, to break the silence. The ultimate yearning of the final petition in this group is that God should speak, enter into dialogue, and offer assurance. The speaker is so daring that out of the tradition of his community, he dares to suggest to YHWH what is to be said and who is to be addressed: "Address me, my soul, *my nephesh*, my life."

As with much of the Psalms, this rhetoric is so familiar and conventional that we do not notice. This simple voice of petition is speaking truth to power and is requiring from YHWH a quite specific answer. The proposed answer cuts through the neglect, silence, and absence of God, and offers assurance that God is back in play—in my life—with enough power and sufficient attentiveness to change everything. The suggested response is a salvation oracle rooted in old liturgic traditions that are best known in the exile-ending proclamation of Second Isaiah:

> But you, Israel, my servant,
>> Jacob, whom I have chosen,
>> the offspring of Abraham, my friend;
> you whom I took from the ends of the earth,
>> and called from its farthest corners,
> saying to you, "You are my servant,
>> I have chosen you and not cast you off";
> do not fear, for I am with you,
>> do not be afraid, for I am your God;
> I will strengthen you, I will help you,
>> I will uphold you with my victorious right hand. (Isa 41:8-10)

For I, the LORD your God,
    hold your right hand;
it is I who say to you, "Do not fear,
    I will help you." (Isa 41:13)

But now thus says the LORD,
    he who created you, O Jacob,
    he who formed you, O Israel:
Do not fear, for I have redeemed you;
    I have called you by name, you are mine.
when you pass through the waters, I will be with you. (Isa 43:1-2)

Israel—and this psalmist—does not doubt that God's self-announcement will change everything, but the self-announcement from YHWH does not come from divine initiative, as our usual Augustinian presuppositions might suggest. Rather, it is the human utterance of insistence that expects, evokes, and listens for divine announcement of truthfulness that initiates the process. Even the expected deployment of YHWH depends on a dialogic initiative by the psalmist.

The psalm proceeds in verses 4-8 with a wish list of imprecations, of bad things proposed to God that God should do to "my enemies." While we treat these statements as wishes of a most regressive kind, notice that in fact the speaker is instructing God on the best way to proceed.

At the end of the imperatives, verse 9 then turns to a human promise. "Then," when God has acted decisively at the point of need, then and only then, promises the psalmist:

Then my soul shall rejoice in the LORD,
    exulting in his deliverance. (Ps 35:9)

The "soul" that rejoices is the same "soul" to whom God was to have said, in verse 3, "I am your salvation." That same self (soul) that has listened for God's assurance is now the self that will speak. That self, "all my bones"—every part of the self that has been addressed by God—will answer back:

All my bones shall say,
    "O LORD, who is like you?
You deliver the weak
    from those too strong for them,
    the weak and needy from those who despoil them." (Ps 35:10)

YHWH is named as the subject of a "formula of incomparability." Who is like YHWH? No one! No one is like YHWH in power. No one is like YHWH in compassionate attentiveness. YHWH is connected to the weak and the needy; it is this voice of need and weakness that speaks, now a second voice in the conversation; now that voice of need has turned to become a voice of gratitude.

After this doxological utterance in verses 9-10, the psalm moves in conventional fashion. On the one hand, in verses 11-14, the speaker is permitted to plead self-absorption as the poem is dominated by first-person pronouns that state need but that also state evidence of righteousness by having cared for the neighborhood. It is the speaker who, when the others were sick, engaged in rites and rituals of grief and healing.

In verse 15, the rhetoric with a disjunctive "but" turns from self-preoccupation to "they," the same "they" who are the subject of imprecations in verses 4-8:

> But at my stumbling they gathered in glee,
>   they gathered together against me;
> ruffians whom I did not know
>   tore at me without ceasing;
> they impiously mocked more and more,
>   gnashing at me with their teeth. (Ps 35:15-16)

They gathered. They tore at me. They mocked more and more. They gnashed their teeth. The poem does not say how this happened; all we know is that they—who remain unnamed—engaged in hostile, antineighborly conduct. Thus, in verses 11-14 the poem is about "me"; in verses 15-16 it is about "they." There is a standoff in this urgent struggle.

But then it becomes clear that this "I-They" presentation is at the most a rhetorical strategy for what comes next in verses 17 and following. Again, the psalmist addresses and names YHWH and issues a large imperative: rescue my *nephesh*! This is the third use of the word *nephesh* (self-soul), the speaking self who now depends completely on YHWH and is without other resources. The speaker in trouble, moreover, makes a promise to YHWH that, immediately upon the rescue for which he has prayed, he will express ample thanks to YHWH:

> *Then* I will thank you in the great congregation;
>   in the mighty throng I will praise you. (Ps 35:18)

But the psalmist is not yet convinced that YHWH "gets it," that YHWH understands the critical urgency of the moment. Now, with YHWH at attention, the speaker returns yet again to portray the enemy that threatens:

> For they do not speak peace,
>   but they conceive deceitful words
>   against those who are quiet in the land.
> They open wide their mouths against me;
>   they say, "Aha, Aha, our eyes have seen it." (Ps 35:20-21)

They—the enemy is now quoted. The enemies speak. Of course they do. Because in this life-or-death conversation, all parties have opportunity to give utterance. They do not speak *shalom*. Rather, in shamelessness they mock "more and more" (see v. 16):

> Aha, Aha,
> our eyes have seen it.

That is what they say in their dismissive scorn. The double use of "aha" is a mock that trivializes and embarrasses. The speaker now in need is utterly exposed and shamed. The enemies have now seen him in ways in which he did not want to be seen. They have seen him as helpless. And, we may imagine, they have also seen that he is resourceless and without an advocate. They are free to bully him because he has no means to protect himself or to injure them. The dismissive utterance of the adversaries, it may be, not only mocks the speaker; but we may infer that the enemies also mock the God of the speaker, who has not come to help. In a shame-oriented society, such voices of derision speak loudly and dangerously.

When the enemy takes part in the conversation in this way, the speaker is again driven to YHWH, again named in verse 22. Now follows a series of urgent petitions, imperatives addressed to the Holy One:

> You have seen, O LORD; do not be silent!
>   O LORD, do not be far from me!
> Wake up! Bestir yourself for *my* defense,
>   for *my* cause, *my* God and *my* LORD!
> Vindicate me, O LORD, *my* God,
>   according to your righteousness,
>   and do not let them rejoice over me. (Ps 35:22-24)

The address is to God; but the verses are dominated by first-person references: my defense, my cause, my God, my Lord. Everything is at stake in this summons issued to YHWH. Only YHWH stands as a protector against another dismissive utterance that, if spoken, would be the unbearable extremity of social humiliation:

> Do not let them say in their hearts . . .
> Do not let them say . . .

Stop this voice sounding in my life. It is a loud, threatening voice, and I cannot bear it. We can imagine the speaker turning to God while covering his ears to resist this social dismantling that is at the brink of utterance. What he fears is that the enemy will say:

> Aha [this is the same word spoken above in v. 21]
> We have our heart's desire.

In fact, this NRSV's phrasing is of only one Hebrew word, "our *nephesh*." Our soul! Our self! The psalmist dreads that his enemies will voice their own satisfied self-affirmation that will signify their triumph and his undoing. The psalmist is afraid that they will gloat: "Do not let them say, 'We have swallowed you up'" (Ps 35:25).

The prayer continues with more imperatives and petitions. But the speaker, having said everything that could be said about the adversary, now knows a coming well being. He knows that he will be "vindicated," that is, treated righteously. He knows this because in the process of the psalm he has heard the assurance of YHWH, for which he prayed in verse 3. He knows because he has given full voice to the adversary and finds the adversary, in such out-loud utterance, less overwhelming than he had imagined. Thus by verse 27 the speaker can now enjoy a sense of well being and can imagine himself now fully and gladly resituated in his congregation. It is that congregation who will join in praise to the God who saves. The congregation will issue one of its standard doxologies:

> Let those who desire my vindication
> shout for joy and be glad,
> and say evermore,

> "Great is the LORD,
> who delights in the welfare of his servant." (Ps 35:27)

This stereotypical phrasing merits close attention, because in it the worshiping congregation connects complex strands of reality. YHWH is praised as "great," but the reason that greatness is acknowledged is because the congregation knows that YHWH has taken delight in the *shalom* of this particular speaker. The final voice is the speaker's resolve to put his own tongue to glad work. The speaker's tongue will be employed—we may imagine "without ceasing"—to celebrate YHWH's righteousness, YHWH's capacity to take an initiative to turn the world of the speaker back to life; the last word is praise all day every day. The very process of the psalm itself permits the speaker to move from urgent need to glad doxology, and we who have paid attention are permitted the same glad move in our life.

Now it may be that I have excessively labored this psalm. But I want to ask, how does that transformation from need to gladness occur? My answer is that the psalmist has constructed and given voice to a *complex conversation that was inchoately present in his life*, as it is inescapably present in every life. I can imagine, given my own compulsive ruminations at night, that the speaker has heard and imagined and uttered all four parts of this conversation; he has done so because these voices are characteristically present to us when our faith becomes honest:

- There is the voice of *the saving God* who will—soon or late—say to the needy one: "I am your salvation" (v. 3).
- There is the voice of *the speaker* who anticipates that in time to come—soon, but not very soon—that he will be able to make a glad affirmation:

> All my bones shall say,
>   "O LORD, who is like you?
> You deliver the weak
>   from those too strong for them,
>   the weak and needy from those who despoil them." (Ps 35:10)

- There is the voice of *the adversary* that rings in our ears. Indeed, the adversary gets the most airtime as we go over the speech of mocking that has been spoken. And as we anticipate an even more threatening speech that is potentially to be uttered, this is what the enemies say that I have already heard:

> Aha, Aha,
> Our eyes have seen it. (v. 21)

But in addition to what they have said, this is what they might say that I cannot bear to hear:

> Aha, we have our hearts desire.
> . . . We have swallowed you up. (v. 25)

This dread-filled exchange, however, does not happen in a vacuum. The psalmist can remember that he is a member of *the community*. And as he can anticipate—with dread—what the adversary might say, so he can anticipate—with elation—what the congregation will say in time to come:

> Great is the LORD,
>   who delights in the welfare of his servant. (Ps 35:27)

During the day, the speaker might imagine his entire life in the single, unified, coherent, manageable self-announcement. But at night that singular coherence falls apart into a cacophony of voices, all of which press for airtime. The speaker finds now that his life is reconstituted as a dialogic transaction in which everything is at stake:

Here speaks *threat* that will undo;
Here speaks *holy intervention* that will rescue;
Here speaks *self in confidence*;
Here speaks *congregation* in a summation of God's goodness toward the
speaker.

This poem is a remarkable artistic achievement. It is of course only a poem.
But it is a poem that bespeaks the contested dialogue that constitutes life in faith
under stress.

We can imagine that this is a *liturgical articulation,* in which all voices are routinely acknowledged as commonplace in faith, for this dialogic faith knows about
the contest between YHWH and the adversaries who vie for control of our lives.

But we can also imagine that behind the commonplace liturgical expression is
the deep pathos of *profound personal struggle* by one haunted with all of these
voices. And newness can come only when these inchoate voices are given freedom
of tongue. It may be that in such a map of turmoil, dispute, and anxiety that the
speaker must play all of the parts, because in some way these are all parts of the self.
But even if it is only the speaker who tongues each role, each speaking part is given
different nuance and inflection because these are identifiable voices in a divided,
conflicted self. Every self that pays attention to the rich internal life entrusted to us
by God knows about being haunted, knows about the voices of threat, knows about
the care of the congregation, knows about the holy possibility of God, and knows
about the work that the self must conduct. The happy reality is that in ancient
Israel, there were venues were all these voices could be given air time.

Liturgical commonplace and pathos-filled struggle of candor surely mark this
psalm. Thus, we may push in a psychological direction. If we do so, I suggest that
this is not an exceptionally disordered life, for every attentive life is a conversation
on its way to articulation. But I do not reduce the psalm to psychology. Let us
imagine that the psalm is *a mapping out of social forces,* a field of complex power
that is real in the perception of faith:

- There really is a yearning needy self;
- There really are voices of dismantling threat, anciently remembered
  and contemporarily uttered;
- There really is a surrounding congregation that has not lost its confidence, buoyancy, or nerve;
- And to be sure, there really is a holy God who waits offstage to be
  summoned to intervene decisively.

This is the world where God has placed us, and the self is characteristically at risk
among these voices. This self at risk makes its tricky way amid all these voices
in a move from need to praise. The voices are real voices. The voices are parts of
the self. The voices sound in nighttime moments of vulnerability. Freud, of course

already, understood that to give concrete utterance to such voices is to rob the negating voices of authority. Conversely, to give utterance is to let healthy reality override the threat.

This psalm, unlike many others, is an affirmation that life is deeply contested, a dialogue in which everything is at stake. Where we fail such pastoral, liturgical articulation, we are fated, I suggest, to a monologic world of repression and denial that can host no newness but that remains in a destructive exchange that stops short of out-loud utterance and thereby has immense and recurring destructive force. The action of such recital is to see that one's life is *an unsettled, unresolved venue* for God's contestation: all parts of the self, all social realities, all forces converge in the utterance that permits newness. The challenge for the teaching pastors of the church is to authorize the conversation that breaks the monologic grip of dominant ideology, whether that ideology be of the military-industrial complex or of our well-meaning mothers. For to break the grip is to forswear control and domination and to enter a practice of vulnerability that is our true human habitat.

I note one other remarkable feature in this psalm. It is a rhetorical strategy that occurs three times: First, in verses 4-8 the psalmist asks God to "do" his enemies, and follows in verse 9 with "then":

> *Then* my soul shall rejoice in the LORD,
>   exulting in his deliverance. (Ps 35:9)

Second, in verse 17, the psalmist petitions God in an imperative to "rescue me from their ravages," and follows in verse 18 with a "then":

> *Then* I will thank you in the great congregation;
>   in the mighty throng I will praise you. (Ps 35:18)

Third, in verse 27, the psalmist describes the praising congregation, and follows in verse 28 with a "then":

> *Then* my tongue shall tell of your righteousness
>   and of your praise all day long. (Ps 35:28)

These three uses of "then" (variously given in the Hebrew text) are in each case a promise to praise God and to give God thanks. But the "then" indicates that the promised celebration and affirmation of God are held in abeyance until God acts to deliver. Indeed, praise of God is consequent to and dependent on God's action of rescue. I cite this rhetorical strategy because it indicates that the psalmist, as the lesser party to the dialogue, has nerve and entitlement to hold his ground in a Joblike fashion and to make demands on the senior party to the dialogue. This means, does it not, that the dialogue is not cheap or easy or facile but consists in a struggle for validation with the outcome held in abeyance for the future. But that, of course, is the character of dialogue that refuses premature conclusion or closure. Dialogic partners wait together, even if not comfortably, for newness to emerge in the process between them, a newness that might to some extent satisfy both parties. In this case that expected emergent satisfaction will be *rescue* for the psalmist and *praise* for God; thus, both parties are enhanced in the eyes of their mutual adversary.

V

The second facet of dialogic life in a monologic environment I will deal with more briefly. It is the capacity of the Psalms—Israel's script for worship and faithful imagination—to move from the *most intent, concrete personal experience* to the *great public agenda of the congregation.* It is the interface of personal and public that concerns us here, that puts the one and the many into a conversation of mutuality. I suggest that this characteristic maneuver in the congregation is an important antidote to both the *privatization* of much of the life of the church and the *loud moral indignation* of the church without the specificities of pathos and hope. The interaction between the two is by way of testimony, of giving specific evidence in the congregation of both need and healing, giving account of individual drama that funds and energizes the work of the active congregation.

We have seen this motif at work in Psalm 35 in two references. In verse 18, after the anticipated rescue by God, the psalmist says:

> Then I will thank you in the great congregation;
>> in the mighty throng I will praise you. (Ps 35:18)

The thanks is an individual matter in which the speaker runs the course of need and the concreteness of divine intervention. But that specific thanks is in "the great congregation," so that we may imagine members of the community gathered around, giving praise for miracles that in a world of monologic control are never evoked, never acknowledged, never celebrated, and never publicly owned. The same motif, less directly expressed, is evident in verse 27:

> Let those who desire my vindication
>> shout for joy and be glad,
>> and say evermore,
> "Great is the LORD,
>> who delights in the welfare of his servant." (Ps 35:27)

The congregation consists in those who "desire my vindication," who are pleased at God's righteous action on my behalf. The speaker can imagine, even in great need, that the congregation is filled with members who care, who are praying for and pulling for and cheering for God to effect a concrete rescue.

When one pays attention to the Psalter, it is clear that even the most personal of prayers are in the horizon of the congregation. Indeed, Fredrik Lindström has vigorously argued that the Psalter is all about *temple theology*, about a place of centered divine presence, power, and attentiveness. This communal sense of the individual is of immense importance in a society that is increasingly organized to resist any notion of the public and to isolate individuals so as to leave us all disconnected and at the mercy of market forces. The effort of the Bush administration to dismantle social security may be taken as a metaphor for the work of monologic society in its effort to preclude the true human functioning of society, for which the Christian congregation may be a microcosm. The congregation is not simply a unit of finance or of power or of tradition. It is the defining unit of human existence whenever we become aware that genuine *security* is inescapably *social*, and the privatization of society, taken theologically, is a decision to be insecure. This dialogic alternative to monologue is to be "members one of another."

I will cite two clear cases of the move from personal to public whereby individual thanksgiving funds the imagination and energy of the entire public.

Psalm 30 is a pure song of individual thanksgiving. At the center of the psalm, the speaker narrates the dramatic experience of:

initial well being:

> As for me, I said in my prosperity,
>   "I shall never be moved."
> By your favor, O LORD,
>   you had established me as a strong mountain. (Ps 30:6-7a)

devastating disruption:

> You hid your face;
>   I was dismayed. (Ps 30:7b)

petition and bargaining with God:

> To you, O LORD, I cried,
>   and to the LORD I made supplication:
> "What profit is there in my death,
>   if I go down to the Pit?
> Will the dust praise you?
>   Will it tell of your faithfulness? (Ps 30:8-10)

resolution and well being:

> You have turned my mourning into dancing;
>> you have taken off my sackcloth
>> and clothed me with joy. (Ps 30:11)

That drama is intensely personal. It culminates, moreover, in the resolve of the recipient of God's mercy to praise and give thanks forever. The speaker refuses silence and joins the practice of utterance, an utterance that goes all the way through trouble to the divine gift of well being:

> So that my soul may praise you and not be silent.
>> O LORD my God, I will give thanks to you forever. (Ps 30:12)

The speaker is totally focused on the journey of the self at the behest of God. The psalm begins in verses 1-3 in a quite intimate, personal testimony:

> I will extol you, O LORD, for you have drawn me up,
>> and did not let my foes rejoice over me.
> O LORD my God, I cried to you for help,
>> and you have healed me.
> O LORD, you brought up my soul from Sheol,
>> restored me to life from among
>> those gone down to the Pit. (Ps 30:1-3)

But then the psalmist moves beyond self in verses 4 and 5. He knows that the joy and elation at his new life is too much for him to celebrate alone. He appeals to his community and recruits others to join in the celebration:

> Sing praises to the LORD, O you his faithful ones,
>> and give thanks to his holy name. (Ps 30:4)

The summons is to "his faithful ones," the ones who are steadfast and keep covenant. They are the ones who are schooled in the dialogic practice of fidelity, for they will of course understand the dramatic turn in his life. They not only will fully appreciate that turn, but they will also know with whom to credit it and how best to say it. Indeed, it is the work of the faithful ones, the congregation, to take up individual cases and magnify and enhance them by full public coverage. And the reason for communal exuberance is that the community knows that divine love outdistances divine neglect or anger. These are the ones who know about the hardness and sadness of the night that seems interminable when the haunting voice of death stalks our bed. They are the ones who have learned amid these voices of the night, and who have no doubt that, as powerful as those voice are, they must flee and yield when God gives the sun:

> For his anger is but for a moment;
>   his favor is for a lifetime.
> Weeping may linger for the night,
>   but joy comes with the morning. (Ps 30:5)

The congregation consists in those who have been there before us and before this speaker. They know of case after case after case of suffering turned to well being and death turned to life, anger to grace, and weeping to joy.

Indeed, Israel is rooted in that characteristic transformative act. The overarching awareness in ancient Israel is, of course, the exile, that harsh moment of displacement. In that context, the poetry of Second Isaiah sounds, on God's lips, a recognition very like our verse 5:

> For a brief moment I abandoned you,
>   but with great compassion I will gather you.
> In overflowing wrath for a moment
>   I hid my face from you,
> but with everlasting love I will have compassion on you,
>   says the LORD, your Redeemer. (Isa 54:7-8)

This is what the congregation knows. It knows, as God here concedes, that there really are moments of divine abandonment when we must honestly say, "My God, my God, why have you forsaken me?" They know, as does the speaker in verse 7, about the hidden face of absence. But they are also able to trust and anticipate that as the sun rises so the great compassion and everlasting love of the Redeemer God are beyond such abandonment.

And if we ask, how does the congregation so confidently know this? The answer is, by *many, many individual testimonies*, to which this one in the psalm is now added. The truth of miracle is not from above in some theoretical imposition. Rather, the truth of miracle is from below, from wonders that are daily, concrete, material, and specific. The congregation is a collection of those who know about miracles, from which it draws deep resilient doxology. And the speaker joins the song, never to try to celebrate the miracle alone. This *security* is indeed *social* without at all minimizing the first-person-singular articulation.

The same dynamic practice occurs in the more familiar Psalm 22. The first part of the psalm is quite intimate and personal and of course struggles with the reality of divine abandonment (vv. 1-21a). As is well known, the psalm turns in the middle of verse 21, with the abrupt, inexplicable affirmation: "From the horns of the wild oxen you have answered me." That simple utterance is affirmation that the prayer of petition in the foregoing verses has been effective. The petition has moved God to overcome abandonment and to answer, that is, to be dialogically present in a context of profound need.

But then the speaker—now rescued, affirmed, and addressed—must find a way to give voice to newness that is commensurate with a need that has been previously expressed. Immediately, the speaker knows that he cannot do this task of acknowledgment by himself but must recruit his companions into the task. He knows how to proceed:

> I will tell of your name to my brothers and sisters;
> > in the midst of the congregation I will praise you. (Ps 22:22)

It is a telling, a narrating, a bearing witness. The first hearers of his resurrection experience are "brothers," that is, fellow members of the covenant who inhabit the congregation. No privatism here! That verse 22 is followed by a much larger invitation to share the joy:

> You who fear the LORD, praise him!
> > All you offspring of Jacob, glorify him;
> > stand in awe of him, all you offspring of Israel! (Ps 22:23)

All celebrate the truth that God hears, answers, and thereby transforms. Ellen Davies has shown how the summons to praise moves in concentric circles into all imaginable human reality as it is recruited into the task.[3] The Bible characteristically moves from the particular embodied truth to the larger communal acclamation as all are drawn into the utterance of joy.

In verse 25 the reference to the congregation in verse 22 is now expanded to be "the great congregation," the same phrase we have seen in 35:18: "From you comes my praise in the great congregation" (Ps 22:25a). Perhaps the move from "congregation" to "great congregation" is from local sanctuary to temple. But the circle expands even more. After that, in verse 27, it is "all the ends of the earth" and "all the families of the nations," all of whom celebrate the rule of YHWH over all nations:

> All the ends of the earth shall remember
> > and turn to the LORD;
> and all the families of the nations
> > shall worship before him.
> For dominion belongs to the LORD,
> > and he rules over the nations. (Ps 22:27-28)

In verse 28 the psalm clearly employs rhetoric that moves out from the personal to the great public affirmation about the rule of God over the nation-states. The psalm accomplishes this transition easily and readily, for both the personal and the public have to do with overcoming alienation for the sake of *shalom*.

In a final leap of inclusiveness, the psalm now refers to praise among the deceased, who are now only remembered, along with the ones only hoped for and not yet born:

> To him, indeed, shall all who sleep in the earth bow down;
> > before him shall bow all who go down to the dust,
> > and I shall live for him.
> Posterity will serve him;
> > future generations will be told about the LORD,
> and proclaim his deliverance to a people yet unborn,
> > saying that he has done it. (Ps 22:29-31)

The whole of creation is gathered around this one speaker. That speaker initiated the process by telling the truth of divine abandonment. The deep reality of divine abandonment, however, did not lead to silence and resignation. Rather, it led to vigorous protest, accusation, and petition that eventuated in divine attentiveness. And if we wonder why abandonment led to speech, it is because everything in this dialogic community leads to speech. Israel knows, and after Israel Freud and Martin Luther King, and many others know, that utterance produces newness. Utterance enlivens social possibility; but it enlivens social possibility because we—all of us—are in the image of the dialogic God. Praise, the alternative voice of this community, is not easy speech; it arises only after the hard trouble is told, truth that is hard on all powerful ears, including the ears of the powerful God.

VI

So imagine the bishops and priests of the church presiding over and empowering communities of utterance who tell truth that leads to newness. We have the script, and we have the venue. It is a ministry of Word. It is a ministry of Word and sacrament, because the sacrament enacts bodily what our words dare say. And every time the bishop or the priest empowers a community of utterance, we commit a subversive act that intends to overthrow the powers of silence. I do not know our way ahead in North American society. But I do know that we live in a silencing culture, growing more silent amid electronic prattle. The empire depends on quiescent taxpayers. The market depends on isolated shoppers. As we grow quiescent and isolated, the human spirit withers; and options for newness grow jaded in fatigue. And then this utterance of truth and possibility, dangerous and welcome, so dangerous as to be unwelcome, but nonetheless urgent.

I finish with the well-known narrative of Bartimaeus. When Bartimaeus heard that it was Jesus of Nazareth, he shouted out, "Jesus, son of David, have mercy on me." Mark reports: "Many sternly ordered him to be quiet, but he cried out even more loudly, 'Son of David, have mercy on me!' " (Mark 10:48). And the rest, as we say, is history. The world is filled with self-appointed librarians who impose coerced silence into our common life. But the cry breaks that open:

> Weeping may linger for the night,
> > but joy comes with the morning. (Ps 30:5)

All these words have been entrusted to us by the Word come flesh, full of grace and truth.

Chapter 11

Spirit-Led Imagination:
Reality Practiced in a Sub-Version

THE PRACTICE OF FAITHFUL WORSHIP is more odd than we often take it to be, familiar as it is to us. In recent times the church has relinquished much of that oddness in a seductive attempt to be current, popular, alternative, or entertaining. It is, I submit, a major task of the church to receive the oddness of our odd holy partner. In this, I would like to delineate something of that oddness that matters for the missional call of the church and that ultimately matters for the well being of the world.

I

Worship is an act of *poetic imagination* that aims to reconstrue the world. By the phrase, "act of imagination," I mean it presents lived reality in *images, figures, and metaphors* that defy our conventional structures of plausibility and that host alternative scenarios of reality that cut beyond our conventional perceptual field. This act of imagination that offers an alternative world is, perforce, a poetic act; that is, it is given to us in playful traces and hints that come at us sideways and that do not conform to any of our usual categories of understanding or explanation. The practice of such poetic imagination that invites us playfully to alternative reality is deeply rooted in old texts, old memories, and old practices; but it requires contemporary, disciplined, informed imagination to sustain alternative vision.

I will cite at some length three *mighty acts of poetic imagination* in the Old Testament that are characteristic acts of worship to which the community returns again and again.

In *Exodus 15:21*—surely one of the oldest poems in the Old Testament—Miriam and the other women, as they departed Egypt and began the journey into the wilderness and eventually to the land of promise, took up tambourines and sang:

> Sing to the LORD, for he has triumphed gloriously;
> horse and rider he has thrown into the sea. (Exod 15:21)

This brief hymn is a characteristic example of the way in which Israel does praise. It invites the community to sing to YHWH. It does not explain, because everyone knows. Everyone knows we have just witnessed an inexplicable triumphant act in the world, and everyone knows that it must be referred to the holy God who is Creator of heaven and earth. Everyone knows, moreover, that the only fitting response to such an awesome turn in the world is to sing, to offer deep-throated, lyrical, prerational exuberance to the giver of life. Miriam and the other women knew before the Wesleys what the Wesleys exhibited so well, that worship is a glad, full, unqualified sense of glad abandonment of our life toward the giver of all life.

This little hymn gives reason for exuberance. YHWH has won a great victory. YHWH has destroyed Egyptian armaments and has overthrown the mighty imperial superpower. Miriam does not know how this has happened and has no mandate to explain. Indeed, Miriam's testimony is not a mechanical response that is connected to what happened. It is, rather, an act of deep imagination, for the overthrow of Pharaoh could be offered, as it has been by critical studies, on other grounds—there was a mighty wind, this was an escape of slaves, there was a lapse in state security, there was a dismissal of surplus labor. All that is of course possible; but no, says this worship leader Miriam. She has imagined and construed the wonder differently, and we will not pause over trivializing explanation. The event is miracle, with marks of holy awe, and it must not be reduced to explanation. It is miracle that invites exuberance and dismay, whereas explanation invites control and management and no doubt another layer of committees.

II

Well, as you might imagine, the hymnal committee, chaired by a man, took up the spontaneous outburst of Miriam and the other women and transposed that originary poetic act into a more set poem. The outcome of such a canonizing process is the so-called Song of Moses in *Exodus 15:1-18*. That poetry begins with the attestation of Miriam in Exodus 15:1:

> Then Moses and the Israelites sang this song to the LORD:
> "I will sing to the LORD, for he has triumphed gloriously;
> horse and rider he has thrown into the sea." (Exod 15:1)

It continues, by way of extrapolation, in verses 2-3 with more hymnic introduction. And then, in verses 4-10, it offers poetic imagination to provide a narrative scenario of the death of Pharaoh. The community of emancipated slaves in generation after generation sings the song and celebrates the overthrow of whoever is the current pharaoh. We watch as the writers dabble with death and settle on a way to characterize the God of the wind who put tyranny to death:

> Pharaoh's chariots and his army he cast into the sea;
>> his picked officers were sunk in the Red Sea.
> The floods covered them;
>> they went down into the depths like a stone.
> Your right hand, O LORD, glorious in power—
>> your right hand, O LORD, shattered the enemy.
> In the greatness of your majesty you overthrew your adversaries;
>> you sent out your fury, it consumed them like stubble.
> At the blast of your nostrils the waters piled up,
>> the floods stood up in a heap;
>> the deeps congealed in the heart of the sea.
> The enemy said, "I will pursue, I will overtake,
>> I will divide the spoil, my desire shall have its fill of them.
> I will draw my sword, my hand shall destroy them."
> You blew with your wind, the sea covered them;
>> they sank like lead in the mighty waters. (Exod 15:4-10)

Nothing explained. Everything stays hidden except the outcome. The outcome to which the narrative leads is that everything has been changed!

The hymnal committee of course took liberties with Miriam's little verse. They added verses. In canonical form, it is not enough to cross the waters. The whole narrative must be told, because the narrative is the screen memory for all of faith. The slaves not only go out. They go in—to the land of promise. Thus, in verses 13-17, these ex-slaves are led "in your steadfast love," led through dangerous valleys of death amid Edomites and Moabites and Ammonites, all those who did not subscribe to this act of imagination, and they arrive safely:

> You brought them in and planted them on the mountain of your own
>> possession,
>> the place, O LORD, that you made your abode,
>> the sanctuary, O LORD, that your hands have established. (Exod 15:17)

It was a long journey, and Israel would have stories to tell all the way along. But the skeletal structure of imagination is now in place. The narrative that scripts this imagination is from slavery to safety, from death to life, from oppression to freedom, the story that has countless variations and that is endlessly sung and then sung again, because the imaginative drama is always required yet again in new circumstance.

The poem is symmetrical: verses 4-10 are about the death of Pharaoh, who can be any face of brutalizing power; verses 13-17 are the arrival at well being. And in between these two units, in verses 11-12, we are offered a formula of incomparability, for no other god has been so allied with slaves:

> Who is like you, O LORD, among the gods?
>   Who is like you, majestic in holiness,
>   awesome in splendor, doing wonders? (Exod 15:11)

It is YHWH, directly, immediately, whose great spirit of power has turned the world. And so the song can culminate in verse 18 with a great mantra of enthronement: "The LORD will reign forever and ever" (Exod 15:18). There has been regime change. A new king is among us, a new king who has no brick quotas and no imperial palaces based on forced labor, a new king that offers a world covenantally arranged. It is no wonder that the men joined the women singing precisely because "he shall reign forever and ever and ever."

So sang Miriam and so echoed Moses. They did not need to say it as they did. But they said it in this particular way, and their way of saying it has become our way of speaking of a new rule of God in the earth, the realm of well being that we regularly enact in worship. We regularly enact it in hope, in defiance, and in resolve. The song is an act of imagination that hopes an alternative, because the data is all against the song. The data indicates old management by alienating superpowers with brick quotas. But for this one moment, over and over, we refuse the data. We enter another zone of reality that must be expressed not precisely, not didactically, but in raw exuberance about large nostrils of wind and kings sinking like lead and populations seized with dread and then settlement and peace. We sing it over and over again against the data of the day. We refuse to give in to the data of the day because we, like them, "desire a better country," a city that has been prepared for us (Heb 11:16).

III

Of course, the rawness that is so indispensable is not everywhere sustained. When the hymnal committee completes its work, the raw specificity from the beginning point is reshaped into a more urbane poetry. Now the specificity is rounded out to a fuller picture, but the tenacity of fidelity is fully sustained. So consider a third script of praise, the astonishing litany of *Psalm 136*.

This litany begins in verses 1-3 with a threefold invitation to "give thanks to YHWH." It knows that the proper stance of Israel before God is one of gratitude, because YHWH is the generous giver of life for Israel and for all of creation. Such thanks in Israel are liturgically constituted by a material offering accompanied by appropriate words. Here we have only the words; thanks are constituted by public testimony that acknowledges YHWH as the giver of gifts and Israel as recipient. The psalm concludes in verse 26 with a like invitation to thank, only now YHWH is not named but is identified as "the God of heaven," that is, the presiding sovereign of all creatures and all gods.

Thus the psalm is framed in verses 1-3 and verse 26 by thanks. Between these two calls of thanks, the body of the psalm, verses 4-25, provides specific grounds of thanks as it recites YHWH's engagement in the world and on behalf of Israel. Well, it turns out that every part of Israel's life that it can remember or imagine *evokes Israel's thanks*. The reason is that in the interpretative imagination of Israel, everything that happens is read as a sign and signal of YHWH's abiding fidelity (*hesed*), so that the world and its historical processes are known to be saturated with divine constancy and stability. Thus, the litany proceeds so that the response to every line, a reprise surely uttered by the community at worship, concerns YHWH's fidelity.

The body of the psalm begins in verses 4-9 with reference to YHWH's great work in *creation*:

> who alone does great wonders,
>> for his steadfast love endures forever;
> who by understanding made the heavens,
>> for his steadfast love endures forever;
> who spread out the earth on the waters,
>> for his steadfast love endures forever;
> who made the great lights;
>> for his steadfast love endures forever;
> the sun to rule over the day,
>> for his steadfast love endures forever;
> the moon and stars to rule over the night,
>> for his steadfast love endures forever. (Ps 136:4-9)

This is followed by a long litany concerning the *exodus deliverance*, a song not unlike Exodus 15 (vv. 10-15), and is followed by the conventional sequence of *wilderness sojourn and entry into the land* (vv. 16-23). The main body of the psalm concludes with a wondrous summary statement in three parts:

> It is he who remembered us in our low estate,
>> for his steadfast love endures forever;
> and rescued us from our foes,
>> for his steadfast love endures forever;
> who gives good to all flesh,
>> for his steadfast love endures forever. (Ps 136:23-25)

In this conclusion, Israel can remember its abasement, surely a reference to exodus slavery, and offers an acknowledgment of divine rescue (vv. 23-24). Surprisingly, this is followed in verse 25 with a reference to creation and the reliable food chain of creation:

> who gives food to all flesh,
>> for his steadfast love endures forever. (Ps 136:25)

We are able to see that this psalmic imagination reflects a larger body of poetry. Thus, the reference to "low estate" readily recalls Psalm 123, which reflects on YHWH's transformative mercy that addresses YHWH's context of contempt:

> As the eyes of servants look to the hand of their master,
> as the eyes of a maid to the hand of her mistress,
> so our eyes look to the LORD our God,
>> until he has mercy upon us.
> Have mercy upon us, O LORD, have mercy upon us,
>> for we have had more than enough of contempt.
> Our soul has had more than its fill
>> of the scorn of those who are at ease,
>> of the contempt of the proud. (Ps 123:2-4)

Verse 25, with its reference to "food for all flesh," moreover, is reminiscent of the great creation hymns that celebrate the abundance of food:

> These all look to you
>> to give them their food in due season;
> when you give to them, they gather it up;
>> when you open your hand, they are filled with good things.
>> (Ps 104:27-28)

> The eyes of all look to you,
>> and you give them their food in due season.
> You open your hand,
>> satisfying the desire of every living thing. (Ps 145:15-16)

All creation is pulsing with YHWH's faithfulness.

This act of liturgic imagination may strike us as routine. It does not, however, need to be so. The world can indeed be imagined differently. It can be imagined with *Hobbes*, as a war of each against all. It can be imagined with *Kissinger* as a world in which might makes right. It can be imagined with *Milton Friedman* as a place of scarcity where we compete for limited goods. It can be imagined as a place of chaos and threat and risk. All such construals are possible and frequently enacted. But not in Israel. Not in this world of worship. Israel reads and imagines and celebrates otherwise, by appeal to its own remembered narrative, a narrative of constant fidelity, such constancy that evokes assured and unanxious gratitude. (There are, to be sure, testimonies in Israel that construe differently; but in this canonical recital, the point is clear.) It is evident that out of the materials of its experience and observation, Israel is engaged in world-making so that Israel ends the psalm in a safe place where gratitude is the appropriate response.

IV

As *Exodus 15* narrates the raw reality of victory and *Psalm 136* shapes that victory into a collage of stylized affirmations, so my third example, *Psalm 107*, at the same time (1) moves from grand communal affirmation to concrete lived experience and (2) goes underneath glad doxology to the vexations that mark every life in God's world.

Psalm 107 begins in verses 1-3 with a summons to thank, not unlike Psalm 136. The specific ground of thanks is that YHWH is "good" and that, as in Psalm 136, his steadfast love endures forever. This is the baseline of faith and the ground of gratitude:

> O give thanks to the LORD, for he is good,
>   for his steadfast love endures forever. (Ps 107:1)

But this psalm goes further. It not only summons to thanks, but it also identifies those who most readily and appropriately will give thanks:

> Let the redeemed of the LORD say so,
>   those he redeemed from trouble
> and gathered in from the lands,
>   from the east and from the west,
>   from the north and from the south. (Ps 107:2-3)

The ones who can make gestures of gratitude are the ones who have been "redeemed from trouble." The reference could be to the oppression of Egypt; but the body of the psalm will make clear that the invitation is to all sorts of human persons. And the parallel refers to all those "gathered," that is, returned from exile and displacement. The rhetoric of verse 3 is inclusive and pertains to all Jews who have been brought home and to all who had lived through God's generous homecoming. The four-directional inclusion recalls Isaiah 43:6, wherein YHWH seeks out the scattered:

> I will say to the north, "Give them up,"
>   and to the south, "Do not withhold;

> bring my sons from far away
>   and my daughters from the end of the earth—
> everyone who is called by my name,
>   whom I created for my glory,
>   whom I formed and made." (Isa 43:6-7)

That rhetorical maneuver acknowledges the God of all gathering:

> Thus says the LORD God,
>   who gathers the outcasts of Israel,
> I will gather others to them
>   besides those already gathered. (Isa 56:8)

These are the ones who are to give thanks to YHWH, because they are the ones who know YHWH's *hesed* firsthand.

The psalm then lines out, in *four case studies*, some particular examples of those who have been alienated and restored. The substance of verses 4-38 is remarkable. First, because of its concreteness of particular cases, and second, because of its capacity to remember, recall, and characterize specific situations of distress. This latter point, as we shall see in some detail, suggests that much of worship in Israel, albeit in incidental venues, consisted in *petitionary truth-telling* that evoked YHWH's redeeming action.

The first case, characteristic of the fourfold stylized report, describes a situation of wonders that are lost in the wilderness without resources:

> Some wandered in desert wastes,
>   finding no way to an inhabited town;
> hungry and thirsty,
>   their soul fainted within them. (Ps 107:4-5)

But they, Israelites that they are, know that a *petition* addressed to YHWH is the appropriate antidote to such dismay: "Then they cried to the LORD in their trouble" (Ps 107:6a). The remarkable movement of the rhetoric indicates that, without pause or pondering of any kind, the deliverance of YHWH follows promptly upon petition:

> and he delivered them from their distress;
> he led them by a straight way,
>   until they reached an inhabited town. (Ps 107:6b-7)

These two rhetorical elements state the substance of Israel's most elemental worship, namely, *cry in need* and divine *response of rescue*. While it will not be true in two subsequent cases I will mention, here the crisis in which the faithful are located has nothing to do with guilt. What counts is not guilt but need. Israel, it is attested liturgically, knew exactly what to do about desperate need, namely, to recognize one's own inadequacy and to turn to the fully adequate LORD.

In a complex and extensive discussion, Karl Barth has asserted that prayer in Christian tradition is "simply asking."[1] Barth continues to say that asking God is "the most genuine act of praise and thanksgiving and therefore worship." More than that, "God does not act in the same way whether we pray or not." Prayer "exerts an influence upon God's action, even upon his existence."

For that reason, it is no surprise that the *cry* of the wilderness wanderers in their hunger and thirst is promptly *answered* with divine deliverance. This is a God who hears and who decisively responds to the need of Israel. Indeed, as Claus Westermann has shown, this structure of "cry-answer" or "cry-save" is the core plot of biblical faith and therefore the core claim of worship. From the finite verbs "deliver" and "lead," Israel at worship—because of countless cases of concrete testimony—can generalize about God's *hesed*. The generalizing affirmation about YHWH, moreover, introduces the crucial term *niphla'oth*, "wonderful acts," acts of transformation that defy our explanation and belong in the peculiar category of miracle. It is thus no wonder that this tightly drawn rhetoric concludes with a summons to thanks. The final verse of the unit returns to the beginning and reiterates the initial need, only now it is need satisfied:

> For he satisfies the thirsty,
>> and the hungry he fills with good things. (Ps 107:9)

Now the governing verbs are of a different sort, "satisfy, fill." These terms, bespeaking the abundance of creation, are very different from the verbs of verses 6-7, "deliver, lead," that attest historical activity. The four verbs together thus witness both to YHWH's disruptive rescue as Redeemer and to YHWH's generous sustenance as Creator.

The plotline of Psalm 107:4-9 provides a sketch of Israel's faith and surely a sequence of right worship: need, cry, rescue, thanks.

That same plotline is reiterated in three additional case studies.

- In Psalm 107:10-16, the stylized sequence goes this way.
  need:

> Some sat in darkness and in gloom,
>> prisoners in misery and in irons,
> for they had rebelled against the words of God,
>> and spurned the counsel of the Most High.
> Their hearts were bowed down with hard labor;
>> they fell down, with no one to help. (vv. 10-12)

cry:

> Then they cried to the LORD in their trouble. (v. 13a)

rescue:

> and he saved them from their distress;
> he brought them out of darkness and gloom,
>   and broke their bonds asunder. (vv. 13b-14)

a response of *thanks*:

> Let them thank the LORD for his steadfast love,
>   for his wonderful works to humankind. (v. 15)

a reprise of *need resolved*:

> For he shatters the doors of bronze,
>   and cuts in two the bars of iron. (v. 16)

In the response of YHWH, the governing verbs are "save," "bring out," "break." And in the reprise it is "shatter," "cut," all verbs of forceful action. These verbs in sum constitute a "wonderful work" (miracle) that is sure to evoke thanks for the inexplicable gift of new life.

- In verses 17-22, the plot is now familiar.
  need:

> Some were sick through their sinful ways,
>   and because of their iniquities endured affliction;
> they loathed any kind of food,
>   and they drew near to the gates of death. (vv. 17-18)

cry:

> Then they cried to the LORD in their trouble. (v. 19a)

rescue:

> and he saved them from their distress;
> he sent out his word and healed them,
>   and delivered them from destruction. (vv. 19b-20)

thanks:

> Let them thank the LORD for his steadfast love,
>> for his wonderful works to humankind.
> And let them offer thanksgiving sacrifices,
>> and tell of his deeds with songs of joy. (vv. 21-22)

In the rescue, the verbs are now "save," "send," "heal," "deliver"; thus, a more extensive cluster of terms. Of greater interest is the fact that the response of thanks is now more extended, having now displaced any reprise that is absent in this episode.

Verse 21 reiterates the familiar formula of thanks for *hesed* and *niphla'oth*. But verse 22 indicates the enactment of thanks in cultic form. Now the thanks is not only verbal but also includes a thank offering, a gift of material significance; and the material gift is matched by telling, that is, by narrating the rescue in verses 17-22. Thus, verse 22 reflects precisely a combination of Word and sacrament.

- The fourth case, in verses 23-32, is quite extended but by now familiar.
  need:

> they saw the deeds of the LORD,
>> his wondrous works in the deep.
> For he commanded and raised the stormy wind,
>> which lifted up the waves of the sea.
> They mounted up to heaven, they went down to the depths;
>> their courage melted away in their calamity;
> they reeled and staggered like drunkards,
>> and were at their wits' end. (vv. 24-27)

cry:

> Then they cried to the LORD in their trouble. (v. 28a)

rescue:

> and he brought them out from their distress;
> he made the storm be still,
>> and the waves of the sea were hushed.
> Then they were glad because they had quiet,
>> and he brought them to their desired haven. (vv. 28b-30)

thanks:

> Let them thank the LORD for his steadfast love,
>   for his wonderful works to humankind. (vv. 31-32)

In this sequence, it is most noticeable that the crisis is credited directly to YHWH, whereby the storm itself that causes the trouble is a wondrous deed wrought by YHWH's command. The verbs of rescue here include "bring out," "make still." The element of thanks is again extended in verse 22 to include extolment and praise in the midst of the congregation. It is clear in all these cases that the *moment of miracle* has now been transposed into a *stylized narrative*, the purpose of which is to instruct, summon, and empower the congregation to participate in this world of miracles, a world of decisively answered prayer.

The psalm concludes with two more generalized affirmations, more or less derivative from these case studies. In verses 33-38, YHWH as Creator is celebrated as the one who turns rivers to deserts and fruitful land to waste and who blesses those who are hungry with all the fruitfulness of creation. The rhetoric is reminiscent of Genesis 1. In verses 39-41 the rhetoric concerns social transformation in a way reflective of the Song of Hannah and anticipatory of the later Song of Mary:

> When they are diminished and brought low
>   through oppression, trouble, and sorrow,
> he pours contempt on princes
>   and makes them wander in trackless wastes;
> but he raises up the needy out of distress,
>   and makes their families like flocks. (vv. 39-41)

Nature is imagined as "creation," and *history* is imagined as an arena for YHWH's revolutionary activity. The psalm concludes in verse 32 with an invitation to wise discernment of this Yahwistic reality, the neglect of which leads to trouble; the final phrase, yet one more time, concerns the *hesed* of YHWH. All of these case studies attest concretely to the divine fidelity that is voiced in the liturgy of Psalm 136.

V

I have taken extended time—perhaps too much—to consider three songs in ancient Israel:

- Exodus 15 is a *victory* song that plots Israel's way from slavery to the land of promise;
- Psalm 36 is a hymn that attests to *YHWH's fidelity* in every sphere of life; and
- Psalm 107 is a song of thanksgiving that brings the fidelity of YHWH close to *concrete lived human experience.*

I have suggested that three highly stylized and, I believe, self-aware poems are accomplishments of daring imagination that read out of and read into lived experience. Given a Yahwistic assumption, every experience that is reported in Israel is understood with reference to YHWH, without whom the event would not be the event that it is. I cite these cases to insist that Christian worship is an act of human imagination that voices, advocates, and insists on *a gospel perception of all lived reality.* The substance of worship is to *tell the story* in the form of many smaller stories, all of them featuring YHWH as the key character. The purpose of such reportage on past events of miracle is precisely so that the contemporary congregation, many seasons later, may participate as directly as possible in *a world of miraculous fidelity* to which the text attests and which YHWH decisively inhabits.

VI

I have deliberately used the term *imagination* because I want to insist that such stylized narrative account is indeed a human construction. The poets put the words together in this particular way. The poets and Levites utilized this pattern of worship in order to reiterate and reenact this advocacy. It happens over and over, every time pastor and choir director get together to pick hymns and all the rest, the work is one of constructive imagination designed to lead the congregation in turn to imagine the world in a certain way. Much worship is informed by tradition and conventional practice; but those who construct such worship must each time *commit an act of imagination* in order to determine what is to be accented and to adapt the advocacy to the specificity of context.

Having said that worship claims our humanly constructed acts of imagination designed to advocate a perspective, we inescapably must ask if it is all "made up," for the "imagination" is tricky. But of course, in the community of faith, to "imagine" does not mean "to make up." It means, rather, to receive, entertain, and host images of reality that are outside the accepted given. If, however, we say we "receive" images, then we may ask, receive from whom? or, receive for whom? The answer we give is that what the psalmists and liturgists imagine and shape and offer is given by God's Spirit, for it is the Spirit who bears witness. It is the Spirit who has given Israel freedom to recognize and acknowledge YHWH as savior from slavery. It is the Spirit who gives us eyes to see and selves to notice the recurring and constant fidelity of God. It is the Spirit who cries out with us that lets us cry out and receive God's rescue. It is the Spirit who moves in the faith of the community and in the artistry of the poet to give voice to the odd truth of our common life.

Or it may be put differently. When Peter confessed Jesus to be the Messiah, Jesus blessed Peter for his confession: "And Jesus answered him, 'Blessed are you, Simon son of Jonah! For flesh and blood has not revealed this to you, but my Father in heaven'" (Matt 16:17). So it is with all the great liturgic claims of the church and with the text from which these liturgic claims arise. It is not "flesh and blood" that has let us see these matters. It is not human insight or imagination. It is rather the self-disclosing God who has let Israel and the church see that the drama of fidelity is God's own act. Thus, the God who is the subject of our testimony and of our worship is also the God who discloses what we know of that truth. It is God—we may say *Father* as in Matthew 16:17 or we may say *Spirit*—who is the subject of our worship and the object of our knowing. That Spirit, moreover, has been present not only in the originary event and at the point of initiation. That same spirit is also present in our own contemporary appropriation of the tradition, present in our interpretation, and present in the imagination that makes contemporaneity possible. We may indeed say that worship is indeed an act of Spirit-led imagination.

VII

But notice what is implied in this notion of Spirit-led imagination. Insofar as our worship is an act of Spirit-led imagination that permits us to see and live differently, it runs *upstream, against the grain of dominant reality*. Worship does not happen in a vacuum but always in response to context.

I submit that in the context of the North American church, worship that is Spirit-led imagination is powerfully over against dominant reality. One way to consider this interface is to consider the three texts that I have considered and to ask what the contrary may be to each of them.

First, in *Exodus 15:21*, and derivatively in *Exodus 15:1-18*, we have seen the joyous celebration of the overthrow of Pharaoh by the God who is incomparable in compassion and power. In the long stretch of the Bible, Pharaoh is not only an historical person but also becomes a metaphor and symbol for all established power that seeks to organize the world against covenantal freedom, justice, and neighborliness.

But imagine the world without this poem. Imagine this world without the incomparable God of freedom and justice and neighborliness who is attested in this song. Imagine that Pharaoh had never been overthrown, could not be challenged, and was never placed in question. Without this dangerous poetic imagination of worship, we have a world in which entrenched, oppressive power is guaranteed to last to perpetuity. Take away the poem and its worshiping practitioners and the slaves are fated forever to brick quotas, reduced to silence without ever a moan or a groan of self-announcement. Take away the tambourines of Miriam and we are left with an unchanging world of unbearable despair.

But of course, that is the world that the dominant narrative of our time offers us. It believes that technological capacity, economic monopoly, and military mastery can keep the world the way it is forever. It believes that control of finance means that wealth and poverty are to be kept as they are, which places most social pathologies beyond redress. And once given that narrative of despair, it is likely that oppressive interpersonal relationships are fated to last, because a heavy dose of authoritarianism maintains equilibrium and yields no change. At best we are left with shopping and entertainment in a world that is closed and fixed, stable but without a chance for hope. And then imagine—imagine—that the congregation, in the wake of Miriam, begins to sing and dance and remember the overthrow of power. It could have been Pharaoh overthrown. Or it could have been Nebuchadnezzar when we left exile:

> When the LORD restored the fortunes of Zion,
>   we were like those who dream.
> Then our mouth was filled with laughter,
>   and our tongue with shouts of joy;
> then it was said among the nations,
>   "The LORD has done great things for them."
> The LORD has done great things for us,
>   and we rejoiced. (Ps 126:1-3)

Or it could have been the power of death when the church joined the Easter laugh and signed on with the Lord of the Dance, the one who has led the dance since the days of Miriam.

Second, *Psalm 136*, that highly stylized liturgy, offers a community of remembering that is able to recall in some grandeur and some close detail the wonders of creation and the dazzlement of exodus, sure that the incomparable God of freedom, justice, and neighborliness is directly at work among us. And from this acute remembering, our singing community has continued with what we take to be the long-term truth of God, that YHWH's fidelity is very, very long-term. This inventory of miracles shows God's fidelity to be concrete and accessible, and so the recital is sandwiched in the psalm by *thanks*, *thanks* to YHWH for his goodness, *thanks* to YHWH who is the Lord of lords, *thanks* to YHWH who is the God of gods, *thanks* to the God of heaven, whose miracles enfold all lived reality. Israel yields itself in glad gratitude, aware and glad to acknowledge that the decisive features of its life of well-being are all a gift:

> It is he who remembered us in our low estate,
>   for his steadfast love endures forever;

and rescued us from our foes,
>   for his steadfast love endures forever;
who gives food to all flesh,
>   for his steadfast love endures forever. (Ps 136:23-25)

But imagine a world without this psalm and without the God attested there. Imagine a group of people who no longer meet to sing and dance and remember fidelity. In that world:

- memory is lost and amnesia is the order of the day, forgetfulness that assumes that we are the ones and only ones, none before us, none to come after us, only us, free to use up all of creation—and its oil!—in our own extravagant way. Moses, of course, knows all about this. He knows that affluence breeds amnesia and the loss of a grounding memory:

    > When you have eaten your fill and have built fine houses and live in them, and when your herds and flocks have multiplied, and your silver and gold is multiplied, and all that you have is multiplied, then do not exalt yourself, forgetting the LORD your God, who brought you out of the land of Egypt, out of the house of slavery. . . . Do not say to yourself, "My power and the might of my own hand have gotten me this wealth." But remember the LORD your God, for it is he who gives you power to get wealth, so that he may confirm his covenant that he swore to your ancestors, as he is doing today. (Deut 8:12-14, 17-18)

- Eat, enjoy, be full enough, forget enough, until we arrive at a place where we no longer say, "This do in remembrance of me" because the "me" of God has been overwhelmed in a vacuum.

- Fidelity disappears in a large binge of self-indulgence. We no longer remember the faithful God; we no longer remember to imitate God in faithfulness; we no longer remember that fidelity is the coin of humanness, and in place of fidelity comes power and greed and cunning manipulation and anxiety, because covenants are reduced to contracts and promises are only conveniences. And our humanness erodes.

- There will be no thanks, no acknowledgement that life is a gift. In a world where memory fails before amnesia and where fidelity gives way to self-indulgence, we imagine the gift to be an achievement or a possession. And where there is no gratitude, there will be no thank offering, no giving of self, no Eucharist, that great meal of thanks. And where there is no sacrament that dramatizes the world as a mystery of abundance, life becomes sheer commodity and human transactions are reduced to market transactions. Matters we have traditionally understood as *social goods*—medical care and education for example—now become only tools of leverage in the service of greed.

The dominant culture all around is one of self-indulgence without fidelity, manipulation without gratitude. And then comes this little body of singers breaking out in Psalm 136. The big narrative of acquisitiveness is shattered and shown to be false. The powers of leverage and manipulation and monopoly are broken. The singing itself is a dangerous protest of dissent from the dominant culture that does not sing, for everything is reduced to formulae; and this body sings its Spirit-led alternative.

Third, in *Psalm 107* we have considered four cases of human disaster and misery, lost in the wilderness, abandoned in prison, sick and without appetite, nearly lost at sea. In that highly stylized account, we have seen that every troubled person becomes a person able to cry out in need and address pain to God. It turns out to be no surprise that God in fidelity answers, reassures, and makes transformation possible. But the trigger in each case is the cry, the capacity to find voice, the sense of entitlement that pain may speak to power and insist on the redress. For that reason, our worship must not be too happy, too well ordered, or too symmetrically serene; for at the heart of our worship is asking in need, being answered, and taken seriously.

But imagine a world without Psalm 107. What if there were no one to sing this great song of thanks, no acknowledgment of rescue grounded in fidelity, no communal awareness that life consists in situations of distress, and above all no recognition of the *cry* of distress that sets in motion the divine mystery of rescue? Imagine a world without cry, without the public processing of pain, without the insistent sense of entitlement that we deserve better than this. Imagine a world that has grown silent and cold toward human pain. Imagine a world totally silenced, no prayers uttered, no hopes voiced, no hosting of the human condition, and consequently, no miracles of newness or healing.

Well, the dominant culture and its narrative account of reality go a long way toward such silence. Just suck it up and get on with your life! If you are in trouble, it is your fault, so get with the program. At most, those in deep need become only a forgotten statistic; "compassionate conservatism" becomes a retaliatory regression with no answering human community and no compassionate turn toward those in need, but only slanderous impatience toward those without power to save themselves.

And then, right in the midst of such systemic silencing, the congregation breaks out in Psalm 107. It recalls disasters, remembers rescues, and gives thanks. But in the center of that recall and remembering is the cry, the urge and energy and authority of out-loud pain that causes the world to regroup in new ways. The congregation gives voice to old distresses resolved by the mercy of God; and in giving voice to old distresses that have been solved, it invites those in present distress to find voice and hope that may yet again move God to act.

The dominant narrative of antineighborly late capitalism moves along without these great texts. The dominant version of reality:

- goes *without Exodus 15* and so imagines that oppressive power is forever;
- goes *without Psalm 136*, with nothing of fidelity, and so gives no thanks; and
- goes *without Psalm 107* and ends in silence that crushes the human spirit.

We, all of us, are to some extent practitioners of that dominant version of reality. It comes at us in many forms, and if we conform to that dominant voice of reality, we may receive its surface gifts of well being and security for a while. There is enough truth in the dominant version of reality for it to maintain its credibility, but only for a while!

VIII

But there is a countertruth that surfaces in Christian worship. It is a small counterpoint without great voice or muscle. It has been a minority perspective for a very long time. The ones who practice the counterpoint know very well that ours is not and will not be a dominant voice. It is a sub-version of reality, one that sounds beneath the loud sounds of the dominant version, one that flies low beneath the radar surveillance of the dominant version.

This evangelical sub-version of reality lives in delicate tension with the dominant version. It sometimes has aspiration to become the dominant version of reality, as in many of the psalms that make sweeping liturgical claims for the God featured in this sub-version. Thus Psalm 117 can imagine all nations celebrating this compassionate sovereign:

> Praise the LORD, all you nations!
> Extol him, all you peoples! (Ps 117:1)

Or Psalm 96 can outline a message of assurance to all nations in the name of this monarch newly come to power:

> Say among the nations, "The LORD is king!
> The world is firmly established; it shall never be moved.
> He will judge the peoples with equity." (Ps 96:10)

But in fact the sub-version is a poetic, elusive, delicate alternative even while the dominant voice of reality prevails in its facts on the ground. Thus the liturgical practice acknowledges the resilience of the dominant version of reality but in the meeting reiterates the sub-version in the liturgy as a viable, credible, choosable alternative. Thus the community:

- *offers Exodus 15* as an alternative to the claim of oppressive power is forever;
- *offers Psalm 136* as alternative of fidelity to a social vision of comparative greed;
- *offers Psalm 107* as an alternative cry to a social coercion of enforced silence.

In every such liturgical utterance, act, and gesture, this sub-version of reality intends to *subvert* dominant versions, to expose them as inadequate if not false, and to empower the community to reengage reality according to this sub-version.

This delicate tension between dominant version and sub-version, I believe, is the true character of worship. Because the claims made in the sub-version, claims such as "Christ is risen," are a deeply felt, eagerly offered truth. And yet in its very utterance the community at worship knows that the facts on the ground, the data at hand, contradict this and gives evidence that the odor of death is still very much in play. It will not do for the church to become cynical and give in to the dominant vision. But it also will not do for the church to become excessively romantic about its sub-version and so to imagine its dominance. Rather, I believe that the worshiping community must live knowingly and elusively in this tension, not cynical, not romantic, but wise and innocent (Matt 10:16), always engaged in negotiation between subclaim and the world the way we find it.

The task and goal of worship and all the nurture that goes with it is to move our lives from the dominant version of reality to the sub-version; finally, that our old certitudes will have been subverted by the work of the Spirit. Judged by the dominant version, life in the sub-version is vulnerable and foolish and exposed.

But the sub-version in the end cannot be judged by the dominant version. In the end, it is judged by the truth of the gospel, by the reality of God whom we attest, and by the truth of our own lives in the image of that God. We are endlessly seduced out of that truth by the dominant version, and so we return again to worship to recite and receive this sub-version that is the truth of our life and the truth of the world.

In the Old Testament, the Psalms vigorously and without apology live out that sub-version and make a claim against the data at hand. Psalm 23 is one familiar presentation of the sub-version that is contradicted by dominant views, but for all of that no less true:

The Lord is my shepherd, I shall not want.
  He makes me lie down in green pastures;
he leads me beside still waters;
  he restores my soul.
He leads me in right paths for his name's sake.
Even though I walk through the darkest valley,
  I fear no evil;
for you are with me;
  your rod and your staff—they comfort me.
You prepare a table before me
  in the presence of my enemies;
you anoint my head with oil;
  my cup overflows.
Surely goodness and mercy shall follow me
  all the days of my life,
and I shall dwell in the house of the Lord
  my whole life long. (Ps 23)

And in the New Testament, none more eloquently lined out the truth of the sub-version than did Paul:

For the message about the cross is foolishness to those who are perishing, but to us who are being saved it is the power of God. For it is written,

"I will destroy the wisdom of the wise,
  and the discernment of the discerning I will thwart."

Where is the one who is wise? Where is the scribe? Where is the debater of this age? Has not God made foolish the wisdom of the world? For since, in the wisdom of God, the world did not know God through wisdom, God decided, through the foolishness of our proclamation, to save those who believe. For Jews demand signs and Greeks desire wisdom, but we proclaim Christ crucified, a stumbling block to Jews and foolishness to Gentiles, but to those who are the called, both Jews and Greeks, Christ the power of God and the wisdom of God. For God's foolishness is wiser than human wisdom, and God's weakness is stronger than human strength. (1 Cor 1:18-25)

Consider your own call, brothers and sisters: not many of you were wise by human standards, not many were powerful, not many were of noble birth. But God chose what is foolish in the world to shame the wise; God chose what is weak in the world to shame the strong; God chose what is low and despised in the world, things that are not, to reduce to nothing things that

are, so that no one might boast in the presence of God. He is the source of
your life in Christ Jesus, who became for us wisdom from God, and righteousness and sanctification and redemption, in order that, as it is written,
"Let the one who boasts, boast in the Lord." (1 Cor 1:26-31)

For this reason it depends on faith, in order that the promise may rest on
grace and be guaranteed to all his descendants, not only to the adherents of
the law but also to those who share the faith of Abraham (for he is the father
of all of us, as it is written, "I have made you the father of many nations")—
in the presence of the God in whom he believed, who gives life to the dead
and calls into existence the things that do not exist. (Rom 4:16-17)

No, in all these things we are more than conquerors through him who
loved us. For I am convinced that neither death, nor life, nor angels, nor
rulers, nor things present, nor things to come, nor powers, nor height,
nor depth, nor anything else in all creation, will be able to separate us
from the love of God in Christ Jesus our Lord. (Rom 8:37-39)

We leave the hearing and speaking of the sub-version and reenter the world that
has not yet come to this alternative. We make our way in compromise and timid-
ity, and in fear and trembling. But then we enter gladly into the voice of the sub-
version, yet again, very sure of our true home and our real identity:

> O come, let us sing to the LORD;
>   let us make a joyful noise to the rock of our salvation!
> Let us come into his presence with thanksgiving;
>   let us make a joyful noise to him with songs of praise!
> For the LORD is a great God,
>   and a great King above all gods.
> In his hand are the depths of the earth;
>   the heights of the mountains are his also.
> The sea is his, for he made it,
>   and the dry land, which his hands have formed.
>
> O come, let us worship and bow down,
>   let us kneel before the LORD, our Maker!
> For he is our God,
>   and we are the people of his pasture. (Ps 95:1-7a)

CHAPTER 12

Wisdom as "Practical Theology"

THE EMBRACE OF "WISDOM" in the congregation of God's people is a way of recovering gospel faith in a hostile cultural environment. Such an embrace of wisdom (1) provides categories through which the congregation may *engage in practical theology*, that is, church practice that is intentional about an ethical component to missional faith, and (2) provides an urgent *alternative* to the many forms of lethal religion that are available to the church.

I

The recovery of "wisdom" in the critical study of scripture and in the life of the church is a major development in the last two decades.

The key player, as in so much of critical Old Testament theology, has been Gerhard von Rad, the great German interpreter who died in 1971. As the dominant figure in Old Testament theology in the mid-twentieth century, von Rad interpreted Old Testament theology around the theme of "God's Mighty Deeds in History," contending that God's self-revelation was through identifiable, transformative initiatives in the history of Israel and in the life of the world, initiatives rightly slotted in Israel as "miracles."[1] Given that accent, it is not surprising that in 1936 von Rad wrote an essay insisting that the Old Testament had no abiding interest in creation theology, but the accent in the Old Testament is characteristically on historical rescue and transformation.[2]

It is not often enough recognized that von Rad shaped his interpretive course in this way (1) under the influence of Karl Barth and (2) in the midst of German National Socialism. Because the ideology of German National Socialism had offered a "blood and soil" natural theology, it was important for Barth and von

Rad to find a grounding for faith outside of "nature," which had been preempted by the ideology of National Socialism. The connection of von Rad's governing insight to that specific context is important for the course of biblical interpretation in the twentieth century. To be sure, von Rad included in his great *Old Testament Theology*, for purposes of completion, an extended section on wisdom.[3] But this did not seem critical to his enterprise, and even though that material in his study presents an important argument, it appeared to be something of an afterthought in his work.

It is a source of great wonder then that von Rad, in his final book, *Wisdom in Israel*, published in 1970, the year before he died, he treated "wisdom" as a full-fledged theological alternative in the Old Testament.[4] It is easy enough to see that in that book von Rad had changed his course in interpretation; it is not often enough noted that von Rad's interpretive context had in fact changed radically. As the accent on historical miracle is necessary to the Nazi context, so a new context of secular globalism placed interpretation in a different environment that required thought about "limit" and "possibility," the core accents of wisdom theology. But the greatness of von Rad's interpretive capacity is his agile readiness and willingness to reformulate his interpretation in light of a new context. The outcome, adumbrated by his colleague Claus Westermann, is the awareness that *historical miracle* and *wisdom* constitute parallel theological perspectives in Scripture that live in some tension with each other.[5]

It turns out that the interpretive move von Rad made in the last year of his life was a harbinger of what was to come in Old Testament interpretation. "Wisdom" as a theological accent point was not just a new fad in scholarship but also a theological perspective deeply in touch with new challenges to church faith, most especially ethical reflection on the new globalism and critical reflection on creation as environment.[6] Both *globalism* and *environmentalism* required a systemic approach to theology, which wisdom provides; for wisdom theology considers the entire "world order" of life as a domain of God's rule in which the human community has a decisive role to play.[7]

I learned a great deal about wisdom after inhaling von Rad through an essay by David Hartman in which I believe he never employs the word "wisdom."[8] Hartman is practically concerned about how Jews (and the state of Israel) deal with the Palestinian crisis. His perspective, however, is not about contemporary political and military strategy but about long-term perspectives in Jewish interpretive history. His chapter sharply contrasts between two perspectives. On the one hand, there is the teaching of Nahmanides (and in contemporary time Rabbi Soloveitchik) who believe that "the very meaning of the Jewish people is to bear witness to the concept of miracle in history."[9] Whereas the God of nature is the God of the philosophers, the God of the Jews is the God of history:

> Israel's story is the source for revolutionary aspirations in history. Messianism is a Jewish innovation. It did not come from Plato and Aristotle.

The Greeks gave us rigor and truth; they gave us the scientific understanding of nature. It was the prophets who gave us a dream which
enabled us to believe that tomorrow could be radically different from
yesterday.[10]

Consequently, "Jews are the people who convey to the world the experience of
miracle."[11] The cosmos, moreover, "is in order when Israel is in its land."[12] "To be
a Jew is to believe in miracles."[13] Hartman critiques this perspective, especially as
it is given contemporary form in Zionist ideology, as a recipe for political narcis-
sism and fantasy that leads to unreal political expectations and eventuates in a
wishful violence.

On the other hand, Hartman sets over against that discernment of miracles the
teaching of Maimonides, who "passionately hated dependency on miracles" and
who sought a natural explanation for what happened in the world:[14]

The big question for Maimonides was, What are the limits of necessity?
How much room is there for freedom in this world? What do the Jewish
people bear witness to? What is their task? It is not to announce miracle
in the world. Their central task, as Maimonides sees it, is to do battle
against every form of idolatry. What infuses the passion of the *Guide of
the Perplexed* is Moses announcing to a people, "Your task is to fight the
false gods of the world. Your task is to fight against fantasy." The priests
of idol worship, what were they? They played on human weakness.
They exploited people who were frightened of their children dying. The
priests told them, "Do this, and your children will live." All paganism
thrives on human vulnerability and fear, on the manipulation of human
weakness.[15]

As I will show in what follows, the questions of *limit* and *freedom* are at the
center of sapiential reflection for Maimonides:

Creation is not the story of how God gave the Jews the land; Creation is
what takes the Jews out of their own story and places them in a cosmic
drama. The Bible begins with Creation in order to teach us that God is
not Jewish, that there is a world which has a drama and a dignity not
defined by the Jewish story. Halevi makes the creation narrative a Jewish
historical story. Maimonides views it instead as a corrective, as a larger
cosmic filter placing limits upon our private story.[16]

It is clear that Maimonides offers a very different interpretive perspective that is
sober about worldly reality and that entertains no escape from that reality or any
illusion about interventions that will deliver from the hard work of justice and
peace in the world.

Hartman's immediate concern is the fact that peace in the Middle East, for Jews, will not come through fantasy or illusionary religious expectation. It will come only through the hard work of political realism. Hartman, of course, does not make any connection to the Old Testament/Hebrew Scripture, for his horizon is of another kind. It occurs to me nonetheless that the principles of Nahmanides and Maimonides correlate very well with the perspectives of "mighty deeds" and "wisdom" that I have noted about von Rad. While "mighty deeds" (von Rad) and "miracle" (Nahmanides) may yield profound passion and hope, it is wisdom (von Rad) and "respect for the given world" (Maimonides) that guides strategic work in the mending of the world. If we transpose models of Scripture interpretation into Hartman's categories, it is possible to say that von Rad led us into a "theology of miracles" as a counter to National Socialism; but then, in a belated season of his work, von Rad led us away from a "theology of miracles" into a stance of "respect for the given world." The change, wrought through von Rad's study and sketched out by Hartman, makes an enormous difference in the life of the congregation.

My own modest contribution to this interface of interpretive perspectives is my essay of 2002 in which I considered the "preacher as scribe."[17] I wrote the essay as I pondered the role of the preacher in the postmodern U.S. church, where the conventional authority of the preacher has largely disintegrated. As a result, the preacher cannot, in very many contexts, be confrontive as truth is addressed to power. Rather, the preacher must engage in textual reflection that invites rumination on traditional perspectives and gives great respect to the listening congregation in its own decision making. That is, wisdom teachers (in the text work of scribes) are not confrontative but are reflective, inviting the congregation to think again, to ponder it, and to redecide in a context of thick meaning.

In that essay, I did not take up in any detail the role of wisdom. But as I consider again von Rad's new direction and the contrasting perspectives offered by Hartman, it is clear that the way of ministry I had championed there had to do with the way of wisdom, a perspective that anticipates no heroic action on the part of God or on the part of human persons but rather anticipates the slow, steady work of "repair," which seeks transformation in a world that is respected for what it is. My own footnote to the work of von Rad and Hartman is an attempt to bring this perspective closer to congregational practice. It is clear in much of the church community in the United States, both of the Right and of the Left, that there is an alienating zeal, shrill and sometimes hysterical, that does not reflect much upon the staying power of natural and social reality. A consequence of such shrillness is that there is much wasted, destructive motion when in fact other perspectives and other resources are available to us. Thus, in what follows—as is generally so in the essays in this volume—I will consider church practice that does not rely on the white-hot heat of miracle but instead asks about *the truth of the world* in light of *the truth of God*.

II

A leading aphorism that succinctly summarizes recent scholarship concerning wisdom in the Old Testament is that of Walther Zimmerli: "Wisdom theology thinks resolutely within the framework of a theology of creation."[18] That is, wisdom teaching, as reflected in the book of Proverbs, is sustained critical reflection on the nature, purpose, and meaning of the creation as it is willed by the Creator. Such theology moves in very large scope but is focused on the material reality that is before us in the world, albeit a material reality shot through with the mystery of divine purpose and power.[19] That purpose and power is not self-evident on the surface but requires close, steady scrutiny that builds understanding from the specificity and detail of the created order. This means that wisdom theology perceives the world as God's world well before it has been divided up into states or parties or sects or people and, in general, refuses to credit particularistic claims. Such a theology is a contrast to most "redemption theologies," which focus on a particular point of rescue and that conjure a missionary zeal to save the world. This does not mean that creation theology is unaware of the "flaw" in creation or its need for "mending." Such a perspective is able to see, however, that such work willed by God and wrought by human agents is a reclaiming of creation as it is willed by God. If we undertake an engagement with creation and reflect on our place in creation *before God* and *alongside other creatures*, we arrive at a very different set of concerns. And we arrive at a very different posture of faith, not guilt-laden on the one hand or too much celebrated as human creatures on the other hand, but one among many creatures invited to be God's faithful, free, responsive creation. Among the themes that are crucial to wisdom-creation faith are these five that have preoccupied interpreters:

First, life is *ordered and sustained* by the Creator God to generate well being (*shalom*) for all creatures; and the innocent-sounding two-line sayings in the book of Proverbs, as von Rad has made clear, in fact testify to the sustaining order of creation. We may cite a proverbial saying that explicitly mentions YHWH:

> The fear of the LORD prolongs life,
>> but the years of the wicked will be short. (Prov 10:27)

This proverb affirms that life is ordered so that "fear of YHWH," that is, adherence to YHWH's governance, is the precondition and assurance of a long life. The wisdom teacher reasons from observations about the durability of a well-ordered life. The negative counterpoint is that "wickedness," that is, disregard for the rule of YHWH and self-preoccupation, lead to a lesser life. There may well be other explanations for such "performance" of life; but the wisdom teachers are devoted to the centrality of YHWH. A joyous, healthy life is a part of the ordering willed by the Creator. No explanation is offered, only a report on what is observed, when that observation is processed through reference to the Creator.

The same sense of created order is evidenced in many proverbs that do not explicitly mention God. Thus in Proverbs 10:30:

> The righteous will never be removed,
>   but the wicked will not remain in the land. (Prov 10:30)

Here the reference is not to God but to the righteous ordering of life, a neighborly ordering that is guaranteed by the Creator. In this saying, it is the quality of life that keeps existence stable (not "tottering"). Conversely, those who mock the neighborhood forfeit their place in society and cannot be sustained in the community. Again, the sage does not explain how or why this is true. It is teaching that insists that there are normative preconditions to a good life. The wise are those who conform their life to that normative ordering and benefit from the blessings of the Creator God. Notice that such a conclusion requires that the wise should keep public life under close scrutiny, that is, to continue social research to discover the order that is not spelled out programmatically but only noticed in the detail of performance. The theological impact of such teaching is quite pragmatic; but it is not mere pragmatism. It is, rather, a reflection of conformity to the true ordering of reality that, in the end, must be honored.

Second, this order establishes that there are *God-ordained givens* that cannot be circumvented or outflanked. These givens are taken as the will of the Creator. The good life consists in knowing, honoring, and conforming to such givens. Thus, it is a given of creation that practicing "hate" causes turmoil whereas "love" covers over many offenses. It is so! It is a given that the wise teachers found to be true in every circumstance. They generalized, but not according to abstract principle. They generalized according to observed cases, so many observed cases that they found it to be true in every circumstance:

> Hatred stirs up strife,
>   but love covers all offenses. (Prov 10:12)

It is a given that is deeply grounded but that shows up in endless specific cases that could be cited. It is a given that one cannot "hate" and have "offenses covered." This particular teaching that *destructive behavior* yields *negative social outcomes* is at the center of wisdom instruction, because the teachers probe the formation and maintenance of viable human communities. A second reflection on the same inescapable social reality is offered in Proverbs 11:11:

> By the blessing of the upright a city is exalted,
>   but it is overthrown by the mouth of the wicked.

The "upright" are those who contribute to public well being. The teachers observed what a difference a contributing member of society can make. Conversely, they noticed that vicious or slanderous talk is profoundly destructive to the community. This is one of many sayings that comments on what is required to make for a good social life. The requirements are intransigent and go all the way to the bottom of ordained reality. Life is not at the bottom supple or malleable, and the wise come to terms with that reality.

Third, closely related to the givens of created reality is the conviction that there are *limits* to what can be known and what can be acted out. In Jeremiah 5:22, the prophetic poem asserts a limit established by the Creator concerning the chaos of the sea:

> Do you not fear me? says the LORD;
>   Do you not tremble before me?
> I placed the sand as a boundary for the sea,
>   a perpetual barrier that it cannot pass;
> though the waves toss, they cannot prevail,
>   though they roar, they cannot pass over it.

Then the poem continues to reflect on the stubborn and rebellious people who have "turned aside and gone away." What follows is an indictment of those who act against the community for self-advancement:

> Like a cage full of birds,
>   their houses are full of treachery;
> therefore they have become great and rich,
> they have grown fat and sleek.
> They know no limits in deeds of wickedness;
>   they do not judge with justice
> the cause of the orphan, to make it prosper,
>   and they do not defend the rights of the needy. (Jer 5:27-28)

The poem nicely juxtaposes *limit* to chaotic waters and *limit* to deeds of wickedness. Both the sea and social acquisitiveness are threats to the created order of life, a violation of all that makes for peaceable well being. The ethical component in this reflection on limit concerns attentiveness to the orphan and the needy that are the special concern of the Creator. This same sense of limit, in sapiential reflection, has to do with money, talk, work, and every aspect of concrete daily life.

In a very different sapiential reflection, the poem of Job 28 observes that the mystery of wisdom is beyond human ken. It observes that the Creator "made a decree for rain" (*hoq*; v. 27); the poem concludes with a note on modest human behavior that is also governed by the divine decree that limits:

> And he said to humankind,
>   "Truly, the fear of the LORD, that is wisdom;
>   and to depart from evil is understanding." (Job 28:28)

Fourth, within that observed reality of *order*, *givenness*, and *limit*, human persons have choice. This *freedom* is not the limitless autonomy of Enlightenment freedom but rather freedom within the ordained limits of creation. The two-line proverbial sayings regularly articulate decisions that have to be made, choices that are exercised, and freedom to make one choice or the other. Thus, one can exercise freedom for "false balances" or "accurate weight" (Prov 11:1), riches or righteousness (Prov 14:4), belittling or silence (Prov 11:12), kindness or cruelty (Prov 11:17), and giving or withholding (Prov 11:24). Everyday human persons as God's creatures make choices and exercise enormous freedom.

That freedom, however, is in context. Such choices bring with them futures that cannot be avoided. Every act of freedom carries inescapable futures, so that present choices must be considered in terms of the futures they inevitably generate. This framing of human freedom in light of consequences is a central conviction of the wisdom teachers; they know that no amount of power or wealth or cunning can avoid that linkage. Klaus Koch has formulated this central moral conviction of creation theology as "deeds-consequences," in which deeds (choices) create their own sphere of life, a connection guaranteed and assured by the Creator.[20]

Fifth, it follows then that freedom carries with it immense *responsibility*; for any act, every choice and act of freedom, brings futures for which the human agent must accept responsibility. Thus, the call to wisdom is a summons to regard oneself as a creature of God who lives in the world of the Creator and is responsive to the will of the Creator that is provided in the order, givenness, and limits wherein choice is exercised. The great temptation that the wisdom teachers recognize is the practice of autonomy wherein one imagines one is unencumbered and free from all constraints. The preferred term for such elemental irresponsibility is "foolishness," action that defies the created order and does damage to the community:

> Fools think their own way is right,
>   but the wise listen to advice.
> Fools show their anger at once,
>   but the prudent ignore an insult. (Prov 12:15-16)

> Fools mock at the guilt offering,
>   but the upright enjoy God's favor. (Prov 14:9)

> The crown of the wise is their wisdom,
>   but folly is the garland of fools. (Prov 14:24)

> Wisdom is at home in the mind of one who has understanding,
>   but it is not known in the heart of fools. (Prov 14:33)

> A fool despises a parent's instruction,
>   but the one who heeds admonition is prudent. (Prov 15:5)

It is that wisdom teaching that shows up in the parable of Jesus wherein the acquisitive subject of the parable is finally described as "fool" by God's voice in the night (Luke 12:20). The wise know that such acquisitiveness, with its sad disregard of the neighborhood, can only end in a sad death.

Conversely, the wise are those whose choices responsibly generate good for the community. Thus, "righteousness exalts a nation" (Prov 14:34). The wise know that those who practice creatureliness responsibly enhance all those around them.

III

It will be clear, with reference to these five themes I have mentioned, that wisdom is indeed "practical theology." It is theology because it understands that daily life is permeated with the good intentionality of the Creator. It is practical in that it concerns real, material, daily social life; because it believes that in the material context, the deep life-or-death issues are played out. Theology in this horizon is practical in the sense that there is no "sectarian language" concerning money, sexuality, power, or social goods. Thus there is no particularistic nuance to the quotidian enactment of a faithful life, nor is there any eschatological proviso about another world or the next world. This is *the world* in which full *creatureliness* is to be practiced.

This practical theology is *pro-community*. It understands that life and creatureliness is designed to upbuild the neighborhood, even if the "neighborhood" is taken in largest scope.

This practical theology believes in *the coherence of all of life* as God's creation, coherence of present and future, coherence of rich and poor, coherence of members of a family, all "members one of another." There is no opting out, no private peace, no secret deal. This perspective might be an important corrective to much church thought and action that is conducted in blatant forms of individualism.

This practical theology takes *a systems approach* to ethics, the "system" being the way in which elements of God's creation are interrelated to each other. The wisdom teachers obviously believe that there is much to learn from other creatures about human creatureliness as concerns, for example, ants (Prov 6:6), eagles and snakes (Prov 30:19), locusts and lizards (Prov 30:27), lions and roosters (Prov 30:30-31), along with ox and donkey (Isa 1:3) and storks and cranes (Jer 8:7). A systems approach, moreover, is reflective of a "deeds-consequence" perspective in which matters are deeply, irrevocably interrelated. This way of thinking may be a powerful corrective of a recurring temptation in the church to take matters "one at a time," whether with reference to economic transactions or the truth of God's grace given in the world. The same systems approach is evident in Israel's doxologies that imagine all creatures together blessed by God and all joined together in praise to God the Creator.

The pragmatism of the wisdom teacher is *relentlessly ethical* in its reflection, concerned with right and wrong, righteousness and wickedness. This is not to say the teaching is moralistic. It is much too worldly wise to fall into moralism. Rather, it insists, in a wide-eyed prophetic way, that every human transaction contains an ethical dimension. The several ideologies alive in the church today tend to exempt issues from ethical concern, as conservatives tend not to think much about ethical dimensions of public economic policy, and liberals tend not to think too much about ethical dimensions of sexual practice. The wisdom teachers require attention to ethical matters, without any commitment to any ideology (unless it is an ideology of social stability), for the wisdom teachers are inherently conservative about social maintenance and social change. This ethical reflection is never completely innocent, but it may go a long way to think behind and beneath usual assumptions. Ethical decisions of all kinds have to do with scarring or mending creation.

IV

I have come to the theme of "practical theology" by the marvelous phrase von Rad uses to describe "foolishness" in the book of Proverbs. He calls it "practical atheism."[21] By that term, von Rad recognizes that no foolish person in that ancient society would ever explicitly or verbally deny the reality and relevance of God.[22] But even when lip service is given to the reality and relevance of God, actions tell otherwise. Thus, the Psalmist can assert of the wicked:

> In the pride of their countenance the wicked say, "God will not seek it out";
>   all their thoughts are, "There is no God."
> . . . .
> They think in their heart, "God has forgotten,
>   he has hidden his face, he will never see it." (Ps 10:4, 11)

And it is the same in Psalm 14:1:

> Fools say in their hearts, "There is no God."
>   They are corrupt, they do abominable deeds;
>   there is no one who does good. (Ps 14:1)

It is action toward the neighbor that exhibits a kind of exploitative autonomy that refuses the torah commands of God. In the same way, I suggest, practical theology is not an enterprise that makes a great deal out of verbal confession, for the wisdom teachers do not do much theology. Rather, practical faith is exhibited in the action of wisdom and righteousness that lives "with the grain" of creation in a way that enhances human community in the larger environment.

It is, then, the work of the congregation of God's people to engage in practical faith that exhibits in action the rule of God. Such a congregation at practice offers a visible and surely compelling alternative to the practical atheism that is exhibited as "foolishness" in our society. In that ancient world, such foolishness worked against the well being of the human community in words of slander and acts of folly, as though there were no normative reality by which to measure human maturity.

The force of practical atheism (foolishness) in the contemporary world will require the interpreter to make important imaginative connections so that this ancient pondering of foolishness is seen to be powerfully contemporary. Here I will mention four dimensions of contemporary foolishness that the practical theology of the congregation may witness against:

1. It is *foolishness* to define social reality in terms of any ideology that overrides the facts on the ground or that must distort the facts to serve ideologically constructed reality. That power of ideology has been variously exhibited in recent time, including militant anti-Communism, contemporary misrepresentations of Islam, and fearful misinformation about the social reality of gays and lesbians, to name only some of the present forms of ideology that exercise authority among us. The maintenance of such ideology, most often done with great passion, regularly serves powerful financial interests that are mostly disguised. While wisdom teaching itself is not free of ideological distortion, it nonetheless seeks to stay focused on the facts on the ground.[23]

2. It is *foolishness* to entrust our future to technological capacity. Various forms of public life are increasingly reshaped according to computerized transactions and the elimination of the human agent. Thus, the practice of medicine and the enterprise of education are increasingly reduced to such practice, whereas wisdom teachers focused primally on face-to-face interaction among neighbors. Beyond such an obvious recharacterization of social relationships, it is clear that our society increasingly seeks to find security and well being through technological capacity. While the development of technology need not be resisted, it does stand under criticism when such modes of interaction are substitutes for the human enterprise.[24]

3. It is *foolishness* to organize the economy in narcissistic ways through an unsustainable standard of living that is based on a limitless sense of entitlement. The proverbs, in their recurring use of a "better" formula, consistently affirm that human engagement is "better" than the accumulation of commodities.

4. From narcissistic commodification, it follows that it is *foolishness* to reduce life to the endless pursuit of consumer goods in a self-indulgent way.[25] Such a pursuit regularly makes promises that it cannot keep about security and well being. Perhaps the most blatant form of such foolishness concerns the use of drugs and body care in the expectation that the costs of time may be endlessly deferred in the maintenance of an artificial self.

All of these dimensions of foolishness—ideology, technology, narcissistic entitlement, self-indulgent pursuit of consumer goods—converge in the society around an unexamined commitment to U.S. exceptionalism. The ideology of U.S. exceptionalism privileges "American" claims in the world and regards as necessary a national security state with endless capacity for exploitative violence.

It is possible to imagine that a congregation that engages in the practice of wisdom theology would become a community of critical reflection without the confrontive propensity of prophetic faith and without the reductive moralism that comes from a simplistic approach to God's commandments. As a community of critical reflection, such a congregation may see past conventional forms of deathliness in our society. It may commit gladly to God's hidden reliable rule, focus on the facts on the ground, and choose futures that promise well being.

V

In such a perspective on life in the congregation, I conclude with mention of three large theological themes that are central to such practice:

First, wisdom has intimate connections to the commandments of God. Indeed, Erhard Gerstenberger has proposed that the *thou shalt not*'s of Mount Sinai (Exod 20:1-17) arose out of specific practice of parents warning children about dangerous behavior to be avoided.[26] The regularity and reliability of such prohibitions came to be regarded as a nonnegotiable truth that is known from God's own decree. Less speculatively, there is through early Judaism a steady movement whereby wisdom teaching comes to be equated with the commandments of YHWH, once the commandments are seen to be not a burden but a glad guidance toward well being. Thus, Moses can assert:

> See, just as the LORD my God has charged me, I now teach you statutes and ordinances for you to observe in the land that you are about to enter and occupy. You must observe them diligently, for this will show your wisdom and discernment to the peoples, who, when they hear all these statutes, will say, "Surely this great nation is a *wise and discerning* people!" (Deut 4:5-6)

Obedience to the commands of YHWH evidences wisdom and discernment, for such an obedient community is seen to be and known to be in sync with the way the world works.

Given that eventual convergence of wisdom and torah, however, we may also note that the ongoing dynamism of torah and wisdom take very different forms. The torah commands continue to receive interpretive nuance to meet new circumstances. This in fact is the purpose and character of the tradition of Deuteronomy. In a quite different mode, the wisdom teachers can continue to coin new proverbs and new ethical conclusions as more empirical evidence invites reformulation. Thus folk societies could develop a keen sense of the things that can either enhance or destroy the community; on occasion, however, such folk judgments turn out to be wrong, thus requiring fresh articulation. Both wisdom and torah commandments intend to defeat autonomy. Both wisdom and torah commandments are tempted to rigorous conformity. That temptation, however, is not a primal concern in a contemporary self-actualizing society, even though some moralism is voiced in response to self-indulgent nonconformity. The important point to grasp is that "new occasions teach new duties," and the work of wisdom teachers is never to issue a final dictum but only to rearticulate in light of new data.

Second, the wisdom teachers thrive on enunciating connections between "deeds and consequences." The book of Proverbs, in some, is such an articulation. But the wisdom teachers themselves also know that such connections once taken as true and settled may sometimes need to be kept under review and revised. In most extreme form this need for review and revision is the issue of theodicy.[27] In the book of Proverbs, the wisdom teachers trust their judgment about the connection of deeds and consequences. The wisdom teachers, however, are no fools, and they know that God's creation does not work according to formula.[28] For that reason one must read beyond the book of Proverbs into other parts of the wisdom tradition. In the book of Ecclesiastes, it is asserted that the connections may be real but they are not discernable or in human grasp. In the book of Job, moreover, there is an ongoing dispute about the validity of conclusions drawn in the book of Proverbs and the way in which new experience contradicts old settlements. Job's friends give voice to the old connections that were long since settled in the tradition of Proverbs, the very connections that are vigorously refuted by the shrillness of Job.

If we take the entire debate of these three sapiential statements, it is clear that wisdom is not a settled conclusion of truth. Rather, it is an ongoing, open-ended process—as open-ended as human experience—whereby steady truth requires new formulation. Practical theology is the capacity to participate in that ongoing formulation, a refusal to terminate the process and a capacity to pay attention to new truth on the ground.

Third, wisdom theology has almost nothing to say about divine intervention or rescue or miracle. It believes, rather, that God is working out God's purposes in steady, faithful, reliable but hidden ways. That hiddenness has not been handed over to any interpretive community, nor does that hiddenness serve any particular community or interest. The wisdom teachers affirm that God is endlessly reliable in making *provision* for all of God's creatures. That reliable provision becomes the subject of Israel's doxology:

> These all look to you
>> to give them their food in due season;
> when you give to them, they gather it up;
>> when you open your hand, they are filled with good things.
>> (Ps 104:27-28)

> The eyes of all look to you,
>> and you give them their food in due season.
> You open your hand,
>> satisfying the desire of every living thing. (Ps 145:15-16)

While congregations will continue to organize themselves in some particularity, wisdom teaching about divine *providence* and divine *provision* always summons the congregation out beyond itself and its particular identity in order to affirm and celebrate the goodness of God's rule in the world. Thus, wisdom endlessly deconstructs our favorite particularities, even though particularity is the hallmark of fidelity.

In the end we must recognize that in the life of the congregation, there is more to faith than the practical theology of wisdom, even as there is more to Scripture than the wisdom traditions. In my judgment, nonetheless, in a socioreligious environment that is saturated with confessional shrillness, the more "cool" reflective posture of wisdom is a scriptural gift to be recovered among us. The wisdom teachers refuse the endless caressing of our favorite miracles and call us to resonance with the steady reliabilities of creation that are always well out beyond ourselves and our control.

PART IV

CANON AND IMAGINATION

Exodus and Resurrection:
Brueggemann on the Canon

Carolyn J. Sharp

THE ESTABLISHMENT of an authoritative list of certain texts as Scripture and the exclusion of other texts as extrabiblical—whether edifying or heretical—has been popularly interpreted as a means of limiting what counts as sacred. But canon, according to Brueggemann, should not be understood only as a hegemonic means by which particular theological values have constrained the Word of God. Brueggemann has acknowledged the ways in which ancient political and theological decisions have erected a protective fence around the scriptural canon, but he also sees a dynamism inherent in the traditioning processes that escapes the control of any official authority. In Brueggemann's interpretive discourse, Scripture enjoys an agency and performativity and purposes all its own. Listen to his reflection on the vitality of the canon as it is received in churchly and academic circles:

> It is the work of *canonical* practice in ecclesial communities and the work of *criticism* in the scholarly community to keep the text available. It is by the ongoing enterprise of religious and scholarly communities that the text lingers over time in available ways. Out of that lingering . . . words of the text characteristically erupt into new usage. They are seized upon by someone in the community with daring. Or perhaps better, the , words of the text seize someone in the community who is a candidate for daring. In that moment of re-utterance, the present is freshly illuminated, reality is irreversibly transformed. The community comes to know or see or receive or decide afresh. What has been *tradition*, hovering in dormancy, becomes available *experience*.[1]

On the topic of canon as elsewhere, Brueggemann privileges a dialogical hermeneutic in which textual witness engages the reading community to create a newness that is of God. In Brueggemann's view, there is nothing closed or static about the notion of canon.

Brueggemann's theological reflections range freely across the Hebrew Scriptures; he strikes unapologetically and with a characteristic boldness into the New Testament as well. His exegetical work is in each instance focused on hearing a particular word in a particular biblical passage, but it is possible to discern larger trajectories shaping his thought and shaping his proclamation across the scriptural canon. Brueggemann challenges idolatry and cultural smugness; he exhorts to obedience; and he promotes *shalom*, the ancient Hebrew concept that encompasses the peace, security, flourishing, and quiet well being of individuals and communities. Across the diverse collection of his writings on canon, two major biblical metaphors may be discerned and tracked. Those metaphors are exodus and resurrection.[2]

What is exodus for Brueggemann? Daring to leave behind the numerous kinds of slavery that diminish who we are, that impoverish our spiritual imagination, that dehumanize others, and that fracture true and godly community. What is resurrection? Rising to new life and alternative possibility, assenting to Scripture's gospel vision with its miraculous hope, its unsettling freshness, its beginning and far horizon in the radically "other" purposes of God. The texts of the Hebrew Scripture call us continually out of servitude—including complacency about the chains we may have forged ourselves—and they call us forth into a world of justice and grace. In his expository work with texts across the canon, Brueggemann has said that his goal is to open "the text to contemporary, faithful imagination. The purpose of such a practice is that the text can guide to *redescription* and inform the *re-imagination* of the world in which we are to practice faith."[3] A canonically shaped imagination, for Brueggemann, requires two essential qualities: vision and courage. Brueggemann suggests that we need to be prepared to see the wild and untamable hand of God at work in ways that undermine our established certitudes. Further, we need to be courageous about what God requires of us: sacrificial obedience lived out in a wilderness landscape in which the gift of covenantal relationship finally becomes real.

The addresses in this last section seek to fund the resistance of the redeemed over against the death-dealing machinations of empire. For Brueggemann, Scripture helps us reclaim our humanness and shows us how to bow before the Holy, teaching us about miracle, poetic subversion, and the drama of hidden hope. Brueggemann muses on the vulnerability of crucifixion and the countercultural gospel of forgiveness, hospitality, and generosity. He urges that believers' acts of artistic imagination make visible the deconstructive holiness of God, which has the power to re-create our totalizing world. He also entreats us to resist the cultural anxiety that fosters exclusion. Here, he draws on Priestly and Deuteronomic tradition to call us anew to care for the poor, reads Esther and Daniel to underline the importance of resolve about identity, and hopes for a renewed cherishing of the scroll—that is, sacred text—that can reconstitute the community of faith. Finally, Brueggemann reflects on how our engagements with Scripture, the ancient creeds, and a beloved hymn can help engraft us into the ongoing life of the Triune God.

In these pieces readers will perceive Brueggemann's enormous creativity and daring in working with a broad range of biblical and ecclesial traditions. He is a master exegete and teacher, to be sure, but his credentials are not the only reason that we continue to listen. We listen because Brueggemann is steeped in the visionary utterances of Scripture to an astonishing degree. We listen because he wears his hermeneutical and theological passions on his sleeve and does not shrink from polemic when the truth demands it. And we listen because he is so clearly a servant of the Word that gives light to the world, and we know that it is precisely and only in such service that we will find perfect freedom.

CHAPTER 13

Hosting Alternative Worlds

THE CHALLENGE OF MAINTAINING a distinctive community of faith and obedience into the next generation is an urgent issue in a society that wants to reduce everything to the lowest common denominator.[1] As urgent as that challenge is, however, it is not a new one. It is an old challenge that is perennially urgent. It is as old as the New Testament church, which struggled to maintain distinctive identity and ethic in an imperial society. And before that, it was an ongoing challenge in Old Testament Israel, for that community struggled to maintain its distinctiveness in a series of imperial contexts; and of course, the engagement for distinctiveness is an always-unfinished Jewish task.

It is the conservative temptation to center on the distinctive community and to create firm boundaries of holiness that issue in a sectarian direction. It is the liberal temptation to risk the boundaries for the sake of participatory engagement in the larger culture and so to jeopardize peculiar identity. In what follows, I will consider some of the ways in which ancient Israel fostered and nurtured distinct identity, because I believe their efforts in this regard are immensely instructive for our own contemporary challenge.

I

In what follows I will consider, in turn, some elements of the three canons of the Old Testament/Hebrew Bible: the Torah, the Prophets, and the Writings. As a common effort in these three canons, I suggest, following William Cavanaugh, that the task of such nurture is to out-imagine the imagination of dominant culture. In Cavanaugh's analysis, it is the imagination of the church in its sacraments that might out-imagine the ruthless generals and their military ideology. It is useful to identify the task as an act of imagination. And that in turn is based on the recognition that the dominant culture's constant desire to overcome the specificity of any subcommunity is also an act of immense imagination. That dominant imagination may be overcome by sustained counter-imagination in a subcommunity with high intentionality. I propose that the dominant world in which the subcommunity undertakes its counter-imagination is marked by:

1. *The shriveling of the human* by the pressures of commoditization;

2. *The failure of the communal infrastructure*, in which the notion of a "public" is mostly driven out by devotion to the "market"; and

3. *The nullification of holiness*, in which everything is reduced to technological control that leaves nothing to the imagination.

If this is a fair characterization of dominant culture in our midst, then the "missional responsibility" of a human subcommunity in response may be:

1. *The enhancement of the human* in ways that energize, authorize, and celebrate our common humanity;

2. *The reconstruction of a neighborly infrastructure* that requires acts of obligation and generosity but that requires, in a prior way, a set of symbols and images that invite an imagined public; and

3. *The recovery of a sense of the holy* that resists every ideological reduction, that opposes every easy absolute, and that affirms a hidden mystery of governance out beyond all of our posturing and contestation.

I propose that the challenge is to host an alternative world that endlessly arises from *narratives, oracles, and dramas* that are inhabited by holy power. That holy power is, in the rhetoric of the Bible, the three-times-holy God who always appears in power just as human power evaporates (see Isa 6:1-3). The capacity to host alternative worlds requires immense artistic freedom and courage and a readiness to hold quite loosely the dominant world which wants to posture as absolute. Indeed, the nurture of alternatives requires the capacity to utter words and hear them, to receive new networks of images that may strike us as odd and strange, and to relinquish old worlds that we have treasured but that no longer command credibility. It may be that the alternative worlds we host may be in direct dispute with absolutized, dominant worlds. Or it may be that when such alternative worlds are hosted with freedom and courage, they are offered alongside the more official worlds. They may not bother to engage with or dispute dominant worlds; rather, they may proceed in the high-minded position that dominant worlds can be safely disregarded in the interest of the world now proposed through narrative, oracle, and drama.

II

I turn first to the Torah of the Hebrew Bible, to the founding materials of Genesis through Deuteronomy. I suggest that the collage of miracles given there with specificity constitutes an alternative to the *uncritically assumed universals offered by hegemonic power.* It is the work of the nurturing community to model and instruct and authorize freedom from these assumed universals by countering them with specific narratives of miracle.

We may identify six texts that occur in the liturgical-instructional context of Israel whereby the young are inculcated into the alternative world of the adults. It is this context that gives distinctive identity to the community. The first three of these usages are lodged in the instructions for Passover, wherein Israel celebrated the exodus narrative as the defining plot for the community. In Exodus 12–13, we are struck with the detailed care whereby the community attends to the liturgic celebration, because the detail of liturgic celebration is the matrix for narratives of miracle. These three texts exhibit the adult community prepared to answer, nurture, and encourage the curiosity of the young in their moments of readiness:

> And when your children ask you, "What do you mean by this observance?" you shall say, "It is the passover sacrifice to the LORD, for he passed over the houses of the Israelites in Egypt, when he struck down the Egyptians but spared our houses." And the people bowed down and worshiped. (Exod 12:26-27)

> You shall tell your child on that day, "It is because of what the LORD did for me when I came out of Egypt." (Exod 13:8)

> When in the future your child asks you, "What does this mean?" you shall answer, "By strength of hand the LORD brought us out of Egypt, from the house of slavery. When Pharaoh stubbornly refused to let us go, the LORD killed all the firstborn in the land of Egypt, from human firstborn to the firstborn of animals. Therefore I sacrifice to the LORD every male that first opens the womb, but every firstborn of my sons I redeem." It shall serve as a sign on your hand and as an emblem on your forehead that my strength of hand the LORD brought us out of Egypt." (Exod 13:14-16)

Each of these texts assumes that the detailed liturgy will evoke the child's question, "Why?" The first answer is that YHWH made a distinction from the general onslaught and so spared the houses of Israel; the second only generally refers to the exodus; but the third answers fully to refer to the tenth plague—the killing of the firstborn—as a show of YHWH's mighty power that produced emancipation from the harshness of slavery. All three texts attest that Israel can remember its specialness, can recall its move from slavery to freedom, and can acknowledge the name of the agent who made the move possible. These are the ingredients of a miracle. That Israel continues to recite this ancient wonder attests that the memory has "abiding astonishment" (Martin Buber), that is, that it continues to energize and summons and empower.[2] One cannot invent such narrative accounts, but they arise in the depth of the community. Israel does not claim that the world teems with such newnesses, but it holds on to a few that are defining, and invites the imagination of the young to be organized and mobilized around these few awesome, inexplicable reference points. Notice that the edge of such recital is a radical social critique that from the outset calls into question the hegemonic power that is a cipher for all dominant power; from the outset, the narrative invites the young to understand its own tense relationship to such power. From its initial self-presentation, Israel is already doing social analysis and social criticism with the very youngest in the community.

Next I cite two texts from Deuteronomy 6. In verses 4-9, Moses teaches the famous Shema of ancient Israel. Israel's faith centers on this imperative verb that positions Israel on the receiving end of reality, recipient of gift and recipient of summons, not the one who takes initiatives. What Israel is to hear is loyalty to YHWH alone against all other loyalties. The imperative thus is a destabilization of other loyalties, which are to be held loosely. The pedagogic provision for this simple, defining imperative is twofold. First, there is a command not unlike the first commandment: "Hear, O Israel: The LORD is our God, the LORD alone. You shall love the LORD your God with all your heart, and with all your soul, and with all your might" (Deut 6:4-5). The young are invited to a simple, decisive loyalty. The one to be loved is the God of exodus, the one who has power and capacity always to be turning the historical process in new directions. Thus, Israel is committed to a singular obedience. And then second, provision is made for what I term "saturation education":

> Keep these words that I am commanding you today in your heart. Recite
> them to your children and talk about them when you are at home and
> when you are away, when you lie down and when you rise. Bind them as
> a sign on your hand, fix them as an emblem on your forehead, and write
> them on the doorposts of your house and on your gates. (Deut 6:6-9)

You shall wear out your children with signs and symbols, and metaphors and logos that fill the air of the domestic environment with a summons to obedience that defies all other obediences. Michael Fishbane suggests that these verses indicate a deep resistance on the part of the young to share in this particular version of reality. But of course, it is always so among the young. And Moses here makes provision that the young should be bound closely to the Lord of the covenant, a binding that is done through keeping, reciting, and literal binding.

The second text of Deuteronomy 6 is in verses 20-25, yet another text evoked by the curiosity of a child:

> When your children ask you in time to come, "What is the meaning of the decrees and the statutes and the ordinances that the LORD our God has commanded you?" then you shall say to your children, "We were Pharaoh's slaves in Egypt, but the LORD brought us out of Egypt with a mighty hand. The LORD displayed before our eyes great and awesome signs and wonders against Egypt, against Pharaoh and all his household. He brought us out from there in order to bring us in, to give us the land that he promised on oath to our ancestors. Then the LORD commanded us to observe all these statutes, to fear the LORD our God, for our lasting good, so as to keep us alive, as is now the case." (Deut 6:20-24)

The instruction, which seems here highly stylized, begins with the child's question. The adult's response is in two parts. First, there is a familiar review of the exodus that attests to YHWH's transformative power, power here that looks not only to freedom but also to well being in the land. Second, the exodus narrative moves on to the Sinai commands; obedience to torah, it is asserted, is the condition of being kept alive. The commands arise, so it seems, directly from the miracles. Miracles have a way of recruiting people to a certain practice of life, and this practice of obedience, congruent with the miracle, makes life possible.

The sixth text of such wonder that I cite is Joshua 4:21-24, a most remarkable text. Here the child's question is evoked by a liturgical reenactment of the crossing of the Jordan River into the land of promise. The children watch the ceremony of setting stones in the river, and eventually they ask about it. The adult answer is in two remarkable parts. The first part, in verses 22-23a, states the memory that Israel did indeed cross the dry Jordan River in order to enter the land of promise:

> [Joshua said] to the Israelites, "When your children ask their parents in time to come, 'What do these stones mean?' then you shall let your children know, 'Israel crossed over the Jordan here on dry ground.' For the LORD your God dried up the waters of the Jordan for you until you crossed over." (Josh 4:21-23a)

But then the additional recital makes a most remarkable and imaginative maneuver: "As the LORD your God did to the Red Sea, which he dried up for us until we crossed over, so that all the peoples of the earth may know that the hand of the LORD is mighty, and so that you may fear the LORD your God forever" (Josh 4:23b-24). The rhetorical pivot is "as." The answer equates the *crossing of the*

Jordan with the *crossing of the Red Sea* in the exodus. The old miracle is recalled; but the old miracle is made immediate by the replication of old miracle in new enactment, thus assuring the dynamism of the memory that is kept immediately contemporary. This is a new miracle, but it is a new miracle that only makes sense when the community is able to recall the old miracle.

The upshot of this twinning liturgical enactment is indicated in verse 24: "so that." As a consequence, all peoples, and not just the Israelites, but also the ones already in the land, shall know that YHWH is mighty. But then second and more urgently, "so that" you may fear YHWH forever. The wonder is given for all to see. But its ultimate purpose is the generativity of a present-tense community that is utterly committed to YHWH.

These texts constitute the educational intention of Israel, for Israel is characteristically needing to work its distinctive identity for its children in a social context where dominant culture gives no heed to Israel's distinctive recital. This effort at distinctive identity is a constant and recurring one for Israel, for Israel has never lived in a social environment devoid of hegemonic challenge.

Israel moves from these few, treasured, peculiar, concrete transformations rooted in YHWH's initiative to construct its entire narrative frame of reference for life in the world. While the initial miracle requires a deep commitment of faith, the larger construction of reality requires an immense liberated imagination. That ongoing act of imagination in the construction of alternative reality defies conventional, dominant reality and insists on a counterreality rooted in claims that are dismissed in principle by dominant imperial culture. I cite two examples of the larger construction of alternative reality.

In Psalm 145, the community exhibits its extended, refined vocabulary for "miracle":

> One generation shall laud your works to another,
>   and shall declare your mighty acts.
> On the glorious splendor of your majesty,
>   and on your wondrous works, I will meditate.
> The might of your awesome deeds shall be proclaimed,
>   and I will declare your greatness.
> They shall celebrate the fame of your abundant goodness,
>   and shall sing aloud of your righteousness. (Ps 145:4-7)

That vocabulary includes "works," "mighty acts," "mighty wondrous works," "awesome deeds," "greatness," "abundant goodness," and "righteousness." All of these terms are rough synonyms. Verses 8-9, moreover, indicate the substance of all these nameable, recitable memories:

> The LORD is gracious and merciful,
>   slow to anger and abounding in steadfast love.

The Lord is good to all,
> and his compassion is over all that he has made. (Ps 145:8-9)

In its construction of an alternative, the imagination of Israel is able to assert that its entire past is shot through with YHWH's grace, mercy, steadfast love, goodness, and compassion. Thus, the category of miracle links together the *key markings of YHWH* and the *concrete reality of lived experience*. It is this connection that subverts the universal hegemonic world that wants to resist references to the holy and that seeks to void the claims of concrete subcommunities.

Second, Psalm 136 is a primal exhibit of Israel's confessional imagination. In that psalm, Israel recites its entire past as a series of transformative initiatives by YHWH. The second half of each verse, moreover, had the community respond to the named miracle with a regularized, generalized answer, "for the steadfast love of YHWH endures forever." Israel is offering in this recital its core memory to its young. But it is also inviting a response of the young that decisively insists on YHWH as the core agent in reality, to which all of human life is a response. The dialogic utterance in liturgy gives voice to the dialogic reality of fidelity that is constitutive for this alternative world.

III

The second canon of the Old Testament—the second way in which Israel inculcates its distinctive identity among its young—is the prophetic canon. While the extended literature of this canon includes long narrative accounts in Joshua, Judges, Samuel, and Kings that we call "history," and while it encompasses many other genres as well, there is no doubt that the root of the canon consists in *oracles of holiness*. These oracles are quite remarkable. They are disciplined, poetic, highly stylized utterances given by uncredentialed people who sense themselves to say (and do) things that challenge all settled certitude. Their words are context-specific; but after the context passes, the words linger and they are heard always again in new ways with reference to new contexts.

The speakers of such oracles are uncredentialed nobodies. They mostly have no social connection but are taken seriously (if at all) because of the content of what they say. The tradition does its best to credential the uncredentialed. It asserts, "Thus says the Lord." By that term the tradition means that these speakers give not their own words but the word of the government of God that has dispatched them. They claim, without any precision or explanation, to have been present in the assembly of the gods, where the big decisions about heaven and earth have been made. And while the power people tend to dismiss these speakers (as in Amos 7:10-17), the ongoing tradition remembers and preserves their words. Indeed, the tradition does more than remember and preserve. It comes to regard these utterances as authoritative and takes them as genuine disclosures of divine will; it eventually treats them as "canonical." The route by which *uncredentialed utterance* becomes *canonical revelation* is hidden from us; it is, however, no doubt important for the maintenance of alternative community. I have called these poems *oracles of holiness*. That is because these oracles are not only uttered in the name and by the authority of YHWH; but they are also speeches that articulate the character, will, purpose, and substance of YHWH. In a word, these oracles make the holy God a decisive player in the public process of the world, for without prophetic oracle, the world could go its own way without reference to divine governance. The offer of *oracles of holiness* in the canon of the prophets does a very different thing from the narratives of *miracle in the first canon*. The narratives of miracle that we have considered tend to be constructions of a counternarrative of reality. Whereas the narratives are constructions, the oracles are characteristically subversive. They speak against settled certitude and established power. The narratives by themselves, so appropriate to the imagination of young children, might only produce a romantic environment of a magic world. But, then, the oracles of holiness come as a heavy dose of subversive realism. They not only voice alternative; they voice deep challenge to the presumed world that the innocent take for granted; for that reason, I would judge these oracles especially germane to the emerging cynicism of adolescents who want to dissent from and challenge all authority. The oracles are designed for conflictual engagement that exposes settled truth as unreliable. I will consider four such oracles that I cite as representative. I here take fairly obvious cases from which generalization may be made.

Amos 4:1-3

Amos is, of course, the earliest of the prophets who are credited with a "book." As nearly as we know, his context was the golden age of the twin monarchies, when Israel and Judah enjoyed an unchallenged autonomy that permitted the self-indulgent economy of the urban elite to prosper. The poet imagines this self-indulgent, unexamined prosperity to be under threat. He is able to anticipate, apparently, the coming reality of the Assyrian imperial threat. But he does not, in the oracles I cite, mention Assyria. He names only YHWH as the adversary of the economy of his own people. This may be among Amos's best-known oracles of holiness:

> Hear this word, you cows of Bashan
>   who are on Mount Samaria,
> who oppress the poor, who crush the needy,
>   who say to their husbands, "Bring something to drink."
> The LORD God has sworn by his holiness:
>   The time is surely coming upon you,
> when they shall take you away with hooks,

> even the last of you with fishhooks.
> Through breaches in the wall you shall leave,
>   each one straight ahead;
>   and you shall be flung out into Harmon,
>   says the LORD. (Amos 4:1-3)

There is a summons to hear, an imperative that echoes the old *shema'* of Deuter-onomy 6:4. "Listen," because something life-or-death is about to be uttered. After the summons, there is a vocative. You "cows of Bashan." This famous address, no doubt sexist, identifies the female members of the urban elite who are taken to be the propulsion for the extravagant consumerism of the privileged community of the city. This vocative is followed by a characteristic indictment in three parts:

> who oppress,
> who crush,
> who say

The poetic development is remarkable. The first two verbs are accents of physical abuse. But the third verb indicates that all the women really do is *speak* in their avarice. Their desires become the motivation for rapacious social policies.

In verse 2, the oracle, characteristically, turns to the intervention of "the LORD God," who has made a policy decision that the poet must announce. The rest of the poetic unit describes a forcible action whereby the ones addressed will be taken captive, treated roughly, and carried away "with hooks," away from the affluent city. This last, which occupies two of the three verses of the oracle, is in anticipation of deportation at the hands of the Assyrians that did happen in the generation after Amos (see 2 Kgs 17).

Notice that the oracle by a nobody (1) does an acute social analysis of consum-erism, (2) anticipates the invasion of a foreign power that will deport, (3) makes a connection between (a) internal greed and (b) external threat, and (4) links the whole to the acute presence of the governance of YHWH. The sum of the oracle is to indicate to the urban economy of Samaria that it is not autonomous but must conform, eventually, to the governance of YHWH.

The oracle, of course, was not taken seriously. The priesthood dismissed Amos as a crank and a troublemaker (Amos 7:10-17). But not only did the contempo-rary presentation of Amos turn out to be true; but also, imagine the poem linger-ing in the community, always to be heard yet again. And now we hear the poem as an up-to-the-minute, contemporary assault on our own unbridled consumer-ism that has produced enemy assault. The poem makes no specific connection; it only haunts us. And our children should not be protected from haunting, in order that they may learn that our settled world is under challenge from the hidden power of God that finally cannot be resisted. It is only a poem, but it lingers in its intrinsic authority.

Micah 3:9-12

Micah shares much with Amos. Except that he is from the south and is concerned with the political establishment in Jerusalem. He is somewhat later than
Amos; he had seen the kingdom of Samaria destroyed, as Amos had anticipated,
and now Micah imagines a parallel fate for Judah in the south. Unlike Amos the
shepherd, Micah appears to have been a peasant farmer.

Those differences, however, are not overly important. Much like Amos,
Micah plants a poem in Jerusalem that continues to haunt and do its work. The
oracle in Micah 3:9-12 begins like that of Amos: *shema'* ("Listen"!) You are
addressed! The addressee here is not consumer women as with Amos; rather,
the poem concerns government leadership in Jerusalem, most likely in the time
of King Ahaz:

> Hear this, you rulers of the house of Jacob
> > and chiefs of the house of Israel . . . (Mic 3:9a)

The address is followed by an indictment introduced by three *who*'s:

> who abhor justice
> who pervert equity
> who build Zion with blood
> > and Jerusalem with wrong.

The indictment concerns the practice of economic injustice. The poetic indictment
presents a slate of failed leadership:

> Its rulers give judgment for a bribe,
> > its priests teach for a price,
> > its prophets give oracles for money;
> yet they lean upon the LORD and say,
> > "Surely the LORD is with us!
> > No harm shall come upon us." (Mic 3:11)

Not only do the rulers, priests, and prophets practice leadership that is corrupt,
dishonest, and exploitative; but also, after that, they then come to the temple to
voice their piety and their confidence in YHWH. These phrases are likely quotes
from a complaint liturgy in the temple. Notice that in the last line of the indictment, concerning complaining, the phrasing is very much like Psalm 46:1, a song
of Zion:

> God is our refuge and strength,
> > a very present help in trouble. (Ps 46:1)

After the detailed and extended indictment, the poem turns with a powerful "therefore" to state the consequences of the indictment:

> Therefore because of you Zion shall be plowed as a field;
> Jerusalem shall become a heap of ruins,
>   and the mountain of the house a wooded height. (Mic 3:12)

The word is that the rapacious injustice of the establishment will result in destruction of the temple city. Again the prophet makes rhetorical linkage between *policies and practices of greed* and the *sorry fate of the temple* in the presentation of the true God.

This is one of the most remarkable of the oracles of divine holiness, for the poet here imagines the termination of the city and the entire concentration of power—royal, priestly, and economic—in Jerusalem. It is important to remember, of course, that this is only poetry. But what poetry! It is an utterance that lingers with power and that cannot be silenced. The poem resurfaced most remarkably a century later, in Jeremiah 26, where that despised prophet is on trial for his life. Micah 3:12 is quoted in Jeremiah 26:18 to the effect that the prophet-poets are not to be executed because they critiqued Jerusalem. Beyond that resurfacing, moreover, it would not surprise if the poem resurfaced in our own time to illuminate the "terrorist" attacks against our established institutions built on an unjust economy. Such poetry never "explains," never reasons by cause and effect. All it does and all it seeks to do is to reread the world in terms of intransigent holiness that will not be mocked.

Isaiah 43:1-7

In the latter part of the book of Isaiah, we have a different sort of poetry. Now the old words of Amos and Micah have come to fruition. Now the institutions of rapacious greed in Jerusalem have been terminated. Now the leading citizens have been deported, and the ones left behind are in a poor condition. How remarkable and how characteristic that such a context again yields poetry. Oracles of holiness emerge just when the community of faith is pushed to extremity. The burden of the poet now is to voice hope in the context of profound despair, and the poet does so by declaring the faithful presence of holiness precisely in a context of despair:

> But now thus says the LORD,
>   he who created you, O Jacob,
>   he who formed you, O Israel:
> Do not fear, for I have redeemed you;
>   I have called you by name, you are mine.
> When you pass through the waters, I will be with you;

and through the rivers, they shall not overwhelm you;
when you walk through fire you shall not be burned,
    and the flame shall not consume you. (Isa 43:1-2)

Israel had ample reason now to conclude that it had been abandoned by the holy
God. The poet, however, subverts deeply felt despair by the utterance, "fear not."
That sovereign declaration intends to veto all the felt, properly discerned despair
of exile. How fantastic that trusted utterance can veto context. But that of course
is the characteristic work of our best poets.

    The poem goes on to imagine a "prisoner exchange":

For I am the LORD your God,
    the Holy One of Israel, your Savior.
I give Egypt as your ransom,
    Ethiopia and Seba in exchange for you.
Because you are precious in my sight,
    and honored, and I love you,
I give people in return for you,
    nations in exchange for your life. (Isa 43:3-4)

Because every Israelite, every Jew, every fugitive, every displaced person in the
community is treasured by YHWH, who is the Lord of the exile, YHWH is willing to "trade" lots of other people for the sake of these beloved exiles.

    And then the poem circles back to its initial unconditional "fear not":

Do not fear, for I am with you;
    I will bring your offspring from the east,
    and from the west I will gather you;
I will say to the north, "Give them up,"
    and to the south, "Do not withhold;
bring my sons from far away
    and my daughters from the end of the earth—
everyone who is called by my name,
    whom I created for my glory,
    whom I formed and made." (Isa 43:5-7)

YHWH wills the well being, homecoming, and restoration of all of God's people.
Some are held in hock to the north and some are held in cultural bondage to the
south. But in every direction, the Lord of the homecoming says, "give up . . . do
not withhold," because these are my sons and daughters.

    What a marvel that we have here entrusted to us the voice of promise: this
"fear not" that overrides context. The "fear not" of the Holy One echoes and
echoes again through the sore spots of history. We are wont, we people of faith,
to imagine that our situation is unbearable. But the "fear not" of Christmas and

Easter ends exile. It is a "fear not" on the lips of the poet that has sustained Jews in many contexts. But after that, the same "fear not" is spoken to the poor, the persecuted, the ill, the failed, the powerless. The poem does not solve anything, but it permits everything. It now, upon utterance, permits departure and home-coming and dancing and singing and amazement. That is why in every context of our culture the familiar cadences of Psalm 23 sound again:

> Even though I walk through the darkest valley,
>   I fear no evil,
> for you are with me. (Ps 23:4)

It is the speaker of "fear not" who invites poetry of buoyancy even among those left behind in Israel. These are the ones who concluded, against all the data:

> The steadfast love of the LORD never ceases,
>   his mercies never come to an end;
> they are new every morning;
>   great is your faithfulness.
> "The LORD is my portion," says my soul,
>   "therefore I will hope in him." (Lam 3:22-24)

The poem precludes despair!

Isaiah 41:21-29

This is a companion piece to Isaiah 41:1-7, but it moves in the opposite direction. The poet knows that his contemporaries are enthralled to Babylonian imperial power, which is legitimated by Babylonian gods. In the face of such raw power, their own power is feeble, and the capacity of the God of Israel is likewise taken to be feeble. The poet knows, further, that Israel will never regain its courage and energy for its own identity of faith until its imagination breaks free of that enslavement to imperial definitions of reality.

Thus, the poet imagines a great trial scene that calls into the dark the Babylonian gods in order to determine if they are real gods. Imagine the courage of a Jewish poet to court the great gods of Babylon:

> Set forth your case, says the LORD;
>   bring your proofs, says the King of Jacob. (Isa 41:21)

Then as prosecutor, the poet interrogates the Babylonian gods:

> Let them bring them, and tell us what is to happen.
> Tell us the former things, what they are,
>   so that we may consider them,

and that we may know their outcome;
    or declare to us the things to come.
Tell us what is to come hereafter,
    that we may know that you are gods;
do good, or do harm,
    that we may be afraid and terrified. (Isa 41:22-23)

In this poetic scenario, of course, these gods give no answer to the questions put by the prosecutor. They are silent. They have no response to make and no breath with which to make it, because they are no gods, not to be feared or honored or obeyed. Thus the verdict given in this imaginary court:

You, indeed, are nothing and your work is nothing at all;
    whoever chooses you is an abomination. (Isa 41:24)

But then, abruptly, the mood of the court changes as the poem moves on. For YHWH now takes the stand, YHWH who was made by the Babylonians to seem so feeble. YHWH testifies in court even without a question asked by the prosecutor. YHWH takes over the courtroom and fills it with sovereign energy:

I stirred up one from the north, and he has come,
    from the rising of the sun he was summoned by name.
He shall trample on rulers as on mortar,
    as the potter treads clay.
Who declared it from the beginning, so that we might know,
    and beforehand, so that we might say, "He is right"?
There was no one who declared it, none who proclaimed,
    none who heard your words.
I first have declared it to Zion,
    and I give to Jerusalem a herald of good tidings.
But when I look there is no one;
    among these there is no counselor
    who, when I ask, gives an answer. (Isa 41:25-28)

It is YHWH who has renovated history, who has summoned Cyrus the Persian to terminate the empire of Babylon and to emancipate the Jews for homecoming. It is YHWH and none other, without help or advice from any of the secret arts of Babylon. It is only YHWH. YHWH's testimony of self-assertion leads, perhaps inevitably, to a dismissive verdict on the Babylonian gods:

No, they are all a delusion;
    their works are nothing;
    their images are empty wind. (Isa 41:29)

The rhetorical aim of the poems is to take away the breath of self-pitying Jews, to authorize and energize a fresh initiative rooted in YHWH's own freedom, the freedom of a recovered identity in the faith that is no longer captive to dominant culture.

These old Jews—like us—lived in a world of assumed absolutes that denied any freedom. The assumed identity among us here has to do with money and power and violence and military domination and the endless permit of consumer commodities. How astonishing that the antidote long known in our community is poetry that testifies to YHWH's holiness beyond the bounds of dominant perception. This community has always known that poetry is the best testimony to the elusive, irascible character of YHWH. So the strategy undertaken in the book of Isaiah is to saturate the young with good, elusive poetry, texts that are familiar and memorized through much repetition. The precondition for such a poetic alternative of course is to desist from so much computer work and computer games and to be face-to-face in testimony that practices relentless imagination. Without any reservoir of such poetry of holiness, faith devolves into a tight moralism that too readily conforms to the realities of the empire.

IV

The first part of the Hebrew Bible, Torah, yields narratives of miracle that provide a base for the nurture of the young. The second part, the Prophets, offers oracles of holiness that subvert our settlements. Now the third part, the Writings, includes the most urbane and sophisticated of Israel's texts, offering *dramas of hidden subversion* that oppose the dominant mood of self-confident control that reduces all of life to technology, that leaves nothing to the imagination, and that so yields a world of pornographic greed, anxiety, and brutality. Our young, by default, may entertain this world of destructive pornography; but they need not, because such a one-dimensional world is not the only one available.

The third canon invites us—and our young—to a world that is thicker and therefore more interesting, more demanding, and eventually more reassuring. It is characteristic of the world of both the wisdom and the Psalms that the utterance of text is playful and teasing, so that much is left to imagination. I will cite three texts briefly before I comment on the book of Job.

First, Psalm 44 is the most candid and harsh of all the lament Psalms. In part I call attention to the genre of lament, and in part I comment on this particular psalm. The genre of lament that permeates the Psalter is most remarkable. It makes clear, in its many uses, that faith is not a flat conformity and submissiveness. It is, rather, attestation that faith is a dialogue, and we, with all of the nerviness that we can muster, are invited and expected to hold up our end of the conversation. The lament makes clear that challenge to the Holy One of Israel is a proper mode of faithful devotion.

In Psalm 44, the first eight verses are a fine affirmation of trust in YHWH. But then in verse 9—and again in verses 17-19—the psalm turns on an abrupt "yet," rather like the German *doch* that contradicts all that has gone before. After the "yet" of verse 9, there follows a long accusation against YHWH, who has not been faithful to Israel:

> Yet you have rejected us and abased us,
>   and have not gone out with our armies.
> You made us turn back from the foe,
>   and our enemies have gotten spoil.
> You have made us like sheep for slaughter,
>   and have scattered us among the nations.
> You have sold your people for a trifle,
>   demanding no high price for them.
> You have made us the taunt of our neighbors,
>   the derision and scorn of those around us.
> You have made us a byword among the nations,
>   a laughingstock among the peoples. (Ps 44:9-14)

This is followed by a "yet" in verse 17 that asserts Israel's faithfulness to YHWH in spite of YHWH's infidelity:

> All this has come upon us,
>   yet we have not forgotten you,
>   or been false to your covenant.
> Our heart has not turned back,
>   nor have our steps departed from your way. (Ps 44:17-18)

And this in turn produces a third "yet" in verse 19 that reiterates YHWH's failure.

Such an articulation might, we expect, lead to the rejection of YHWH and the abandonment of faith. And there are indeed celebrated cases among us wherein someone has experienced an abandonment of faith that has led to a total of rejection of faith. But not here! What surprises us is that YHWH is still definitional for the speaking community. For after the rhetorical assault on YHWH, the poem reverses direction and offers petition to YHWH that is full of hope:

> Rouse yourself! Why do you sleep, O LORD?
>   Awake, do not cast us off forever!
> Why do you hide your face?
>   Why do you forget our affliction and oppression?
> For we sink down to the dust;
>   our bodies cling to the ground.

> Rise up, come to our help.
> > Redeem us for the sake of your steadfast love. (Ps 44:23-26)

The last word of the psalm is *hesed*. On the one hand, Israel counts deeply on YHWH's fidelity; on the other hand, YHWH is summoned to fidelity and is held accountable for enacting it in this context of emergency. This dialogic capacity with YHWH eschews both our conventional conformity in faith and our reactive autonomy that voids faith. The nurture of our young into a capacity for free, responsible, courageous, energetic dialogic engagement is crucial for the sustenance of faith.

Second, *Proverbs 21:30-31*. Listen to this little drama of *hidden subversion*:

> No wisdom, no understanding, no counsel,
> > can avail against the LORD.
> The horse is made ready for the day of battle,
> > but the victory belongs to the LORD. (Prov 21:30-31)

Nothing known can prevail against the staying power of YHWH, not human failure or human cunning or human intelligence. This is a remarkable statement anytime, certainly remarkable in the modern situation that fully trusts that "knowledge is power." The first lines of this statement teach that the mystery of God will outflank all our best learning.

But then in verse 31, the Proverb becomes specific and comments on "military intelligence." Good military planning means strategy and supplies, good horses, and good chariots that make overwhelming advantage in sheer power. The last line of the proverb does not surprise us after the debacles in Vietnam and then in Iraq, both debacles springing from deep military intelligence coupled with titanic ignorance and limitless pride. The last line is this: "but the victory belongs to the LORD" (Prov 21:31b). We cannot make the world happen on our terms. Such wisdom instruction in the ancient world was aimed at young men who would soon come to power. Such wisdom instruction, read belatedly in our time, is addressed to U.S. arrogance that imagines we can work our will anywhere in the world. Our arrogance can produce killing fields and endless casualties, including our own, without even mentioning the prisons. We are able to work much violence. But outcomes are different, not readily given over to us. So the proverb invites subversion of our best intelligence and planning and power, an odd curbing of the human that ancients credited to the Almighty. The young learn, as they watch the news and read the Proverbs, that the future of the world has not been fully turned over to us. Hiddenness keeps alternative outcomes in reserve, and faith is knowing that reserve without trying to administer it.

Third, *Proverbs 22:2*. I picked this Proverb at random:

> The rich and the poor have this in common:
> > the LORD is the maker of them all. (Prov 22:2)

The wisdom teachers think realistically about life in the world. As a consequence, "money" keeps coming up in their teaching. The common view, surely, is that wealth is the great social differentiation. That is why we work so hard to get ahead. That is why we frantically place our first graders in the best schools and in the best tennis camps. That is why we dress to exhibit our "class" and our classi-ness. That is why we relocate to better neighborhoods. That is why, according to tax laws and mortgage arrangements, the gap between rich and poor becomes even greater. That is why we make new laws against immigrants in order to pro-tect our economic and cultural advantage in the world—to ensure that the rich and the poor have nothing, or as little as possible, in common.

The wisdom teachers, of course, knew all about that. They will not give in to such facts on the ground because their work is to enact little dramas of hidden subversion that give the lie to our usual impressions. The rich and the poor, against all appearances, have one irreducible thing in common—the same God is creator of all, has willed all to existence, and continues to give life to all.

Is that all we have in common? Well, we are left to ponder. If that is all we have in common, then we are free, for the future of creation, to go our own ways and to make the most we can of it. But if that is the extrapolation we make, then the prov-erb is hardly worth uttering. Surely the point is greater than that. Surely the wisdom teachers mean to say that rich and poor are finally together in economic life, have engagement with each other and responsibility for each other. The prophet accom-plishes at least the connection between money and God and has the immediate effect of making money problematic at best, for the work and the will of the Creator God is ultimate and curbs the differentiating power of money. Our propensity to absolutize money and its power to socially differentiate is immediately called into question. And of course, we may infer much more from the proverb. We may infer that the rich and poor are under common assurance and under common mandate to construct and manage and value a "public" sphere together, to share together what is necessary to all and what is possessed by none. The proverb is surely subversive of our widespread assumptions that inform social practice and social policy among us. The proverb is clear that the young must be invited to the conviction that money is at best penultimate in a world of creaturely commonality.

Fourth, the poem of Job, of course, is the *great drama of hidden subversion*. The premise of the poem is that Job and Job's friends together share a set of certi-tudes about how the world works. Job and his friends had learned from the book of Proverbs and the book of Deuteronomy and from Psalm 1 that *obedience pro-duces well being* and *disobedience produces trouble*. That of course is the premise of every community, every corporation, and every family. Conform and prosper! Work well and get a bonus. Mow the lawn and get the car:

> Happy are those who do not follow the advice of the wicked,
> or take the path that sinners tread,

or sit in the seat of scoffers;
but their delight is in the law of the LORD,
    and on his law they meditate day and night.
They are like trees planted by streams of water,
which yield their fruit in its season,
    and their leaves do not wither.
In all that they do, they prosper. (Ps 1:1-3)

Of course, things go amiss. Job—even more than his friends—had learned from
the tradition of lament Psalms that it is right and proper to dispute with YHWH—
as in Psalm 44—when the world does not perform properly. Thus, much of Job's
speech is a defiant challenge to YHWH. At the outset, the poem subverts the
cocksure moral symmetry of Job and his friends.

The big surprise, however, comes only late in the book. By chapter 38, finally
speaks the whirlwind. We wait for YHWH to engage in contestation with Job
about moral symmetry. Perhaps God in the whirlwind will confirm Job's point
and Job's virtue and reward him. Perhaps the God of the whirlwind will expose
the sins of Job that have remained hidden to Job and to his friends. Either way, it
will be a great contest, and we will watch, hoping to see the defeat of this prideful
moralist.

But such a divine response would remain fully in character for Job and would
only reinforce the urgency of the dispute. It turns out that the holy voice from
the whirlwind will not engage either Job or Job's friends in their agenda of moral
symmetry. It turns out that this holy voice directly contradicts Job's tradition of
moral certitude and will not pursue a dispute grounded in self-confidence and
control—the sort of control that leads to a technical approach to life and leaves
nothing to the imagination. It turns out that this holy voice, the most extreme
voice in ancient Israel, is wholly uninterested in Job's ethical questioning. YHWH
will have no part in such a dispute and so stunningly subverts and deconstructs
the entire tradition. YHWH asks Job to unlearn the symmetrical traditions of
Deuteronomy and the clear teaching of the book of Proverbs and to face the awesome sublimity of the mystery of the Creator. Job is not invited to dispute but
now is questioned by the Creator about the depths of creation, about which Job
knows nothing. Job is not now an agent of certitude but is pushed off into a world
he does not understand and cannot manage. For all his prideful certitude about
his proper role and place in the world, Job is sharply reduced to silence. It is
either defiant or submissive silence, but either way it is silence. Job is left to brood
about the wonder and majesty of God and the derivative wonder and majesty of
God's creation. He is, by divine rhetoric, robbed of his self-confidence. He has
opened up to him (and to us) a wondrous world of imagination that lies beyond
our control and our explanation. And there Job remains, destabilized, addressed,
questioned, and finally unresolved before a God who will be God.

V

I suggest that the three canons provide resources for nurture in distinctive identity. Each wave of canon forms an urgent and critical alternative to dominant reality:

- Torah is a collage of narratives of miracle as alternative to unexamined universals that are always in the service of hegemony;
- Prophets offer oracles of holiness that challenge every world of absolutism, imagining harsh dissent from a world that is badly ordered and offering hope in a context of despair;
- The Writings present dramas of hidden subversion that move against a pornographic reductionism that thrives on self-confident control but that completely misses the larger reality of the Creator and the creation.

The nurture and evocation of distinct identity is urgent in our time of globalization and the reduction of the particular. I finish with two texts, however, that warn against a distinctive identity that retreats from public engagement:

First, *Jeremiah 29:4-9*. Jeremiah writes the deportees in Babylon and counsels them on life in displacement. He warns that there will be no return to normalcy, and Jews must get used to marginalization. But then he advises that they focus on the *shalom* of Babylon, for in the *shalom* of Babylon will be Jewish *shalom*. For all of Israel's distinct identity, engagement from that perspective is an urgent responsibility for those in the distinct community.

Second, *Daniel 4:19-37*. Daniel is a Jew with a distinct identity in the service of Babylonian power. He is fearful before the great King Nebuchadnezzar, but he is willing to play his role as a wisely engaged Jew. He is able—wise Jew that he is—to interpret the dream of Nebuchadnezzar after all of the official "intelligence" of the regime has failed in the interpretive task. But Daniel not only interprets. He dares to give advice to the great Babylonian king, advice that arises exactly from his Jewishness. Nebuchadnezzar's regime is under threat and Daniel urges: "Therefore, O king, may my counsel be acceptable to you: atone for your sins with righteousness, and your iniquities with mercy to the oppressed, so that your prosperity may be prolonged" (Dan 4:27). For all imperial posturing, this wise Jew knows that the secret to well being is *mercy to the oppressed*. Such counsel must have sounded strange to Nebuchadnezzar, for empires do not traffic in mercy and do not notice the oppressed. But Daniel knows, and he is ready to bear public witness from a peculiar angle of faith.

That, I suggest, is what we may hope for our children concerning the gift of identity in our faith. Nurture is saturation about the God to be served, the God of justice. It is clear that a good rendering of this version of reality is now urgent among us. But we do not lose heart!

CHAPTER 14

Impossible Talk/Impossible Walk

HERE IS AN IDEA about the vocation of the church:

To dream the impossible dream;
To speak the impossible word;
To act the impossible act.

I

Since the formation of Israel at Sinai, the biblical community of faith has always lived in tension with the empire and has always had to struggle to create and maintain space for the freedom, energy, and courage to live out its vocation in the world.[1] Even though we now sense the matter acutely, our time in the church is not peculiar; it is like the community of faith always is—co-opted, domesticated, intimidated, and seduced by dominant culture.

Already in the wilderness, earliest Israel wanted to return to the imperial slavery of Egypt; it had found the alternative of covenant too difficult (Num 14:2-4).

In the displacement of Babylon, Jews struggled to sing "the Songs of Zion" in a strange land (Ps 137:3-4). They did so at great risk; the evidence shows that some found it easier to give up such a demanding identity and signed on with the imperial economy.

The New Testament offers enough evidence that the early church, at its best, boldly bore witness to gospel truth in the face of the Roman Empire; but in many other ways it found such boldness too demanding and abandoned the project (see 2 Tim 4:10).

We are, moreover, still coming to terms with the fact that the churches of the Reformation never found it easy or simple—or even possible—to follow the sensibilities of the Radical Reformation but remained closely attached to the safety of establishment power.

And now, many of us think that the great ecclesial issue is that the claims of the gospel have been collapsed in our society into "the American Dream." What is promised to us in our faith is everywhere much assumed—by liberals and by conservatives—to be permeated with consumer entitlement, technological advantage, and military preeminence, all packaged as U.S. "exceptionalism."[2] If that intertwining of the American Dream and the promises of the gospel is a correct characterization, then it is the task of evangelical faith, in this time and place, to distinguish the promises of the gospel from and, in important ways, over against the American Dream. In order to do that, we are back to the basics about *the walk that must be walked* and *the talk that must be talked*.

II

In thinking about "back to basics," it occurred to me that in his pastoral-lyrical First Letter to the Corinthians, Paul frames his letter by the two great claims of faith that contradict the truth of the empire.

At the outset, Paul frames his address to the church in terms of *the crucifixion of Jesus*, recognizing that a "theology of the cross" is a stumbling block and a scandal.[3] While that statement of Paul is centered in Christ, the concern of Paul is powerfully ecclesial: "Consider your call" (v. 26). In the cross, the Messiah enacts an alternative to the empire; the Messiah is vulnerable and must suffer at the hands of the empire. The cross is the acknowledgment and manifestation that submission to the power of the empire is not defeat but is the mode through which newness comes. Since that awesome Friday, the church has been preoccupied with the truth of triumph through vulnerability that the empire resists but that is at the core of our faith.

At the conclusion of his letter to the church, Paul frames his address with a lyrical, even if somewhat convoluted, affirmation of *the resurrection of Christ*; again, the claim is christological, but the intent is ecclesial:

> When this perishable body must put on imperishability, and this mortal body must put on immortality, then the saying that is written will be fulfilled:
>
> > "Death has been swallowed up in victory."
> > "Where, O death, is your victory?
> >   Where, O death, is your sting?"

The sting of death is sin, and the power of sin is the law. But thanks be
to God, who gives us the victory through our Lord Jesus Christ. Therefore, my beloved, be steadfast, immovable, always excelling in the work
of the Lord, because you know that in the Lord your labor is not in vain.
(1 Cor 15:54-58)

The victory of Easter is the ground for "excelling in the work of the lord." As
resurrection faith is "not in vain," so Easter labor is "not in vain." The Easter
labor that Paul commends—that is specified and detailed in the chapters of the
epistle—is that Christians are to live and act in the community in ways that refuse
imperial modes of power and that in fact subvert the power assumptions and
value system of the empire.

The two framing affirmations—*crucifixion* that leads to call and *resurrection* that leads to Easter labor—summon the church to a life that the empire has
declared impossible. It is impossible that Messiah should die or that Messiah's followers should—in foolishness and in weakness—"reduce to nothing the things that
are" (1 Cor 1:28). The empire cannot entertain an existence outside of the pursuit,
management, and maintenance of power; but the church is called to vulnerability.
It is, as a counterpoint, impossible that Messiah should be raised from the dead
or that Messiah's followers should be steadfast and immovable in their practice of
"faith, hope, and love," while their greatest habit is self-giving love in the world.

The empire—always and everywhere—has declared that the embrace of vulnerability and loss is not a viable way to be in the world. This message of life
through domination is everywhere in the American empire from ads for military
recruitment to ads that beat the aging process to the virility of sports stars to the
promise of financial security through investment. The sum of all these offers is
the creation of a "virtual world" of control and well being in which there are *no
losses* (crucifixions) and in which there are *no surprises* (resurrections). The offer
is a steady-state management that is never "inconvenient" but celebrates limitless
capacity for Americans to "have it all."

What an impertinence, in the midst of such an imperial seduction of "power,
wealth, and wisdom," for Paul to invite Gentile Christians and Jewish Christians (across imperial distinctions) to "consider your call" to cruciform life and to
"excel" in the Easter work of the Lord! In his pastoral counsel in the epistle, Paul
details the alternative, subversive practice of humanness grounded in the gospel
that the empire can neither resist nor permit. From its inception, the church has
been called to live a life that the empire has known to be "impossible."

III

Evangelical life in tension with the empire—as an alternative to empire, as a sub-
version of empire, as life outside the seduction of empire—has always consisted,

for the faithful, in disciplines of humanness that the quid pro quo calculus of the empire cannot tolerate. Among those disciplines of humanness that belong to this countercommunity, I can identify three that are the most obvious, the most demanding, and the most resisted by empire.

This intentional subcommunity within the empire practices *forgiveness*. Likely the church's mandate to forgive is rooted in the ancient Israelite practice of "year of release" whereby debts are cancelled in a disciplined and regularized way (Deut 15:1-18).[4] There is good reason that in the Lord's Prayer we variously pray for pardon of "sins," "trespasses," "debts," for the theological mandate has economic roots. Forgiveness is an act that breaks the vicious cycles of alienation and permits starting again. It is an act made possible by the Easter *novum* that asserts that death, guilt, and resentment have no more "sting." And so the early church is urged to practice forgiveness, for the community of crucifixion and resurrection knows that there is the slippage of the Spirit that lets us escape the endless score-keeping of empire. Since the empire is an endless game of "king of the mount," there can never be forgiveness but only a deep file of affronts, a grimness about "law and order," and harshness about "three strikes and you're out," all designed to keep power arrangements legitimate and intact. For good reason, Hannah Arendt, the great Jewish political philosopher, has asserted that the newness in the Christian gospel is not resurrection but forgiveness.

This intentional subcommunity within the empire practices *hospitality*. It believes that the human community on the earth should be a visibly welcoming home that excludes none. On the horizon of Paul, that means most especially a welcome that breaks down the wall of separation between Jews and Gentiles (Gal 3:28; Eph 2:14). Behind Paul it means for Jews the acceptance of those who are "unclean" in cultic society and those who are unqualified in civil society. Indeed, Jesus' dangerous violation of the rules of acceptance evoked hostility, for dominant society is committed to the exclusion of any "other."

The empire, of course, cannot practice such hospitality. It is committed to gradations of humanness, with some degraded. And therefore access to goods and power requires a rigorous grid of qualification, either by money, pedigree, education, or more blatantly, race or gender. The empire is arranged for the exclusion of the unwelcome, whether gays in the military or immigrants or any who do not conform to the rigorous merit system.

The church, with its grounding in the vulnerability of Friday and the surprise of Sunday, does not take such gradations seriously but imagines a kind of shared legitimacy of all persons in the community. One can see in the Bible and in the long story of the church the slow and grudging embrace of such possibility, for the church has very often imitated the inhospitality of the empire. There is no doubt, however, that in principle the church is committed to hospitality for all, even if practice runs slowly behind principle.

This intentional subcommunity within the empire practices *generosity*. It does so in imitation of and in response to the self-giving of God, who holds nothing back of compassion and mercy for the well being of the world. The deep rootage of generosity is found in creation faith wherein we confess that God has ordered creation for overflowing fruitfulness in which the Creator God assures enough for all:

> The eyes of all look to you,
>   and you give them their food in due season.
> You open your hand,
>   satisfying the desire of every living thing. (Ps 145:15-16)

Thus, table prayers are acknowledgments of divine generosity, the awareness that all that we have is a gift that is freely given, so that we in turn may give.[5]

The empire, of course, cannot be generous. For generosity subverts power arrangements and interrupts our various calculations about merit and qualification. While the Creator God gives free meals, the empire offers no free lunch (except to those who have access to manipulate the levers of distribution). The power of the empire, in our society, is deeply committed to market ideology in which there is no sustaining social fabric but only a ruthless capacity for what one takes to be scarce goods. Such logic, for example, evokes state-ordered violence in the pursuit of scarce oil. In less dramatic fashion, that same ideology of scarcity evokes policies of parsimony to be sure that none of the unentitled get anything extra, most especially health care.

But the church knows better. Even the widespread church practice of meals for homeless persons, timid and limited as such efforts are—given the density of the problem—attests to the church's deep awareness that all are welcome and that generous sharing of resources is a bodily attestation to the good news of the generosity of the Creator God.

When we consider these three taken-for-granted subversive activities of *forgiveness*, *hospitality*, and *generosity*, we can already see a practical theology that contradicts the primal assumptions of the empire. The church, with only modest permit from the empire, characteristically enacts these habits of wild imagination. I suggest, however, that the leadership of the church faces two interpretive tasks with reference to these defining acts of obedience. First, the church should be more intentional in its recognition that these subversive practical habits are not incidental to the church but are its primal characteristics. The church distinguishes itself by these acts in a society that is unforgiving, inhospitable, and unwelcoming. Second, the practical habits that the church willingly undertakes in many places should be understood and interpreted more systemically as impingements on public policy. For the most part, church members lack the capacity to imagine faith in such systemic categories, but the materials are all present for such work. Thus:

- It is no big reach to convert *forgiveness* into prison reform
  (see Ps 107:10-16; 146:7);

- It is easy enough to move from *hospitality* to immigration policy (see Deut 14:28-29; 23:15-16);
- It is obvious that *generosity* relates to health care policy for the "unqualified."

It is not enough, though it is something, that the church should practice its primal habits locally and one-on-one. Historically, the great habits of the church have impinged on public policy, have occasionally instructed the empire, or invited the empire into alliance in the disciplines of humanness.[6]

IV

In the empire, these practical habits are indeed "impossible," for the empire has other commitments that preclude forgiveness, hospitality, and generosity. And because church members—liberal and conservative—are willy-nilly adherents of empire, the practical question is how such church folk can walk such a walk. The simple thesis I propose is that the walk cannot be walked without the talk being talked. Jews—and after them Christians—have always known that speech leads reality, that talk evokes the walk, that the talk—if it is to empower subversive intentionality—must be bold, imaginative, and direct enough to challenge the imperial talk that is all about fear, greed, and control.

Thus, the talk of the church—in sermon, in liturgy, in study—is what Robert Alter has termed "a culture of interpretation" in which the church probes old memories, traditions, and texts and finds new meanings that are interesting, dangerous, and compelling. It is certain that the empire cannot be subverted unless there is a capacity for freedom and boldness in the church to talk alternatively to the ideology of control in the empire. Thus, the first faithful enterprise in the church is not reasoning according to the requirements of the empire but rather narrative, song, and oracle that invite the church out beyond the borders of the empire.

The narrative of the church is characteristically presented as challenge to the empire. Thus, the old narrative of Israel has as its locale the power of Pharaoh: "After a long time the king of Egypt died" (Exod 2:23). What follows is a narrative out beyond Pharaoh: "Let my people go" outside the empire to an alternative life. The narrative of Jesus characteristically begins when "a decree went out from Emperor Augustus" (Luke 2:1); and we confess, "under Pontius Pilate." The narrative of faith always has the empire in purview; but it does not linger over the empire. It goes its own way in joy and freedom, in surprise and vulnerability. With the context of these "big stories," there are "little stories" of gift and surprise (miracles), all of which remember the enactment of that which the empire has declared to be impossible. The work of such a narrative is to recruit listeners into an alternative imagination, so that actions and policies may reflect a reality of freedom, mercy, and justice that remains off limits in the empire.

The song of the church outlines in lyrical fashion an alternative existence grounded in gift. That song stretches from Miriam, in her exultant victory, to Hannah, in her expectation of Messiah, to Mary, in her gladness for the child to come:

> And Miriam sang to them:
>> "Sing to the LORD, for he has triumphed gloriously;
>> horse and rider he has thrown into the sea." (Exod 15:21)

> Those who were full have hired themselves out for bread,
>> but those who were hungry are fat with spoil.
> The barren has borne seven,
>> but she who has many children is forlorn.
> The LORD kills and brings to life;
>> he brings down to Sheol and raises up.
> The LORD makes poor and makes rich;
>> he brings low, he also exalts.
> He raises up the poor from the dust. (1 Sam 2:5-8)

> He has brought down the powerful from their thrones,
>> and lifted up the lowly;
> he has filled the hungry with good things,
>> and sent the rich away empty. (Luke 1:52-53)

These are no innocent "praise hymns" but are attestations to a world beyond imperial administration.

The oracle of the church is poetry by the uncredentialed, to whom "words are given": "Thus saith the LORD." The oracles, so far as pedigree is concerned, come from nowhere. They tell the *truth* of Friday, that loss is coming among those who have chosen death. With equal force they tell the *hope* of Sunday wherein there is an ongoing chorus of those who can say, "I have a dream" . . . of plowshares and pruning hooks, of new covenant when sin is remembered no more, of dry bones turned to homecoming, of newness over the nations who are healed so that there are no more tears.

The *narrative, the song, the oracle* entrusted to the church conjure a new zone of freedom in which *forgiveness, hospitality,* and *generosity* are not odd or scandalous but rather are the only appropriate conduct. What happens through such utterance is that the listening community departs (exodus!) the rigorous world of contained possibility offered by the empire and lives into the world of impossibility that, in the moment of utterance, is heard and received as possibility.

The church wrought through such speech is of sacramental proportion. In such acted speech, we watch while the Holy One *takes* our little lives. We watch while our lives are submitted to a Friday *breaking* and end in Sunday *blessing.* We watch as the Holy One *gives* our lives back to us in generosity. These four verbs of sacramental freight—*he took, he broke, he blessed, he gave*—are the truth of our new life (Mark 6:41; 8:6). Each act in this drama is a dangerous, risky one, never sanctioned by empire. The congregation that relies on the sacrament has been transported into gratitude (Eucharist) that leaves ungrudging and unanxious.

The Jewish counterpoint to Christian *Eucharist* may be *Sabbath*, work stoppage that refuses to let life be defined by the rhythms of production and consumption on which the empire relies. Sabbath time and Sabbath space, Sabbath practice and Sabbath freedom are an antidote to imperial anxiety. As we are rendered unafraid, there is energy of another kind given, energy for the disciplines of humanness.

<h1 style="text-align:center">V</h1>

Thus, I imagine the church to be a venue for the practice of such *talk* and the envisioning of such *walk*. In church, what we do is constituted by *Word and sacrament*, *talk* and *walk* that are freighted with authority that the empire cannot resist or administer. It is all uphill, since we who practice such authority are ourselves too much enthralled by the empire. Even given that, however, the newness happens in church as nowhere else. It happens because the Spirit comes there like the wind. The Spirit comes and invites us be a *catholic unity*. The Spirit comes there and creates a *communion of saints* among the members. The Spirit comes there and enacts *forgiveness*. The Spirit comes there and invites hope of a *bodily Easter* kind with *eternity* writ among us. That is why we dare confess:

> I believe in the Holy Spirit,
> the holy Catholic Church,
> the communion of saints,
> the forgiveness of sins,
> the resurrection of the body,
> and the life everlasting.

The acts we commit in church generate, by the mercy of God, new life. In the generation of new life, moreover, the church becomes unlike the empire; for the empire—like the Egyptians of ancient time—is without Spirit:

> The Egyptians are human, and not God;
>   their horses are flesh, and *not spirit*.
> When the LORD stretches out his hand,
>   the helper will stumble, and the one helped will fall,
>   and they will all perish together. (Isa 31:3)

The empire cannot create community because it specializes in fear. It cannot enact forgiveness, because it depends on coercion. It cannot practice bodily futures, because it is too preoccupied with maintaining the present. It is here and there possible that when the church has its freedom, the empire can be addressed and impinged on, because even the ideology of empire finally cannot withstand the self-giving of Friday or the new life of Sunday. The empire is not a very welcoming venue for the church. But it has been—since Egypt and Bethlehem and Calvary—the inescapable host for Friday and Sunday. Much that is urgent has been entrusted to us who are talkers and walkers—more than the empire has ever thought to be possible.

CHAPTER 15

Faithful Imagination
as Sustained Subversion

IMAGINATION IS THE CAPACITY to picture (image!) the world out beyond what we take as established given.[1] Imagination is an ability to hold loosely what the world assumes and to walk into alternative contours of reality, which we have only in hint and trace. Imagination is the peculiar province of artists, artists of all kinds; it is for that reason that artists are always at the edge of causing trouble, always seen to be troublemakers whom establishment types view with suspicion. The vocation of the artist is to provide a *sub-version* of reality that insistently *subverts* the ordinary.[2]

Behind the artist, however, is a stirring of mystery that evokes and summons and authorizes. The artist knows that there is *more* and *other* that is not available until it is evoked and rendered. Not all artists have a name for that *more* and *other*, but in theological discourse we say that the artist is led by the spirit of God's own holiness, so we may judge that the artist is "in-spired," that is, occupied by the spirit of God's holiness. One could, through such a conviction, insist that all artists are involved in a theological exercise. Here, however, I want to reverse the proposition: all serious theological efforts are in fact *acts of artistic imagination*, acts of "more" and "other" that are, when faithful, rooted in God's own spirit that refuses any close commitment to an established, given world. The artist and the theological interpreter, in very different modes, are led by God's restless, deconstructive holiness out beyond the familiar.

I

I begin with this affirmation: the life, death, and resurrection of Jesus—and the church's ongoing teaching of that cluster of events—constitute an act of immense imagination that intends to subvert all settled social arrangements and power structures.[3]

It is a primal Christian confession that Jesus "suffered under Pontius Pilate, that he was crucified, dead, and buried." They executed him! They executed him because he threatened their order, their advantage, their security systems. He did that because he *out-imagined* them!

Pilate was the official Roman *imaginer*. It was his task to make gestures and speeches and commit public acts that brought all social reality and all social power under Roman authority and Roman explanation. His responsibility as governor was to imagine all social reality in a *total* package and system from Rome. He is a "totalizer," so that nothing could exist or be imagined outside of Roman aegis. His administration is so totalizing that we may say he is totalitarian, as is every force of interpretation that claims the whole of reality.[4] Pilate's effective totalizing is evident in the insistence of the crowd at the trial, "We have no king but Caesar" (John 18:15). The crowd had had its imaginative capacity completely contained in the claims of Rome. Such totalizing is accomplished by a monopoly of power and technology but finally by a mode of interpretation that claims to be final and beyond question. Such totalizing imagination is possible because people submit to it, either out of conviction or out of cynical conformity. The totalizing imagination may be proposed by those in power, but it depends on the collusion of those who submit. The *imaginers* and the *submitters* make common cause for the sake of security and order.

Jesus constituted a dangerous problem for such a totalizing act of imagination, and the authorities were on to him very quickly. Thus, in Mark 1:14-15, he had announced the "kingdom of God": "Now after John was arrested, Jesus came to Galilee, proclaiming the good news of God, and saying, 'The time is fulfilled, and the kingdom of God has come near; repent, and believe in the good news'" (Mark 1:14-15). By Mark 2:7, they had accused him of blasphemy, and by Mark 3:6, the Pharisees conspired with the Herodians against him, how to destroy him. They recognized his subversive threat from day one. He asserted the order and shape and future of the world differently in a way that discredited both the claims of Rome and the claims of local officials who relied on Rome and who colluded with the empire.[5]

Jesus imagined the world differently through his teaching. He said:

- The new regime is like a man who had two sons and welcomed the renegade home who had violated the norms of acceptable society (Luke 15:22-24).

- The new regime is like the owner of a vineyard who paid "the usual daily wage" to his workers without consideration of when they came to work (Matt 20:1-16).
- The new regime is like a dinner party to which outsiders and losers off the street are invited (Luke 14:25-24).
- The new regime is a place that welcomes little children, the ones who have no practical productive value for society (Matt 19:14).
- The new regime is like a bridegroom who arrives in the middle of the night at the home of the bride. He surprises everyone and finds out who has stayed up, fully prepared for his arrival (Matt 25:1-13).
- The new regime is like yeast that bubbles and grows with its own intrinsic energy, not needing to be managed or administered (Matt 13:33).

His teaching was immediately recognized for what it was, a dangerous articulation of an alternative social practice. It was dangerous because it led his listeners—who had uncritically accepted conventional rules of social engagement—to have a second thought, to imagine that their own lives could be different. His teaching was elusive so that the listeners were left free to make connections and fill in the space, so elusive that the authorities did not find it easy to incriminate him even while he called their very existence into question.

Jesus' imaginative teaching of new regime was matched by his actions. His actions were *imaginative performances* of an alternative way in the world. He worked on small scale, one modest incident at a time. The sum of those actions is considerable; but more important than the sum of those actions is the emancipated energy he set loose among those who were called to participate with him in his performance of an alternative world:

- He performed a *world of inclusiveness* by his readiness to eat with people who had been declared impure and unacceptable (Mark 2:16).[6]
- He performed a *world of welcome* in which disqualified sinners without religious or social merit would be at home (Luke 19:1-10).
- He performed *a world with a long neighbor reach* in which strangers came into his purview and were made stakeholders in new social possibilities (Mark 7:24-30).
- He performed *a world of radical discipleship* in which his simple "follow me" was a bid for loyalty and risk, with the downside of abandoning old loyalties to parents, to home, to tradition, to religious and political authorities (Mark 10:17-23).

He preferred traveling lean and without anxiety, because he inhabited a world of generosity, a creation ordered as a gift that keeps on giving.

He worked by small, terse *teaching* and by *actions* that were open-ended enough that "moral lessons" were to be calculated by listeners and observers. He operated by small gestures that we have come to call "miracles." His life was so filled with the *power of rehabilitation* that, everywhere he went, life bloomed and defenders of the old regime were left embarrassed and exposed as frauds. He emitted energy beyond explanation. They asked him, as they watched his imaginative performance, "Are you the one?" (Luke 7:19). He refused a direct answer. He simply called their attention to the evidence that was there for all to see: "And he answered them, 'Go and tell John what you have seen and heard: the blind receive their sight, the lame walk, the lepers are cleansed, the deaf hear, the dead are raised, the poor have good news brought to them'" (Luke 7:22). The world he generated by his presence teemed with restorative energy. His capacity for rehabilitation was in such contrast to the old regime that in fact had no power to bring well being, security, or joy. He imagined and performed the world differently, to show that the world was under alternative management. He made available to those he touched a whole new set of possibilities that the imagination of the Roman governor had declared to be impossible.

The issue is joined! No totalitarian regime can tolerate such subversive teaching and actions that incite the populace against the status quo. The populace sensed that his talk and his walk mocked establishment certitude and had immense social implication. The issue is clear: "Every day he was teaching in the temple. The chief priests, the scribes, and the leaders of the people kept looking for a way to kill him; but they did not find anything they could do, for all the people were spellbound by what they heard" (Luke 19:47-48). He was highly visible in public places, as if courting a confrontation. Luke's report portrays the anxious leaders of the old regime engaged in plotting against him. But the key word in the report is "spellbound." Those who were on the underside of the old regime were mesmerized by the possibilities they sensed in Jesus.

Jesus is treated, according to the narrative, as every unmanageable subversive is treated in the history of official abusiveness. He is brought to trial. The trial before the governor from Rome is a dance of competing imaginations, one *settled* in power, the other *open* in possibility. The Gospel writers—in their own vivid narrative imagination—provide us with something like a transcript of the trial proceedings:[7]

> Pilate: Are you the king of the Jews?
> Jesus: Who wants to know?
> Pilate: What have you done?
> Jesus: My kingdom is not from here.
> Pilate: Are you a king?
> Jesus: You say so . . . but I am to tell the truth.
> Pilate: What is truth?

The governor is bewildered by Jesus, because he has been pushed beyond his comfortable categories of control. Pilate wonders in a moment when his power reaches its limit:

> Which one of us is doing reliable imagination?
> Who is organizing the world according to adequate, trustworthy images?

Pilate does not know the answer to the vexing questions posed by the presence of Jesus:

> Pilate: Where are you from?
> Jesus: [No answer.]
> Pilate: Do you not know that I have power to release or to execute you?
>   Do you know who I am? Do you know with whom you are dealing?
>   Do you know that I have the entire power of Rome behind me?
> Jesus: You have no power over me unless it is given from above.

This statement must have caused the governor to pause; and it causes the later reader to wonder as well. Is the power of the regime God-given? And if it is not, does that regime have legitimacy?

> Jesus would not play the games of the governor;
> Jesus would not submit to the power of the old regime;
> Jesus would not submit to the traditions of settled certitude.
> He would not do so because he imagined the world differently.

Jesus grew up imagining differently, because from his infancy he had heard his mother Mary singing to him. She sang an alternative version of reality that is rooted deeply in Judaism that has behind it the Old Testament. She sang:

> He has shown strength with his arm;
>   he has scattered the proud in the thoughts of their hearts.
> He has brought down the powerful from their thrones,
>   and lifted up the lowly;
> he has filled the hungry with good things,
>   and sent the rich away empty. (Luke 1:51-53)

Mary, his mother, sang of the God who has subverted all dominating power and all settled economics. Mary did not blink at moving her praise of God into the public spheres of politics and economics. That same connection of *doxology* and *political economy* is everywhere in the old tradition of Israel. Mary taught him this counterintuitive stuff; and because of that, he could not accept established versions of social reality. He could not curb his emancipated, spirit-led imagination in order to submit to settled assumptions. He played out—in talk and in walk—this counterintuitive version of reality. His followers called it "gospel," news that the world in truth is not organized as they say it is.

He taught in bits and pieces. He acted locally and concretely. But he drew all of his ad hoc teaching and his ad hoc performances into an elusive phrasing, "kingdom of God." The phrase offers a political image; but the phrase is also freighted with traces of revelation and hints of holy mystery that do not usually connect to the political. His entire ministry is committed to an alternative way in the world, a way that appeals outside the ordinary and, in the process, delegitimates settled authority. He called disciples to walk his elusive walk with him. He called his disciples to sign on for his imagined world of which they could have only glimpses. He called them to enact "impossibilities" that the power of God would make possible. He set in motion a subversion of the known world that is led by *imagination* but that takes *concrete, bodily form* in the world, so concrete that it unnerves the managers of old power.

My theme is imagination and the kingdom of God. But I transpose it into a contest of competing imaginations, for the old world is also an act of sustained imagination. Indeed, the old order has been imagined for so long and with such certitude that we come to regard it as a substantive given. It is in fact a consensus imagination of signs, symbols, and gestures that we take as a given. And when we entertain the oddness of Jesus, we can see that his performance begins to expose "settled reality" as a fragile act of imagination.

I take my lead from William Cavanaugh and his extraordinary book *Torture and Eucharist*.[8] Cavanaugh reflects on the sorry story of Chile under the regime of Augusto Pinochet and his generals. That regime instituted a massive, shameless rule of terror and intimidation that was sustained by torture. It created a state of total surveillance, in which none—not even in families—could trust anyone, because society was filled with informers. The purpose of the torture and surveillance, concludes Cavanaugh, was to make trust impossible and so to preclude any form of community.[9] And when community is made impossible, there is nothing left but the totalism of the state.

Eventually, after much too long, the Roman Catholic bishops became alert to the crisis created by Pinochet. They responded, finally, to the crisis by seeing that the Eucharist, with its mystery of generous abundance, was an antidote to torture. In the Eucharist, people began to be drawn into community where they could again entrust their lives to each other. And when community was revitalized, the lethal state of intimidation became less a threat.

What may interest us is the way in which Cavanaugh interprets this context, which he does through a reading of the novel *Imagining Argentina*. The novel asserts,

> They can only see the conflict in terms of fantasy versus reality.
> Carlos on the other hand rightly grasps that the contest is not between

imagination and the real, but between types of imagination, of the generals and the opponents. . . . Carlos realizes he has been living with the
imagination of the generals. . . . As long as he accepts what the men in
the car imagine, we are finished. . . . We have to believe in the power
of imagination, because it is all we have, and ours is stronger than
theirs.[10]

To participate in the Eucharist is to live inside God's imagination.

I appeal to the conclusion drawn by Cavanaugh because it illuminates the
situation of Jesus before Pilate as he enacted an alternative kingdom that placed
the kingdom of Pilate and of Rome in jeopardy. It was inevitable that Pilate
would execute Jesus, because totalitarian imagination cannot tolerate alternative, subversive imagination. The teaching and the action of Jesus, taken in all
its parts together, is the enactment of an alternative imagination that insists
that the transformative power of the holy God is alive in the world. It is a sovereign power that finally will prevail, albeit through vulnerability. And therefore
it merits and evokes loyalty. To enter the kingdom of God, so Jesus tells his
disciples, is to talk the talk and walk the walk of this alternative imagination,
an imagination that bespeaks forgiveness, generosity, vulnerability, abundance,
and finally justice.

II

Jesus did not enact this subversive counterimagination de novo. And therefore
we may *read backward* to the sources of imagination that shaped, nurtured, and
sustained Jesus and his movement.

When we read backward from Jesus and the teaching of the New Testament,
we come, in the Old Testament, first of all, to *the book of Daniel*, likely the latest
literature of the Old Testament.[11] In that collection of heroic tales, we come to
Nebuchadnezzar, the great, brutal totalizer of his time. Whatever may be said of
the history of Nebuchadnezzar in the book of Daniel, he is, in this literature, a
cipher for abusive, self-serving power. He demands total allegiance from Daniel
and his friends:

> Nebuchadnezzar said to them, "Is it true, O Shadrach, Meshach, and
> Abednego, that you do not serve my gods and you do not worship the
> golden statue that I have set up? Now if you are ready when you hear
> the sound of the horn, pipe, lyre, trigon, harp, drum, and entire musical
> ensemble to fall down and worship the statue that I have made, well and
> good. But if you do not worship, you shall immediately be thrown into a
> furnace of blazing fire, and who is the god that will deliver you out of my
> hands?" (Dan 3:14-15)

But Daniel would not give in to such a requirement, because he knew of another governance. He responds to the demand of Nebuchadnezzar:

> Shadrach, Meshach, and Abednego answered the king, "O Nebuchad-
> nezzar, we have no need to present a defense to you in this matter. If our
> God whom we serve is able to deliver us from the furnace of blazing fire
> and out of your hand, O king, let him deliver us. But if not, be it known
> to you, O king, that we will not serve your gods and we will not worship
> the golden statue that you have set up." (Dan 3:16-18)

His refusal, a characteristic Jewish refusal, is grounded in the conviction of another God, another governance, another regime.

This is the same Daniel who, in another narrative, is summoned to interpret the nightmare of Nebuchadnezzar. Daniel was afraid to tell Nebuchadnezzar the meaning of his dream, because the news is not good. But finally he must announce to Nebuchadnezzar the meaning of the dream, that his governance cannot resist the larger governance of the God of heaven:

> This is the interpretation, O king, and it is a decree of the Most High
> that has come upon my lord the king. You shall be driven away from
> human society, and your dwelling shall be with the wild animals. You
> shall be made to eat grass like oxen, you shall be bathed with the dew of
> heaven, and seven times shall pass over you, until you have learned that
> the Most High has sovereignty over the kingdom of mortals, and gives it
> to whom he will. (Dan 4:24-25)

It is a hard lesson for the totalizer, but one that the rhetoric of "kingdom of God" in the Bible continually attests. Daniel, the Jew, does more than announce to Nebuchadnezzar the sovereignty of the Most High. He also offers to Nebuchadnezzar a characteristically Jewish admonition about how to respond to that divine sovereignty: "Therefore, O king, may my counsel be acceptable to you: atone for your sins with righteousness, and your iniquities with mercy to the oppressed, so that your prosperity may be prolonged" (Dan 4:27). The key issue in this alternative governance is *mercy and righteousness to the oppressed*. These are the marks of the kingdom of God. Daniel intrudes on raw power and speaks the truth of mercy, a truth that always checks and subverts raw power. The point of this governance is reiterated in the narrative:

> You shall be driven away from human society, and your dwelling shall
> be with the animals of the field. You shall be made to eat grass like oxen,
> and seven times shall pass over you, until you have learned that the Most
> High has sovereignty over the kingdom of mortals and gives it to whom
> he will. (Dan 4:32)

The end of the tale is remarkable. In due course, after abjection and humiliation, Nebuchadnezzar is restored to power: "When that period was over, I, Nebuchadnezzar, lifted my eyes to heaven, and my reason returned to me" (Dan 4:34a).
His reason returned. He recovered his sanity. He had become insane with his
imagined autonomy. The measure of his sanity, moreover, is that he breaks out in
doxology to God:

> I blessed the Most High,
>   and praised and honored the one who lives forever.
> For his sovereignty is an everlasting sovereignty,
>   and his kingdom endures from generation to generation.
> All the inhabitants of the earth are accounted as nothing,
>   and he does what he wills with the host of heaven
>   and the inhabitants of the earth.
> There is no one who can stay his hand
>   or say to him, "What are you doing?" (Dan 4:34b-35)

His "reason" is the recognition of his proper place in the world, subject to the
ultimate rule of God Most High who is marked by truth and justice that overrides
all human pretension:

> Now, I, Nebuchadnezzar, praise and extol and honor the King of heaven,
> for all his works are truth,
>   and his ways are justice;
> and he is able to bring low
>   those who walk in pride. (Dan 4:37)

This narrative fantasy exhibits the way in which Nebuchadnezzar—unlike
Pilate—came to learn enough about the rule of God to recover his penultimate
governance.

If we read behind the book of Daniel and that fictional account of Nebuchadnezzar to the historical Nebuchadnezzar in the sixth century BCE, we will come to
the figure of Cyrus, the great Persian king who ended Babylonian imperial power
and who is regarded in the Old Testament as the great rescuer of Israel. There is
no doubt that in this rendition of Cyrus as rescuer, there is a great deal of political
calculation on the part of contemporary Jewish interpreters. They were eager to
have a friendly imperial power at hand. Without denying that knowing calculation, we can listen to Israel's poetic acknowledgement of Cyrus. In the poetic
imagination of Israel, YHWH speaks:

> I stirred up one from the north, and he has come,
>   from the rising of the sun he was summoned by name.
> He shall trample on rulers as on mortar,

> as the potter treads clay.
> Who declared it from the beginning, so that we might know,
>   and beforehand, so that we might say, "He is right"?
> There was no one who declared it, none who proclaimed,
>   none who heard your words.
> I first have declared it to Zion,
>   and I give to Jerusalem a herald of *good tidings*. (Isa 41:25-27)

The claim is that it was YHWH who "stirred up" Cyrus. In the purview of the Isaiah tradition, this is the "gospel news," that YHWH has authorized and summoned a world leader with power to turn the course of human history.[12]

We know, from many sources, that Cyrus initiated the great Persian Empire that was the dominant force in the world for over a century, until its defeat at the hands of the Greeks at Marathon and Salamis. When one takes this dominance in terms of realpolitik, there is no doubt that Cyrus and the Persians after him were wise administrators and ruthless military agents. That was enough to have a season of domination. Cyrus knew no more than this, and thought no more than this.

In the Bible, however, all such historical reality is processed through the imagination of Israel and is taken as a venue for the workings of God. With reference to Cyrus, Israel, in the lines of Isaiah, affirms a most remarkable imaginative act.

> Thus say the LORD, your Redeemer,
>
> . . . .
>   who says of Cyrus, "He is my shepherd,
>   and he shall carry out all my purpose";
> and who says of Jerusalem, "It shall be rebuilt,"
>   and of the temple, "Your foundation shall be laid." (Isa 44:24, 28)

In this poetry, it is YHWH who has dispatched and authorized Cyrus for the purpose of the restoration of Jerusalem. And in the next verse, the poetry of Isaiah goes further:

> Thus says the LORD to his
>   *anointed*, to Cyrus,
> whose right hand I have grasped
> to subdue nations before him
>   and strip kings of their robes,
> to open doors before him—
>   and the gates shall not be closed. (Isa 45:1)

Most remarkably, this poetry has God identify the Persian Cyrus as "my anointed," which in Greek is rendered as "my Christ." This is, to be sure, an act of poetic imagination. But what an act it is, whereby world history is transposed so that even great world leaders are recruited for the purposes of YHWH in the historical process! When Isaiah is finished, Cyrus has become an agent and a regent in the kingdom of God, the realm of public power that will be ordered according to the purpose of God. It is a great poetic stretch, but the outcome is to assert that Cyrus, not unlike Jesus after him, is performing a governance other than his own. In the purview of the poetry, the governance in which Cyrus is at work is a governance about restoration and transformation toward justice.

When we read back further into the Old Testament, behind Nebuchadnezzar and behind Cyrus, we come to *the prophet Jeremiah*, whom we may take as representative of the prophetic practice of the kingdom of God. The prophets are fundamentally poets. They set out to imagine a world other than the one that is visible in front of us. But their imagination is thoroughly grounded in the social scene that is before them. In Jeremiah 22, we may consider a poetic oracle in which the prophet deals with kings in Jerusalem, the ones who, in prophetic perspective, had set Jerusalem on a path of self-destruction. In verses 13-15a, Jeremiah offers a poem that is addressed to King Jehoiachim. We get a flavor of the subversive imagination of the kingdom of God when we consider the odd behavior of offering a *poem* to a *king*. The poem begins with "woe," a term that means big trouble is coming that will lead to death. The "woe" is followed by five participial verbs that describe the failed conduct and policy of the king:

Woe to him:

- who builds his house in unrighteousness and his upper rooms with injustice. The word pair "righteousness and justice" refers to covenantal solidarity. The negative, "unrighteousness and injustice," refers to the disregard of covenantal solidarity;
- who makes his neighbors work for nothing;
- who does not give them their wages. The question of the kingdom of God is always about economics, and the generous treatment of the poor. The prophet sees that the king is so well off because of cheap labor policies;
- who says, "I will build myself a spacious house with larger upper rooms";
- who cuts windows for it, panels it with cedar, and paints it with vermillion.

The point being royal, extravagant, exhibitionist self-indulgence. And then the poet poses for the king a rhetorical question:

- Do you think you are a king because you have a cedar panel office?
- Do you think you count for something because you have a big car and a deep portfolio?

The poem amounts to a delegitmation of the king, an exposé of his fraudulent rule.

Then the poem turns, most spectacularly, to the father of the king, the previous king, Josiah (vv. 15b-16). Unlike Jehoiachim, his father, Josiah, is reckoned as a good king:

> Did not your father eat and drink,
>   and do justice and righteousness?

This is the same word pair used above, only this time used positively. This is what makes for valid governance: "He judged the poor and the needy." That is, he intervened for them and had policies that protected them. The contrast of son and father makes the crucial point about "kingdom" when it is related to "God." The kingdom of God occurs when there is justice and righteousness toward the vulnerable. It is enacted through a human agent—like Josiah—but it is in sync with the will and purpose of God.

The point is reinforced in the next chapter of Jeremiah, in a poem wherein Jeremiah anticipates a coming time with a better king. "Behold the days are coming . . ." A conventional formula for hope:

> I will raise up from David a Righteous Branch;
> He will deal wisely and execute justice
> And righteousness in the land. (Jer 23:5)

We Christians sometimes read this as though it were an anticipation of Jesus, the Branch of David. But in the first instance, this is not an anticipation of Jesus but a Jewish conviction that God will restore valid leadership. The important point, yet again, is a governance marked by justice and righteousness, that is, a commitment to the common good whereby the weak and the strong, the poor and the rich are bound together in creating an infrastructure in which all are safe and none are under threat. Wherever governance becomes preoccupied with self-serving advantage, with the pursuit of extravagance, with the protection of the elites, with the exhibition of wealth or power, we may be sure it is a kingdom that is disassociated from the will of God.

If we read back behind Daniel, Cyrus, and Jeremiah, we will come to *the Psalter*, where Israel at worship in Jerusalem sings of the coming kingdom of God. Psalm 96 is a typical song of enthronement, whereby worship in the temple is a doxological act of recognizing the coming rule of God and in a liturgical way effecting the rule of God.[13]

The psalm begins with a summons to praise YHWH, the God who has just now come to power as king. It names the name of YHWH three times (vv. 1-2a):

> Sing to YHWH a new song,
> Sing to YHWH, all the earth,
> Sing to YHWH.

It continues with three imperatives that refer to YHWH's name, salvation, glory, and marvelous works (vv. 2b-3):

> Bless his name,
> Tell of his salvation,
> Declare his glory among the nations,
> His marvelous works among all peoples.

Then, in verses 5-6, the psalm contrasts the majesty, strength, and beauty of YHWH with the other gods, who are pitiful frauds who do not merit attention. If kept within the liturgy, this contrast is dramatic. But it cannot be contained there. It inevitably spills over into political rhetoric. And when it spills over, it becomes an invitation to a revolutionary subversion of all other power.

I believe that the principle accent in the psalm is to be found in verse 10: "Say among the nations, 'YHWH has just become king.'" This way of translating the line means that this hour of liturgy is the moment when, by the praise of Israel in the temple, YHWH comes to new power and authority. This liturgy is understood as a political act of effecting the new governance of YHWH and at the same time swearing allegiance to it. That new governance—which amounts to regime change—is to be asserted among all nations.

This is "the good news" of the gospel, a new governance that will make the world right. This "good news," of course, is not good news for old regimes. It is bad news for Nebuchadnezzar and for Cyrus and for Rome and for any who thought they could govern in injustice and unrighteousness. Thus, in the New Testament, when we observe Jesus committing acts of feeding and forgiving and healing, what we witness are signs of the new governance of God that will turn the world to justice, righteousness, compassion, and mercy. And one can see in the gospel narratives how "the old powers" immediately want to stop him because the coming regime of God's justice and righteousness is a threat to all old self-serving regimes.

In Psalm 96, the new regime is marked by equity, righteousness, and truth:

> He will judge the peoples with *equity*.
> . . . .
> He will judge the world with *righteousness*,
>   and the peoples with his *truth*. (vv. 10, 13)

The psalm reports, in glad doxology, the wild reception the new regime receives from the various creatures:

> The heavens are glad,
> The earth rejoices,
> The sea roars its approval,

The field exults,
The trees of the forest sing for joy. (vv. 11-12)

The sea and the fields and the trees celebrate; they recognize that the new king is the Creator God, who will care for all creation. The new king will stop the pollution of the oceans, will stop the exploitation of the fields, will stop the deforestation of the trees. The new king will enact policies that let the world be safe and creation whole again. No wonder there is joy in heaven and on earth. The Christmas carol echoes the psalm: "Let heaven and nature sing . . ."

If we read back behind Daniel and Cyrus and Jeremiah and the Psalms, finally we will come *to Moses and his dealings with Pharaoh*. In the Old Testament, Pharaoh is the grand totalizer who, in totalitarian ways, had a monopoly on food and land (Gen 47:13-26). Such a regime inevitably must depend on cheap labor to sustain itself. Moses, who identifies with that cheap labor force that served the regime of Pharaoh, is stirred to action by a voice he hears amid the burning bush (Exod 3:1-6). He is stirred enough to be able to envision another place for existence beyond the reach of Pharaoh, a land flowing with milk and honey (Exod 3:8). It is as though he walked away from the burning bush and declared, "I have a dream." He moved to turn the *vision* and the *dream* to *policy*. Moses forced the political-economic issue on Pharaoh, who responded with immense resistance; for he did not want to lose his supply of cheap labor. Moses proceeded to the departure with no technology or with no official power or credential. He committed an enormous act of political imagination and persuaded some of his fellow laborers to wall into the alternative dream with him. He entertained the thought of a world outside Pharaoh's system of exploitative labor. And so he said, on behalf of the new God who had authorized him: "Let my people go!" (Exod 5:1). Let them go, outside the Egyptian kingdom of death. Let them go to the possibility of new life that cannot be received in a system of violent exploitation.

The exodus narrative is a contest between the old regime of Pharaoh—a regime that became a metaphor for all exploitative governance—and the new rule of YHWH that ensures well being to all its adherents.[14] The drama of the contrast passes through all the plagues of frogs (Exod 8:1-15) and gnats (Exod 8:16-19) and flies (Exod 8:20-24). They come, finally, to the edge of the water that is the edge of the empire. And when they have crossed the waters, Moses sings freedom, Miriam and her sisters shake their tambourines and dance, and all offer doxology to YHWH:

Sing to YHWH,
for he has triumphed gloriously,
The horse and its rider he has thrown into the sea. (Exod 15:21)

The Song of Moses in Exod 15:1-18 is longer than the Song of his sister Miriam in verse 21. Moses sings the entire narrative of faith all the way from slavery to the new land of well being. He sings of the death of Pharaoh, who sinks like lead to the bottom of the sea:

> At the blast of your nostrils the waters piled up,
>   the floods stood up in a heap;
>   the deeps congealed in the heart of the sea.
> The enemy said, "I will pursue, I will overtake,
>   I will divide the spoil, my desire shall have its fill of them.
>   I will draw my sword, my hand shall destroy them."
> You blew with your wind, the sea covered them;
>   they sank like lead in the mighty waters. (Exod 15:8-10)

The song moves toward its great doxological conclusion wherein Moses and all of Israel sing of the new rule of YHWH: "The LORD will reign forever and ever" (Exod 15:18).

The exodus event is the route by which YHWH comes to power in the world. This liturgy of the exodus is the way in which YHWH is regularly celebrated as king. In Christian practice, moreover, Easter is the version of the same enthronement whereby the kingdom of God comes to visibility. This verse 18, I suspect, is the one from which Handel's *Messiah* took the great phrasing of the Hallelujah Chorus, "And he shall reign forever and ever and ever." The "Hallelujah" names YHWH as the new king. It also implies, undoubtedly, do not praise Pharaoh or any of the kings who practice injustice and unrighteousness, for they have been dethroned and are no longer legitimate forces in the world.

Notice that in the drama of Moses and Pharaoh, and in all of the derivative exchanges that I have cited, the action is poetic and elusive. It has, to be sure, political, economic, and military spin-offs, but it is first of all imagination that subverts. The process of imagination is to delegitimate and then to acknowledge newness. The poetry is a way to sign on for the new obedience and new loyalty to the new regime that lives by song and by metaphor and by poem. The old regime regularly refuses the poem and resists the song. The contest continues, and we are recruited into the contest for the new regime. The old regime always tries to eliminate the poets in order to stop the alternative imagination. What they find, however, is that poetry is enormously elusive—and will have its say.

III

In Christian affirmation, the substance and the reality of the kingdom of God pivots on Jesus of Nazareth. By his imaginative word and his imaginative action he subverted all conventional practices of power and all conventional claims for truth. I have proposed that while Jesus' enactment of the kingdom of God is defining in its force and authority, his enactment arises from Israel's long tradition of subversive imagination. For that reason I have *read back* from Jesus, all the way to Moses to whom YHWH, the Lord of the new regime, disclosed divine name, divine purpose, and divine power.

But in order to engage and appropriate this tradition of subversive imagination, we need now to *read forward* from Jesus concerning all those who have enlisted in subversive imagination in order to enact the kingdom of God:

We may begin by reading forward from Jesus to the book of Acts. As the evangelist Luke has arranged it, the book of Acts is the "second volume" after his volume on Jesus, the "second act" in the drama of the kingdom of God. In the book of Acts the early church was propelled by the Holy Spirit, by the Spirit of Jesus. They were preachers and healers. By their actions and their sermons, they attested that the world was under new management (see, e.g., Acts 2:22-24; Acts 4:1-2). So bold and daring was their testimony that they were regularly brought to trial and given opportunity to attest to their faith (Acts 4:3; Acts 21:27-36; 24:1-9). It is clear that by their performance of the new governance, they made all establishment governance nervous concerning its grip on authority. It is for that reason that they were said to be turning the world upside down (Acts 17:6). They did so simply by asserting the resurrection of Jesus and making the claim that the old powers of death were no longer capable of defining reality. They attested that new power had been turned loose in the world that evoked new patterns of social practice and new waves of truth.

Read forward beyond the Bible, and we will find the continuing surge of those who have heard the voice in the bush and have caught the vision of the new land and have invested their lives in a dream that lingers and that here and there comes to fruition. Many of those dreamers belong to the traditions of the Bible and to church faith. But many do not, because the coming regime of God is not a churchy thing. It is a human thing, and *all sorts of human persons* have joined the enactment of subversive alternative. It is likely, moreover, that if we knew more, we would discover that there are among *nonhuman creatures*—apes and geese and whales and radishes and melons—also creatures of God who have joined this dangerous enterprise. We do know that in some nonhuman species there are those who are more nurturing and more ready to contribute to the common good. And we do know that nonhuman creatures are summoned to the same doxology of the new regime:

> Praise the LORD from the earth,
>   you sea monsters and all deeps,
> fire and hail, snow and frost,
>   stormy wind fulfilling his command!
> Mountains and all hills,
>   fruit trees and all cedars!
> Wild animals and all cattle,
>   creeping things and flying birds!

Kings of the earth and all peoples,
>   princes and all rulers of the earth!
Young men and women alike,
>   old and young together!
Let them praise the name of the Lord,
>   for his name alone is exalted;
>   his glory is above earth and heaven. (Ps 148:7-13)

Imagine that. The new regime is welcomed and embraced by sea monsters and fruit trees and cattle and wild animals and creeping things and flying birds—all gladly come to terms with the Creator and the new creation. In his teaching about this newness, Jesus observed that sparrows shun anxiety because they trust the goodness of God, and lilies are unworried because they know about the reliability of God. Indeed, we might imagine that of all the creatures it is the human species that has the most difficult time welcoming the new regime, because we continue to have the illusion that we could organize the world better—or at least according to our own interests and predilections.

We do not know so much yet about nonhuman creatures and their embrace of God's kingdom. We know enough to imagine it. But we can confine ourselves to the human species where we have some clear evidence.

First, we can name *the great bishops* in the early church who, according to historian Peter Brown, invented the social category of "the poor" in order that those with power and resources would notice and take responsibility for vulnerable brothers and sisters.[15] And we know from Moses and Jeremiah and Daniel that notice of the poor is a sign of the kingdom.

Second, we can notice that in the great sixteenth century, the thoughtful monk *Martin Luther* dared to say that it was grace and not bargaining commodities that is the clue to the world, a grace that embodies the new rule of God. And *the pesky Mennonites* came soon alongside Luther and bore witness to the truth that kingdom action happens outside the order of power. These latter have, since then, worked beyond the halls of power for the sake of mercy and compassion and reconciliation.

Third, when we look more closely at our own time and place, it is clear that the new regime is not without witnesses and adherents among whom we can easily name *Dietrich Bonhoeffer*, who risked life in confession for the lordship of Jesus against the old regime of evil. And Archbishop *Oscar Romero*, who challenged and challenged until the forces of evil caught him at the Communion table and killed him. And Bishop *Desmond Tutu*, with his easy laugh and his ready heart, refused the regime of apartheid and joined the walk to freedom and fife. The modern history of the world is one of violence; and where violence pertains, there we will find those who refuse to accept and who risk for the sake of alternative.

Fourth, alongside those I have mentioned, there is of course *Martin Luther King*, who dreamed the dream and walked the walk and who refused to give in to the power of hate and violence; he created new possibilities among us, some of which have become law in our land.

After we have named Dietrich and Oscar and Desmond and Martin, we are bound to say that there are *legions of saints*, over time and now—some whose names we do not know, some we know—who have surged on with the new regime.[16] These are the ones who have embodied hospitality and generosity and forgiveness and mercy and compassion and justice, who have made a different life in the world possible. Some have run great risks, some have played it safe, but the whole company has determined to join the procession toward newness out beyond the rule of Pharaoh, out beyond the truth of the Roman Empire, out beyond the commoditization of society, out beyond the zone of hate and violence and exploitation and oppression and abuse.

We are bound to notice, moreover, that not all of the saints are found in the church, because God's generative spirit works where it will.

The call has reached those great spirits whom we have come to call *the Masters of Suspicion*: Sigmund Freud, who learned that human freedom came in truthfulness, and Karl Marx, who came to know that economic justice is a deep truth in the human community that cannot be done on the cheap.[17]

And in our time, *Václav Havel*—without religious connection—wrote his novels and poems that caused a shift of power in Eastern Europe. And *Nelson Mandela*, rooted in a religious tradition quite other than ours, maintained a dignity of self and a zone of freedom in the face of human degradation in order to create a new society. You can add to that list of prophets and martyrs any number of poets and artists who have refused to conform to the rule of Herod and the brick quotas of Pharaoh and have taken the road less traveled that has led, over and over, via wilderness, to new creation.

IV

And now *us* vis-à-vis the *kingdom of God*. In the great chapter of Hebrews 11, the writer names many of the great names of faith in ancient Israel. And after that long list, the chapter ends this way: "Yet all these, though they were commended for their faith, did not receive what was promised, since God had provided something better so that they would not, apart from us, be made perfect" (Heb 11:39-40). The conclusion drawn is a most astonishing one. All of those great characters that lived courageous faith depend on us for validation and "perfection." Through our courageous faith, they will be "made perfect." Without our courageous faith in our own context, their risky faith will have been in vain. The purpose of this chapter that lists the risk-runners of the past is not simply an act of memory. The chapter is written in order to summon contemporary persons of faith to courage in their daily lives.

We are carriers of faith in the kingdom of God along with that whole company of risk-takers, or perhaps we are their grandchildren. We are children of the vision of Moses and the Song of Mary and the Dream of Martin. And we, like them, are haunted by the question of Pilate, the governor:

> What is truth?
> Which imagination is reliable?

Those questions, very old and most contemporary, are the central questions of the educational process in which we are engaged:

> Whose truth will you accept?
> Whose imagination will you inhale?

The matter is always a current one, and it is a current one now: it is easiest to sign on with the totalizers in the national security state, who are echoed by the religious totalizers who know all the answers ahead of time. Or it is easiest to refuse such totalizing commitments and drop out and imagine autonomous freedom to go one's own way, as though the world began when we were born. Or it is easiest to grow cynical, utilize the system and make money but not believe or care at all.

But of course, when we gather around the biblical imagination concerning the kingdom of God, we are immediately placed in profound tension with all of these ready temptations. The matter of imaginative, subversive, demanding claim is peculiarly urgent among us:

- *The matter is urgent* because our consumer economy reduces every-thing and everyone to a commodity, just as Pharaoh had done.
- *The matter is urgent* because U.S. militarism now stalks the earth and generates resistance among local cultures and local economies; the enormous, unrestrained power of the U.S. military is itself a reflection of the pervasive violence that marks our society.
- *The matter is urgent* because the public infrastructure of our soci-ety—health, education, housing, jobs—are all at risk, and we increas-ingly seek to go "on the cheap" about everything except military assertiveness.
- *The matter is urgent* because our use and abuse of the earth is rapa-cious and cannot be sustained, even in the interest of a growing economy.

And then there is this counterimagination that has been "counter" since Moses at the burning bush. This counterimagination refuses and resists, but then imagines and acts generatively. We can read back from Jesus as far as Moses. We can read forward from Jesus as far as Martin Luther King and Desmond Tutu. But finally, the metaphor focuses on Jesus, who in his initial utterance gathered the entire tradition of faith for his moment of self-announcement: "Now after John was arrested, Jesus came to Galilee, proclaiming the good news of God, and saying, 'The time is fulfilled, and the kingdom of God has come near; repent, and believe in the good news'" (Mark 1:14-15). This claim at the beginning of the life of Jesus pushes us to the pivot point at the end of his life in the exchange with Pilate the governor:

> *Either* to stand with the totalizers,
> *or* to walk with the subverters,
> because there is no middle ground.

The kingdom of God:

- is a cipher for a world of impossibility grounded by God;
- is an act of imagination that calls into question dominant imagination;
- is an act of imagination that is powered by God's own spirit;
- is an act of imagination that remains elusive and cannot be reduced to blueprint; thus, Jesus articulated it as parable;
- is an act of imagination that, soon or late, puts its carriers at risk;
- is an act of imagination on which the future of the world depends. The world cannot be reduced to commodity, power, violence, and aggressive self-regard. It depends on the holiness of God who makes our self-securing efforts inescapably penultimate and sure to fail.

Pilate's question is still on the table. The question in our time, as in every time, evokes poets and such who act and suffer, who hope and wait, and who do not, even in the long run, lose heart or give in.

CHAPTER 16

Scriptural Strategies against Exclusionary Absolutism

GOD HAS PLACED THE U.S. CHURCH in a situation of enormous risk.[1] It is a risk brought on mostly because of policies and attitudes rooted in a conviction of exceptionalism, but it is nonetheless a risk that is deep and broad, and generative of enormous anxiety. The by-products of that systemic anxiety include, on the one hand, denial among those who do not want to face the risk and, on the other hand, despair among those who see the risk but can imagine no way beyond it. The two by-products of anxiety, denial and despair, have resulted in a variety of strategies aimed at exclusionary absolutism, based on the fearful assumption that elimination of the "other" will ease the anxiety and bring well being and security.

I have no doubt that the matrix of anxiety, denial, despair, and exclusionary absolutism is a dense and complex social phenomenon well beyond my under-standing. But since religion is much at play in this matrix and since it impinges on the life and faith and missional energy of the church, all of us must consider it well. Thus, I consider the self-selection into Red and Blue communities of hous-ing, jobs, schools, and churches to be a matter of enormous concern. Even a scrip-tural exegete must wonder about the issue, even though scriptural exegesis is far from the center of our most common concerns.

I understand, of course, that there is no easy interface between the contempo-rary "Big Sort" and Scripture, but I will seek to make a useful connection through this thesis:[2] the temptation to exclusionary absolutism is an old and deep and recurring seduction in the community of faith. But one can also detect scriptural strategies—by which I mean interpretive strategies undertaken by those who put the Bible together—that seek to resist such exclusionary absolutism that is char-acteristically rooted in anxiety. I will use my time and energy to consider three such interpretive strategies, with the suggestion that these same strategies are now available in our interpretive practices and may be useful in present circumstance for the sustenance and maintenance of church unity and church fidelity.

I

The first such strategy I mention is the recognition that, nearly to the bottom of the tradition, interpretation was conducted in pluralistic modes that refused any simple settlement in a single unitary interpretive voice. I say "nearly to the bottom of the tradition," because at the very bottom there was a singular unity. In the Old Testament, as von Rad has made clear, that singular unity attested, "He brought us out of Egypt with a strong hand and an outstretched arm and brought us into a good land."[3] In the New Testament church, as C. H. Dodd among others has seen, that singular unity affirmed, "He was crucified according to scripture and raised, according to scripture on the third day."[4] Or as we say,

> Christ has died,
> Christ is risen,
> Christ will come again.

At bottom unity. But as soon as the community, Israel, or the church has uttered an interpretive syllable about any of these mantras, the tradition has gone pluralistic. That is why I say, "nearly to the bottom."

That pluralism in the Old Testament has been featured and articulated in a way familiar to you in the so-called Documentary Hypothesis, that is, JEDP. I assume that most people do not sit around and think about JEDP; but the terms, Germanic in articulation, reflect an interpretive strategy that resists exclusionary absolutism. When most of us went to seminary, the matter of JEDP was used to explain and identify the evolutionary development of Israelite religion from primitive to sophisticated, from polytheism to monotheism, from magic to ethics. J, we said, was early, polytheistic, and magical; D was sophisticated, monotheistic, and ethical. I would not take time with this if that were still a viable hypothesis. Current scholarship, however, takes the sources, JEDP, to be contemporary with each other and not arranged in a sequence; rather, they are seen as deeply rooted competing interpretive trajectories, all of which are early, all of which are late, all of which vie for airtime as the true rendering of the bottom-line credo. Particular attention is now given to D and P, and I will exposit these, when taken together, as a textual strategy for pluralism that resists exclusionary absolutism.

At Sinai, all of Israel remembered exodus, all of Israel received the Decalogue, and all of Israel swore allegiance to the covenant. Within a nanosecond of Sinai, however, Israel discovered that the Sinai data permitted and required interpretation; as soon as Israel took the first step into interpretation, Israel found itself in a pluralistic practice of how to render, perceive, and teach Sinai. That competitive pluralism over time organized itself into two powerful interpretive trajectories, the Priestly and the Deuteronomic. We can imagine that both of these interpretive offers were loud, credible, and insistent. The Primary Narrative of Israel's memory from Genesis through 2 Kings, the narrative from creation to exile, divides into two sections, divided at the Jordan River and the entry into the land of promise.

It is now agreed that the Priestly tradition, very old in Israel and made contemporary in sixth-century exile, dominates the first four books, Genesis through Numbers. It is this tradition that authorized the ritual practices of Sabbath and circumcision. And as you know, it is this Priestly tradition that offers the holiness accent of Exodus and Numbers and most especially Leviticus. It was a deep conviction of the priests that Israel must create a holy environment if it wanted to host the holiness of God, and therefore the accent is on purity and cleanness. Conversely, what is unclean and impure constitutes an affrontive abomination to God and will drive out the holy God, who will not dwell among an unholy people.

Thus, the many repetitions of Leviticus are an attempt to organize the ritual life of Israel—and derivatively, the civic life of Israel—as a suitable locus for God's holiness. As you know, the long (tedious) section of text in Exodus 25–40 concerns the construction of a priestly tabernacle where the glory of God may bivouac. That narrative moves to the culmination of Moses' work in Exodus 40, the final chapter, where it is happily affirmed: "Then the cloud covered the tent of meeting, and the glory of the LORD filled the tabernacle. Moses was not able to enter the tent of meeting because the cloud settled upon it, and the glory of the LORD filled the tabernacle" (Ex 40:34-35). This text is followed in Leviticus 1–7 with an inventory of proper sacrifices that pertain to every dimension of relationship with God, in Leviticus 8–10 with a concern for proper priesthood, In Leviticus 16 with the proper disposal of sin in Yom Kippur, and in Leviticus 18–26, which scholars term the "Holiness Code," with regulations for every aspect of life. As you also know, Leviticus 18–20 has received most recent attention because chapters 18 and 20 concern sexuality and the two chapters sandwich the commandment in chapter 19 to love neighbor as self.

Mary Douglas, the most prominent Leviticus scholar of present time (an anthropologist and not a biblical exegete herself), has written of "purity and danger," in which she proposes that purity is an agenda to which a community gravitates when it perceives itself under threat.[5] It is possible, so the priests contended, to organize a communal practice according to purity that will be a fitting habitat for God's abiding holy presence.

The second part of the Primary Narrative of Genesis—2 Kings is dominated in Deuteronomy, Joshua, Judges, Samuel, and Kings by what scholars call "Deuteronomic theology," that is, interpretation that is rooted in the book of Deuteronomy. The book of Deuteronomy, unlike the Priestly materials I have cited, does not claim to be God's word but is, rather, Moses' exegetical commentary on Sinai. In the book of Deuteronomy, the Ten Commandments are reiterated in chapter 5. And then, after some hortatory sermons by Moses, the Decalogue is exposited in the legal corpus of Deuteronomy 12–25. It is thought by some scholars that the central teaching of the Deuteronomic commandments is "the year of release" in Deuteronomy 15:1-18. That commandment provides that at the end of every seven years debts against poor people must be canceled. That is, the poor are released from debt in order that they may viably participate in the economy and in order that the community does not form a permanent underclass. That extended commandment is of interest to us:

- because Moses says that you must always do the release because there will always be poor people: "The poor you have always with you" (v. 11; see Mark 14:7);
- because if you do this, there need be no poor people in the community (v. 4);
- because the commandment utilizes five infinitive absolutes, the most intense verbal form, suggesting the intensity of the commandment (vv. 4-5, 8, 10), and
- because the commandment warns against tightfisted hard-heartedness toward the poor, evidence of resistance to the commandment (v. 7).

But the point is this. Deuteronomy is concerned with economic justice of a distributive sort, so that communal goods may be made available to all members of the community, most especially including the poor.

That focus of interpretation of Sinai receives extended exposition in Deuteronomy. In chapter 14, for example, the tithe is designed as a festival for the poor:

> Every third year you shall bring out the full tithe of your produce for that year, and store it within your towns; The Levites, because they have no allotment or inheritance with you, as well as the resident aliens, the orphans, and the widows in your towns, may come and eat their fill so that the LORD your God may bless you in all the work that you undertake (14:28-29; see 16:11, 14).

A variety of miscellaneous commandments in Deuteronomy are designed to protect the poor, culminating in chapter 24 with attention to the "triad of the vulnerable" (widows, orphans, sojourners) and with reference to the three money crops (wine, grain, and olive oil):

> When you reap your harvest in the field and forget a sheaf in the field, you shall not go back to get it; it shall be left for the alien, the orphan, and the widow, so that the LORD your God may bless you in all your

undertakings. When you beat your olive trees, do not strip what is
left; it shall be for the alien, the orphan, and the widow. When you
gather the grapes of your vineyard, do not glean what is left; it shall be
for the alien, the orphan, and the widow. Remember that you were a
slave in the land of Egypt; therefore I am commanding you to do this.
(24:19-22)

In sum, the Deuteronomic tradition concerns economic justice so that the economy is subordinated to and made to serve the infrastructure of the neighborhood.
Obedience to Sinai has to do with a countercultural practice of economic justice.

Now, I have taken this long on these two parts of JEDP in order to make a
simple but defining point concerning our topic. Nearly to the bottom of the tradition there is interpretive pluralism in the tradition that moves in the direction of
sacerdotal purity or societal justice, together with all of the derivatives that these
two commitments evoke in terms of liturgy, ethics, and public policy. The reason
these twinned moral trajectories may interest us is that they readily translate into
our own preferred categories of conservative and liberal (or progressive), into a
tradition of equilibrium and a tradition of transformation, or in present company,
into Red and Blue. As the canon of Scripture was finally formulated, these traditions divided between themselves the Primary Narrative of Genesis—2 Kings,
which we may reckon as the oldest and most authoritative text of Israel, and
derivatively of the church. I wish to draw five conclusions about this interpretive
pluralism that may continue to instruct us.

First, both of these traditions are there in the biblical text. Both are "biblical."
And both are accorded high and binding authority.

Second, neither of these trajectories was able to win or to crowd the other
out. Neither was granted ultimate authority, either because the canon makers
exercised wisdom or because neither could, as we say in sports, "finish." Because
both are there, this means that neither one can claim high moral or theological
ground over the other, because both are kept in the final form of the text, in a
penultimate status.

Third, both traditions contain enough of the other accent that it represents
a tip of the hat, a recognition, or even a concession to the validity of the other
trajectory (consider James in Acts 15). Thus, the holiness tradition of the priestly
trajectory includes the remarkable text of the Jubilee year in Leviticus 25. The
festival is called "holy to you" (v. 12) and so fits the bill of holiness. But it is odd
in the Priestly account and concerns the political economy.

Conversely, Deuteronomy 14 offers a full inventory of clean and unclean animals, befitting a Priestly agenda:

You may eat any clean birds. But these are the ones that you shall not
eat: the eagle, the vulture, the osprey, the buzzard, the kite, of any kind;
every raven of any kind; the ostrich, the nighthawk, the sea gull, the

hawk, of any kind; the little owl and the great owl, the water hen and
the desert owl, the carrion vulture and cormorant, the stork, the heron,
of any kind, the hoopoe and the bat. And all winged insects are unclean
for you; they shall not be eaten. You may eat any clean winged creature.
(14:11-20)

And then comes the conclusion: "For you are a people holy to the LORD your
God" (14:21). Again, the accent is odd, against the grain of the tradition in which
it is situated.

Fourth, each of these trajectories issues in a strong hope-filled prophetic articulation. On the one hand, Ezekiel, a child of the Priestly tradition, describes the
way in which a polluted temple required the departure of YHWH's holiness
(Ezek 8–10). In the end, with careful delineation of priestly authority, Ezekiel can
anticipate the full return of the glory to the temple, so that the book of Ezekiel
ends with the new name for Jerusalem, "YHWH is there" (48:35). On the other
hand, Jeremiah, child of Deuteronomy, can discern the destruction of Jerusalem
due to the exploitation of the widow, orphan, and sojourner. And eventually, Jeremiah can envision a new covenant in which all members of Israel keep the torah
of Deuteronomy that is written on their hearts: "I will put my torah within them,
and I will it write it on their hearts; and I will be their God, and they shall be my
people" (Jer. 31:33). It is instructive that these two sons of the canon variously
hope, each in his own trajectory, that the future will be a renewed temple with
indwelling presence, or the future will be a renewed community of neighborly
justice. Both are there, and neither Jeremiah nor Ezekiel was resolved to excommunicate the other.

Fifth, the teachers of the church, enthralled by the classical tradition of theology or by the bewitching power of systemic theology, have in my judgment
ill-served the church by teaching that biblical faith is a seamless package of coherent truth. It is, in my judgment, much more faithful and much more pastorally
helpful to exhibit the Bible in its disputatious pluralism in order to show that no
trajectory has the power or the authority to be the ultimate. The core claim at
bottom is a simple one. But it evokes and requires and permits and authorizes
interpretation that is defyingly pluralistic. The household of faith with its Red
and Blue contentions is faithful to the P and D trajectories. The exclusionary
absolutism of either Red or Blue is a betrayal of the very structure of biblical
faith. Such absolutism is to fall into the Enlightenment trap of drawing singular
conclusions rather than engaging in dialogic processes. And if church people are
seduced into such absolutism, it is in some large measure because they have been
taught that by the church teachers in their refusal to do the hard work of living
with penultimate judgments that are always a membrane away from the bottom
of the singular claim. The pastoral recognition that goes with this awareness is
that human persons, like the Bible, each and all, are conundrums of dispute that
refuse final settlement.

II

The second scriptural strategy against exclusionary absolutism that I suggest and review is that the preferred mode of interpretation in our time and place is not *the Babylonian exile* but more properly the *Persian period of flexible negotiation.* I pay particular attention to this because the mode of the "Persian period" is a relative innovation in scholarship.[6] When most of us were in seminary, the Persian period was not even on the syllabus, so little was known about it.

The Babylonian period and its theological categories have been clear and well known and compelling among us for a long time. It was a rendering of the history of Jerusalem generated by a small group of elite fanatics who were deported to Babylon, who seethed in displacement, who yearned for return to Jerusalem, and who became the moving force in the formation of Judaism. This group of fanatics, like every group of fanatics, took its own experience of deportation (exile) and their passionate hope of return and imposed that experience as the governing truth for all Jews, whether they had been deported or not, whether they had ever left Jerusalem or not.

This model of faith depends on absolute clarity vis-à-vis Babylon without any compromise. The clarity is (1) that Babylon is an unmitigated evil, and (2) Israel is the chosen, forgiven people who are the unique carrier of God's way in the world. This contrast between *good, forgiven Israel* and *evil, condemned Babylon* leads to a radical either/or that invites courage and daring hope and a sense of blessed exceptionalism that requires risk and defiance.

This model of *exile and restoration*, imposed on the raggedness of lived experience as defining ideology, is best known in the poetry of Second Isaiah, partly mediated through Handel's *Messiah.* In this rendering, Babylon is rejected as an arrogant, self-serving imperial power whose haughtiness, the characteristic haughtiness of a superpower, is critiqued and rejected:

> You said, "I shall be mistress forever,"
> . . . .
> who say in your heart,
>   "I am, and there is no one besides me;
> I shall not sit as a widow
>   or know the loss of children"—
> . . . .
>   You said, "No one sees me."
> . . . .
>   "I am, and there is no one besides me." (Isa 47:7, 8, 10)

Alternatively, Israel is the blessed recipient of God's salvation oracles that give assurance of God's rescuing attentiveness:

But you, Israel, my servant,
> Jacob whom I have chosen,
> The offspring of Abraham, my friend;
You whom I took from the ends of the earth,
> and called from its farthest corners,
saying to you, "You are my servant,
> I have chosen you and not cast you off";
do not fear, for I am with you,
> do not be afraid, for I am our God;
I will strengthen you, I will help you,
> I will uphold you with my victorious right hand. (Isa 41:8-10)

Do not fear, for I have redeemed you;
> I have called you by name, you are mine. (Isa 43:1)

This beloved Israel, moreover, is called on to learn "the arts of departure." The departure from a rejected empire permits a self-discernment as YHWH's holy people:

Depart, depart, go out from there!
> Touch no unclean thing;
go out from the midst of it, purify yourselves,
> you who carry the vessels of the LORD,
For you shall not go out in haste,
> and you shall not go out in flight;
for the lord will go before you,
> and the God of Israel will be your rear guard. (Isa 52:11-12)

For you shall go out in joy,
> and be led back peace;
the mountains and the hills before you
> shall burst into song,
> and all trees of the field shall clap their hands. (Isa 55:12)

What strikes one in the poetry is the certitude, singularity of purpose, and a radical either/or. This rhetoric invited the community to a sturdy ideology of "us" against the world, and the conviction that all of God's future promises are designed precisely for this singular community. The point is to be distinguished from the world in order to receive a special future from God.

It is of course a leap from that poetic vision to Red and Blue. But I think not too much. I believe that the Red and Blue passions in our society carry with them an inchoate sense of self-congratulation as a carrier of what is true and faithful and best and a corresponding sense that the way to remain unsullied is to have no serious engagement with "the other." In such a horizon, the other, Red or Blue, is not perceived as a part of the community of chosen destiny but is perceived as the imperial "other" that offers a distorted view of reality that is to be avoided.

While the other party may not be demonized that clearly, at the very least it has nothing worthwhile to contribute and therefore no attention need be paid. The "Babylonian model" leads to a virtue of being "put upon" by the other party, so Jew as victim of empire, Red or Blue as victim of Red or Blue. I think this model of self-congratulations is so pervasive that we do not reflect on it. I suggest it is a model designed out of self-interest that has been made culturally and theologically normative among us.

In place of that Babylonian model that became normative for Judaism, I suggest that we pay attention to the long Persian period of Jewish faith that extended from Cyrus in 540 to Alexander the Great in 333, thus a period of two hundred years. Unlike the Babylonian model of *exile and restoration*, the Persian period yielded a practice of *accommodation and resistance* that required uncommon agility, not unlike that modeled in *Fiddler on the Roof*. According to this model, the church must nurture people in agility, persons who have no intransigent point but are capable of responding imaginatively to new circumstance and challenge without digging in anywhere too deeply.

Three matters are clear about the Persian period that contrasts with the Babylonian:

First, it was a very long period that required Jews to have patience and staying power, without any restoration as it had been envisioned by the poetry. This is in contrast to the Babylonian period, according to the ideological model, that was short and then over.

Second, whatever may have been the historical reality (and scholars dispute the point), in Jewish articulation the Persian government was benign in its treatment of Jews, utilizing an imperial policy of supporting local traditions, including the local Jewish tradition of "the God of Heaven." According to the data, Persia permitted the Jews to return home, funded much of the restoration of the city, and paid for the newly built temple in Jerusalem. As a result, there is in the Old Testament no prophetic oracle that condemns Persia, while we have many oracles that condemn Babylon.

Third, at the same time, we know that Persia taxed the Jewish colony heavily, so much so that Ezra could say in his prayer:

> Here we are, slaves to this day—slaves in the land that you gave to our
> ancestors to enjoy its fruit and its good gifts. Its rich yield goes to the
> kings whom you have set over us because of our sins. They have power
> also over our bodies and over our livestock at their pleasure, and we are
> in great distress. (Neh 9:36-37)

Such a prayer warns us not to take too seriously the portrayal of Persia as benign.

Fourth, given that demanding imperial-colonial relationship, Persia could be perceived as the rescuer of Israel that was helplessly held by Babylon. At the end of 2 Chronicles 36, the final verses of the Hebrew Bible, Cyrus is remembered as the one who issued the edict permitting Jews to go back home. And Second Isaiah ups the rhetorical ante in 45:1 by declaring that Cyrus is YHWH's anointed, that is, his Messiah, that is, his Christ. The functions that had pertained to David have been transferred to the Gentile deliverer.

There is evidence that some Babylonian Jews resisted deliverance by a Gentile, perhaps in a defiant posture of wanting to wait for a Jewish deliverer. But the poet (or better YHWH) will have none of that resistance to a Gentile deliverer:

> Woe to you who strive with your Maker,
>   earthen vessels with the potter!
> Does the clay say to the one who fashions it, "What are you making"?
>   or "Your work has no handles"?
> Woe to anyone who says to a father, "What are you begetting?"
>   or to a woman, "With what are you in labor?"
> Thus say the LORD,
>   the holy One of Israel, and its Maker:
> "Will you question me about my children,
>   or command me concerning the work of my hands?" (Isa 45:9-11)

All of these data concerning the Persian Empire have suggested to scholars that the Persian period is in fact the generative, creative era of ancient Israel, leading to the formation of the canon of the Hebrew Bible and the formative decisions concerning the future of Judaism. For our purposes, what strikes one is that the old Babylonian model of *exile and restoration* accompanied by *defiance and departure* is no longer the order of the day. If there is to be a restoration, it will be funded and authorized by the Persians. Clearly, defiance is inappropriate in such a circumstance; and departure of a geographical kind is irrelevant, for wherever Jews might go, including to Jerusalem, they were still in Persia. Thus the exile-restoration model of a radical either/or had to be displaced by a model of both/and, both Jews and empire, both Jerusalem and Persia, and I would extrapolate, both Red and Blue, because a Babylonian either/or is incongruent with social, ecclesial reality.

The new model in the quasi-benign imperial context is one of accommodation and resistance that required immense agility, more agility than a simplistic either/or required or permitted. Great accommodation was required to the unyielding facts on the ground. And sufficient resistance was undertaken to sustain a distinct Jewish self-awareness, or what Michael Fishbane has recently termed "mindfulness," in a society committed to mindlessness.[7] It is in the Persian period, most likely, that Judaism developed the disciplines of Jewishness that fostered and sustained a distinct identity, but they are disciplines that did not preclude a great deal of accommodation.[8]

It is the judgment of many scholars that the appropriate mode of Jewishness in the Persian period is not the utterance of defiant oracles but rather the telling of narratives that evidence agile negotiation in a social environment that did not permit the throwing down of a defiant gauntlet.[9] Here I will consider three such narratives that bespeak accommodation and resistance rather than exile and restoration.

There is a propensity among scholars now to date much of the Old Testament to the Persian period. Among such texts that are increasingly situated in the Persian period is the Joseph narrative of Genesis 37–50. As you know, this story turns on the capacity of Joseph to interpret the dream of pharaoh after the imperial intelligence community had failed to read the intelligence of the dream adequately. Pharaoh, in Jewish imagination, is the cipher for every imperial power, no doubt including Persia. The Persians have power but cannot decode hidden revelation. As you know, Joseph reads the dream that is a nightmare of coming scarcity. There is surely irony in the dream: the one with the most dreams of lacking what is needed! With the completion of the dream interpretation, Joseph, in anticipation of Richard Cheney, nominates himself to preside over imperial food policy: "Now therefore let Pharaoh select a man who is discerning and wise, and set him over the land of Egypt" (Gen. 41:33). That much we all know.

But we most often do not read on to chapter 47, where Joseph, as food czar, implements a policy of imperial monopoly, systematically taking from the peasant labor force their money, their cattle, and their land, and eventually their bodies, as they are reduced to slavery:

> So Joseph bought all the land of Egypt for Pharaoh. All the Egyptians
> sold their fields, because the famine was severe upon them; and the land
> became Pharaoh's. As for the people, he made slaves of them from one
> end of Egypt to the other. . . . They said, "You have saved our lives; may
> it please my lord, we will be slaves to pharaoh." (47:20-21, 25)

The antidote to anticipated scarcity is state monopoly that culminates in slavery. And because of deep anxiety about hunger, the slaves express gratitude for their new status as slaves.

A son of Jacob manages the entire process of economic centralization. Most remarkably, the narrative utters not a word of criticism against Joseph for his exploitative policy. Recent commentators, following von Rad, have focused on the claim that Joseph fed his brothers (Gen. 45:1-8). If, however, we look at the narrative in larger scope, here is a Persian-period Jewish story featuring a wise Jew who fully accommodated himself to imperial reality and gave his life and career over to resolving imperial anxiety about scarcity. It is no wonder that Leon Kass, in his recent commentary, speaks of the complete "Egyptianization" of Joseph, the full accommodation of Jewishness to imperial requirement.[10] Given all of that, Joseph is still reckoned in the narrative as a full-fledged practitioner of the covenant who is an adequate carrier of Jewish hopes for the future. The Joseph narrative lives at the extreme "accommodation" end of the spectrum of the accommodation-resistance model of faith.

Perhaps at the other extreme is the *story of Esther*, who manages her Persian access point to the great benefit of the Jews. There is no doubt that the Esther narrative is Persian in setting, set in the world of Ahasuerus, perhaps Artaxerxes. As the story goes, Esther becomes the Persian queen because she is "fair and beautiful" and has a powerful political uncle, Mordecai. As she becomes queen, we are told: "Esther did not reveal her people or kindred, for Mordecai had charged her not to tell" (2:10). In the plot of the book, Haman, a Persian political operator, is planning to get the Persian authorities to eliminate all Jews. It is only by the intervention of Mordecai that his plot is foiled. But his effectiveness depends on the cooperation of Esther; she must run the risk of exposing her own Jewishness and thereby risk her status in the empire. Mordecai wants her to go public:

> Do not think that in the king's palace you will escape any more than all
> the other Jews. For if you keep silent at such a time as this, relief and
> deliverance will rise for the Jews from another quarter, but you and your
> father's family will perish. Who knows? Perhaps you have come to royal
> dignity for just such a time as this. (4:13-14)

Esther is persuaded. At great personal risk, she makes her Jewish identity visible and is prepared for what that may cost her: "Go, gather all the Jews to be found in Susa, and hold a fast on my behalf, and neither eat nor drink for three days, night or day. I and my maids will also fast as you do. After that I will go to the king, though it is against the law; and if I perish, I perish" (4:16). This paragraph is the turning point in the narrative wherein we arrive at a new interface of Persia and Judaism, of empire and distinct identity. Esther had fully accommodated herself to the empire. Her new resolve does not quite amount to resistance, except that her articulation of Jewish identity now makes her an awkwardness in the empire, for what can empire do with such distinct identity? From that decision the plot unfolds. Haman, who had thought to execute the Jews, is now himself executed. Esther's action has caused the empire to mobilize on behalf of Jews. Now it is not Jews in service to the empire (as with Joseph); now it is empire in the service of Jews. The narrative ends with a Persian permit that the Jews are free to kill their enemies with imperial approval, an act that eventuates in the Festival of Purim, the great festival of Jewish self-assertion (9:18-32).

It is clear that Esther embodies a model very different from that of Joseph. Here there is less accommodation and much more self-assertion. That perhaps amounts to resistance, if we take Jewish self-declaration as itself an act of resistance against imperial reductionism.

The third character I mention is *Daniel*, who has much in common with Joseph. While the narrative situates him vis-à-vis Nebuchadnezzar, it is likely a Persian period piece, though you may know that much historical criticism links the narrative to the Maccabean crisis of the second century. In a series of narratives, Daniel operates vis-à-vis the empire.

In chapter 2, Daniel, not unlike Joseph, interprets the dream for Nebuchadnezzar. It is a dream of a succession of kingdoms, each of which is in turn destroyed. As with Joseph, the imperial sages could not read the dream; but here Daniel intervenes to save the imperial intelligence community that the king wanted to execute for its failure.

The narrative culminates with Nebuchadnezzar's recognition of Daniel and Daniel's Jewish God:

> Then King Nebuchadnezzar fell on his face, worshiped Daniel, and com-
> manded that a grain offering and incense be offered to him. The king
> said to Daniel, "Truly your God is God of gods an LORD of kings and
> a revealer of mysteries, for you have been able to reveal this mystery!"
> (Dan 2:46-47)

And beyond that theological affirmation, Daniel is a huge political success in the empire:

> Then the king promoted Daniel, giving him many great gifts, and made
> him ruler of the whole province of Babylon and chief prefect over all
> the wise men of Babylon. Daniel made a request of the king, and he
> appointed Shadrach, Meshach, and Abednego over the affairs of the
> province of Babylon. But Daniel remained at the king's court.
> (Dan 2:48-49)

The narrative exhibits the way in which a Jew uses his peculiar Jewish gifts of interpretation both to gain promotion in the empire and to serve the benefit of the empire. In this narrative, there is no conflict between Jewish advancement and imperial well being.

The narrative in Daniel 3, by contrast, features strong resistance to empire. Here Daniel's three friends, Shadrach, Meshach, and Abednego, refuse to bow down to imperial icons and rely on deliverance from their own God. They are, as a result of such resistance, thrown into the fiery furnace but come out unharmed. The fact that they are unharmed by the worst that the empire can think to do evokes from Nebuchadnezzar another theological affirmation: "Blessed be the God of Shadrach, Meshach, and Abednego, who has sent his angel and delivered his servants who trusted in him. They disobeyed the king's command and yielded up their bodies rather than serve and worship any god except their own" (3:28). And again, the theological affirmation is followed by political gains for the Jewish people:

> Therefore I make a decree: Any people, nation, or language that utters blasphemy against the God of Shadrach, Meshach, and Abednego shall be torn limb from limb, and their houses laid in ruins; for there is no other god who is able to deliver in this way. Then the king promoted Shadrach, Meshach, and Abednego in the province of Babylon. (3:29-30)

Here it is resistance that is the order of the day; but it is resistance that does not attack the empire. The outcome is a positive one because their resistance is linked to the reality of the God they serve.

In chapter 4, Daniel is again a dream interpreter. Here, after he has interpreted the dream, he dares to give advice to Nebuchadnezzar, advice that is quintessentially Jewish; it derives precisely from Sinai and the prophetic tradition: "Therefore, O king, may my counsel be acceptable to you: Atone for your sins with righteousness, and your iniquities with mercy to the oppressed, so that your prosperity may be prolonged" (4:27). This utterance is a remarkable intrusion of Jewish ethical conviction into a self-serving empire that had little ethical sensibility.

The narrative unfolds so that Nebuchadnezzar suffers because of his arrogance. But when his "reason retuned" (v. 34), it issues in a doxology to the king of heaven. Indeed, in the horizon of the narrative, imperial sanity is recognition of the God to whom the Jews attest. The great emperor is in a posture of self-yielding praise:

> Now I, Nebuchadnezzar, praise and extol and honor the King of heaven,
>   for all his works are truth,
>   and his ways are justice,
> and he is able to bring low
>   those who walk in pride. (4:37)

The Daniel narratives show a Jew in the empire with freedom, courage, and imagination. If we ask about the source of such freedom, courage, and imagination, we may turn back to Daniel 1, the opening narrative, wherein Daniel is a recruit for civil service in the empire. This narrative offers the grounding for all that follows. For it is reported that Daniel refused the rich food of the imperial training table and negotiated permission to live on a Jewish diet of vegetables and water. The narrator reports: "But Daniel resolved that he would not defile himself with the royal rations of food and wine; so he asked the palace master to allow him not to defile himself" (Dan 1:8). The key word is "defile." He would not compromise his Jewishness for the sake of empire. He maintained his Jewish identity through

Jewish disciplines that the empire barely permitted. It is this refusal, I submit, that subsequently gave Daniel ground for effective life in the empire. That initial narrative on Daniel concludes in this way:

> And among them all, none was found to compare with Daniel, Hananiah, Michael, and Azariah; therefore they were stationed in the king's court. In every matter of wisdom and understanding concerning which the king inquired of them, he found them ten times better than all the magicians and enchanters in his whole kingdom. And Daniel continued there until the first year of King Cyrus. (1:19-21)

The final note makes a connection to the Persian, Cyrus.

I suggest that the character of Daniel is not as accommodationist as Joseph and not as militant as Esther and so perhaps occupies a median position. But if we take the three Persian narratives all together, what we have are rich models for faithful survival and effectiveness in the empire, a faithfulness and effectiveness that requires enormous agility. For our purposes, the point to accent in this Persian context is that there is no radical either/or, no strident polemic, no attempt to excommunicate others who operate differently, but a recognition of a common danger and a common possibility that pertains to the entire community. It is my thought that such a model of accommodation and resistance in place of exile-restoration goes a long way beyond our usual internecine combat that is here rendered passé. The true situation of Christians in the U.S. is in a dance of agility that is not propelled by passionate ideology but by a steadfast resolve about identity and a shared awareness of the vulnerability of faith in the midst of the hegemony of empire.

III

The third scriptural strategy against exclusionary absolutism that I consider is a shift from *prophetic proclamation* to *scribal interpretation*, a shift I have laid out in an article in the *Scottish Journal of Theology*.[11] Of course, all of us value prophetic ministry and prophetic preaching, and the most zealous of the Red and the most vigorous of the Blue will most fervently engage in prophetic rhetoric concerning their grasp of truth against the enemies of that truth.

Prophetic rhetoric aims to confront and divide and sort out. Prophetic rhetoric is on the one hand vigorous in its articulation of what scholars call "speeches of judgment," which consist in an indictment for violation of torah and a sentence of divine judgment to come. The package of indictment and sentence is rooted in old covenantal traditions of divine commandment and divine sanctions (curses). We are of course familiar with such prophetic confrontations:

Nathan to David;
Elijah to Ahab;
Isaiah to Ahaz;
Amos to Amaziah;
Jeremiah to Jehoiachim.

Every one of these utterers against the "cows of Bashan" knew that big trouble was coming for the self-indulgent, who were not "vexed over the ruin of Jacob." And no doubt that capacity for righteous indignation has continued with the pope keeping the emperor standing in the snow, and Luther, "Hier ich stehe," and Martin Luther King before the sheriffs. I do not for an instant denigrate such moral passion.

Conversely, prophetic promises are large and clear concerning homecoming and new covenant and new Jerusalem and new temple and new heaven and new earth, and even passing allusion to new life after death. The promissory passion of the prophetic tradition matches the moral conviction. And the Red and Blue communities can continue that vigor, Reds most often about sexuality and Blues most often about economics. In the Old Testament such rhetoric required a king and an urban elite as counterpoint and target. When Israel ended that political arrangement, prophecy tended to dry up. There is no doubt that, as Israel moved into displaced Judaism, the initiative for leadership passed from the prophets to the scribes, who were allied with the wisdom teachers and whose principle task was the continued interpretation of the textual tradition that operated, if not authoritatively, at least as a consensus funding for imagination. My judgment is that the vigor of the prophetic becomes less viable as Israel was *decentered* from power and as circumstance of *marginality* made it unseemly and impractical for Israelites (now Jews) to use their fragile energy excommunicating each other when the community could ill afford to lose any.[12]

Mutatis mutandis, I propose that our situation in the U.S. church is not unlike that, decentered from power and situated in marginality. For me it follows, by way of analogue, that it is unseemly and impractical for the church to use its fragile energy excommunicating each other when the community can ill afford to lose any. That shift means that internal disputes over moral questions are dealt with less intensely, and it means that all parties are aware that present interpretations are not final interpretations. The classic example among us of interpretation being excessively final is the vigor mobilized in the defense of slavery on a biblical basis. My own seminary, Columbia Seminary, and its great theologian James Henley Thornwell used immense energy on that project, with as much moral fervor as one could mount on any issue. And of course, that seminary and its constituency are still processing the awareness that it was wrong. The scribes, unlike the prophets, were aware of the elusiveness of faithful interpretation and the precarious notion of truth, especially when it is inescapably allied with economic interest and a hunger for power. I do not suppose that I would persuade any to abandon prophetic vigor; my purpose is to consider scribal activity enough to suggest it as a viable alternative. Scribes are fundamentally scroll people who understand that the normative scrolls require ongoing work and continue to be a gift that keeps on giving.[13] The scribes are characteristically neither "strict constructionists" nor "originalists" but are concerned to let the text have its fresh contemporary say. I will mention four texts:

1. It is possible that the tradition of Deuteronomy is scribal, as Moshe Weinfeld has proposed, though not provably so.[14] In any case Deuteronomy is a revision, a rereading of Sinai, in the interest of contemporaneity: "Not with our ancestors did the LORD make this covenant, but with us, who are all of us here alive today" (Deut 5:3). The dynamic of the tradition of Deuteronomy (unlike that of the Priestly tradition) is a dynamism that can be traced through the whole text, as each new generation had to do it all over, albeit informed by their predecessors.

2. In Jeremiah 36, we have the remarkable narrative account of how the scroll of Jeremiah—the book of Jeremiah—came into existence. Jeremiah dictates it to Baruch the scribe, who then reads it in public and is summoned to answer for the scroll in official councils. It is Baruch the scribe and not Jeremiah the prophet who answers for the scroll. I make only two observations about the narrative. First, the scroll was read to King Jehoiachim, who ostentatiously cut it up with a pen knife and threw it, a little at a time, into the fireplace. This is the first instance we have of the shredding of documents. Power wants to eliminate the scroll. Second, after the shredding, we are told that Jeremiah redictated the scroll to the scribe. And the narrative ends with these ominous words: "Many similar words were added to them" (36:32). The scroll is not disposed of. The scroll is not fixed and final. It is open and elastic, and it is the work of scribers to see that "many other words" might be added. Many scholars believe that this narrative maneuver from Jeremiah to Baruch constitutes a huge historical turn in which the impetus for religious leadership is passed from prophet to scribe, and it is the task of the scribe to keep the scroll contemporary through the ongoing exercise of imagination.

3. The second scribe I mention is Ezra, who is reckoned by the rabbis to be second only to Moses in the tradition. David Halivni, moreover, has proposed that the text of Moses was "damaged" and it was the work of Ezra to heal and restore the scroll to its full, generative future.[15] In Nehemiah 8, we are offered a narrative that many scholars, following von Rad, regard as the founding moment of Judaism, as the scribe Ezra convenes the entire community before the Water Gate in Jerusalem and reads to them the book of the law, the scroll of the torah. The remarkable description of this public act is that with the Levites, Ezra "helped the people to understand the law, while the people remained in their places. So they read from the book, from the law of God, with interpretation. They gave the sense, so that the people understood the reading" (Neh 8:7-8). This is a remarkable hermeneutical act, perhaps the origin of the sermon, certainly an exercise in exegesis. They read—in order to understand—with interpretation—

to give sense—so that they understood. The refounding of the restored community depends on exegetical interpretation, which perforce went beyond old memory to let it be contemporary. This public reading that produced weeping (v. 9) and then joy (v. 12) led to a celebration of the Festival of Booths, thus word that led to sacrament. The narrative ends this way: "And day by day, from the first day to the last day, he read from the book of the law of God" (Neh 8:18). It is all about the text, its reading, its hearing, its exegesis, its interpretation, its openness to the contemporary. Notice how scribal this is. Prophets do not propound texts. They offer oracles that sort it out in original ways. But textual interpretation summons the whole community—all who could understand—to receive fresh identity from fresh hearing. Judaism characteristically pushes behind the prophetic oracle to torah narrative and commandments. I think this is exactly what is now required in a church where prophetic oracles are mostly uttered and heard by the already convinced in the particular sect that holds the truth.

4. It is a quick stretch from Baruch via Ezra to Jesus. My fourth scribal text is the parabolic collection that Jesus gives to his disciples in Matthew 13, a text that is peculiar to Matthew. In this sequence there is

> the parable of weeds and wheat (vv. 24-30),
> the mustard seed (vv. 31-32),
> yeast (v. 33),
> sowing seed (vv. 36-43),
> hidden treasure (v. 44),
> great pearl (vv. 45-46),
> fish in a net (vv. 47-50).

When Jesus finished his sequence of parables, he says to the disciples, "Have you understood all of this?" And they answer, "Yes." And then he says, "Therefore every scribe that has been trained for the kingdom of heaven is like the master of a household who brings out of his treasure what is new and what is old" (Matt 13:52). Clearly, the scribes, often linked to the Pharisees, have gotten mostly bad press. But here it is positive. These are peculiar scribes "trained for the kingdom of heaven," that is, committed to the Jesus project. These parables are the curriculum for such scribes. When we take the sum of these parables, which are bracketed by the "wheat and tares" and "fish in a net," the conclusion is that the wheat and tares must be left to grow together until the final harvest and the good fish and bad will be sorted when the angels come and separate out the evil. There will be a Big Sort. But it is not given over to human agents. Human agents are to let it be, confident that God and God's angels are adequate deciders.

In the meantime, free of obligation to sort, true scribes have a different function, to bring out of the treasure "what is old and what is new." Old in context is the faith of Israel. What is new is the coming of the kingdom in Jesus. And from that model, we may say what is old is the reliable tradition of the church;

what is new is where the Spirit leads beyond the settled tradition. Scribes are situated exactly at the hinge of the old and the new. There is no clear guide about old and new; but it clearly requires freedom and fidelity and agility to keep the action going between old and new. That of course is what the rabbis always do. Of course, that is what every lively parish always does. Of course, that is what everyone in psychotherapy always does. Of course, that is what we do all the time in our personal relationships, not settled in what is old, not easy with what is new, but brooding in negotiation about old and new, repeated formulae and fresh insight, and awaiting the Big Sort that will come later. I suspect that the good scribe would say that the work of conservatives is to treasure what has been settled; the work of liberals is to make new connections. We are all in a negotiation together, and we are all willing to leave the Big Sort to God and to God's angels.

We are able to see Jesus the scribe practicing exactly such a repertoire in his old/new in the Sermon on the Mount. Of the verse about the old and new in the treasure, Daniel Harrington adds in his exposition: "The message of patient tolerance and leaving to God the settling of scores is timely today also. For a world in which so many conflicts occur on the basis of religion, race, ethnic identity, and so forth, this is sound advice."[16]

IV

I am no sociologist, only an exegete. But I believe we can see in Scripture itself practices that are pertinent to the Big Sort among us:

- A recognition that *the foundational tradition is pluralistic*, that neither the voice of justice nor the voice of purity can easily claim high moral ground;
- A location in the Persian context of *accommodation and resistance* with a practice of agility, a rejection of a Babylonian model with its strident either/or;
- A *practice of scribal interpretation* that refuses the bold invectives and bold promises of the prophetic, but continues to watch for newness in the old text that is given in imagination.

The sum of these strategies, I believe, is to recognize that our work is characteristically penultimate, well short of any absolute. It is my judgment that the church, in all quarters, must repent of its lust for the absolute. But surely the rabbis, and the church fathers after them, understood that there are no final interpretations. And surely we have learned in the twentieth century that final interpretations are a dangerous step along the way to the final solution. In my church, the United Church of Christ, we have now adopted the slogan, "God is still speaking," which means in that liberal context that God has something new to say about sexuality.

The logo for that slogan is a comma, suggesting that after the received truth of Scripture there is not a period but a comma.

But my church is tempted to disregard everything in front of the comma. The task for Red and Blue in the church, conservatives and liberals, is to recognize that because the Spirit is on the move, we must pay attention to both sides of the comma, not just what is old and not just what is new. That is what it means to be a scribe trained for the kingdom. Those who cherish only what is old or only what is new are doing something other than serving the kingdom. Of course, Anglicans have long known that a proper check on absoluteness is the message Oliver Cromwell sent to parliament, "I beseech you by the bowels of Christ to think that you may be mistaken." It is the hard-hearted refusal of the church to entertain that thought that leads to an Easy Sort. The gospel summons to more openness, thickness, and complexity than that.[17]

CHAPTER 17

A Life and a Time
Other than Our Own

PREACHING IN THE COMING CENTURY will be a demanding challenge for the preacher.[1] We do not know what changes are to come among us soon—technologically, electronically, sociologically, militarily, economically. Nobody can guess what particular responses the preacher and the church are to make in such an environment of profound change. But try this as a thesis. Preachers in the coming century of rapid and deep change are to keep doing what serious preachers have always done at their best, namely,

> to engraft folk into the life and times of the holy God, whom we name as Father, Son, and Spirit.

If we go back to the church's earliest narratives in the book of Acts, the preaching and the resultant baptisms drew folk into a different venue for life, a venue that caused *radical sharing* and *radical testimony* before the authorities. And if we push behind that earliest preaching to the memory of Jesus, it is clear that Jesus summoned folk to follow him in a different walk, a different walk that was on a collision course with the way things were said to be.

I

So consider the *life and times of the holy God*. The life of the holy God is with the rejoicing angels in heaven, where they sit around and read torah all day. But the life of the holy God also consists in deep engagement with the world that God makes and loves:

For thus says the high and lofty one
>   who inhabits eternity, whose name is Holy:
> I dwell in the high and holy place,
>   and also with those who are contrite and humble in spirit,
> to revive the spirit of the humble,
>   and to revive the heart of the contrite. (Isa 57:15)

And that deep engagement with the world—like the intimate interaction of spouse and spouse or parent and child—is an engagement of agony and ecstasy, of alienation and reconciliation, of anger and forgiveness, of exasperation and possibility. It is in the very character of this God—unlike the "unmoved mover" of ancient time or the phantom "pulse of new age religion" and its many forms—to invest fully in a way that evidences *sovereignty as vulnerability* and *grace as demanding truth-telling*.

So consider the "times" of the holy God. Against much that is static about God in popular theology, this God has times and seasons, and for this God there is a season for everything. There is a season for creating and blessing; there is a season for saving and rescuing; there is a season for commanding and covenant-making; there is a season for judgment and banishment; there is a season for forgiveness and homecoming; there is a season for planting and building; there is a season for hurt and for hope. There are many seasons, and each one is infused with governing intentionality and self-abandoning generosity.

The life and times of the holy God—who is known to us as awesome Father, as enfleshed Son, as hovering Spirit—is constituted by a thick, complex drama that is grounded and open. It is grounded in resolves that are as deep as the foundation of the world; it is as open as God's resolve for newness, all the way to a new heaven and a new earth, all the wonder as far as new life out of death.

So consider: that we may be "engrafted," to be spliced into that life. Repeatedly, Israel, human persons, nations, all creatures are invited to the life and times of the holy God, whom we name as Father, Son, and Spirit:

- Already in Genesis 1:22, God addresses creatures of water and sky, great sea monsters at every living thing, and says, "Be fruitful." Join me in the work of creation.
- Already in Exodus 4:22-23, God speaks of Israel and says, "Israel is my firstborn son. . . . Let my son go that he may worship me."
- Already in Joshua 24:15-16, the invitation is in the mouth of Joshua:

> Now if you are unwilling to serve the LORD, choose this day
> whom you will serve, whether the gods your ancestors served in
> the region beyond the River or the gods of the Amorites in whose
> land you are living; but as for me and my household, we will serve

the LORD. Then the people answered, "Far be it from us that we
should forsake the LORD to serve other gods." (Josh 24:15-16)

- Already in prophetic utterance, Israel is invited back to the work of
  justice that operates in the life of God:

  For thus says the LORD to the house of Israel:
  Seek me and live. (Amos 5:4)

  Seek good and not evil,
      that you may live;
  and so the LORD, the God of hosts, will be with you,
      just as you have said. (Amos 5:14)

- Already in Isaiah 55:6-9, God addresses recalcitrant, despairing exiles:

  Seek the LORD while he may be found,
      call upon him while he is near;
  let the wicked forsake their way,
      and the unrighteous their thoughts;
  let them return to the LORD, that he may have mercy on them,
      and to our God, for he will abundantly pardon. (Isa 55:6-7)

- Already in Matthew 11:28-30, Jesus summoned the world-weary:

  Come to me, all you that are weary and are carrying heavy bur-
  dens, and I will give you rest. Take my yoke upon you, and learn
  from me; for I am gentle and humble in heart, and you will find
  rest for your souls. For my yoke is easy, and my burden is light.
  (Matt 11:28-30)

And of course, the invitation to be engrafted goes on. The engrafting consists
in a ready embrace of a thick, complex interactive life with many seasons, each
of which brings with it an appropriate response. The ones invited are summoned
to be "with God" in all their seasons, to sing exuberant, self-forgetting praise in
company with all creatures, to join in weeping lament and righteous indignation
over the injustice so evident in the world, to work the repertoire of praise and
lament, to live a life of self-forgetting before God and self-asserting before God,
to bring the neighbor along in praise and protest.

But engrafting also entails departure from other narrative accounts of reality.
The preacher is always summoning and empowering folk to make a move out
beyond failed narrative accounts of the world. Thus, the preacher is situated, now as
always, between old failed narratives and the new narrative of the three-named God.

The preacher seeks ways to exhibit the adequacy of the new narrative of the life and times of God and to help people recognize—even as they already know in traces and hints—other narratives that are inadequate. All the while, as the preacher advocates and persuades and exposes, the preacher's own life is stretched too far, often still clinging to the narratives of leanness that give no rest or new life. I cannot imagine a time in a long life of the church or in the long story of God's times when such engrafting was more difficult—or more urgent—or trickier, or more glorious. Notice, please notice, how I seek to change the subject of our preaching away from the human predicament, away from our several ideologies of conservatives or liberals, away from the troubles of the world—because the subject of our preaching, when it is "news," is about the God who persists in engagement with us, both for us and over against us.

II

Since my subject is the life and times of God, I thought I would begin this exploration by considering the times of God in three masterful articulations of our faith, and then consider in greater detail the three principal seasons of God's life. First then, *three masterful articulations* of God's seasons, articulations that remain, for all their problematic character, found reliable for us.

The Nicene Creed

The creed, wrought under the emperor, traces God's times in three seasons. The trinitarian structure is a given of the church's preaching, even when we are aware of the endless ways we are able to betray or distort that claim.

So says the creed, *God the Father Almighty* was there before all and is responsible for all. Heaven and earth, visible and invisible—no exceptions—result from the making of God. It is this one who has the whole world—no exceptions—in safe hands.

So says the creed, *the only begotten Son of God.* This long, second paragraph with which the council struggled is shaped dramatically. It begins with a wondrous poetic flight because the times of God require poetry:

> God of God,
> light from light,
> very God of very God.

This council struggled to assert the Son's divinity. The paragraph ends in soaring fashion, "whose kingdom will have no end." But between "God of God" and "has no end," there is the narrative of suffering and death, life in the matrix of Roman power.

So says the creed, *the Spirit is Lord and giver of life*. Notable here is that the Spirit "spoke by the prophets," as though Israel's truth-tellers are the ones who give life.

> The Father responsible for all.
> The only Son facing the empire;
> The Spirit giving life through truth-telling.

We watch as this God moves through God's times from *making* to *suffering* to *giving life*.

The Apostles' Creed

This one, more familiar, also is trinitarian in structure.

So says the creed, tersely, *God the Father Almighty . . . maker*. This formulation does not make the sweep of Nicaea, but of course the same is implied. Before all, God! It all is, because of God's power and God's will and God's purpose—nothing outside!

So says the creed, *only Son of God*. This ancient symbol was not so preoccupied with the Arian problem, so the christological exercise is less intent. The second season in God's life begins with the Spirit vis-à-vis Mary and ends with judgment over all, over the quick and the dead. And between the Spirit's fecundity and the vision of a great final court, there is again the governor and suffering, the same drama.

So says the creed, *the Spirit*, and from the Spirit comes the great five points of hope for new life, two concerning the church, two concerning the final things of resurrection and eternal life, and the fifth between these four—two of which are on ecclesiology, two on eschatology. The central one is *forgiveness*, as though the defining season in God's life concerns forgiveness, reconciliation, atonement, homecoming, acceptance. The creed, typically, has no curiosity about how all of this happens because the Spirit surges beyond explanation.

In both creeds that tell the story of God's life and God's times, there are no other actors. Well, there could not be, because this is God.[2] All other parties—the creation, the human person, the church—are acted upon, recipients of God's sovereign action in the world.

Wesley's "Love Divine, All Loves Excelling"

After the two great creeds, I selected one other exemplary rendition of God's life and times. I selected this one simply because it is my favorite and it seems to me most comprehensive in its artistic persuasiveness, namely, Charles Wesley's "Love Divine, All Loves Excelling." Wesley knew here and everywhere that the life and times of God can only be rendered in the poetic, and he does it majestically.

The hymn begins with the mystery of divine love that excels beyond any other love that we can imagine. That love, that overflowing self-giving, is the joy of heaven. That means that the angels, the saints, the lesser gods, the watchers, and the holy ones exalt in the reality of God's self-giving.

But by the second line of the first stanza, Wesley, preacher that he is, must move on "to earth come down." The focus here, as at Nicaea, is on the second season, when the divine love enjoyed in heaven takes "humble dwelling" among us. Or as Wesley says, "in us. . . . Fix in us." It is Jesus now, second season, second person, but nothing here about birth, only a wondrous showing forth of divine love:

> Thou art all compassion,
> pure unbounded love.

You can sense Wesley searching for words and phrases and images to say what our words will scarcely carry, because our words are a "humble dwelling" for what is true.

It is this Jesus, this divine love in humble dwelling, who is now addressed through the petitioner's petition: "Visit us." Visit us with your rescue, your salvation, your healing, your forgiveness, your transformation. Wesley's vision is pietistic, ". . . every trembling heart." This inwardness is parallel to "fix in us" voiced earlier. The divine love that is pure and unbounded indwells human persons.

The second stanza moves to the Spirit, again inward, ". . . every trembling heart." The language is inward and individualistic, but it recognizes that the spirit of God finds habitat not only in every human heart but also in every *troubled* human heart. It is the wont of God in the third season to inhabit our troubled selves. The consequence of such breathing of new life is to bring us to the inheritance of promised rest. The goal of the Spirit is to bring us home to full well being, surely beyond troubles. The Spirit treats the troubled as *heirs* of old promises to which God has sworn fidelity.

But the journey to our true home is not too easy. There is a recognition that we will not get home safely until this same transformative God overcomes our yearning to sin, our inclination to organize our times against God's time and our life against God's life. God can change all of that, which is why the imperative is uttered, "Take away" what we crave to keep.

When that is taken away, this God—not any alternative idol—can be all in all, alpha and omega, every yearning from A to Z. The end of this time as a gift of the Spirit is like beginning time—with hearts at liberty. In between there have been troubled hearts, troubled in fear and anxiety and compulsion and alienation; but the prayer is to restore us to initial liberty, utterly at ease, as daughters and sons come home to the family with no vexation.

In the third stanza, Wesley moves beyond the trinitarian formula to bid for the full return of God as savior: "Come, Almighty, to deliver." In imagery not unlike that of Ezekiel, this petition asks for a "sudden" return of God to the earth, to

God's temple for a permanent habitat, that God should be always present among us. The response to such priestly sacramental presence is that the congregation pledges to receive the returned deliverer and to give its life over to the worship of God:

> Thee . . . always blessing;
> serve thee (as the heavenly troop of angels serve thee);
> pray and praise thee without ceasing.

The last phrase of verse three returns to the beginning of the hymn, "glory in thy perfect love." The congregational response to the return of God's glory is reminiscent of Psalm 23:

> Surely goodness and mercy shall follow me
>   all the days of my life,
> and I shall dwell in the house of the LORD
>   my whole life long. (Ps 23:6)

Life is transformed into glad liturgical activity, all of life devoted to God alone.

It would have been enough to end with the third stanza and the culmination of "perfect love." But Wesley has one more series of imperative to address to this divine love. It is a petition to "finish" the first creation; we are told in Genesis 2:1 that it was finished on the sixth day. The tabernacle, replica of creation, it is reported in Exodus 39:32 and Exodus 40:33 was "finished" by Moses. And in John 19:30, Jesus asserts that "it is finished." But the new creation remains unfinished. And so the church prays,

> that the new creation will be established in its fullness,
> that we be "pure and spotless," that is, without blemish and able to
>   abide in the midst of God's holiness,
> that all will be "perfectly restored" in God,
> that we will be transposed into our rightful places in heaven,
> that we will be finally lost, in wonder, love, and praise.

After recognition of the trinitarian formula, several things strike one about this rendition of God's life and history:

- It requires a *mass of thick images* to get it said, and we never forget that it is poetry.
- The hymn is dominated by *imperatives*:

> fix in us,
> visit us,
> enter every trembling heart,

breathe O breathe,
let us inherit,
let us find promised rest,
take away the love of sinning,
be Alpha and Omega,
set our hearts at liberty,
come Almighty,
let us all renew,
return . . . never, never more leave,
finish then,
let us be pure and spotless,
let us see thy great salvation.

- Imagine *praise as petition* (Ps 51)! Why petition? Because the exuberant congregation that praises stands before the holy God as suppliant, needing resources that it cannot muster for itself, requiring intervention that it cannot initiate, presenting itself as an impatient community of waiting, seeking to mobilize by petition the faithfulness and goodness of God.[3]
- The plot of the hymn clearly moves from *divine love* through *embodiment* to *culmination*, exactly the shape of the trinitarian creeds to which I have referred.
- All of life is transposed into worship. One could, if one did not know Charles Wesley, conclude that this is otherworldly escapism. But of course this could not be so for Wesley, who was totally rooted in the economic realities of his time and place. His, rather, is a piety that responds to the old catechism question: "What is man's chief concern?" Or "What is the goal and purpose of human life?" The answer is: "To glorify God and enjoy God forever." It is the prayer of this congregation of troubled hearts or the cries of liberated hearts that God will govern in a way that makes such an existence of worship a joy on earth as it is a joy in heaven.[4] The hymn moves from creation and, like the creeds, awaits the fullness of God's Godness among us.
- Nicaea ends:

  We look for the resurrection of the dead
  and the life of the world to come.

- The Apostles' Creed has it:

  I believe in the resurrection of the body
  and the life everlasting.

- Wesley concludes:

> Finish then thy new creation
> that we may be lost in wonder, love, and praise.

The preacher's task is to engraft folk into that rendition of reality.

III

So how shall the preacher proceed? Well, one can outline the drama in various ways. In Jewish tradition, Franz Rosenzweig outlines it in three seasons, as creation, revelation, and redemption.[5] It is not far from that Jewish rendition to the creedal structure of Nicaea and the Apostles' Creed. If we are careful against the temptation of modalism, we may outline the drama of God's life and times as creation, embodiment, and kingdom so that the historical moment of embodiment is framed by a memory of initiating divine love and a hope of culminating divine love. I propose that it is the preacher's task to *frame* our moment of *embodiment* by a memory and a hope; when that is done, the preacher and the congregation will soon come to see that such framing permits a completely different articulation of our moment of embodiment in the historical process.

Following the creeds and Wesley's first line, it is the preacher's chance to frame contemporary life in terms of *the wonder* and the *mystery of creation*. The affirmation of the three-named God as Creator receives only terse expression in the two creeds, and in Wesley's hymn not much more:

- "of all things visible and invisible";
- "creator of heaven and earth";
- "all loves excelling, joy of heaven."

That is all. It remains for the doxological tradition of Israel and the church to flesh out the mystery of creation, the inscrutable wonder that we—and all creatures in heaven and on earth—are because of the self-giving flow of God's love. It is the preacher's task to frame life in such a miracle out beyond us. To that end, I mention eight texts, four from each of the testaments:

1. *Psalm 145* is the richest attestation to the work of the Creator in the Psalter. I call attention only to verses 4-7, because those verses offer a rich and effusive vocabulary that was necessary for Israel's faith:

> One generation shall laud your works to another,
>   and shall declare your mighty acts.
> On the glorious splendor of your majesty,
>   and on your wondrous works, I will meditate.

> The might of your awesome deeds shall be proclaimed,
>> and I will declare your greatness.
> They shall celebrate the fame of your abundant goodness,
>> and shall sing aloud of your righteousness. (Ps 145:4-7)

Notice the cluster of terms: works, mighty acts, majesty, wondrous works, awesome deeds, greatness, abundant goodness, righteousness. Roughly, the terms are all synonyms, though of course with varied nuance. All of them speak of God's sovereign capacity to exercise originary power to call into existence that which does not exist. This cluster of terms bespeaks awesome power; but in the end, it is "goodness" and "righteousness," that is, qualities of a blessed, fruitful, prosperous life. The term "wondrous works" in verse 5 is as close as the Bible comes to "miracle," an act of surpassing wonder that lies outside our rationality and our capacity for explanation. The language of doxology must be as extravagant as is the God of creation extravagant in self-giving generosity. When Israel begins to detail the content of these wonders, the psalm speaks of the rule of God's kingdom and then witnesses to the scope of well-being given by the God of all miracles:

> Your kingdom is an everlasting kingdom,
>> and your dominion endures throughout all generations.
> The LORD is faithful in all his words,
>> and gracious in all his deeds.
> The LORD upholds all who are falling,
>> and raises up all who are bowed down.
> The eyes of all look to you,
>> and you give them their food in due season.
> You open your hand,
>> satisfying the desire of every living thing.
> The LORD is just in all his ways,
>> and kind in all his doings.
> The LORD is near to all who call on him,
>> to all who call on him in truth.
> He fulfills the desire of all who fear him;
>> he also hears their cry, and saves them.
> The LORD watches over all who love him,
>> but all the wicked he will destroy. (Ps 145:13-20)

These verses exhibit the generosity of the Creator God toward all creatures, with a final footnote of strictness, showing that the creator God is no "nice uncle"; "but all the wicked he will destroy."

2. The breathtaking doxology of Psalm 145 is matched by the lyric of *Psalm 104*, the other great creation psalm. The inventory of all creatures concludes with a mention of wine, bread, and oil, the stuff of sacraments:

> You cause the grass to grow for the cattle,
>   and plants for people to use,
> to bring forth food from the earth,
>   and wine to gladden the human heart,
> oil to make the face shine,
>   and bread to strengthen the human heart. (Ps 104:14-15)

After that inventory, three notices are important:

First, God is the great guarantor of order against the threat of chaos:

> Yonder is the sea, great and wide,
>   creeping things innumerable are there,
>   living things both small and great.
> There go the ships,
>   and Leviathan that you formed to sport in it. (Ps 104:25-26)

Leviathan has been domesticated, good news for all the other creatures!

Second, food comes from the Creator:

> These all look to you
>   to give them their food in due season;
> when you give to them, they gather it up;
>   when you open your hand,
>   they are filled with good things. (Ps 104:27-28)

Food is the most elemental sign of the Creator's sustenance of the creatures. And all the junk food in the world is no fill-in for the good gifts that the creatures receive from God's open hand.

Third, most spectacularly, the psalm asserts that all of life depends on the gift of God's breath:

> When you hide your face, they are dismayed;
>   when you take away their breath, they die
>   and return to their dust. (Ps 104:29-30)

The two uses in the NRSV "breath" and "spirit" render the same term, *ruah*. The lines portray God as a reliable iron lung that continues to breathe the world to vitality. Recall Wesley's second verse:

> Breathe O breathe thy loving spirit
> into every trouble heart.

It is the Creator who gives food and who gives oxygen, without which we die. Like little birds with wide open mouths, all creatures are dependent, and God is faithful. It is no wonder that the psalm moves finally to unqualified praise:

> I will sing to the LORD as long as I live;
>> I will sing praise to my God while I have being. (Ps 104:33)

That move is not unlike Wesley's last line. The ones given the sustaining tokens of bread, wine, and oil are lost in wonder, love, and praise, lost along with all creatures, who receive life as given, moment by moment, all day long and all through the night.

3. *Psalms 148 and 150* voice contextless exuberance with endless summons to praise. That is how the Psalter ends:

> Praise the LORD!
> Praise the LORD from the heavens;
>> praise him in the heights!
> Praise him, all his angels;
>> praise him, all his host!
> Praise him, sun and moon;
>> praise him, all you shining stars!
> Praise him, you highest heavens,
>> and you waters above the heavens! (Ps 148:1-4)

> Praise the LORD!
> Praise God in his sanctuary;
>> praise him in his mighty firmament!
> Praise him for his mighty deeds;
>> praise him according to his surpassing greatness! (Ps 150:1-2)

It is, however, *Psalms 146 and 147* that supply the ground for such doxology with abandonment. These psalms, penultimate in the collection, recite the wonders of the Creator-deliverer God:

> The LORD sets the prisoners free;
>> the LORD opens the eyes of the blind.
> The LORD lifts up those who are bowed down;
>> the LORD loves the righteous.
> The LORD watches over the strangers. (Ps 146:7b-9a)

> The LORD builds up Jerusalem;
>> he gathers the outcasts of Israel.

> He heals the brokenhearted,
>   and binds up their wounds.
> He determines the number of the stars;
>   he gives to all of them their names.
> . . . .
> He covers the heavens with clouds,
>   prepares rain for the earth,
>   makes grass grow on the hills.
> He gives to the animals their food,
>   and to the young ravens when they cry.
> . . . .
> He grants peace within your borders;
>   he fills you with the finest of wheat.
> He sends out his command to the earth;
>   his word runs swiftly.
> He gives snow like wool;
>   he scatters frost like ashes.
> He hurls down hail like crumbs—
>   who can stand before his cold?
> He sends out his word, and melts them;
>   he makes his wind blow, and the waters flow. (Ps 147:2-4, 8-9, 14-18)

Israel gives celebrative voice to the awareness that in every sphere of reality it is the generative force of God that causes life to function well. That good news pertains to Israel and to the outcasts; it also pertains to the brokenhearted, to the stars, to the grass, to the rivers. It is the Creator who causes wind to blow and water to flow.

4. I cannot resist, in my list of Old Testaments texts, the amazing verse in Job 40:15.[6] Since I have mentioned the taming of Leviathan in Psalm 104, I mention this reference to Behemoth, the great hippopotamus who is wild, ferocious, majestic, demanding, imperious, and dazzlingly impressive. And the Creator God says to Job in the presence of Behemoth:

> Look at Behemoth,
>   which I made just as I made you;
>   it eats grass like an ox. (Job 40:15)

Look at this ferocious creature; and get a sense of powerful, untamed creatureliness, the kind of creature willed by the unanxious Creator. And then God says that creature is *just like you, Job*!

5. In the New Testament, I begin with the obvious texts in which Jesus performs the work of the Creator, *Mark 4:35-41*. The disciples are in a boat at sea, terrified by the storm. When they awaken Jesus, he says, "Peace, be still" (v. 39). Well, he

really said to the waters, "Shut up." He said that to chaos, and the wind ceased. And then he said to his boat mates: "Why are you afraid? Have you still no faith?" (Mark 4:40). Have you no confidence that the creation must answer to the Creator God, who is here bodied in the boat with you? No wonder, as Mark reports, "they were filled with awe." They wonder who this is. And the church has said about this storm-stilling one, "God from God, true God from true God," the Creator.

6. In *Mark 6:30-43 and 8:1-10*, Jesus twice performs the wonder of food. He feeds crowds; he has great surpluses left over when he is finished. He accomplishes this sacramental act by the great verbs of the church: he took, he blessed, he broke, he gave. What he did in this freighted moment is that he kick-started creation again in its abundance. And every time the church blesses and breaks, it sees again creation fully restored to its true abundance. And we, like all teachers, are satisfied along with "the desire of every living thing" (Ps 145:16).

7. In *Matthew 6:25-34*, Jesus invites his disciples to trust themselves to the Creator. Trust in the Creator is the alternative to anxiety about precarious creatureliness. He commands, "Do not be anxious." Then he attests that the birds and flowers and all other creatures trust that the Creator-Father God knows everything that is needed. It is only Gentiles—those outside this narrative—that attempt to secure themselves.

8. In critical reflection on the church's memory, Paul gathers up all the fragmented data of the memory and is able to assert of Jesus: "For in him all things in heaven and on earth were created, things visible and invisible, whether thrones or dominions or rulers or powers—all things have been created through him and for him. He himself is before all things; and in him all things hold together" (Col 1:16-17). More than that cannot be claimed. This Jesus is the clue and key to the coherence of all creation. Life will hold. Life is not shattered or in jeopardy or meaningless because the Son—the one in the second paragraph—enacts, embodies, and assures that life is pure, trustworthy gift.

IV

So how shall the preacher proceed? Well, the preacher frames the moment of embodiment *by hope as by memory*. The story of God's life and times is propelled by a divine resolve that reaches into the future. That future receives utterance in the classic recitals:

- We look for the life of the world to come;
- I believe in the resurrection of the body and life everlasting;
- Creation will be finished, pure and spotless.

Of course, these phrases are open to world-escaping otherworldliness, immortality and life after death with our loved ones, and all of that. While none of that is precluded, it is not the point of accent in the story of God's times. Rather, the gospel is the announcement of the coming "kingdom," the historical realm of God's governance in the world (see Mark 1:14-15). That is why the church continues to pray, "Thy kingdom come, thy will be done." The church awaits the divine gift of a human community that will perform its life according to the will of the creator. It is promised that, soon or late, the world will come to be the world God intends, a world summarized as the fullness of *shalom*:

> Steadfast love and faithfulness will meet;
>   righteousness and peace will kiss each other.
> Faithfulness will spring up from the ground,
>   and righteousness will look down from the sky.
> The LORD will give what is good,
>   and our land will yield its increase.
> Righteousness will go before him,
>   and will make a path for his steps. (Ps 85:10-13)

This this-world account is pervasive in the Old Testament. Gerhard von Rad has proposed that the first full narrative of Israel's faith is the story of Abraham's promise of land that comes to fulfillment in the book of Joshua:[7]

> Thus the LORD gave to Israel all the land that he swore to their ancestors that he would give them; and having taken possession of it, they settled there. And the LORD gave them rest on every side just as he had sworn to their ancestors; not one of all their enemies had withstood them, for the LORD had given all their enemies into their hands. Not one of all the good promises that the LORD had made to the house of Israel had failed; all came to pass. (Josh 21:43-45).

The land, with peaceableness, is a gift of God's promise.

That same sense of landed well-being is evident in the final verses of the Hebrew Bible, according to its own ordering of books. In Jewish tradition, the Bible ends with the verses of *2 Chronicles 36:22-23*, a permit of Cyrus the Persian that displaced Jews are free to return to Jerusalem. In this tradition Jerusalem is the expectation of newness as a gift of God in fulfillment of God's promises:

> In the first year of King Cyrus of Persia, in fulfillment of the word of the LORD spoken by Jeremiah, the LORD stirred up the spirit of King Cyrus of Persia so that he sent a herald throughout all his kingdom and also declared in a written edict: "Thus says King Cyrus of Persia: the LORD, the God of heaven, has given me all the kingdoms of the earth, and he has charged me to build him a house at Jerusalem, which is in Judah.

> Whoever is among you of all his people, may the Lord his God be with
> him! Let him go up." (2 Chron 36:22-23)

Now even the empire is allied with God's people in bringing history to its concrete
fulfillment.

But of course, the Jews who trust the promise and cherish the land are under
no illusion. They know that their life in the world is one of dispute, conflict, and
contestation. So they wait. They wait because the world is under promise, a promised finish in Jerusalem. Nowhere is this promise for Jerusalem more powerfully
voiced than in the book of Isaiah, a book that reaches its final form among exiles
and returnees. The Jerusalem promise forms the bookends of the book of Isaiah.

In *Isaiah 2:2-4*, prophetic imagination looks into God's intention for Jerusalem. The ultimate hope for Jerusalem is that the city—now the place of torah
instruction—will be the epicenter of international history; all nations will come
there for torah instruction. And what they will learn is peace:

> He shall judge between the nations,
>   and shall arbitrate for many peoples;
> they shall beat their swords into plowshares,
>   and their spears into pruning hooks;
> nation shall not lift up sword against nation,
>   neither shall they learn war any more. (Isa 2:4)

This coming Jerusalem, at the center of the coming world of God, will be a society disarmed, a peaceable kingdom in which lions and lambs will be peaceably
together, and none will practice brutality any longer toward their neighbors.
There will be a glad end of all hostility; Micah adds to the poem the awareness
that this coming peaceable future will perforce feature a lower standard of living
without aggressive acquisitiveness:

> but they shall all sit under their own vines and under their own fig trees,
>   and no one shall make them afraid;
>   for the mouth of the Lord of hosts has spoken. (Mic 4:4)

At the other end of the book of Isaiah, in *Isaiah 65:17-25*, we have the most
sweeping hope of the Old Testament, a new heaven and a new earth, and a new
Jerusalem as the epicenter of the new earth. The poem proceeds to characterize
the coming regime of peaceableness in quite concrete, urban ways. It will be a
region of societal well being without infant mortality, without acquisitive economics, with the old curses of Genesis 3 rendered null and void because the earth
will be under the aegis of blessing. The visionary poem concludes with two notes,
(1) full, immediate attentiveness from God and (2) complete reconciliation:

> Before they call I will answer,
>> while they are yet speaking I will hear.
> The wolf and the lamb shall feed together,
>> the lion shall eat straw like the ox;
>> but the serpent—its food shall be dust!
> They shall not hurt or destroy
>> on all my holy mountain,
>>> says the LORD. (Isa 65:24-25)

Israel and all humanity are headed for a season of ultimate well-being, in which there will be no ground for conflict, enmity, anxiety, or brutality.

Jesus, according to Christian confession, initiates this new order, this earthly regime change for the "kingdom of God." While the rhetoric of newness is sweeping, the specificity of newness in the narrative is one leper at a time, one blind person at a time, one poor person at a time, as lives are resituated by the divine power and promise into a new zone. Jesus had done enough to make others wonder if he were indeed the edge of God's newness. For that reason, John asks, and Jesus answers John. There are no creeds yet, no christological formulations. There is only the neighborly data: "And he answered them, 'Go and tell John what you have seen and heard: the blind receive their sight, the lame walk, the lepers are cleansed, the deaf hear, the dead are raised, the poor have good news brought to them'" (Luke 7:22). Jesus' presence, so they discerned, is surging with end-time transformational power. That is how the future will be under God's governance, healed, whole, forgiven, cleansed. The inventory in Luke 7:22 builds to its climax, "The dead are raised." One could not go beyond that affirmation except that Jesus does go beyond it. There is one miracle even beyond resurrection. The final note is, "The poor have good news," good news of debt cancellation and rehabilitation into the economy. And then Jesus adds enigmatically: "And blessed is anyone who takes no offense at me" (Luke 7:23).

Why would his listeners be offended at such rehabilitative practices? Well, because the enactment of God's promise will wipe out all the possibility of power politics and economic leverage and military intimidation. What is coming in God's future outflanks the way we have organized the world, and one can see the alternative already in play in this bodied son.

The news on Easter day is that the world is not without God, not without this bodied edge of God's holiness alive and loose in the world. Easter may be the culmination of the gospel story in the four accounts; but it is only the beginning of that newness. As a consequence, the gospel writers puzzle about how to conclude their writing in order to leave it open-ended. I mention only the conclusion of Matthew wherein the disciples worship the risen Jesus and then he charges them: "Go therefore and make disciples of all nations, baptizing them in the name of the Father and of the Son and of the Holy Spirit, and teaching them to obey everything that I have commanded you" (Matt 28:19-20a). This great missional mandate is toward the future. The obedience now commanded is to invite participation in the new regime of God's governance initiated in Easter. Baptizing in the three-named God is the access point to the new age. The work of the disciples is exactly to recruit and engraft folk all over the world into the new peaceable regime now made possible by torah obedience. It is a risky venture among those "offended," and so Jesus adds: "And remember, I am with you always, to the end of the age" (Matt 28:20b). The final promise is full presence and accompaniment. The assurance of full presence sounds a lot like Isaiah 65:24:

> Before they call I will answer,
>> while they are yet speaking I will hear. (Isa 65:24)

It sounds, moreover, like Wesley's last phrase,

> Till we cast our crowns before thee,
> lost in wonder, love, and praise.

The destiny of the disciples is full companionship and attentiveness from this agent of God's holy newness.

The theme of divine presence, a stunning reversal of the absence known among us, is crucial in the lyrical rhetoric of Paul. After Paul's careful assertion about baptism and the new life, he finishes his relentless insistence with a confident, lyrical statement of divine presence:

> No, in all these things we are more than conquerors through him who
> loved us. For I am convinced that neither death, nor life, nor angels, nor
> rulers, nor things present, nor things to come, nor powers, nor height,
> nor depth, nor anything else in all creation, will be able to separate us
> from the love of God in Christ Jesus our Lord. (Rom 8:37-39)

What preacher among us has not fallen back on this poetry in the face of death? It is too bad that we have consigned Romans 8 to funerals in the same way that we have slotted 1 Corinthians 13 to weddings. The text is usable at funerals, but it is not a funeral text. It is an assertion, rather, that newness has begun to crowd in on creation; and while creation groans in labor, the decisive act is already completed. The world, as God's coming regime, is not without God, and that changes everything for those who are already authorized and empowered to live according to the new governance, unafraid, courageous, and ready to trust. Paul's affirmation about the coming of age of presence is reminiscent of Israel's affirmation in Psalm 27:

> The LORD is my light and my salvation:
>> whom shall I fear?

> The LORD is the stronghold of my life;
>   of whom shall I be afraid? (Ps 27:1)

It is promised that our lives will be kept safely for all time to come by this presence that works the new creation. It is no wonder that all things work together for good for those who are called according to his purposes (Rom 8:28).

Finally, inevitably, I mention the ultimate promise of the New Testament in *Revelation 21*, a riff on the poetry of Isaiah 65: "Then I saw a new heaven and a new earth; for the first heaven and the first earth had passed away, and the sea was no more. And I saw the holy city, the new Jerusalem, coming down out of heaven from God, prepared as a bride adorned for her husband" (Rev 21:1-2). The future is not a private, individualistic future. It is a new epoch in the history of the world. The church knows that the old earth cannot be sustained. The church knows that the old Jerusalem is frayed around the edges, and the church knows that the old heaven is too filled with the dispute among the gods. This promise is of a God who makes all things new. There will be no more sea, no threat of chaos, no anxiety. There will be no more death and no tears and no mourning. The new epoch is one of glorious well being, and it is as sure as the God known in creation.

The church, with its appropriation of the traditions of ancient Israel, has found many poetic ways to speak about God's coming regime of new life: Easter, second coming, new creation, lion and lamb. The words tumble out because we have more to say than any set of our words will allow. God will be God, and that is the best news available.

V

It is the preacher's task *to frame our life*. From the first article of the creed, the preacher pushes back to the mystery of creation and the flood of miracles that constitute a blessed life. In the third article of the creed, the preacher pushes forward to resurrection and eternal life. But all such framing talk is in order that the church can be led to freedom and courage, within the frame, for life with the bodied one from the second paragraph of the creed.

The language between the framing of beginning and ending is terse. Nicaea offers a breathtaking phrase:

> And was made man.

Or more currently, "became truly human." The creed moves immediately from virgin birth to Pontius Pilate. It is not different in the Apostles' Creed,

> Born of the Virgin Mary,
>   suffered under Pontius Pilate,
>   was crucified, dead, and buried.

It is remarked often enough that the life of Jesus, the narrative offered by the evangelists, is reduced by the creed to a comma. But what a comma! "Was made man, crucified, suffered, died, and was buried." But the route from birth to suffering and death is all the venture of the human condition. So the preacher takes us into the human condition and invites the church, now framed between miracles and promises, to live its humanness differently, as did he:

- It is this Jesus who understood the neighbor to be the epicenter of gospel obedience;
- It is this Jesus who spoke truth to power;
- It is this Jesus who bent social institutions to the service of human need;
- It is this Jesus who practiced his life with children and widows and orphans and other valueless nonproducers;
- It is this Jesus who called Rome into question and offered an alternative governance;
- It is this Jesus who argued with the other rabbis for the sake of the good news;
- It is this Jesus who taught poetically in order not to be slotted by the ideologues;
- It is this Jesus who embodied God's vulnerability, God's edgy attentiveness in the world, God's crash course on newness that summons.

So the preacher explicates the comma of the creeds, creating huge space between the miracle of creation and the promise of culmination. The preacher knows that when the ultimate framing is clear enough, there can be transformation in the season of the comma. Indeed, we are told that

- knowing where he had come from,
- knowing where he was going,
- he took a towel!

Well, what else, says the preacher, did you think he would take?

Wesley is no more forthcoming about the middle paragraph than are the creeds. He says only, in the second stanza,

> Breathe O breathe thy loving spirit,
> into every troubled breast.

"Was made man . . . meets . . . 'the troubled breast,'" troubled about greed and disorder, troubled about foreclosures and bad diagnoses, troubled about life displaced in a strange world. Beyond personal anxieties, Wesley knew that troubled breasts arise from poor healthcare policy and poor educational resources and poor welfare assistance and vengeful military policy. The preacher not only acknowledges troubled breasts that belong to the human predicament but also invites well-framed people to be active protagonists in the midst of these contradictions. We are all in the process of becoming truly human, being made in the image of the one who is the firstborn image of God's holiness.

I take *Psalm 103* as a gospel exploration of being truly human and being sustained therein. The truly human are sustained by the faithfulness of the three-named God:

> who forgives all your iniquity,
>   who heals all your diseases,
> who redeems your life from the Pit,
>   who crowns you with steadfast love and mercy,
> who satisfies you with good as long as you live
>   so that your youth is renewed like the eagle's. (Ps 103:3-5)

The Psalm identifies the great issues of the troubled human breast. On the one hand, there is *guilt* that is met by divine forgiveness:

> He will not always accuse,
>   nor will he keep his anger forever.
> He does not deal with us according to our sins,
>   nor repay us according to our iniquities.
> For as the heavens are high above the earth,
>   so great is his steadfast love toward those who fear him;
> as far as the east is from the west,
>   so far he removes our transgressions from us.
> As a father has compassion for his children,
>   so the LORD has compassion for those who fear him.
> For he knows how we were made;
>   he remembers that we are dust. (Ps 103:9-14)

On the other hand, there is *mortality*, which is overridden by steadfast love that is from everlasting to everlasting:

> As for mortals, their days are like grass;
>   they flourish like a flower of the field;
> for the wind passes over it, and it is gone,
>   and its place knows it no more.
> But the steadfast love of the LORD is from everlasting to everlasting
>   on those who fear him,
>   and his righteousness to children's children,
> to those who keep his covenant
>   and remember to do his commandments. (Ps 103:15-18)

Those who have the human predicament *framed by miracle and by promise* are authorized to a present tense of freedom and courage in order to live a life big with the blessing of God:

> The LORD has established his throne in the heavens,
>   and his kingdom rules over all.
> Bless the LORD, O you his angels,
>   you mighty ones who do his bidding,
>   obedient to his spoken word.
> Bless the LORD, all his hosts,
>   his ministers that do his will.
> Bless the LORD, all his works,
>   in all places of his dominion.
> Bless the LORD, O my soul. (Ps 103:19-22)

VI

It is my view that the preacher has only a few things to say but a myriad of ways in which to say them. It is my view that in our time and place the utterance of the preacher is urgent:

1. *The framing of life by creation and miracle* is urgent because without such framing in creation the primary option is self-sufficiency, self-invention, and self-security. Where there are not wondrous gifts to begin to sustain life, human existence becomes a rat race for domination.

2. *The framing of life by promise and culmination* is urgent because when such framing culmination is unuttered, we are left without hope in the world and left with a deep nihilism. And clearly those who have no more than the nihil become dangerous and destructive forces.

3. *The articulation of courage and energy for obedience* between framing creation and framing culmination is urgent because without a deep probing of "becoming truly human," we are left with an alternative framing that produces a present tense of mindless autonomy and anxious conformity. Thus the preacher has the good news of an alternative:

- *creation* miracles as alternative to *self-sufficiency*;
- culminating *promises* as alternative to a *fate of nihilism*;
- an offer of *the truly human* as an alternative to *autonomy and conformity*.

I imagine that in the twenty-first century, like every other century, the moment of preaching utterance is a deeply freighted moment in the life of the world and in the life and times of God. We may take care not to trivialize that thick moment by shrill ideology or by moralism or by mere entertainment. Preaching is, rather, a moment of truth-telling concerning the most elemental matters, elemental but immediately and urgently contemporary.

VII

The preacher's task is to *engraft* folk into this narrative of *originary miracle, culminating promise,* and *human intentionality.* To engraft folk into this narrative requires *relinquishment* of other narratives, notably the modernist narrative of control. Because that *embrace* and *relinquishment* is so difficult and demanding, it cannot, for the most part, be done frontally. The capacity to entertain an alternative to the dominant narrative, perchance to embrace it, is evoked, hosted, and practiced by imagination, construing possible, choosable, embraceable reality beyond the presumed given. Perhaps Jesus' parables are as good an example as we have of emancipative articulation of an alternative that is noncoercive but powerfully subversive. Such acts are perforce *poetic* (not given to precision and closure), *playful* (not coercive or insistent), and are more likely to be narrative *performances* in which both the teller (preacher) and listener can assume one or more roles in the drama and move through the scenes to a new reality. Thus, good preaching is in some sense a theater of the absurd, street theater, gorilla theater, a refusal to accommodate settled assumptions. It follows that such a "performance" is not closely tied to "contemporary issues," is not strong advocacy for any particular behavior or morality, but seeks to go below such immediacy to long-term "redescription." The task of performance is not to close oneself to certitude but to open oneself to possibility because no serious relinquishment or new embrace is possible until an alternative is hosted as a real possibility.

To that end, I have considered in some specificity three texts that bring my larger advocacy down to concrete cases: Psalm 131, Isaiah 49:8-16a, and Matthew 6:24-34. The obvious place to begin is Jesus' invitation to his disciples in the Sermon on the Mount, where he summons them away from anxiety in order to trust in the generous Father God. Since that is such an obvious beginning point, I choose rather to begin with Psalm 131, a brief psalm of trust:

> O LORD, my heart is not lifted up,
>   my eyes are not raised too high;
> I do not occupy myself with things
>   too great and too marvelous for me.
> But I have calmed and quieted my soul,
>   like a weaned child with its mother;
>   my soul is like the weaned child that is with me. (Ps 131:1-2)

The poem—it is a poem—situates the speaker in a context not unlike that of a very young, weaned child with his mother. The image is of total trust, confident in mother, clean, fed, safe, cared for. That image is chosen over against the alternative in verse 1:

> heart lifted up,
> eyes raised high,
> occupied with great things.

The temptation—here rejected—is one of aggressive ambition, the need to assert and dominate and control. And, says this calm speaker, I decided not to go down that road. I decided to opt out of ambition-cum-anxiety and to settle for a life of quiet well being. I could do that because I have entrusted myself to a God who is like a mother, there before me, there after me, capable, attentive, trustworthy, the pure alternative to anxiety.

It takes no great imagination to see that the psalm voices a harsh critique of a can-do society that is driven by money and power in the interest of control and domination and being on top of the heap. The implied critique concerns aggressiveness, unrestrained acquisitiveness, and perhaps even military domination, all acts that keep us endlessly unsafe and anxious in the world. The psalmist has decided not to live on "Orange Alert." The psalmist can do otherwise because *the Mother God* makes it not necessary to secure oneself.

That reading of the psalm is surely the assumption of the teaching of Jesus. The disciples can trust *the Father God*, who knows what they need. The disciples can be in solidarity with lilies and pigeons and other trusting creatures. They are all contrasted with Solomon who, in all his glory, was still marked by aggressiveness, acquisitiveness, and greedy entitlement. The psalmist has broken with the dominant system by yielding to the Mother God. The disciples are to break with the dominant system by trusting the Father God.

The capacity of those who break with the dominant system, says the poet in Isaiah 49, permits them to be,

- a covenant to the people,
- an emancipation of prisoners,
- a gatherer of displaced persons,
- an agent of compassion and comfort.

Clearly, the authorization and empowerment of that poem equips people to be remakers of the world. People who continue in the dominant system of aggressive acquisitiveness and entitlement cannot do anything to remake the world. And, says Jesus to his disciples, you cannot have it both ways; you cannot serve two masters.

The preacher is always articulating the evangelical possibility that is out beyond the horizon of the dominant narrative. The preacher is always inviting folk to choose and redecide:

- to decide about *foundational miracles or self-sufficiency,*
- to decide about *culminating promises or fated nihilism,*
- to decide about an *emancipated life of glad obedience or a life of anxiety.*

There are no two ways about it. It is the glorious task of the preacher that the preacher, along with the whole people of God, can be engrafted into the life of the Father of all miracles, the bodied Son of obedience, the promise-keeping Spirit. The world waits in its hopeful resistance for such good preaching.

With Thanks to

Lowell H. Zuck

RETROSPECT

THERE ARE MANY WAYS to publish a book. The least demanding way is to get someone else to do the heavy lifting. That is the case with this book. Carolyn Sharp has taken on most of the demanding chores of compiling and editing, and I am most grateful to her. She has been, all along the way and in her several introductory essays, consistently generous and affirmative of my work, though she would of course have critical differences if the case were pressed.

More than that, she has rightly seen, in depth, what I have been trying to do in my several expositions over time and, indeed, has helped me to see some aspects of the trajectory of my work that I myself had not fully understood. She has of course seen that I have struggled, as most people in our discipline have struggled, with the tricky interface of the critical and the confessional. I have never intended to scuttle the critical process, and I do not think that critical work is unimportant or "bankrupt," as one mantra has it. But I do think, as many now do, that it has acute limitation. Thus, our confidence in the modernist critical project has waned considerably. As much as I can judge, it is only interpreters who have been wounded by church authoritarianism and thereby pushed to skepticism who continue to imagine that there is high ground for what they think is "objective scholarship." Because my venue of interpretation and my passion have been the church and, more specifically, seminary education, my reading has been in a confessional mode. (Of course, what passes for "objective scholarship" is also in a confessional mode, only with reference to modernist rationality.) Because my interest has been consistently practical, that is, aimed at *praxis*, it is inescapable that much of my work has moved toward advocacy. That is because I believe both that our society is in huge trouble and that there are compelling resources of faith and practice in the biblical text that may permit serious engagement with that deep social crisis. The critical project is both to situate texts contextually as best we can and to critique the various lethal ideologies that pervade the text. As we are able, provisionally, to sort out context and ideology, we are able as well to see how the text imagines lived reality differently when the God of Israel (the God of the church) is taken to be an active character and effective agent in the world. Such an act of imagination requires an intentional epistemological act, and there is no doubt that both the textual community and the communities funded by the text continue to commit that epistemological act, though we may try to conceal it as best we can. Thus, the Bible seems to us as strange as it does (so Karl Barth referred to "the strange new world of the Bible") because we have everywhere among us accepted modernist rationality as normative. As we have learned over and over again from Barth, the break with that rationality is a deeply subversive act that is funded and evoked by the text. Consequently, practical interpretation, that is, interpretation that leads to practice, is inevitably pushed beyond critical contextual and historical questions to theological questions about the character and agency of God, for whom there is no room in modernist rationality. When that move toward the character and agency of God is taken seriously, as I have attempted to do, one moves, perforce, toward advocacy in some way or another.

My own growth in perception, understanding, and courage has been a long, slow process—aided and abetted by engaged students—of moving into and then beyond critical categories. I can identity some influences on my practice of interpretation that continue to be evident in my work. It is impossible to overstate the importance of Jewish scholarship in more recent time that has summoned Christian interpreters like myself away from thin critical work. That is, the summons is not only not to be so unwittingly and blatantly "Christian" but also not to rely on critical work that has been, in its long history, a handmaid of Christian interpretation. When I began my work a long time ago, even though we read Abraham Heschel and Martin Buber, Jewish interpretive work was hardly on the horizon, and even now folk like me have only an impressionistic glimpse into it. But the strictures of Jon Levenson and the work on thick tradition by Michael Fishbane have been most important to me, permitting me to recognize that the text is irresolvably multivalent and cannot be reduced to a single reading. That means that I, and many alongside me, have much unlearning to do about how to read texts that are invariably thick, multilayered, and conflicted.

I pause over my most important teachers, because I am able to see that what I have been taught has converged for me in a quite distinctive practice of interpretation. While I am continually grateful to my teachers, the particular way of interpretation reflected in these essays is distinctly my own. Of course, my access to the wondrous, surging capacity of the text was entrusted to me most especially by my teacher James Muilenburg, who insisted, almost alone at that time among major people in the field, that we should be reading the text rather than books about the text. Muilenburg's "rhetorical criticism" has been defining for me even though I have not practiced it in the "pure" form that he intended. I have learned from him how deeply and intimately speech and reality are intertwined, a point also accented in the remarkable exchange between Franz Rosenzweig and Eugen Rosenstock-Huessey. Thus, as I have asserted, in a way not very well articulated, the God of Israel lives on Israel's lips and has as much freedom and authority as Israel's bold lips are able to voice. And of course, it is not different in the early church with the witness of the evangelists and the apostolic preachers. Consequently, the study of the detail of the text matters because in the end it is a theological rendering. Beyond Muilenburg's enormously important methodological contributions, I have learned from him about the dramatic performance of the text, so that he was indeed a "performer" who did not resist being "foolish" for the sake of the "truthfulness" of the text. My own work reflects that conviction and some of that performative "foolishness."

In a retrospective, I may be permitted the lining out of my teachers who came before and after Muilenburg in my learning. Before Muilenburg, from the outset, was my father, August, not a learned man but a convinced, passionate witness who understood intuitively about "the big stuff." I learn, more and more in my old age, about his decisive impact on me. Th. W. Mueller was my sociology teacher who helped me to understand the decisiveness of the social construction of reality and the urgency of social justice in the midst of such constructive action. In seminary, Allen Wehrli introduced me, in his peculiar narrative capacity, to the ways in which the biblical text required and permitted immense imaginative freedom, and Lionel Whiston walked me into the first English translations of the work of Gerhard von Rad, which has been defining for me. I am able to see, at this distance, that this sequence of teachers constituted a long tutorial to prepare me for Muilenburg's way with the text and his way through the text to the God of the text.

After Muilenburg, I can identify two teachers in particular. I team-taught with Douglas Meeks for a number of years and learned from him about the profound seriousness of theological work. And then, by happenstance, the world of interpretation was opened to me through the writings of Paul Ricoeur, with whom I have spent an endless amount of time trying to understand his density. Ricoeur made available to me the generative force of imagination, which in evangelical parlance amounts to "the work of the Spirit." We are led beyond ourselves in ways that we do not understand or anticipate. As Israel has known since the flood narrative, there can be an "evil imagination of the heart," just as Paul counseled that the spirit must be "tested" (in this case, by critical study). No doubt more than once I have engaged in "evil imagination" that has been forcibly "tested" by critical reviewers. But in sum, it is my sense that imagination—the move beyond reductionism and criticism—has helped us to see that serious interpretation that matters is finally not "science" but "art." The long-term attempt of our discipline to be "scientific" has been useful and necessary. But that is never the end of the story. And the scholars who want to keep the lid on imagination through critical study finally do not fully discern how the text works, nor do they honor the reality of the primary "Resident" in the text.

In the wake of Ricoeur, I have been and wanted to be instructed by a number of important teachers, notably liberationists, feminists, and, more recently, postcolonial interpreters. Because of who I am (white, male, tenured), it has always been for me a matter of "catching up" with more subversive perceptions. I have, nonetheless, no doubt that such a stance is the wave of a faithful future in interpretation. Such teachers have taught me that our work is always contextual and never innocent and that advocacy is an inescapable part of serious interpretation of serious texts. This means, regularly, that part of the interpretive process is always unlearning. I believe such work urgent precisely because our society—and the church within that society—has so much to unlearn in a process that is always both painful and emancipatory.

Professor Sharp has nicely settled on the term "disruptive" for the God who inhabits the text and for the interpretive work derived from and that bears witness to that Disruptor.

That is precisely how I understand my work and how I understand what characteristically happens among us (and to me) in doing interpretive work that is theologically serious. Such interpretation often results in a disruptive surprise that leads both to unlearning and to advocacy, while much of modern rationality (to which we are commonly and variously committed) functions to fend off that very disruption. The God who occupies the biblical text (and who, we Christians say, is peculiarly evident in the disruptive presence of Jesus) was and is, as Judith Shilevitz nicely puts it, "the ungovernable reality" that always again meets Israel and the church. I suppose that "ungovernable reality" is best attested by the enigmatic divine name in Exodus 3:14, where we continue to be at a loss for translation. The textual tradition that follows that enigmatic declaration, moreover, is the long-term process of decoding and summarizing that name and then being yet again surprised by more loss and more gift.

That disruptive dimension of reality has been, in modest ways, named and processed in my own life especially by the generosity of Gerald Jenkins, my long-term therapist, friend, and eventually colleague. Jenkins has sat attentively and patiently with me while I have resisted the demands of such disruption and now and then have embraced such disruptiveness. I am not overly proud of how I responded to that disruptiveness (who is?!), nor overly confident about being a faithful interpreter of that disruptive presence who outruns all our categories and is at the core of life and of faith (who is?!). But I do know that it has been engagement with this text—reading and studying—that has been a guide and source for the subtext of disruption in my own life.

Two specifics: First, like every Old Testament teacher, I am routinely and often asked about "the violence of God" in the Old Testament. There is now an expansive literature that seeks either to understand or to explain away that reality in the text. These attempts variously appeal to an evolutionary hypothesis that God gets "better and better" in human perception over time in a way that permits us to reject the offensive texts as primitive misperceptions that have been "superseded." I have no solution to the problem, except to suggest that "the violence of God" in the text attests the continuing drama of God's holiness that may not be explained away as human misperception simply because it is a deep affront to us—as it is! The payout of taking that "violence of God" with theological seriousness may be to recognize that I (and we) are variously constituted exactly in the image of this God who struggles with the seduction of violence. While that violence is surely affrontive and scandalous, it belongs, in this witness, to theological reality, and we need to ponder it rather than wish it away. I find the truth of that testimony congruent with how life is; and consequently, I am not convinced by easy attempts to escape the testimony.

Second, of late I have turned to the book of Daniel, a world and a book that are largely unfamiliar to me. I am struck by the role of the "magicians" in the narrative who serve in the court of Nebuchadnezzar. ("Magicians" is the familiar translation of the term that is derived from "engraving tool," that is, those learned in the art of writing and thus more generally learned). The "magicians" in Daniel 1:20 and 2:2, at the end of the Old Testament, have as their counterpart the magicians of Pharaoh at the beginning of Israel's text (Genesis 41:8, 24; Exodus 8:15 [v. 18 in English translation]; 9:11). In both cases, at the court of Pharaoh and at the court of Nebuchadnezzar, the "magicians" constitute the "intelligence community" of the royal court that is supposed to know about matters that other members of the court cannot discern. In both pieces of literature, the "magicians" are found to be inadequate to their task. In the Genesis narrative, they cannot decipher Pharaoh's dream. In the Exodus narrative, they cannot match the wonders of Moses and Aaron. In the Daniel narrative they cannot know or interpret the dreams of the king. In each case, of course, the alternative to the failed, discredited officials is an uncredentialed person of faith (Joseph the Hebrew, Moses the mighty Hebrew performer, Daniel the Jew), each of whom has a large capacity, unmatched in the empire, to understand and interpret and accomplish what the royal company cannot manage.

I have come to think that much of the quarrelsome anxiety in our culture, and not least among us "urban elites" who inhabit our discipline, is not unlike that of the ancient "magicians" who are identified by their learning and intend to be schooled in the arts of controlling the disruptive. We imagine that the more we know, the more we can control, whether it is in science or even in Scripture study. At the same time, there is, I believe, a pervasive anxiety in the recognition that for all our knowing and for all our learning, we are missing the real stuff. We know that there are real limits to our learning before the mystery that is beyond our control. Thus, our common "learnedness" perhaps does not give us access to what it is that we most need to know. The world of power (and scholarship) cannot do without the learned "magicians." But our recognition of the limit of such capacity may permit us some freedom to let the text run beyond our explanatory control. It is precisely when we are pushed beyond our explanatory control that we may find life given, bread broken, and wine poured out. That is what I have attempted in the statements of this collection.

It remains for me to "acknowledge." I am of course deeply indebted to Carolyn Sharp for her willing steadfastness throughout the process of this publication. I am grateful to Neil Elliott and his colleagues at Fortress Press, notably Michael West, for their willingness to bring out this book, but more, for their long-term readiness to publish my work. And I am, yet again, grateful to Tia Foley, who has brought most of these essays to publishable form.

I have dedicated this present book to Lowell Zuck, my first church history teacher and my long-term colleague. It has taken me a very long time to understand what Zuck, in his irenic, ironic way, has been trying to teach us about our particular theological rootedness. His gentle testimony to German Pietism, as it came to be embodied in the Evangelical Synod of North America (1866-1934) and eventually became a part of the United Church of Christ, has greatly aided me in discerning the ways in which I have inhaled that tradition that refused excessive theological preoccupation, that innocently took the biblical text as the defining resource and impetus for faith, that early and readily settled the potential struggle with historical criticism, and that relentlessly cared about the disadvantaged and the powerless. It is from this tradition, I am now able to see, that there is a convergence in my work of the themes of imagination, justice, and patient passion for the biblical text in all its oddness. It is clear that these several themes, so largely defining for my theological roots and so well exposited by Zuck, permeate my work. It is not a great stretch for me to see the connections between that tradition and practice and contemporary modes of spiritual life that fund compassion and that require interpretation that Ricoeur has termed "post-critical." I am grateful to Zuck for his witty patience, as he has always waited graciously for the rest of us to catch up with what he already has known.

NOTES

A bibliography of Walter Brueggemann's works cited in this volume begins on p. 381.

Introduction: The Uncompromising Theology of Walter Brueggemann

1. " 'Othering' with Grace and Courage," 1.
2. *Deep Memory, Exuberant Hope*, 4; emphasis original.
3. *Theology of the Old Testament*, 736.
4. *Pathway of Interpretation*, 110–11.
5. *Theology of the Old Testament*, 107.
6. *Pathway of Interpretation*, 17.
7. *Texts Under Negotiation*, 59.
8. *Theology of the Old Testament*, 117; emphasis original.
9. *Texts Under Negotiation*, 70.
10. "Psalms and the Life of Faith: A Suggested Typology of Function," in *Psalms and the Life of Faith*, 10–11.
11. Ibid., 21.
12. Ibid., 15, 23.
13. *Theology of the Old Testament*, 123.
14. Ibid., 400.
15. *Texts Under Negotiation*, 12.
16. *Theology of the Old Testament*, 122; emphasis original.
17. *Deep Memory, Exuberant Hope*, 122.
18. *Pathway of Interpretation*, 25–26.
19. *Interpretation and Obedience*, 19.
20. Ibid., 175.
21. *Introduction to the Old Testament*, 24.
22. "Othering" with Grace and Courage," 1.
23. "Duty as Delight and Desire," 35.
24. *Introduction to the Old Testament*, 27.
25. See *Mandate to Difference*, 65–66.
26. *Introduction to the Old Testament*, 23; emphasis original.
27. *Deep Memory, Exuberant Hope*, 5; emphasis original.
28. *Theology of the Old Testament*, 711.

Part I. Torah

Demand and Deliverance: Brueggemann on the Torah

1. *Old Testament Theology*, 37.
2. Ibid., 82; emphasis original.
3. *Introduction to the Old Testament*, 23.
4. Ibid., 17; emphasis original.
5. Ibid., 21.
6. "Covenant as a Subversive Paradigm," 46.
7. *Texts Under Negotiation*, 38.

1. Summons to a Dialogic Life

1. This paper was presented at the Presbyterian Covenant Network in Minneapolis.
2. On the Jewishness of Freud's contribution, see Susan A. Handelman, *The Slayers of Moses: The Emergence of Rabbinic Interpretation in Modern Literary Theory* (Albany: SUNY Press, 1982), 123–52.
3. There has been a dramatic reconception of psychotherapy in recent time in which the therapist is personally engaged in the process rather than a disengaged, "objective" listener.
4. Martin Buber, *I and Thou* (New York: Touchstone, 1996). On the way in which "meeting" became the primal theme of Buber's life, see Martin Buber, *Meeting: Autobiographical Fragments* (ed. Maurice Friedman; London: Routledge, 2002).
5. See Charles Taylor, *Sources of the Self: The Making of the Modern Identity* (Cambridge: Harvard University Press, 1989).
6. Emmanuel Levinas, *Totality and Infinity: An Essay on Exteriority* (Pittsburgh: Duquesne University Press, 1969).
7. Jürgen Moltmann, *The Crucified God: The Cross of Christ as the Foundation and Criticism of Christian Theology* (San Francisco: Harper & Row, 1974).

2. Exodus: Limit and Possibility

1. Walter Isaacson and Evan Thomas, *The Wise Men: Six Friends and the World They Made* (Touchstone Books; New York: Simon & Schuster, 1986).
2. Erich Voegelin, *Israel and Revelation: Order and History 1* (Baton Rouge: Louisiana State University Press, 1956).
3. Peter Ochs, "Talmudic Scholarship as Textual Reason: Halivni's Pragmatic Historiography," in *Textual Reasonings: Jewish Philosophy and Text Study at the End of the Twentieth Century*, ed. Peter Ochs and Nancy Levene (Grand Rapids: Eerdmans, 2002), 120–43; David Weiss Halivni, "Response to 'Talmudic Scholarship as Textual Reasoning,'" in ibid., 144–49.
4. It is Terence E. Fretheim, "The Plagues as Ecological Signs of Historical Disaster," *Journal of Biblical Literature* 110 (1991): 385–95, who has called our attention to the ways in which the plague narrative is to be read as creation theology and as a disturbance of the environment willed by the Creator.
5. Barbara Green, "The Determination of Pharaoh: His Characterization in the Joseph Story," in *The World of Genesis*, ed. Philip R. Davies and David J. A. Clines (Sheffield: Sheffield Academic Press, 1998), 150–71, has described the ways in which the Joseph narrative cunningly deconstructs Pharaoh against all of his pretensions to the contrary.
6. Emmanuel Levinas, *Totality and Infinity: An Essay on Exteriority* (Pittsburgh: Duquesne University Press, 1969).
7. Slavoj Žižek, *The Universal Exception* (New York: Continuum, 2006), 159: The problem, of course, is that in today's global sociopolitical circumstances it is practically impossible

effectively to call into question the logic of Capital: even a modest sociodemocratic attempt to redistribute wealth beyond the limit acceptable to Capital "effectively" leads to an economic crisis, inflation, a fall in revenues, and so on.

8. The deconstructive dimension of Yahwistic faith is evident, for example, in 1 Kings 8. In that narrative a high claim is made for the patronage and presence of YHWH in the Jerusalem temple "forever"; the deconstructive counterpoint is voiced in verses 9 and 27, thus precluding the totalizing claim of verses 12-13.

9. On the many problematic articulations of divine presence, see Samuel L. Terrien, *The Elusive Presence: Toward a New Biblical Theology* (New York: Harper & Row, 1978).

10. See Kathleen M. O'Connor, *Lamentations and the Tears of the World* (Maryknoll: Orbis, 2002).

3. Sabbath as Antidote to Anxiety

1. This lecture was presented at a Clergy Conference of the Episcopal Diocese of Atlanta.

2. The reference is, of course, to Paul Tillich, *The Courage to Be* (2nd ed.; New Haven: Yale University Press, 2000).

3. Erich Voegelin, *Israel and Revelation: Order and History 1* (Baton Rouge: Louisiana State Press, 1956) has utilized the term "paradigmatic" for Israel's early historical memory. By such a usage Voegelin acknowledges that that historical memory will not stand the scrutiny of modern critical methods but it nonetheless is defining for Israel's imagination and hope. See also Yosef Hayim Jerushalmi, *Zakhor: Jewish History and Jewish Memory* (Seattle: University of Washington Press, 1982).

4. The literal Hebrew is "do evil," so that both YHWH and Pharaoh are accused of "doing evil" to Israel.

5. Michael Walzer, *Exodus and Revolution* (New York: Basic, 1985), 149.

6. Terence E. Fretheim, *God and World in the Old Testament: A Relational Theology of Creation* (Nashville: Abingdon, 2005) 48–53.

7. On the way in which the seven speeches correlate with the seven days of creation, see Peter J. Kearney, "The P Redaction of Exod 25–20," *Zeitschrift für die alttestamentliche Wissenschaft* 89 (1977): 375–87, and Joseph Blenkinsopp, *Prophecy and Canon: A Contribution to the Study of Jewish Origins* (Notre Dame: University of Notre Dame Press, 1977) 54–69.

8. See S. Dean McBride Jr., "Polity of the Covenant People: The Book of Deuteronomy," *Interpretation* 41 (1987): 229–44.

9. See Stephen Kaufman, "The Structure of the Deuteronomic Law," *Maarav* 1 (1979): 105–58.

10. See Patrick D. Miller, "Luke 4:16-21," *Interpretation* 29 (1975): 417–21.

11. Reference may be made to almost any writing of Wendell Berry; see for example, *The Gift of Good Land: Further Essays Cultural and Agricultural* (San Francisco: North Point, 1981). Berry has made a powerful case that agribusiness manages land in a way that makes it less productive. In poetic idiom ancient Israel had already understood this point.

12. On this same contradiction between piety and social practice, see Isaiah 58:1-4, wherein workers are oppressed in the midst of much religious practice.

13. Philip Carrington, *The Primitive Christian Catechism: A Study in the Epistles* (Cambridge: Cambridge University Press, 1940).

4. The Countercommands of Sinai

1. This lecture was given at Luther Theological Seminary on January 15, 2009.

2. William S. Morrow, *Protest Against God: The Eclipse of a Biblical Tradition* (Hebrew Bible Monographs 4; Sheffield: Sheffield Phoenix, 2007) has made a powerful case that in the later period of the Old Testament the capacity to cry out to God and against God was

gradually stifled and transposed into repentance whereby the one who suffers does not protest but confesses sin. Morrow judges that this transposition is the work of the interpretive elites who wanted to protect the honor of God and so shifted the rhetoric away from protest to confession. In the exodus narrative, that shift has not yet been accomplished.

3. On this remarkable verse, see Brian S. Rosner, *Greed As Idolatry: The Origin and Meaning of a Pauline Metaphor* (Grand Rapids: Eerdmans, 2007).

4. Wendell Berry, *The Way of Ignorance and Other Essays* (Berkeley: Shoemaker & Hoard, 2005), 62–63.

PART II. PROPHETS

Refusal and Redescription: Brueggemann on the Prophets

1. *Reverberations of Faith*, 161.
2. "Jeremiah: Portrait of the Prophet," 7.
3. *Prophetic Imagination*, 16.
4. *Prophetic Imagination*, 99.

5. Every City a Holy City: The Holy City in Jeopardy

1. This presentation was offered as the P. C. and Janie Enniss Lectures at Central Presbyterian Church in Atlanta.

2. It is now passé to view these pentateuchal layers as "documents." But it is still the case that those layers of tradition represent different theological perspectives and advocacies. See the survey of common opinion by Richard Elliott Friedman, *Who Wrote the Bible?* (New York: Harper and Row, 1987).

3. Robert R. Wilson, *Prophecy and Society in Ancient Israel* (Philadelphia: Fortress Press, 1980), 270–74.

4. On the history of these traditions, see Gerhard von Rad, *Old Testament Theology*, vol. 2, *The Theology of Israel's Prophetic Traditions* (San Francisco: Harper and Row, 1965), 147–75.

5. There is no doubt that this poetry is a direct, perhaps liturgical response to the long cry of grief voiced in the book of Lamentations.

6. See Wilson, *Prophecy and Society*, 231–51.

7. There is no doubt that the book of Jeremiah is shaped under the decisive impact of the Deuteronomic tradition, on which see Ernest W. Nicholson, *Preaching to the Exiles: A Study of the Prose Tradition in the Book of Jeremiah* (Oxford: Blackwell, 1970). But behind that evident literary accomplishment, there is now no doubt that Jeremiah himself moved in and was shaped by that lively tradition that amounted to nothing less than a subversive alternative to the royal establishment and its urban-royal-temple ideology.

8. This is made explicit in Jeremiah 7:9 with its specific reference to the decalogue; beyond that, the cadences and accents of Jeremiah are reminiscent of Deuteronomy.

9. Frank Crüsemann, *The Torah: Theology and Social History of Old Testament Law* (Edinburgh: T & T Clark, 1996), 224–34.

10. See Walter Brueggemann, "Secretary of Woe," *Sojourners* 31, no. 4 (2002): 30–33.

11. See Wilson, *Prophecy and Society*, 282–86.

6. Every City a Holy City: The City of Possibility

1. This presentation was offered for the P. C. and Janie Enniss Lectures at Central Presbyterian Church in Atlanta.

2. It is startling that the crisis became the milieu for the most generative literature in ancient Israel. It is of course striking that Israel, in its defeat, was not driven to despair and

silence; it was, rather, propelled to vigorous imaginative speech. See Ralph W. Klein, *Israel in Exile: A Theological Interpretation* (Overtures to Biblical Theology; Philadelphia: Fortress Press, 1979).

3. On "forgive and forget" in contemporary framing, see the poignant statement of Miroslav Volf, *The End of Memory: Remembering Rightly in a Violent World* (Grand Rapid: Eerdmans, 2006).

4. Walt Whitman, *Leaves of Grass* 324. See my discussion of the poetic lines in *Finally Comes the Poet: Daring Speech for Proclamation* (Minneapolis: Fortress Press, 1989).

7. Prophetic Ministry in the National Security State

1. This address was delivered at the Festival of Homiletics in Nashville, Tennessee.

2. See the exposition of Paul Lehmann, *The Transfiguration of Politics: The Presence and Power of Jesus of Nazareth in and over Human Affairs* (New York: Harper & Row, 1975), 48–70.

3. Jürgen Moltmann, *The Crucified God: The Cross of Christ as the Foundation and Criticism of Christian Theology* (New York: Harper & Row, 1974).

4. Reference may usefully be made to Jon D. Levenson, *Resurrection and the Restoration of Israel: The Ultimate Victory of the God of Life* (New Haven: Yale University Press, 2006). Levenson offers a critique of "rationalistic" Jews who are embarrassed by the claim of resurrection and explain it away. There is, of course, a powerful parallel in Christian tradition and in contemporary interpretation.

5. See Alan E. Lewis, *Between Cross and Resurrection: A Theology of Holy Saturday* (Grand Rapids: Eerdmans, 2001).

6. John Bright, *A History of Israel* (4th ed.; Louisville: Westminster John Knox, 2000), 363.

7. Abraham J. Heschel, *Who Is Man?* (Stanford: Stanford University Press, 1965), 112–14.

8. On the dramatic symmetry of this poem, see David J. A. Clines, "Hosea 2: Structure and Interpretation," *Studia Biblica 1978*, ed. E. A. Livingston (Sheffield: JSOT, 1979), 83–103.

9. On the prophetic "otherwise," see Walter Brueggemann, *Testimony to Otherwise: The Witness of Elijah and Elisha* (St. Louis: Chalice, 2001).

10. On the significance of this phrase for my work, see Walter Brueggemann, *Finally Comes the Poet: Daring Speech for Proclamation* (Minneapolis: Fortress Press, 1989).

11. On the "empire of death," see James Boyd White, *Living Speech: Resisting the Empire of Force* (Princeton: Princeton University Press, 2006). White takes a phrase from Simone Weil to refer to coercive social arrangements as "empire of force." White's usage is close in intent to my own phrasing here. The phrase refers both to actual power arrangements and to the less visible social and symbolic practices that preclude hope and new possibility.

8. The Land Mourns

1. This paper was presented through the Lutheran Campus Ministry at Northern Michigan University, in Marquette, Michigan.

2. See Walter Brueggemann, *Solomon: Israel's Ironic Icon of Human Achievement* (Columbia: University of South Carolina Press, 2005).

3. On the connection between Pharaoh and the violation of creation, see Terence E. Fretheim, "The Plagues as Ecological Signs of Historical Disaster," *Journal of Biblical Literature* 110 (1991): 385–96.

4. Even such a modern rationalist as Francis Fukuyama, *Trust: The Social Virtues and the Creation of Prosperity* (New York: Free, 1996) has come to see that underneath rational management an important component of trust is indispensable for the proper working of the human economy.

5. On the generative potential of the Bible as a "classic" text, see David Tracy, *The Analogical Imagination: Christian Theology and the Culture of Pluralism* (New York: Crossroad, 1981).

6. I have here followed the conventional rendering of the text. In the Hebrew there is no "alas" in verse 4, it being appropriated from verse 1. This rendering is unexceptional but should be noted for precision.

7. This point is at the center of the writings of Wendell Berry, in his novels as in his essays. For his programmatic statement, see *The Gift of Good Land: Further Essays Cultural and Agricultural* (San Francisco: North Point, 1981).

8. See the acute analysis of Renita J. Weems, *Battered Love: Marriage, Sex, and Violence in the Hebrew Prophets* (Overtures to Biblical Theology; Minneapolis: Fortress Press, 1995) on this point.

Part III. Writings

Skepticism and Doxology: Brueggemann on the Writings

1. *Introduction to the Old Testament*, 273.
2. *Pathway of Interpretation*, 94.
3. *Introduction to the Old Testament*, 308.
4. *Theology of the Old Testament*, 318.
5. *Introduction to the Old Testament*, 358.
6. *Mandate to Difference*, 77.
7. "Psalms 9–10: A Counter to Conventional Social Reality," 230–32; emphasis original.

9. A Necessary Condition of a Good, Loud Lament

1. This address was presented at a conference at the Montreat Conference Center: "Reclaiming the Text: Recovering the Language of Lament."

2. Claus Westermann, "The Role of the Lament in the Theology of the Old Testament," *Interpretation* 28 (1974): 25.

3. See Hermann Gunkel, *An Introduction to the Psalms* (Mercer Library of Biblical Studies; Macon: Mercer University Press, 1998).

4. Claus Westermann, "Struktur und Geschichte der Klage im alten Testament," *Zeitschrift für die alttestamentliche Wissenschaft* 66 (1954): 44–80.

5. Claus Westermann, *Praise and Lament in the Psalms* (Atlanta: John Knox, 1981).

6. Erhard Gerstenberger, *Der Bittende Mensch: Bittritual und Klagelied des Einzelnen im Alten Testament* (Wissenschaftliche Monographien zum Alten und Neuen Testament 51; Neukirchen-Vluyn: Neukirchener Verlag, 1980).

7. Erhard Gerstenberger, "Psalms," in *Old Testament Form Criticism*, ed. John H. Hayes (San Antonio: Trinity University Press, 1974), 179–223; idem., *Psalms Part 1 with an Introduction to Cultic Poetry* (Forms of the Old Testament Literature 14; Grand Rapids: Eerdmans, 1988); idem., *Psalms Part 2 and Lamentations* (Forms of the Old Testament Literature 15; Grand Rapids: Eerdmans, 2001).

8. Rainer Albertz, *Persönliche Frömmigkeit und offizielle Religion* (Calwer Theologische Monographien 9; Stuttgart: Calwer, 1978).

9. Patrick D. Miller, *They Cried to the Lord: The Form and Theology of Biblical Prayer* (Minneapolis: Fortress Press, 1994).

10. *Interpretation* 28 (January, 1974).

11. See n. 2.

12. Michael Jinkins, *In the House of the Lord: Inhabiting the Psalms of Lament* (Collegeville: Liturgical, 1998); Kathleen D. Billman and Daniel L. Migliore, *Rachel's Cry:*

Prayer of Lament and Rebirth of Hope (Cleveland: United Church Press, 1999); Stephen P. McCutchan, *Experiencing the Psalms: Weaving the Psalms into Your Ministry and Faith* (Macon: Smyth & Helwys, 2000).

13. Harold Fisch, *Poetry with a Purpose: Biblical Poetics and Interpretation* (Bloomington: Indiana University Press, 1988), 108–11.

14. See Ann Weems, *Prayers of Lament* (Louisville: Westminster John Knox, 1995).

15. Brad D. Strawn and Brent D. Strawn, "From Petition to Praise: An Intrapsychic Phenomenon?" (paper presented in the Psychology and Biblical Studies section at the national meeting of the Society of Biblical Literature, Denver, Colo., November 2001).

16. On the hypothesis, see the summary of Miller, *They Cried to the Lord*, ch. 4.

17. Kathleen M. O'Connor, *Lamentations and the Tears of the World* (Maryknoll: Orbis, 2002) xiv.

18. Ibid., xv.

19. Patrick D. Miller, "Deuteronomy and Psalms: Evoking a Biblical Conversation," *Journal of Biblical Literature* 118 (1999): 3–18.

20. Simone Weil, quoted by Alexander Nava, *The Mystical and Prophetic Thought of Simone Weil and Gustavo Gutierrez: Reflections on the Mystery and Hiddenness of God* (Albany: SUNY Press, 2001), 32.

21. On the theme of destructive silence, see Walter Brueggemann, "Voice as Counter to Violence," *Calvin Theological Journal* 36, no. 1 (April 2001) 22–33.

22. Charles T. Mathewes, "Judging Judgment: An Apophatic Approach: Reconsidering the Role of Mainline Churches in Public Life," *Theology Today* 58 (2002): 555–56.

23. James Plastaras, *The God of Exodus* (Milwaukee: Bruce Publishing, 1966).

24. O'Connor, *Lamentations and the Tears of the World*, 5.

25. Ibid., 57.

10. The Fearful Thirst for Dialogue

1. This paper was presented to a North American conference of Episcopal bishops in Windsor, Ontario.

2. George Steiner, *Real Presences* (Chicago: University of Chicago Press, 1989), 225.

3. Ellen Davies, "Exploding the Limits: Form and Function in Psalm 22," *Journal for the Study of the Old Testament* 53 (1997): 93–105.

11. Spirit-Led Imagination: Reality Practiced in a Sub-Version

1. See the discussion of John Hesselink, "Karl Barth on Prayer," in Karl Barth, *Prayer* (ed. Don E. Saliers; 50th anniversary ed.; Louisville: Westminster John Knox, 2002), 75–84, and his references to Karl Barth, *Church Dogmatics* III/3, from where the following quotes are drawn. On "the cry," see James L. Kugel, *The God of Old: Inside the Lost World of the Bible* (New York: Free Press, 2003), 109–36.

12. Wisdom as "Practical Theology"

1. Gerhard von Rad, *Old Testament Theology*, vol. 1, *The Theology of Israel's Historical Traditions* (San Francisco: Harper and Row, 1962). The program worked out in that volume was adumbrated by von Rad in "The Form-Critical Problem of the Hexateuch," in *The Problem of the Hexateuch and Other Essays* (New York: McGraw-Hill, 1966), 1–78, originally published in 1938.

2. Gerhard von Rad, "The Theological Problem of the Old Testament Doctrine of Creation," in *Problem of the Hexateuch*, 131–43, first published in 1936.

3. Von Rad, *Old Testament Theology*, 1:418–59.

4. Von Rad, *Wisdom in Israel* (Nashville: Abingdon, 1972).

5. Claus Westermann, "Creation and History in the Old Testament," *The Gospel and Human Destiny*, ed. Vilmos Vajta (Minneapolis: Augsburg Publishing House, 1971), 11–38; idem, *What Does the Old Testament Say About God?* (Atlanta: John Knox, 1979).

6. The most important scholar on wisdom traditions in the United States, one largely responsible for the emergence of wisdom as an interpretive option in Old Testament studies, is James Crenshaw. Among his many publications on wisdom, see, as representative of his work, *Urgent Advice and Probing Questions: Collected Writings on Old Testament Wisdom* (Macon: Mercer University, 1995).

7. See my summary of this recent scholarship, Walter Brueggemann, "The Loss and Recovery of 'Creation' in Old Testament Theology," *Theology Today* 53 (1996): 177–90. Of special importance in this connection is the work of H. H. Schmid and Rolf Knierim cited in my discussion.

8. David Hartman, *Conflicting Visions: Spiritual Possibilities of Modern Israel* (New York: Schocken, 1990).

9. Ibid., 234.

10. Ibid., 235.

11. Ibid.

12. Ibid., 235–36.

13. Ibid., 236.

14. Ibid.

15. Ibid., 237.

16. Ibid., 238.

17. Walter Brueggemann, "Four Proclamatory Confrontations in Scribal Refraction," *Scottish Journal of Theology* 56 (2003): 404–26.

18. Walther Zimmerli, "The Place and Limit of the Wisdom in the Framework of the Old Testament Theology," *Scottish Journal of Theology* 17 (1964): 148.

19. On the way of God in the wisdom traditions, see Lennart Bostrom, *The God of the Sages: The Portrayal of God in the Book of Proverbs* (Coniectanea Biblica Old Testament 29; Stockholm: Almqvist & Wiksell International, 1990).

20. Klaus Koch, "Is There a Doctrine of Retribution in the Old Testament?" in *Theodicy in the Old Testament*, ed. James L. Crenshaw (Philadelphia: Fortress Press, 1983), 57–87.

21. Von Rad, *Wisdom in Israel*, 65.

22. On atheism as a distinctly modern possibility, see Michael J. Buckley, *At the Origins of Modern Atheism* (New Haven: Yale University Press, 1987).

23. One such obvious ideological tilt among the wisdom teachers is the commitment to patriarchy, an unexamined assumption, on which see Claudia V. Camp, *Strange and Holy: The Strange Woman and the Making of the Bible* (Journal for the Study of the Old Testament Supplement 320; Sheffield: Sheffield Academic, 2000).

24. The classic study is that of Jacques Ellul, *The Technological Society* (New York: Alfred A. Knopf, 1965).

25. For a dramatic, prophetic assault on self-indulgent consumerism, see Reverend Billy, *What Would Jesus Buy? Fabulous Prayers in the Face of The Shopocalypse* (New York: PublicAffairs, 2006); Bill Talen, *What should I do if Reverend Billy Is in My Store?* (New York: New, 2003).

26. Erhard Gerstenberger, *Wesen und Herkunft des sogennanten 'apodiktischen Rechts' im Alten Testament* (Wissenschaftliche Monographien zum Alten und Neuen Testament 20; Neukirchen-Vluyn: Neukirchener, 1965).

27. On the problematic of every attempt at theodicy, see Terrence W. Tilley, *The Evils of Theodicy* (Eugene: Wipf and Stock, 2000).

28. Gerhard von Rad, *Wisdom in Israel*, 98–101, has identified six proverbial sayings that acknowledge the mystery of God's way that lies well beyond sapiential calculation.

Part IV. Canon and Imagination

Exodus and Resurrection: Brueggemann on the Canon

1. "Texts That Linger, Words That Explode," 1; emphasis original.
2. Brueggemann articulates this overtly in an essay titled, "Our Story Tells Us What to Do," but these themes are visible in much of his other work as well. His interest in reformation—and the necessary challenge that must always precede reformation—lies at the heart of his understanding of the exodus story and his view of what the resurrection of Christ demands of us.
3. *Pathway of Interpretation*, 76; emphasis original.

13. Hosting Alternative Worlds

1. This address was given to the Oblate School of Theology in San Antonio.
2. Martin Buber, *Moses: The Revelation and the Covenant* (Atlanta Highlands: Humanities Press International, 1988) 75.

14. Impossible Talk/Impossible Walk

1. On "faith and empire," see Walter Brueggemann, *Theology of the Old Testament: Testimony, Dispute, Advocacy* (Minneapolis: Fortress Press, 1997), 492–527.
2. Concerning the current exploitation of U.S. "exceptionalism," see Gary Dorrien, "Consolidating the Empire: Neoconservatism and the Politics of American Domination," *Political Theology* 6, no. 4 (October 2005): 409–28.
3. On a "theology of the cross" in context, see Douglas John Hall, *The Cross in Our Context: Jesus and the Suffering of the World* (Minneapolis: Fortress Press, 2003).
4. On the connection between the old provision of Moses and forgiveness as a theological motif, see Patrick D. Miller Jr., "Luke 4:16-21," *Interpretation* 29 (1975): 417–21.
5. On the theological significance of table prayers in a contested situation, see Mark Douglas, *Confessing Christ in the 21st Century* (Lanham: Rowman & Littlefield, 2005), 235–39.
6. To cite one example of such impingement on public policy, Peter Brown, *Poverty and Leadership in the Later Roman Empire* (Lebanon: University Press of New England, 2002) has shown the remarkable way in which the early bishops of the church created the category of "the poor" as a political reality that required public attention.

15. Faithful Imagination as Sustained Subversion

1. This address was given at Mt. Vernon Nazarene University, Mt. Vernon, Ohio.
2. My own work on imagination includes *The Prophetic Imagination* (Philadelphia: Fortress Press, 1978), *Hopeful Imagination: Prophetic Voices in Exile* (Philadelphia: Fortress Press, 1986), and *Texts under Negotiation: The Bible and Postmodern Imagination* (Minneapolis: Fortress Press, 1993).
3. In contemporary Calvinist thought, these two core themes have been definingly exposited in the dense discussions of Jürgen Moltmann, respectively, in *Theology of Hope: On the Ground and the Implications of a Christian Eschatology* (New York: Harper & Row, 1967), and *The Crucified God: The Cross of Christ as the Foundation and Criticism of Christian Theology* (New York: Harper and Row, 1974).

4. I use the phrase "force of interpretation" with reference to the consideration of the *Iliad* by Simone Weil as a "poem of force," on which see James Boyd White, *Living Speech: Resisting the Empire of Force* (Princeton: Princeton University Press, 2006).

5. There is a growing literature on the ways in which "empire" has been a recurring reality in Christian theology and interpretation. See Richard A. Horsley, *Jesus and Empire: The Kingdom of God and the New World Disorder* (Minneapolis: Fortress Press, 2003), Elisabeth Schüssler Fiorenza, *The Power of the Word: Scripture and the Rhetoric of Empire* (Minneapolis: Fortress Press, 2007), Joerg Rieger, *Christ and Empire: From Paul to Postcolonial Times* (Minneapolis: Fortress Press, 2007), Kwok Pui-lan et al., eds., *Empire and The Christian Tradition: New Readings of Classical Theologians* (Minneapolis: Fortress Press, 2007).

6. On this text see Fernando Belo, *A Materialist Reading of the Gospel of Mark* (Maryknoll: Orbis, 1981) 110–11. Belo's general thesis is pertinent to the argument made here.

7. See the classic exposition of the trial narrative of the Gospel of John by Paul Lehmann, *The Transfiguration of Politics* (New York: Harper & Row, 1975) 48–70.

8. William T. Cavanaugh, *Torture and Eucharist: Theology, Politics, and the Body of Christ* (Oxford; Blackwell, 1998).

9. Elaine Scarry, *The Body in Pain: The Making and Unmaking of the World* (Oxford: Oxford University Press, 1985), makes the case that torture is for the "unmaking" of the world and the dismantling of the subject of torture.

10. Lawrence Thornton, *Imagining Argentina* (New York: Doubleday, 1987), quoted by Cavanaugh, *Torture and Eucharist*, 278–79.

11. Reading backward from the New Testament of course leads into a very complex historical scene reflected in a great complexity of literary evidence. By focusing on the book of Daniel, I leap over much of that complexity. My argument, however, does not require working through that enormous complexity, but only a focus on texts.

12. On the "gospel" in the Isaiah texts, see Walter Brueggemann, *Biblical Perspectives on Evangelism: Living in a Three-Storied Universe* (Nashville: Abingdon, 1993), ch. 1.

13. On the liturgical performance of such songs of enthronement, see J. J. M. Roberts, "Mowinckel's Enthronement Festival: A Review," in *The Book of Psalms: Composition and Reception*, ed. Peter W. Flint and Patrick D. Miller Jr. (Leiden: Brill, 2005), 97–115.

14. On the continuing force and significance of the exodus narrative, see Michael Walzer, *Exodus and Revolution* (New York: Basic, 1985).

15. Peter Brown, *Poverty and Leadership in the Later Roman Empire* (Lebanon: University Press of New England, 2002).

16. The declaration of the Lord to Elijah that there will be "seven thousand in Israel" who have not bowed to Baal is an anticipation of this recognition of the legion of saints who remain faithful in every generation (1 Kgs 19:18). The assurance, then and now, is an antidote to self-pity and to a sense of being left all alone in fidelity.

17. The phrase is from Paul Ricoeur, *Freud and Philosophy: An Essay on Interpretation* (New Haven: Yale University Press, 1970). See a commentary on Ricoeur's argument by Dan T. Stiver, *Theology after Ricoeur: New Directions in Hermeneutical Theology* (Louisville: Westminster John Knox, 2001) 137–59.

16. Scriptural Strategies against Exclusionary Absolutism

1. Presented to a Continuing Education event of the Episcopal House of Bishops at Kanuga.

2. I have made my argument in what follows by way of an engagement with Bill Bishop, *The Big Sort: Why the Clustering of Like Minded America is Tearing Us Apart* (Boston: Houghton Mifflin, 2008). Bishop observes the pattern of the way in which U.S. residents are choosing to live and work and study and worship with like-minded people, Red or Blue. Thus, the term "Big Sort" refers to this self-selection process that divides our society.

3. Gerhard von Rad, *The Problem of the Hexateuch and Other Essays* (New York: McGraw-Hill, 1966), 3–8.

4. C. H. Dodd, *The Apostolic Preaching and Its Developments* (New York: Harper & Brothers, n.d.), 7–35.

5. Mary Douglas, *Purity and Danger: An Analysis of the Concepts of Pollution and Taboo* (London: Routledge & Kegan Paul, 1966); idem, *Implicit Meanings: Essays in Anthropology* (London: Routledge & Kegan Paul, 1975), 249–75, 276–318. See the comments on her work as it pertains to Leviticus by Lester L. Grabbe, *Leviticus* (Old Testament Guides; Sheffield: Sheffield Academic, 1993), 56–62.

6. On recent scholarship of the period, the best access is through Jon L. Berquist, *Judaism in Persia's Shadow: A Social and Historical Approach* (Minneapolis: Fortress Press, 1995); idem, ed., *Approaching Yehud: New Approaches to the Study of the Persian Period* (Semeia 50; Atlanta: Society of Biblical Literature, 2007). See also Daniel L. Smith, *The Religion of the Landless: The Social Context of the Babylonian Exile* (Bloomington: Meyer Stone, 1989), and Daniel L. Smith-Christopher, *A Biblical Theology of Exile* (Overtures to Biblical Theology; Minneapolis: Fortress Press, 2002).

7. Michael Fishbane, *Sacred Attunement: A Jewish Theology* (Chicago: University of Chicago Press, 2008), 82–84 and passim.

8. The practice of Jewishness amid the empire is not unlike the "hidden transcripts" identified by James C. Scott. See Scott, *Weapons of the Weak: Everyday Forms of Peasant Resistance* (New Haven: Yale University Press, 1985); idem, *Domination and the Arts of Resistance: Hidden Transcripts* (New Haven: Yale University Press, 1990). Such disciplines deliberately stay beneath the radar of the empire.

9. See the pioneering work of W. L. Humphreys, "A Lifestyle for Diaspora: A Study of the Tales of Esther and Daniel," *Journal of Biblical Literature* 92 (1973): 211–23, followed by Smith, *The Religion of the Landless*, 153–78, and Berquist, *Judaism in Persia's Shadow*, 221–32.

10. Leon R. Kass, *The Beginning of Wisdom: Reading Genesis* (New York: Free, 2003), 569 and passim.

11. Walter Brueggemann, "Four Proclamatory Confrontations in Scribal Refraction," *Scottish Journal of Theology* 56, no. 4 (2003): 404–26.

12. I do not suggest that there was no zeal to judge other members of the community. Psalm 1 is commonly taken to be a late Psalm that reflects internal dispute in the community concerning the real torah keepers (the righteous), and the "wicked," who did not measure up. I do suggest, however, that such a propensity did not halt the more generous way in which the canon was shaped.

13. On the defining role of the scribes, see Philip R. Davies, *Scribes and Schools: The Canonization of Hebrew Scriptures* (Library of Ancient Israel; Louisville: Westminster John Knox, 1998), and Karel Van der Toorn, *Scribal Culture and the Making of the Hebrew Bible* (Cambridge: Harvard University Press, 2007).

14. Moshe Weinfeld, *Deuteronomy and the Deuteronomic School* (Oxford: Clarendon, 1972).

15. David Weiss Halivni, *Revelation Restored: Divine Writ and Critical Responses* (Boulder: Westview/Perseus, 1997), and Peter Ochs, "Talmudic Scholarship as Textual Reasoning: Halivni's Pragmatic Historiography," *Textual Reasonings: Jewish Philosophy and Text Study at the End of the Twentieth Century* (ed. Peter Ochs and Nancy Levene; Grand Rapids: Eerdmans, 2002), 120–43. There is no agreement about the nature or extent of the scroll that Ezra read, though it is not impossible that it was the full form of the Pentateuch. Indeed, Richard Elliott Friedman, *Who Wrote the Bible?* (New York: Harper and Row, 1987), suggests that Ezra authored the Pentateuch, a view informed by rabbinic scholarship.

16. Daniel J. Harrington, *The Gospel of Matthew* (Sacra Pagina; Collegeville: Liturgical, 2007), 210.

17. It is clear that there is no single motif of the famous "Christ and Culture" model that is adequate for such circumstance. Indeed, the agility required precludes a settlement in any

single mode of Christ and Culture. I am glad to mention two studies that pertain to the line of my argument in this paper. See Donn Morgan, *Fighting with the Bible: Why Scripture Divides Us and How It Can Bring Us Together* (New York: Seabury, 2007), and Brad Hirschfield, *You Don't Have to be Wrong for Me to Be Right: Finding Faith Without Fanaticism* (New York: Crown, 2007).

17. A Life and a Time Other than Our Own

1. This address was given at the Festival of Homiletics, Minneapolis.

2. This recognition of the singularity of God in the creed calls to mind the poetic admonition of Alan Paton, "Meditation for Young Boy Confirmed," *Christian Century*, October 13, 1954, 1238, to his son:

> Do not address your mind to criticism of the Creator, do not pretend to know His categories,
> Do not take His Universe in your hand, and point out its defects with condescension.
> Do not think He is a greater potentate, a manner of President of the United Galaxies,
> Do not think that because you know so few human beings, that He is in a comparable though more favorable position.
> Do not think it absurd that He should know every sparrow, or the number of hairs of your head,
> Do not compare Him with yourself, not suppose your human love to be an example to shame Him.
> He is not greater than Plato or Lincoln, nor superior to Shakespeare and Beethoven,
> He is their God, their powers and their gifts proceeded from Him,
> In infinite darkness they pored with their fingers over the first word of the Book of His Knowledge.

3. Karl Barth, *Church Dogmatics* III/3 (Edinburgh: T & T Clark, 1960), 268, has asserted that "prayer, or praying, is simply asking." More than that, Barth, *Prayer* (ed. Don E. Saliers; 50th anniversary ed.; Louisville: Westminster John Knox, 2002), 13, concludes:

> God is not deaf, but listens; more than that, he acts. God does not act in the same way whether we pray or not. Prayer exerts influence upon God's actions, even upon his existence. . . . But one thing is beyond doubt: it is the answer that God gives. Our prayers are weak and poor. Nevertheless, what matters is not that our prayers be forceful, but that God listens to them. That is why we pray.

4. Samuel Wells, "Rethinking Resurrection: For Better or For Worse," *Journal for Preachers* 31, no. 3 (Easter 2008): 41–48, has suggested a characterization of joy in heaven that connects forcefully with the best joys of earth.

5. Franz Rosenzweig, *The Star of Redemption* (Notre Dame: University of Notre Dame Press, 1970, 1971), 93–265.

6. See Samuel E. Balentine, "'What Are Human Beings, That You Make So Much of Them?' Divine Disclosure from the Whirlwind: 'Look at Behemoth,'" in *God in the Fray: A Tribute to Walter Brueggemann* (ed. Tod Linafelt and Timothy K. Beal; Minneapolis: Fortress Press, 1998), 259–78.

7. Gerhard von Rad, *The Problem of the Hexateuch and Other Essays* (New York: McGraw-Hill, 1966), 71–77.

ACKNOWLEDGMENTS

Chapter 1 was a lecture given at Luther Theological Seminary in St. Paul, Minnesota, in 2009.

Chapter 2 was given at a clergy conference at Lipscomb University in Nashville, Tennessee, in 2008.

Chapter 3 was an address to the clergy conference of the Episcopal Diocese of Atlanta, Georgia, in 2007.

Chapter 4 was presented to the Presbyterian Covenant Network in Minneapolis in 2008.

Chapters 5 and 6 were originally offered as the P. C. and Janie Ennis Lectures at Central Presbyterian Church in Atlanta in 2002.

Chapters 7, 16, and 17 were delivered at Festival of Homiletics meetings in Nashville, Tennessee (2007), Atlanta (2009), and Minneapolis (2008), respectively.

Chapter 8 was an address for Lutheran Campus Ministry at Northern Michigan University in Marquette, Michigan, in 2007.

Chapter 9 was presented at a conference on "Reclaiming the Text: Recovering the Language of Lament" at the Montreat Conference Center in Asheville, North Carolina, in 2002.

Chapter 10 was delivered to the North American Conference of Episcopal Bishops in Windsor, Ontario, in 2005.

Chapter 11 was given at a United Methodist conference on worship at Christ United Methodist Church, Manhattan, New York, in 2005.

Chapters 12 and 14 are previously unpublished.

Chapter 13 was first an address to the Oblate School of Theology in San Antonio, Texas, in 2004.

Chapter 15 began as a lecture given at Mount Vernon Nazarene University in Mount Vernon, Ohio, in 2008.

Chapter 16 was presented to a Continuing Education event of the Episcopal House of Bishops at Kanuga in North Carolina in 2009.

Bibliography of Walter Brueggemann's Works Cited

"Covenant as a Subversive Paradigm." Chap. 2 in *A Social Reading of the Old Testament: Prophetic Approaches to Israel's Communal Life*. Edited by Patrick D. Miller. Minneapolis: Fortress Press, 1994.

Deep Memory, Exuberant Hope: Contested Truth in a Post-Christian World. Minneapolis: Fortress Press, 2000.

"Duty as Delight and Desire: Preaching Obedience That Is Not Legalism." Chap. 3 in *The Covenanted Self: Explorations in Law and Covenant*. Edited by Patrick D. Miller. Minneapolis: Fortress Press, 1999.

Interpretation and Obedience: From Faithful Reading to Faithful Living. Minneapolis: Fortress Press, 1991.

An Introduction to the Old Testament: The Canon and Christian Imagination. Louisville: Westminster John Knox, 2003.

"Jeremiah: Portrait of the Prophet." Chap. 1 in *Like Fire in the Bones: Listening for the Prophetic Word in Jeremiah*. Edited by Patrick D. Miller. Minneapolis: Fortress Press, 2006.

Mandate to Difference: An Invitation to the Contemporary Church. Louisville: Westminster John Knox, 2007.

Old Testament Theology: An Introduction. Nashville: Abingdon, 2008.

" 'Othering' with Grace and Courage." Chap. 1 in *The Covenanted Self: Explorations in Law and Covenant*. Edited by Patrick D. Miller. Minneapolis: Fortress Press, 1999.

"Our Story Tells Us What to Do." Chap. 5 in *Peace*. Understanding Biblical Themes. St. Louis: Chalice, 2001.

A Pathway of Interpretation: The Old Testament for Pastors and Students. Eugene: Cascade, 2008.

The Prophetic Imagination. 2nd ed. Minneapolis: Fortress Press, 2001.

"Psalms and the Life of Faith: A Suggested Typology of Function." Chap. 1 in *The Psalms and the Life of Faith*. Edited by Patrick D. Miller. Minneapolis: Fortress Press, 1995.

"Psalms 9–10: A Counter to Conventional Social Reality." Chap. 11 in *The Psalms and the Life of Faith*. Edited by Patrick D. Miller. Minneapolis: Fortress Press, 1995.

Reverberations of Faith: A Theological Handbook of Old Testament Themes. Louisville: Westminster John Knox, 2002.

"Texts That Linger, Words That Explode." Chap. 1 in *Texts That Linger, Words That Explode: Listening to Prophetic Voices.* Edited by Patrick D. Miller. Minneapolis: Fortress Press, 2000.

Texts Under Negotiation: The Bible and Postmodern Imagination. Minneapolis: Fortress Press, 1993.

Theology of the Old Testament: Testimony, Dispute, Advocacy. Minneapolis: Fortress Press, 1997.

INDEX OF BIBLICAL REFERENCES

NEW TESTAMENT

Index of Authors
Cited in the Text